For Tom Murnane —

An impressive coalition builder,

Fondly.

Brian

Jan 1, 1997

Powered by Coalition

Brian O'Connell

Foreword by John W. Gardner

—〜— **Powered by Coalition**

The Story of
INDEPENDENT SECTOR

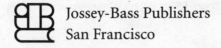

Jossey-Bass Publishers
San Francisco

Substantial discounts on bulk quantities of Jossey-Bass books are available to corporations, professional associations, and other organizations. For details and discount information, contact the special sales department at Jossey-Bass Inc., Publishers (415) 433–1740; Fax (800) 605–2665.

For sales outside the United States, please contact your local Simon & Schuster International Office.

Jossey-Bass Web address: http://www.josseybass.com

 Manufactured in the United States of America on Lyons Falls Turin Book. This paper is acid-free and 100 percent totally chlorine-free.

Library of Congress Cataloging-in-Publication Data

O'Connell, Brian, date.
    Powered by coalition: the story of INDEPENDENT SECTOR/
Brian O'Connell; foreword by John W. Gardner.
      p. cm.—(The Jossey-Bass nonprofit sector series)
    Includes bibliographical references and index.
    ISBN 0-7879-0954-8 (acid-free paper)
    1. INDEPENDENT SECTOR (Firm) 2. Voluntarism—United States.
3. Associations, institutions, etc.—United States. 4. Nonprofit
organizations—United States. I. Title. II. Series: Jossey-Bass nonprofit sector series.
HV97.I47026   1997
361.7'63'09753—dc21   96-51318

HB Printing   10 9 8 7 6 5 4 3 2 1   FIRST EDITION

~~~ Contents

Foreword   ix
John W. Gardner

Preface   xiii

Acknowledgments   xvii

The Author   xix

Introduction: The Significance of Voluntary Action
in America   1

Part One: The Beginnings of INDEPENDENT SECTOR   11

1   Serious Challenges to Nonprofit Organizations
in the 1960s and 1970s   13

2   Searching for a Course   21

3   The Organizing Effort   35

4   The Birth of INDEPENDENT SECTOR
and the Defining First Year   55

Part Two: The Power of Association   71

5   The Strength of Coalition: A Quintessential Example   73

6   Battles and Cooperation with Government   84

7   Telling the Sector's Story   106

8   Fostering Research on the Sector   121

9   Promoting Effectiveness, Openness, and Accountability   134

10   Making the Most of the Meeting Ground   148

Part Three: Lessons and Afterthoughts   155

  11 Building, Energizing, and Maintaining Large
      and Diverse Coalitions   157

  12 Hopes Not Realized and Other Regrets   174

  13 A Personal View of the Future   182

Appendixes   191

  A Roster of Charter Members   193

  B The Start-Up Funders   199

  C 1995 Membership Roster   201

  D Board Members 1980–1995   217

  E Staff Members 1980–1996   223

     Bibliography   225

     Index   229

—ᴧᴧᴧ— Foreword

Brian O'Connell has written extensively in this and other books about the attributes of the independent sector, so I shall comment only briefly on that subject.

Ever since colonial days, foreign visitors have commented on the extraordinary impulse of Americans to form voluntary groups and invent nongovernmental institutions to serve community purposes. Out of that impulse has come an incredible variety of such institutions—libraries, museums, hospitals, symphony orchestras, great universities, adoption services, religious organizations, civic groups, the 4-H clubs, and so on.

In 1978, when we were just launched on the preliminary discussions that led eventually to INDEPENDENT SECTOR, I wrote:

> Thanks to the institutions of the non-profit sector, not only can citizens participate in the concerns of American life, they can participate at the grassroots level—and in doing so contribute importantly to the preservation of vital communities. There is in grassroots community activity the opportunity for sympathetic personal attention to shared problems.
>
> Crucial to the metabolism of a healthy private sector are groups and patterns of social interaction that rarely occupy space on the front page—the family, religious congregations, coherent neighborhoods, social groups that still preserve a "sense of community."
>
> The past century has seen a more or less steady deterioration of American communities as coherent entities with the morale and binding values that hold people together. Our *sense of community* has been badly battered, and every social philosopher emphasizes the need to restore it. What is at stake is the individual's sense of responsibility for something beyond the self. A spirit of concern and caring for one's fellow beings is virtually impossible to sustain in a vast, impersonal, featureless society.

All experience shows that our shared values survive best in coherent human groupings (the family, the neighborhood, the community). We must recreate a society that has its social and spiritual roots firmly planted in such groupings—so firmly planted that those roots cannot be ripped out by the winds of change, nor by the dehumanizing, automatizing forces of the contemporary world.

The sector is a source of deep and positive meaning in our national life. If it were to disappear, we would be less distinctively American. The sector enhances our creativity, enlivens our communities, nurtures individual responsibility, stirs life at the grassroots, and reminds us that we were born free. Its vitality is rooted in good soil—civic pride, compassion, a philanthropic tradition, a strong problem-solving impulse, a sense of individual responsibility, and, despite what cynics may say, an irrepressible commitment to the great shared task of improving our life together.

It's a sector in which you're allowed to pursue truth, even if you're going in the wrong direction; to experiment, even if you're bound to fail; to map unknown territory, even if you get lost; a sector in which we are committed to alleviating misery and redressing grievances, to giving rein to the mind's curiosity and the soul's longing, to seeking beauty where we can and defending truth where we must, to honoring the worthy and smiting the rascals (with everyone free to define worth and rascality), to combating the ancient impulse to hate and fear the tribe in the next valley, to finding cures and consoling the incurable, to preparing for tomorrow's crisis and preserving yesterday's wisdom, and to pursuing the questions others won't pursue because they're too busy or lazy or fearful or jaded.

It's a sector for seed planting and path finding, for lost causes and for causes that yet may win, and in the words of George Bernard Shaw, "for the future and the past, for the posterity that has no vote and the tradition that never had any, for the great abstractions, . . . for the eternal against the expedient, for the evolutionary appetite against the day's gluttony, for intellectual integrity, for humanity."

After about a year and a half of preparatory study, it took fifteen months for the representatives of the various parts of the sector to create an organization that could serve as common ground for all of them and others like them. Our purpose was to serve the sector. The organizations of the sector are independent and intend to remain so. What we set out to create was a "meeting ground" for the diverse institutions of the sector, a place where they could gather to discuss common problems and plan appropriate action. The sector is tumultuous in its variety, and we did not set out to make it neater. It contains profound differences of view, and we did not intend to create an overall harmony. We were confident that members would find a core of significant shared goals and values, and in fact they did.

When one reflects on the fact that the creation of INDEPENDENT SECTOR involved two distinguished organizations voting themselves out of existence, one knows that much negotiation and selfless statesmanship was involved. The negotiations were delicate and the discussions long. Nothing came easy. But as often happens, individuals of large vision and steadfast character rallied around and made it happen. The debt was particularly heavy to Bayard Ewing, Kenneth Albrecht, Philip Bernstein, Homer Wadsworth, and James Lipscomb. They had the strength and stature among their colleagues to bring independent constituencies into a common venture, and they deserve to be listed among the founders of INDEPENDENT SECTOR.

Brian O'Connell and I worked in the closest partnership to develop the initial vision and to shape the alliances that would bring the vision to reality. I estimate that some thirty-three months elapsed from the first conversations Brian and I had on the subject to the launching of the new organization, and our conversations ranged from the broadest social perspectives to the smallest organizational details. It was an equal partnership in every way. We shaped it and launched it together.

But once the organization was launched, Brian's burdens grew immensely heavier, and mine (as chairman of the board) only moderately heavier. It fell to Brian to bring us through all the ailments of an infant organization and to cope with the tough problems of emerging adulthood. As I said on INDEPENDENT SECTOR's tenth anniversary: "Tommy Henrich, a great ballplayer of my generation, said 'Catching a fly ball is a pleasure. Knowing what to do with it after you catch it is a business.' Launching an organization is an adventure. But transforming it into a vital institution that gains strength with every passing year takes more than an adventurer. It calls for an inspired leader-manager."

And Brian fit the role of "inspired leader-manager," with spectacular results.

As a task of coalition building, the formation of INDEPENDENT SECTOR was in a class by itself. The nonprofit sector tests the limits of diversity, and we didn't want the organization to shrink from that diversity. That made for noisy meetings and tense interactions in the early days. From the beginning, Brian and I understood that trust was a crucial ingredient in the success of the venture, and we functioned accordingly. We took great pains to be open with all parties and totally consistent in our dealings—no surprises, no hidden agendas.

An overwhelming reason for the success of INDEPENDENT SECTOR was the character and attributes of Brian O'Connell himself. He is one of the ablest leaders I have ever known, particularly in the dimensions so crucial to contemporary leadership—the capacity to cross boundaries, the gift for dealing with diversity, and skill in finding common ground and shared values. It is not possible to exaggerate the importance of steadiness and predictability in dealings with a highly diverse constituency. Brian moved as a trustworthy and trusted figure in widely diverse parts of the sector, always reaching out, always listening, always exercising extraordinarily good judgment. He was meticulous in explaining his actions, in consulting all stakeholders, in setting policies—always fair, always with a sense of humor.

He saw the sector in a broad perspective. He understood in depth and breadth the nature of the nonprofit sector and its diverse parts. He saw its problems and its possibilities. And it is much to our benefit that he has taken the time to tell the story.

February 1997   JOHN W. GARDNER
Founding Chairperson
of INDEPENDENT SECTOR

—ᴎ— **Preface**

In the summer of 1995, seventeen years to the month after our first discussion about the need for some greater connectedness within the sprawling third sector, John Gardner and I stole away for two days to share thoughts and recollections about what had occurred in the blur of those intervening years.

My immediate task was to gain the benefit of John's advice on the history of INDEPENDENT SECTOR that I had been asked to write. I had even prepared an agenda. I wanted his thoughts about the book's scope, tone, and thrust and his recollections of facts, events, and people.

Eventually, those purposes were well served, but before we could make headway on any of them, it became clear that each of us needed to get down to such basic wonderments as why we had even taken on the challenge, why we had gambled so much on such a long shot, and why it had succeeded after all. It wasn't part of our plan for the time together, but we couldn't seem to look back without probing those bedrock considerations, and that started with a lot of brutally candid "Why in the world did we . . . ?" and "How did it ever . . . ?"

It wasn't that we hadn't known what we were getting into. It was more that we knew and still went ahead. And our candor was not just in admitting our doubts but also in admitting a confidence in ourselves that in retrospect appears audacious.

At times in that conversation, we asked each other genuinely and uncertainly whether we had been gamblers or visionaries, foolhardy or courageous, reckless or calculated.

We let it all hang out—two battle-scarred survivors admitting to fear and to bravery. In the end, we admitted we had thought we could win, that the cause was worth the gamble, and that the time and climate seemed right. But we also admitted that in fact we had been audacious, reckless, and foolhardy, tempered with at least some doses of courage, confidence, and vision.

We acknowledged that we had been risk takers, but that we had not blindly followed an impulse. We had thrown caution to the wind not for the daring but because something unusual seemed to be in the air.

Looking back, the origins are terribly complex, but the essential dilemma was startlingly clear: something had to be done to preserve and strengthen America's independent sector, but nothing was likely to succeed.

The obstacles and the problems, presented to us with intensity and in a growing litany, had dogged all previous efforts at creating an umbrella: a sector so broad that it defied commonality; antipathies and worse between many of the players; the disdain of university officials for grassroots organizers and vice versa; the determination of funders to keep their distance from grant seekers; fear of the very size of a coalition large enough to span the sector; lack of confidence that such a group could really do anything about the sector's problems; reluctance to pay for still another layer of representation and structure; and on and on.

Perhaps the only thing that kept us at it in those early days was that though almost everyone assured us that every solution was foreclosed, they were equally determined that something had to be tried. The contradiction suggested a chance that maybe some of the obstacles in our way could be overcome. That helped to keep us at least curious about what, if anything, might be done to ease resistance, and that in turn led to further exploration. Gradually, we moved to a consideration of whether the unnamed somebody who "ought to do something" might be us. Then it was even more urgent to look at whether there really were signs in the wind to make this attempt any more promising than all the others.

Essentially, what gnawed at us and nudged us toward commitment were six key observations. First, we found widespread conviction that the sector occupied an important place in American society, and that it deserved to be further nurtured and developed. Second, it was clear that the problems facing the sector were threatening and pervasive and constituted a potential rallying point for common endeavor. Third, a growing roster of impressive allies was ready to sign on as soon as we did. Fourth, other key figures, despite being negative or pessimistic, seemed willing to at least keep an open mind.

The fifth salient fact was that the National Council on Philanthropy and the Coalition of National Voluntary Organizations were in a position to provide some institutional underpinning. And finally, though various prior efforts may have failed to achieve ambitious goals to unite the sector, what they had accomplished and what had been learned from them could be built on.

Beyond those positive signs, there were less tangible factors that helped tip the scales. Though we didn't actually say it to each other until seventeen years later, John and I felt that each of us would come to the task better prepared than those who had preceded us, or at least with unique experience behind us. Furthermore, the two of us seemed to represent many of the varied assets and balances necessary to the teamwork that the next stages would require.

We also agreed that the time and circumstances would probably never be better for such a project, and finally a feeling grew in both of us that it was simply the right thing to do.

So after much more testing, lining up of allies, and persuasion of other important figures to keep an open mind, we finally threw our hearts over the fence and took off on what turned out to be one hell of a ride.

Years later, after we had survived excruciating complications and crushing work schedules to see the confederation achieve impressive impact and stature, I would hear people describe the organization's founding and development as so natural that it had just fallen into place. At those moments, I didn't know whether to weep, scream, or kill.

The better outlet was to tell a story.

A farmer had taken over a long-neglected property. The fields were barely distinguishable, covered with weeds and trees. The barn had pretty much collapsed, with much of the wood deteriorating or lost to theft. The house leaned so badly, it seemed beyond renovation.

After years of struggle, the farmer finally brought the place to the point where he wanted to show it off to his parson. With great pride, he took the reverend to the fields now laden with produce, and the parson proclaimed, "The Lord doth provide."

The farmer took the reverend to the barn, wonderfully renewed and full of bellowing livestock, and the parson declared, "Praise the Lord."

Finally, the minister was taken to the house, now safe and cozy, and he intoned, "The Lord works in wondrous ways."

With some exasperation, the farmer responded, "Meaning no disrespect to you, reverend, or the Almighty, but I just wish you could have seen this place when God had it to Himself."

Let me tell you the way I remember it.

Chatham, Massachusetts   BRIAN O'CONNELL
February 1997

᪥ Acknowledgments

John Gardner was, as usual, wonderfully encouraging and helpful at every stage of this long project, including remembering, prodding me to bring out the personal and passionate sides of the story, and making suggestions even for scope and style. For all of that, and for his willingness to write the Foreword, my considerable appreciation. In a previous book, dedicated to him, I expressed acknowledgment and gratitude for all he has meant to the existence and vitality of INDEPENDENT SECTOR. I referred to him then as "mentor, partner, and friend," and I think of him always with appreciation, admiration, and affection.

Ann Brown O'Connell, too, has been a significant factor in this book and in the creation and development of IS. An earlier book was also dedicated to her, and now as then, I acknowledge her indispensable contributions and her abilities, warmth, enthusiasm, and total support. I'm forever grateful.

I'm indebted to Sharon Stewart at IS for her substantial help in locating and organizing a great deal of resource material necessary to the book, and to Sheila McColgan at the Filene Center at Tufts for her tireless work in processing the many drafts that were necessary to try to get the story right.

Alan Shrader at Jossey-Bass was critical, efficient, and kind—a rare and awfully nice combination in an editor. Susan Williams, assistant editor of Jossey-Bass's Nonprofit Sector Series, and Xenia Lisanevich, production editor, were also impressively professional and friendly.

I'm also grateful to the Ford, W. K. Kellogg, and Charles Stewart Mott Foundations and to the Lincoln Filene Center at Tufts University for providing support that helped make the book possible.

Though their mention here is far, far short of what is deserved, I also want to acknowledge the thousands of people and organizations who helped build INDEPENDENT SECTOR and all that it has been able to achieve. Each one deserves to be named and thanked. We were powered by their individual caring and joint action.

—*B.O.*

Dedicated to the members of INDEPENDENT SECTOR *and its volunteer and staff leaders. Coalitions derive their strength from the participation and commitment of the members, and they make the most of their missions and opportunities through good leaders loyal to the members.* INDEPENDENT SECTOR *has been blessed with an abundance of both.*

⸺ The Author

Brian O'Connell is founding president of INDEPENDENT SECTOR and professor of public service at the Lincoln Filene Center for Citizenship and Public Affairs at Tufts University, Medford, Massachusetts. He served as president and chief executive officer of INDEPENDENT SECTOR from 1980 to 1995.

He received his B.A. degree (1953) in liberal arts with a major in English from Tufts University, and did graduate work in public administration at the Maxwell School of Citizenship and Public Affairs at Syracuse University.

Before joining INDEPENDENT SECTOR, he served as president of the National Council of Philanthropy and executive director of the Coalition of National Voluntary Organizations. For twelve years, he was executive director of the National Mental Health Association. During that time, he was an organizer and first chairman of the National Committee on Patients' Rights. For the prior dozen years, he was with the American Heart Association, and on leaving was director of its California affiliate.

O'Connell served as chairperson of the organizing committee for CIVICUS: World Alliance for Citizen Participation, and as the first head of its executive committee. Among his current positions are board memberships at the Ewing Marion Kauffman Foundation, the National Academy of Public Administration, and Tufts University; he is also on the advisory boards of the Peter Drucker Foundation and the Advertising Council.

He was previously a board member at the Points of Light Foundation, the Hogg Foundation, the National Assembly of Voluntary Health and Social Welfare Organizations, the Family Service Society of San Francisco, and the California Health and Welfare Association; and he was chairperson of the 1989 Salzburg Seminar on nongovernmental organizations.

O'Connell is an elected fellow of the American Public Health Association and the National Academy of Public Administration and has received several honorary degrees, including a doctorate of humanities from Fairleigh Dickinson University and a doctorate of laws from Indiana University. He is also director emeritus of the National Mental Health Association.

Among other honors he has received are the John W. Gardner Leadership Award of INDEPENDENT SECTOR; the Weston Howland Award for Citizenship of the Lincoln Filene Center; the Gold Key Award of the American Society of Association Executives; the Award for Professionalism of United Way of America; the Chairman's Award of the National Society of Fund Raising Executives; and the Distinguished Alumni Award of Tufts University.

Throughout his career, O'Connell has bridged the worlds of action and writing. Among his eleven books are *The Board Member's Book* (1985); *Effective Leadership in Voluntary Organizations* (1976); *America's Voluntary Spirit: A Book of Readings* (1983); *Board Overboard: Laughs and Lessons for All but the Perfect Nonprofit* (1996); *People Power: Service, Advocacy, Empowerment* (1995); *Philanthropy in Action* (1987); and with Ann Brown O'Connell, *Volunteers in Action* (1989).

Introduction
The Significance of Voluntary Action
in America

———

Fifty percent of all Americans are active volunteers, and they give an average of four hours a week to the causes of their choice. The base of participation is broad and spreading.

Three out of four of us are regular contributors of money to charitable causes. We give more than $900 per family each year. Almost 90 percent of the giving comes from individuals. Foundations and business corporations, as important as they are, represent only 10 percent of all that is contributed. People of all incomes are involved, and contributors at the lower end of the scale are more likely to be generous than the better off.

We are the only country in the world where giving and volunteering are pervasive characteristics of the population.

The recipients of our time and money are as varied as neighborhood improvement societies, overseas relief agencies, private schools and colleges, conservation and preservation groups, community foundations, religious institutions, hospitals, community mental health clinics, environmental organizations, recreational centers, civil rights groups, museums, fraternal benevolent societies, and the United Way.

There are more than a million charitable organizations officially registered with the Internal Revenue Service, but that number doesn't include most religious congregations, mutual assistance groups, or local chapters of large national organizations such as the American Cancer Society. Also excluded are the less formal groups concerned and involved with everything from prenatal care to cemeteries. Altogether, the total is at least two million organizations, and growing.

In the composite, an almost dizzying array of charitable activities exists. Americans inform, protest, assist, teach, heal, build, advocate, comfort, testify, support, solicit, donate, canvass, demonstrate, guide, feed, monitor and in a hundred other ways, serve people, communities, and causes.

Even more important than the impressive statistics is the evidence of our impact on the country's problems and aspirations.

From the earliest discussions of the possible creation of what became INDEPENDENT SECTOR, John Gardner said repeatedly, "Out of our pluralism has come virtually all of our creativity" and "Virtually every significant social idea of the past century in this country has been nurtured in the nonprofit sector. If the sector were to disappear from our national life, we would be less distinctly American."

Most often when examples of the sector's impact are cited, they relate to the distant past and to such issues as slavery, women's suffrage, and child labor laws. As real and important as those examples are, their constant repetition tends to support the notion that things of significance have not occurred since. It is my distinct experience that in just the past twenty-five years, there has been an absolute explosion of citizen impact on a vast range of human needs. We organize now to serve every conceivable aspect of the human condition and are willing to stand up and be counted on almost any public issue. We mobilize to fight zoning changes, approve bond issues, advocate pro life or pro choice, improve garbage collection, expose overpricing, enforce equal rights, or protest wars. In very recent times, we have successfully organized to deal with the rights of women, conservation and preservation, learning disabilities, conflict resolution, Hispanic culture and rights, the aged, voter registration, the environment, Native American issues, the dying, experimental theater, international understanding, population growth, neighborhood empowerment, control of nuclear power, consumerism, and on and on. Our interest and impact extend from neighborhoods to the ozone layer and even beyond.

When I became head of the National Council on Philanthropy and the Coalition of National Voluntary Organizations, and later after INDEPENDENT SECTOR was formed, I found I was called on regularly to provide briefings, testimony, articles, and speeches about the role and impact of philanthropic and voluntary initiative. However, I found there were relatively few telling examples at hand that brought the generalizations to life. That's when Ann Brown O'Connell and I set out to pull together specific examples of gifts and volunteers that had made a large difference in many fields.

For *Philanthropy in Action,* we amassed about 2,500 examples of gifts that struck us as particularly impressive. From these, we selected approximately 300, within thirteen disparate categories of impact. The categories included the discovery of new knowledge; the support and encouragement of excellence; the fostering of human potential; the relief of human misery; the preservation and enhancement of democratic government and institutions; the improvement of communities; the nourishment of the spirit; and the creation of tolerance, understanding, and peace.

For *Volunteers in Action,* we collected about 4,000 profiles of impressive service and sifted these to about 400, in the following categories: serving those most in need; lifting people toward self-reliance; advocating and empowering; cooperating in mutual dependence and assistance; exercising religious belief; and serving other causes and places—from arts to zoos. As we stated in our introduction to that book, "It is the composite of the work of millions of volunteers that adds up to the compassion, spirit, and power that are the quintessential characteristics of voluntary action in America. Everyone can make a difference, and a great many people do."

It is almost equally important to recognize what these opportunities for service mean to the kind of people Americans are. I submit that all this voluntary participation strengthens us as a nation, strengthens our communities, and strengthens and fulfills us as individual human beings.

The historian Merle Curti, in "American Philanthropy and the National Character," summarized it this way: "Emphasis on voluntary initiative . . . has helped give America her national character. . . . All these philanthropic initiatives give support to the thesis that philanthropy has helped to shape national character . . . [by] implementing the idea that America is a process rather than a finished product."

What comes through from all of the great citizen movements of our history is that the participation, the caring, the evidence that people can make a difference, add wonderfully to the spirit of our society. Inez Haynes Irwin, in her book *The Last Days of the Fight for Women's Suffrage,* repeatedly refers to the *spirit* of those women, not only in deciding on their task and accomplishing it, but in responding as human beings to their success: "They developed a sense of devotion to their ideal of freedom which would have stopped short of no personal sacrifice, not death itself. They developed a sense of comradeship for each other which was half love, half admiration and all reverence. In summing up a fellow worker, they speak first of her spirit, and her spirit is always *beautiful,* or *noble* or *glorious.*"

From where does all this generosity stem? Obviously, ours is not the only participatory society in the world. Giving, volunteering, and nonprofit organizations exist in most countries, but nowhere else are the numbers, proportions and impact so great.

The comparative studies are sketchy, but what facts there are indicate that this country's degree of organized participation is unique. In a 1986 speech, "A Global View of Philanthropy," J. D. Livingston Booth of Great Britain, then president of Interphil (International Standing Conference on Philanthropy) said, "Outside the United States there is very little recognition that an independent voluntary sector even exists, let alone that it has a wholeness, a role, and a significance in free societies."

Why is there so much more of this activity here? It's not easy to sort out, but if we hope to sustain it into future generations, we need to understand the phenomenon better than we do. The research and literature are sparse, but one can begin to piece together some of the explanation.

Most often, the participation is attributed to our Protestant ethic and English ancestry; but as important as they were, they are only two of many sources. What we identify as Christian, or Judeo-Christian, impulses were also brought to our shores by other waves of immigrants, whether they came from Sweden, Russia, China, or India, and whether they followed Jesus, Moses, Mohammed, or Buddha.

One of the largest roles of voluntary organizations is religious expression and its protection. In the 1993 edition of INDEPENDENT SECTOR's report *From Belief to Commitment,* which was based on the largest study ever undertaken of the community service role of religious congregations, extensive documentation showed that religious congregations are the primary service providers for neighborhoods. It is my experience that the poorer the community, the larger that role. Beyond the exercise of religious freedom and the provision of community services, religious congregations have been and continue to be the places where moral issues are raised and pursued. In his mid-nineteenth-century observations of the American scene, Alexis de Tocqueville saw this country's voluntary organizations, especially religiously affiliated ones, not so much as service providers but as "the moral associations" where such values as charity and responsibility to others were taught, and where the nation's crusades took root.

A good 50 percent of our country's community service and advocacy is related to the activities of churches, synagogues, temples, and mosques, and to the initial and continuing protections of freedom of religion. Many people dismiss this huge portion of the voluntary sector as being concerned largely with salvation. But religious congregations take on a different and larger significance when they are considered as meeting grounds, as forums of conscience, and as promoters of organized neighborliness.

As important as religious influences have been, we can't ascribe our tradition of voluntary action solely to the good example set by religion. The realities of pure need and mutual dependence and assistance cannot be overlooked. The Minute Men and the frontier families practiced pretty basic forms of enlightened self-interest. To portray our history of volunteering as relating solely to goodness may do justice to the best of our forebears, but it ignores the widespread tradition of organized neighborliness dictated by hardship.

It would be quite wrong to assume that all the characteristics and traditions of voluntary action were imported. In *American Philanthropy,* historian Robert Bremner makes clear that the Indians treated the Europeans with far more "Christian" goodness than they received in return. Reading his descriptions of the kindly way in which the Indians greeted the intruders and helped them adjust to their new environment, one is absolutely wrenched out of prior notions about imported goodness.

The settlers came into a country where there was little structure, and they had a chance to start all over again. For most people, for the first time in generations, the family hierarchy was absent. There were few restraints imposed by centuries of laws and habits, and yet the newcomers were terribly interdependent. In the absence of families and controlling traditions, they addressed their dependence and gregariousness by becoming, as Max Lerner described it, "a nation of joiners." New institutions, whether they were churches, unions, granges, fire companies, or other types of organization, became the networks for socializing and mutual activity.

It's also important to realize that the settlers were people determined never again to be ruled by kings or emperors or czars, and thus were suspicious of any central authority. They were resolved that power should be spread. This meant that voluntary institutions took on a large share of what was done in other countries by governments. In an article titled "What Kind of Society Shall We Have?" Richard W. Lyman, former president of the Rockefeller Foundation, former chairperson of IS, and now president emeritus at Stanford University, reminded us of Edmund Burke's description of "the little platoons" of France, which provided greater flexibility for fast action and became the new Americans' own way for achieving dispersion of power and organization of mutual effort.

As more and more people experienced the benefits of so much citizen participation, including the personal satisfactions that such service provides, they became all the more committed to this kind of participatory society. Along the way, they constantly renewed their faith in the basic intelligence and ability of people.

We have never found a better way of safeguarding freedom than placing responsibility in the hands of the people and expecting them to fulfill it. We may be disappointed at times in their performance, and we may be concerned that the people won't make the right decisions for themselves, their families, and their communities, but there is wisdom and comfort in Thomas Jefferson's advice: "I know of no safe depository of the ultimate powers of society, but the people themselves; and if we think them not enlightened enough to exercise their control with a wholesome discretion, the remedy is not to take it from them, but to inform their discretion by education."

Our founders really meant, and we continue to subscribe to, what is written in the Declaration of Independence. We do believe in the rights and power of people, and these convictions cause us to stand up and be counted on a broad array of issues, and to cherish and fiercely defend the freedoms of religion, speech, and assembly.

If we accept that our patterns and levels of participation and generosity contribute importantly to our national life, it is essential to understand and nurture all of the roots that give rise to such participation. One of the basic jobs is to be sure that the American people understand that, in addition to government and commerce, there is this third way by which we address our national problems and aspirations.

Among the very best teachers of the essentiality of civic engagement was the educator and philosopher John Dewey. In *The Ethics of Democracy*, Dewey concluded that "democracy is not an alternative to other principles of associated life. It is the idea of community life itself." Dewey's biographer, Robert Westbrook, states, "Dewey was the most important advocate of participatory democracy, that is, of the belief that democracy as an ethical ideal calls upon men and women to build communities in which the necessary opportunities and resources are available for every individual to realize fully his or her particular capacities and powers through participation in political, social and cultural life."

More recently, Robert Bellah and the several other authors of *The Good Society* wrote: "It is central to our very notion of a good society that it is an open quest, actively involving all its members. . . . Indeed, the great classic criteria of a good society—peace, prosperity, freedom, justice—all depend today on a new experiment in democracy, a newly extended and enhanced set of democratic institutions, within which we citizens can better discern what we really want and what we ought to want to sustain a good life on this planet for ourselves and the generations to come."

One of the unanticipated roles of INDEPENDENT SECTOR has been to serve as a resource for people from other countries who are eager to learn more about our philanthropy and voluntary action. These individuals are not necessarily unhappy with their own political structures, but they are keenly aware that an important aspect of freedom and influence is missing when there isn't a buffer or independent sector. They find it at best restrictive and at worst oppressive when there is only the one governmental system for education or health and no tradition of independent service and criticism.

Many of us who were involved in the creation of CIVICUS: World Alliance for Citizen Participation learned very quickly that citizen service and influence are increasingly viewed as essential underpinnings of effective societies. In the initial exploratory sessions, our committee, representative of twenty-one diverse countries, found itself unable to agree on the use of terms like *philanthropy, civil society,* and *voluntarism* because each term had negative connotations in some parts of the world. But in the end, Miklós Marschall of Budapest pointed out that though we couldn't agree on specific terms and practices, we all seemed to be acknowledging that there is a distinct correlation between the degree of citizen participation in a society and that society's effectiveness. With the articulation of that common notion, the committee was able to move toward the establishment of the organization. Under the CIVICUS umbrella, countries will emphasize indigenous organizations, philanthropy, civil society, voluntarism, grassroots activity, or some combination of these things.

At about the same time CIVICUS was being formed, Vaclav Havel, president of the Czech Republic, captured the importance of this growing worldwide interest in citizen participation when he said, "The modern era is at its height, and if we are not to perish of our modernness we have to rehabilitate the human dimension of citizenship."

At the time I am writing all this about worldwide attention to civic engagement, there is a great debate swirling in higher education circles in the U.S. about whether it is the business of universities to teach citizenship and about the citizen's responsibility to society. Some don't think this subject is scholarly enough.

When that astounding notion was first surfacing in the 1980s, I was invited to give the keynote address at the American Association of Higher Education's national conference, and I took the opportunity to say:

> The United States is the longest-lived democracy in the history of the world. This democracy has provided almost all of us with greater freedom and opportunity than any nation human beings have ever known. Among the crucial factors that foster and preserve that democracy and those freedoms are active citizenship and personal community service. No leader or leadership institution—particularly no educator or educational institution—can presume that fostering active citizenship to prolong our democracy and to extend those glorious freedoms for those who come after us is someone else's business.

Despite my belief in and passion about active citizenship and the independent sector in America, I have learned that it is essential not to suggest that nonprofit activity is more important or can take the place of democratic government. We lose our perspective on the sector and society when we exaggerate the importance of private philanthropy and voluntary organizations, particularly when we separate them from the public sector or even put them ahead of our responsibility to democratic government. An active voluntary sector can help preserve and enhance our democratic principles, but it doesn't transcend them. More attention from the schools and the public at large will help to increase understanding of how this country does its public business. In some quarters, there is an exaggerated idea of what voluntary organizations should and can do and what government should not do. Some see voluntary effort as getting in the way of governmental responsibility. Others preach that voluntary organizations should do it all. Obviously, we need both strong government and a strong voluntary sector, but we won't have either if the public does not understand their relative roles and its responsibility to each.

One of the immediate consequences of confusion about who should do what in our society is a reduced emphasis on the independence of voluntary organizations. Caught between the efforts of voluntary organizations to attract government dollars and government's growing efforts to regulate nonprofit activity, the quintessential contribution and quality of independence are being compromised. There are many contributions that nonprofit institutions make, including providing services and acting as vehicles through which the government fulfills some of its public responsibilities, but the largest contribution is the opportunities they provide for innovation, excellence, criticism, and where necessary, reform. These opportunities rest on a basis of independence.

At the time IS was being formed, John Gardner spoke to the Council on Foundations about the issue of independence:

> Perhaps the most striking feature of the sector is its relative freedom from constraints and its resulting pluralism. Within the bounds of the law, all kinds of people can pursue any idea or program they wish. Unlike government, an independent sector group need not ascertain that its idea or philosophy is supported by some large constituency, and unlike the business sector, they do not need to pursue only those ideas which will be profitable. If a handful of people want to back a new idea, they need seek no larger consensus.
>
> Institutions of the nonprofit sector are in a position to serve as the guardians of intellectual and artistic freedom. Both the commercial and political marketplaces are subject to leveling forces that may threaten standards of excellence. In the nonprofit sector, the fiercest champions of excellence may have their say. So may the champions of liberty and justice.

Although it is important not to exaggerate the worth of voluntary effort, it is also important not to underestimate how much this participation means to our opportunities to be unique and free as individuals and as a society. Through our voluntary initiative and independent institutions, ever more Americans worship freely, study quietly, are cared for compassionately, experiment creatively, serve effectively, advocate aggressively, and contribute generously. These treasures of our common life are constantly beautiful and must remain beautifully constant.

PART ONE

The Beginnings
of INDEPENDENT SECTOR

Serious Challenges to Nonprofit Organizations in the 1960s and 1970s

T he post–World War II period marked the coming of age of citizen participation and the establishment of a staggering number of associations and institutions through which people could express their collective views on what society should be—and their power to usher it into being. These included colleges, community foundations, civil rights groups, environmental organizations, fraternal societies, neighborhood theaters, corporate public services, museums, self-help participants, veterans' organizations, neighborhood development alliances, and thousands of others.

By the 1960s, participatory democracy began to include all parts of society. Americans were organizing to influence every conceivable aspect of the human condition. They were also willing to stand up and be counted on almost any public issue.

A few examples may help to emphasize what an empowering period this was:

• The civil rights battles of the 1960s provided the model and the courage for a great many other groups determined to be empowered and included in the freedoms and opportunities of democracy.

• The success of the March of Dimes and then of all the other major health organizations, including the American Cancer Society and National Mental Health Association, created a new, effective force of ordinary citizens—as described in Richard Carter's book *The Gentle Legions.*

• The moral indignation of individual parents of retarded children achieved blistering force through the National Association for Retarded Children and set the organizing example for everyone else determined to provide better services and understanding for people with autism, spina bifida, dyslexia, and hundreds of other seemingly incurable conditions.

Americans of all backgrounds and economic conditions began to realize that they too could make a difference by joining forces around the crises, problems, and causes that concerned them. Over more than a century, voluntary participation had moved by stages from the early days of Lord and Lady Bountiful through the period of an elite and concentrated power structure, to the 1960s and 1970s when we came to accept that participatory democracy was everybody's business. We owe a tremendous debt to Dorothea Dix, the crusader for the mentally ill, and other heroes of her kind, and to the community fathers who served so many causes, but the greatest accolades should be reserved for those in the here and now, when democracy has become more fully alive, with the population joining in the traditions of service and reform.

Given this burgeoning of all forms of civic engagement, it was perplexing, bewildering, and frightening for those involved to find themselves and their institutions increasingly questioned, criticized, and attacked. Explanations came slowly but would have profound influence on the future of nonprofit endeavor.

Waldemar A. Nielsen was the first to grasp the reasons and consequences of this alarming development. Author of the seminal study *The Golden Donors,* Nielsen had been the sector's foremost observer and chronicler. Beginning in the mid-1970s, he began to sound alarms, which reached the screeching point with publication of *The Endangered Sector* in 1979. The book presented a chilling picture of government's increasing control of the activities of voluntary associations and institutions through money, mandates, regulation, penalties, political influence, intimidation, and even witch hunts. Nielsen provided specific examples from the sector as a whole and from institutions devoted to education, science, health, social action, culture, and the arts. Almost all of the activities described were compounded by the increasing dependence of these institutions on government financing.

Nielsen also pointed out the general failure of private foundations to defend the independence of these organizations and to be in the forefront of protecting rights and promoting services for people most in need.

The threatening title of the book and the enumeration and elaboration of danger signs drove even the most ardent supporter of nongovernmental activity into confusion and defensiveness.

People like Nielsen who had been part of the action for several years had seen negativism heating up during a series of governmental hearings and investigations, particularly directed to foundations.

In "The Rocky Road to Regulation," an article that appeared in the Robert Wood Johnson Foundation's twentieth-anniversary report in 1992, Terrance Keenan provided a valuable recap of ominous events that began as far back as 1916 but really boiled over in the mid-1960s. It is revealing that at least as much of the antagonism and regulation was caused by foundations that abused their public responsibilities as was caused by regulators who didn't happen to like what foundations did or didn't do.

Pre-1960s inquiries included the Walsh Committee of 1916, which considered the request of the Rockefeller Foundation to become a federally chartered institution. In turning down the request, the committee recommended that sweeping regulatory powers be imposed on the governance of foundations.

The Cox Committee in 1952 investigated whether foundations promoted "un-American activities." (It is fascinating that Walsh assumed that foundations were guilty of preserving control of society by the wealthy, and Cox believed that funders wanted to tear apart the comfortable status quo. What a change in just thirty-five years!)

The Reece Committee in 1953 pursued a broader mandate to determine whether foundations used their resources for nonexempt purposes, subversive activities, political activities, propaganda, or the influencing of legislation. That committee's recommendations foreshadowed the Tax Reform Act of 1969 in proposing that foundations be treated as a separate class of charitable institutions; come under a mandatory annual payout of their assets, including capital gains; be prohibited from investing more than 5–10 percent of their holdings in any one enterprise; and be prohibited from all political activities.

The problems and decisions of the 1960s developed out of three primary events: the Patman investigations, the U.S. Treasury Department's *Report on Private Foundations,* and the Tax Reform Act of 1969. Because of their significance to the climate of the time and the continuing lessons they present, I'll try to summarize each of them.

Representative Wright Patman of Texas was chairman of the House Select Committee on Small Business. His investigations of foundations, which lasted throughout the 1960s, revealed a number of instances of self-dealing and other abuse, and his committee issued seven recommendations for reform.

First, the life of a foundation should be limited to twenty-five years. Second, foundations should be prohibited from engaging in business, either directly or indirectly. Third, an "arm's length" relationship should be enforced between donors and foundations. Fourth, foundations should be limited to ownership of no more than 3 percent of any corporation and should be prohibited from voting their stock. Fifth, charitable deductions should be denied to donors who controlled foundations until the money was actually used for charity. Sixth, capital gains should be treated as income, not capital. And seventh, foundations should be prohibited from influencing political campaigns through voter registration drives.

Patman's findings and recommendations drew the attention of Congress and the media, and subsequently the House Ways and Means Committee and the Senate Finance Committee jointly requested a Treasury Department report. That 1965 report listed six major problems with foundation philanthropy:

1. *Delay in benefit to charity.* Accumulation of income was cited, as well as investments in low-yield assets, such as land.

2. *Ownership of business.* A for-profit company could set up a foundation, then create a subsidiary of the corporation financed through tax-exempt dollars from the foundation.

3. *Family use of foundations to control corporate and other property.* A donor, for example, could grant a foundation stock in a company, reap a large tax deduction and lower his or her equity in the company, thereby reducing estate taxes.

4. *Questionable investments.* Foundations were investing tax-exempt funds in speculative securities.

5. *Self-dealing.* Donors used foundation assets for self-advantage, such as buying control of another company.

6. *Unlimited donor control.* Donors and families could control a foundation in perpetuity. There was no limit to their tenure on the board.

The Tax Reform Act of 1969 was the culmination of all this probing and contained a long list of provisions. For example, the act denied to foundations the same favorable tax deductions as those allowed for gifts to public charities; imposed a 6 percent annual payout requirement; restricted lobbying activities; and required an annual information report to be filed with the IRS.

Although many foundation officials still consider the 1969 act as harsh and grossly overreaching, others like Nielsen believe that much in the process and final results was healthy, and that on balance, foundations came out fairly well. Everyone is pretty much agreed that the investigations produced an awful scare and horrible publicity. They also revealed that the foundation world, which generally thought of itself as attractively charitable and above the reach of repressive regulation, wasn't ready for this dose of populism, criticism, and governmental intrusion.

The criticisms and concerns were not restricted to foundations, nor did they originate only from government. Many grassroots groups, emerging leaders, and unpopular causes were aggressively hostile to both grant-making and voluntary groups considering them to be elitist or indifferent. In just one example, the Donee Group, which described itself as "a coalition of public interest, social action, and volunteer groups," was able to force its way into the activities of the Filer Commission (Commission on Private Philanthropy and Public Needs, 1973–75), and even issued a report of its own that was distributed with the commission's primary report. The Donee document, *Private Philanthropy: Vital and Innovative? or Passive and Irrelevant?* concluded that the Filer Commission was too focused on "preserving the status quo," and that it had failed to adequately "assess public needs."

It wasn't only liberals and the new crop of activists who were stridently critical. From the conservative and establishment side, people like Richard C. Cornuelle of the National Association of Manufacturers expressed their own alarm about voluntary groups surrendering to government many responsibilities that belonged best to private initiative. In his book *Reclaiming the American Dream,* published in 1965, Cornuelle presaged the Republican revolution of the mid-1990s—the "Contract with America"—when he proposed that the independent sector take back its traditional role in and responsibility for community service. His call for reclaiming the American Dream concluded with the words: "Through it [the independent sector] we can restore the supportive circle whereby America originally put its unique emphasis on personal dignity. We can again insure our freedom by limiting the powers of central government. Being free, we can move to ever higher planes of prosperity and ever greater human aspirations. We can, as we learn how, focus our growing prosperity directly and imaginatively on real human needs."

Many ardent supporters of voluntary initiative balanced their positive views with concerns about some of the sector's weaknesses. For example, in his foreword to *America's Voluntary Spirit*, John Gardner cautioned: "My observations about the positive aspects of the sector are not intended to gloss over the flaws that are evident in its institutions and organizations. Some nonprofit institutions are far gone in decay. Some are so badly managed as to make a mockery of every good intention they might have had. There is fraud, mediocrity, and silliness. In short, the human and institutional failures that afflict government and business are also present in the voluntary sector."

In my own study of the state of things, reported more fully in the next chapter, I came up with a litany of concerns and criticisms, including the degree of government funding and consequent influence; government rules and regulations that went far beyond any contracted obligations of voluntary organizations to perform specified services; challenges to advocacy rights; reduction or removal of exemption from property taxes; proposed taxes on endowments; limitations on deductions of contributions; the concept of "tax expenditures" (the belief that because the government loses money when people deduct charitable gifts from their taxes, it should have more control over where that money is channeled and how it is spent); and concerns about unfair competition between businesses and nonprofit organizations.

In addition, I listed other factors that provoked criticism of our organizations, including the illegal and irresponsible behavior of some groups; general questioning of the effectiveness of philanthropic and voluntary organizations; and the growing skepticism in the country about all institutions, including church, government, media, politicians, and big business. I said, "It is to be expected that institutions which perform public functions will receive a great deal of scrutiny. Even when they perform openly and effectively, they will not escape suspicion, and where they are perceived to be secretive, unresponsive, or ineffective, there will be cynicism and scorn."

Much of my review pointed up the pain felt by leaders of philanthropy and voluntary action, who believed deeply in the importance and worth of the sector but recognized that all their experience and conviction were being challenged by skeptics and even cynics who questioned whether giving is a loophole or charity a rip-off. They also had to acknowledge that they were the object of criticism from emerging groups that couldn't get a fair share of the charitable pie and from reporters who were looking behind the tired rhetoric used to rationalize tired programs. They recognized also that the number and intensity of such criticisms caused a lot of people to wonder whether the automatic assumptions that volunteering is good and that voluntary activity is better than government were perhaps themselves tired shibboleths.

At that stage, the National Organization for Women was pronouncing that volunteering was a bummer; Treasury officials were saying that private philanthropy was a raid on the U.S. Treasury; health agencies were suing the United Way for monopoly; boiler room solicitations were annoying the hell out of everyone who owned a telephone; and better-organized consumers were calling down a pox on everybody not delivering services to human beings who hurt.

As if those weren't enough problems for leaders of voluntary effort, there were also the realities that many strong advocacy organizations were making government officials and agencies extremely nervous and defensive, and that some nonprofit organizations, even at the level of the Sierra Club and Ford Foundation, were being accused of engaging in illegal political activity.

In addition, as the sector became larger, more involved, and more visible, it attracted attention—and that certainly included escalating criticism of what it was doing or not doing and of whom it was including or not including.

Faced with all these attacks, the sector found there was little research to bolster a factual case for its worth, and there was no clear and pervasive voice speaking out on its behalf.

People in the sector believed passionately in the value of what they were about and its relevance to a free society. They also agreed that despite the obviousness of the good their sector did, many policy makers and opinion molders increasingly put them on the defensive. There was a consequent assumption that if someone could just better organize the sector to tell its story, the wind would shift.

In a very short period of time, those involved in voluntary action went from an appreciation of the inherent goodness of giving and volunteering to a recognition that that appreciation was far from universally shared.

I didn't quite agree that we were "the endangered sector," but I did agree that unless we could improve ourselves, strengthen public perceptions of us, and educate people about the importance of this voluntary, independent sector, our unique contributions to the American experience would be tragically reduced. At that point, like many others, I turned to considerations of whether anything could be done about it.

CHAPTER TWO

Searching for a Course

The 1978 study I undertook of the state of the sector was part of a review I had been asked to do by the National Council on Philanthropy and the Coalition of National Voluntary Organizations. Those two groups were interested in identifying ways in which they might collaborate to better address their mutual interests in philanthropy and voluntary action. The unusual origins of that assignment are part of the history.

Earlier that year, I had indicated to my board at the Mental Health Association that I felt twelve years as national executive director were long enough for them and for me, and that with almost a year's notice, I planned to step down.

I had intended to do this after ten years, but when our board member Rosalynn Carter became first lady, it was essential to keep the team intact to capitalize on her commitment and prominence. Incidentally—but not incidental to the IS story—John Gardner chaired and I served on the small committee that worked with President and Mrs. Carter to set up the enormously influential Mental Health Commission that she headed.

Two years later, with the commission established and with the association enjoying new heights of visibility and influence, it was a better time to deal with a leadership change. Also, by then I had been a health association executive for twenty-five years, including a dozen years with the American Heart Association, finishing as its California director. At age forty-eight, it was time to do something different—and, I hoped, a bit less chaotic! It was a scary time for the organization and me, but there was about a year to adjust and to plan for our separate futures.

To locate my next job, I talked to at least fifty people who might help steer me to possible opportunities or to other individuals who might have leads. In that way, I was brought to the attention of Ken Albrecht, head of contributions and public service at Equitable Life, and Bayard Ewing, volunteer head of the National Information Bureau and a significant leader in many national voluntary efforts. I had known both, but not in their current leadership roles, respectively with the National Council on Philanthropy (NCOP) and the Coalition of National Voluntary Organizations (CONVO). It turned out that NCOP's president had died shortly after taking over, and CONVO's board felt it needed a change of director. Both Kenneth and Bayard expressed interest in exploring my possible candidacy, but from what I knew about each, I didn't feel either opportunity was what I was hoping for.

I had known that when CONVO was formed a few years earlier, there had been some consideration of establishing it as part of NCOP, but nothing had come of the idea. It's my recollection that when I learned each was searching, I asked permission to let the other know, just in case that might lead to reconsideration of joint effort. I didn't do this with my own situation in mind. My memory and notes remind me that I didn't think even a merger of the two would offer sufficient opportunity or the more sensible setting I was looking for.

Subsequently, Ken and Bayard, after discussions with others, asked if I would at least take a look at what they might do, separately or jointly, in their next stages of staffing and programming. Because I was still in a more than full-time job, as well as facing the stark reality of being off the payroll by year-end, I was reluctant to take on even that much, but I thought the examination could be done in a few weeks, and it appeared important and fascinating to see if I could help facilitate what might be a sensible amalgamation. I don't remember if I had any sense that Ken and Bayard hoped I would become more interested in their prospects, or if somewhere in the back of my mind then was a glimmer of interest, but if either was the case, it was subliminal.

At that point, Bayard and Ken were eager to make decisions. Each board was engaged in its staff search, and each was facing organizational uncertainties that seriously threatened financial support. For these reasons, each of them hoped it would be possible for me to come forward with clear recommendations fairly quickly so that action might be taken shortly after Labor Day, not many weeks away. As I should have expected, any review of such serious and complicated issues had to be intense, and the challenge of the task was compounded in this case by the very tight timetable.

I interviewed forty people, including leaders of the two organizations and other prominent and informed figures, and I corresponded with about forty others. Before long, it became apparent that my review would involve three levels of examination, ranging from very specific and immediate to very general and long-range. The first was the immediate futures of CONVO and NCOP. The second was current and prospective issues, events, and activities within philanthropy and the broader voluntary sector, including the question of who was already doing and planning what. The third concerned what, if anything, was needed and could be done to strengthen giving, volunteering, and the overall worth and impact of the philanthropic voluntary sector.

As indicated in Chapter One, it was obvious right away that the study had to start at the broadest level and work backwards to organizational specifics.

Predictably, there were many different ideas about what was needed to strengthen the sector, but there was resounding unanimity that something substantial had to be done. Indeed, there was a general impression that the sector was in dangerous disarray.

Most people with whom I talked began by pointing out the exasperating contradiction that despite the worth of philanthropy and voluntary action in America, there seemed to be an alarming increase in the number of skeptics and even cynics in key places such as Congress, state and local legislatures, and the media, who either didn't know about the worth, doubted it, or knocked it. Added to these legitimate concerns were the illegitimate actions of even the Palatine Fathers, who had been caught at fraudulent fund-raising, and it was no wonder that a public conditioned to rip-offs wondered about our motives and worth.

Many people pointed to the Filer Commission for evidence of the importance of the voluntary sector. Officially named the Commission on Private Philanthropy and Public Needs, and known for its chairman, John H. Filer, CEO of Aetna Life and Casualty and later a chairperson of INDEPENDENT SECTOR, it began its work in 1973, and in 1975 issued a report and book, *Giving in America: Toward a Stronger Voluntary Sector.*

The commission laid out its views of the "virtues of nonprofit activity and philanthropic giving" and made recommendations for protecting and expanding them. Among the findings, these were foremost:

> The *voluntary sector* is a large and vital part of American society, more important today than ever. But the sector is undergoing economic strains that predate and are generally more severe than the troubles of the economy as a whole.

> Giving in America involves an immense amount of time and money, is the fundamental underpinning of the voluntary sector, encompasses a wide diversity of relationships between donor, donations, and donee, and is not keeping pace.

The commission's primary concerns related to tax policy, and therefore most of its recommendations were for revisions in the tax code, such as allowing those who do not itemize their tax deductions (generally those who use the short form) to be able to deduct their charitable contributions.

The commission also recommended "that a permanent national commission on the nonprofit sector be established by Congress to examine philanthropic priorities, determine ways to increase private giving, and establish means of insulating voluntary organizations from political and bureaucratic pressures."

Half the new commission's membership would be named by the president and the other half by the presidential appointees themselves. Half the funding for the commission would come from government and half from private sources.

Less well known than the Filer Commission was the Peterson Commission, which dealt largely with the giving side of the sector. That group was formally named the Commission on Foundation and Private Philanthropy, and its report and related book, issued in 1970, were called *Foundations, Private Giving, and Public Policy.* It was known for its chairman, Peter G. Peterson, CEO of Bell & Howell and later, Secretary of Commerce.

This study also chronicled the benefits of private philanthropy and the threats to it. For example, the report stated: "We believe that government should not venture to do those things which private citizens and private institutions can do as well or better. . . . Our society, therefore, is in obvious need of private philanthropic institutions standing outside the frame of government but in support of the public interest."

The commission focused on ways to stimulate an increase in funds, with an emphasis on strengthening foundations. It, too, proposed the establishment of a governmental body to pursue those ends.

Though it's hard to determine just why the kinds of commissions called for by both groups never came to pass, I believe an important factor was that the permanent bodies as proposed would have been part of government or likely controlled by it, and there was an instinctive reaction that what was needed for this sector had to be independent of government.

The Filer Commission (with its related Donee Report) and the Peterson Commission provided observations, criticisms, and recommendations that represented valuable guidance for my immediate study, and later for the organizing committee that created INDEPENDENT SECTOR. Through all my interviewing and reading I heard four critical needs expressed repeatedly. What people in the field wanted was greater influence in Washington; research to prove their case; capacity to get that case to the American people; and a meeting ground and communication mechanism so that those working in this vast and disparate sector would have a better grasp of who was doing and thinking what.

Of these four, the first, involving influence in Washington, was by far the top priority.

Beyond the four, there were scores of roles and activities urged on some responsible entity: standard setting, executive search, technical assistance, management consulting, creation of career pathways, training, organizational development, and improvement of the climate for corporate giving. The list went on and on, but at least in the four critical needs and basic functions, there seemed to be general agreement that a much better mechanism was needed.

The second part of my study considered whether anybody could really do anything to vastly improve the climate and resources for private initiative for the public good. This in turn led me to study past and current efforts that had been organized for those purposes.

It became abundantly clear that there was no shortage of existing efforts. Indeed, for quite a while, I was stumped as to how there could be so much activity when those I interviewed, including most of the leaders of those various existing efforts, called for exponentially more. As I sorted it out, I realized that the contradiction existed because most of those already involved saw how very much more needed to be done, the competition for money and roles kept many of them weak, and some of those groups hoped that they would be catapulted into far larger roles. Nevertheless, the question loomed larger all the time: what more could NCOP and CONVO do in any configuration, or what could they do in novel ways, that would make much of a difference?

In a very helpful book, *Modern American Philanthropy,* Jack Schwartz had provided a good survey of early efforts to deal with criticisms of the sector, including descriptions of some of the organizations set up to rally the defense. Jack was the long-time president of the American Association of Fund-Raising Counsel (AAFRC) and had been a board member of both NCOP and CONVO. This is a summary of his much fuller description:

• The 501(C)(3) Group was formed in the late 1950s to bring together nonprofit leaders concerned with tax policies. In 1971, the group funded the initial study by Martin Feldstein on the effect of taxes on charitable giving, which concluded that charities would lose more than government would gain if charitable gifts were not tax-deductible. The 501(C)(3) Group existed until the early 1980s, when the participants agreed that INDEPENDENT SECTOR should assume its functions.

• AAFRC's project "A Campaign for Philanthropy" was organized in 1971. It attracted considerable attention, but not the leadership necessary for success.

• The campaign evolved into the "Coalition for the Public Good," led by Bayard Ewing, with staff support from United Way of America. It was to address tax reform, communication and cooperation within the broad spectrum of the sector, and involvement of top volunteer trustees of member groups.

• In 1976–77, the chances dimmed that the government might establish the kind of commission called for by the Peterson and Filer reports. Even the much less ambitious Advisory Committee on Private Philanthropy and Public Needs, which had been organized within the Treasury Department, had been dissolved.

• During 1976, several groups began to explore the establishment of something like the commission, but as a private body, outside government, so that it would be "removed from the danger of political influences." Those involved included the 501(C)(3) Group, Coalition for the Public Good, National Council on Philanthropy, Council on Foundations, AAFRC, United Way, and many others. The hope was still to achieve a commission, or at least in the interim "to combine the professional resources of our organizations to address the shared concerns about the current state and future capacity of American philanthropy."

• In 1977, the Coalition for the Public Good was reconstituted as the Coalition of National Voluntary Organizations (CONVO) with plans to greatly expand participation, funding, and programs.

At the time of my study in 1978, I looked at many other groups whose missions, activities, and views were intertwined.

The Committee for the Third Sector was also seeking a possible successor organization to the Filer Commission to improve the climate for philanthropy and to support research. Some I interviewed urged me to recommend that NCOP and CONVO fold into such an entity. Indeed, it was that kind of proposal that made me realize the situation was far more complicated than could be resolved by my hurried study.

The National Center for Voluntary Action (NCVA) had retreated from an earlier, very ambitious role and was concentrating on consultation, technical assistance, publications, and building coalitions around specific issues. Finances were a very real problem, in part because the chaotic proliferation of like-minded groups caused confusion among funding sources.

The National Information Center on Volunteerism (NICOV) had carved out very useful space for itself, providing consultation and technical assistance to voluntary agencies and others, but it was finding that the service didn't pay for itself, and it was again looking for foundation and government support. NCVA and NICOV were considering a merger around their joint consultation and technical assistance roles.

The Alliance for Volunteerism was moving from Boulder, Colorado, to Washington, D.C., with the hope that by better serving the voluntary sector in Washington, its functions and financing would become clearer.

The National Committee for Responsive Philanthropy, the successor organization to the Donee Group of the Filer Commission, was determined to broaden the participation and impact of donees and consumers so that there would be a fairer distribution of the charitable dollar and so that programs and services would be more sensitive to the needs of persons to be helped.

The Institute for Voluntary Organizations started as a profit-making venture and was then in the process of rebirth as a voluntary nonprofit organization.

The Center for a Voluntary Society had recently run out of funds after identifying major research issues that needed to be addressed if the sector was to be understood and strengthened.

The Aspen Institute's "Pluralism and the Commonweal" program emphasized Aspen's interest in developments in philanthropy and the voluntary sector.

Involvement, Inc., worked with businesses to develop their participation in voluntarism. It helped to obtain corporate sponsorship of volunteer programs and to mobilize employees in volunteer efforts.

ACTION's Office of Voluntary Citizen Participation (OVCP) was just opening. It would have a multimillion dollar annual budget to stimulate use of volunteers within government, voluntary action outside government, and research. The initial priority was to help advance the Carter administration's urban policy.

The Association of Voluntary Action Scholars was trying to stimulate greater research and the practical application of scholarly findings.

The American Enterprise Institute (AEI) was giving important attention to the voluntary sector. A major four-year study had been launched under the general title "To Empower People," with the more formal heading "The Role of Mediating Structures in Public Policy."

Under Kingman Brewster and John Simon, Yale had launched a new effort and had already raised $1 million of a projected $10 million to support research and interchange under the general title "Mapping the Third Sector."

The Council on Foundations had expanded its efforts for impact in Washington and to provide interchange among a broader spectrum of donors.

The Brookings Institution was considering moving into the all important arena of interrelationships among the voluntary, governmental, and business sectors, one possible focus being corporate support of voluntary activity.

The Carter administration had expressed particular interest in individual initiative and the voluntary sector. Voluntarism was one of Rosalynn Carter's four major projects.

Even this listing didn't cover the waterfront, but I hoped it was sufficiently inclusive to delineate some of the principal players and to highlight concerns about proliferation and competition. I commented, "It is surely an indication of the intense needs that are perceived that so many groups are trying to find a place in the sun."

The third part of my study dealt with NCOP and CONVO's histories, missions, governance, members, funding, budgets, staff, programs, similarities, and differences, and my candid view of their strengths and weaknesses.

NCOP was twenty-four years old and was made up primarily but not exclusively of funders, especially from the corporate side. Its programs, including an annual conference on philanthropy, involved both donors and donees. Its mission was "strengthening and enriching private resources to better meet public needs." It was housed in New York City.

CONVO was just three years old, having grown out of the Coalition for the Public Good. It was made up primarily but not exclusively of leaders of voluntary organizations, but its programs related to both voluntary and philanthropic groups. Its mission was "to maximize the contributions of the voluntary sector in meeting America's human needs, and to enrich the quality of American society." It was housed in Washington, D.C.

Though my section on "similarities" was much longer than the one on "differences," the latter were significant, including the different locations; NCOP's almost twenty-five-year history versus CONVO's newness; and CONVO's priority of government relations contrasting with NCOP's aversion to it.

My assessment of the prospects for closer collaboration was based on a number of findings:

• There was a distinct impression that the two organizations were compatible, but although a few of my interviewees favored immediate merger, most preferred something short of that, at least for a while.

• Because most of those interviewed hoped that something significant could be done in and for the sector, they believed that whatever happened between CONVO and NCOP could represent first, important steps in the right direction.

• Despite CONVO's false start, many people believed that it had the kind of broad constituency essential to national impact.

• NCOP had the forum (the national conference) and the potential for even greater communication, and it had the important interest of many corporate givers.

• I came away with the impression that people felt that for the overall job to be done, CONVO had the more significant constituency and NCOP the better record.

• Even those who were discouraged by or critical of one or both organizations agreed that there was a job to be done. They concluded that the two didn't have too much to lose by trying some new arrangement.

• Overwhelmingly, those interviewed believed that the coincidence of the vacancies in the top staff jobs of the two organizations should be viewed in the perspective of the larger needs of the field, and that therefore this rare opportunity should be seized to try to build something better.

Although, as I came down to the wire, I was far from confident that I had explored all aspects of the situation, I was nevertheless able to draw up a list of thirteen distinct options that the organizations and the sector as a whole could consider:

1.   *Continue as is.* Obviously, it was an option just to let things develop along current lines without attempting to forge any larger meeting ground or liaison.

2.   *Try to reconstitute one of the existing organizations so that it could become a larger and better meeting ground, communicator, and lobbyist.* An attempt could be made to persuade all those who believed that something better was needed to get behind whichever existing organization seemed most likely to bring it off.

3.   *Unite CONVO and NCOP in a way that would represent a major first step toward a possible new and large combine.*

4.   *Push for the kind of quasipublic permanent commission called for by the Commission on Private Philanthropy and Public Needs.*

5.   *Create such a commission within the private sector.*

6.   *Let ACTION and the Carter administration see what they could do.* In addition to letting the new Office of Voluntary Citizen Participation see what it could accomplish, a move could be made to convince the president to establish within the White House a special assistant for the voluntary sector.

7. *Continue as is, but try to strengthen each association organizationally, programmatically, and financially.* Under this option, there would not be a more formal union but, without prejudice, each would be encouraged to go its own way and do the very best possible job in the important mission it had.

8. *Dissolve one or both organizations.* One or both boards might decide that the immediate and potential contribution did not justify the time and expenditure involved and therefore the organization(s) should dissolve.

9. *Disband one or both organizations for the purpose of delivering the assets to someone else in the field.* CONVO might wish to disband but turn its assets over to NCOP to strengthen its future, or vice versa. Both might disband and turn their assets over to a third group, such as NCVA or the Alliance or some new organization that might try to carry on their functions and missions.

10. *Have CONVO and NCOP merge with each other to form a new organization.* The boards might decide that the fullest possible collaboration is indicated, and that the two should go ahead and merge immediately.

11. *Have each merge with another organization.* NCOP might wish to consider merging with the Council on Foundations, the Conference Board, or someone else, and CONVO might consider joining with the Alliance, NCVA, or someone else.

12. *Create a common secretariat.* The two boards might agree to a common office and staff as an interim means of proceeding and as a tentative step toward possible later merger. A management committee made up of equal numbers from both organizations could be established to handle the details.

13. *Create a new league or combine that would serve as the secretariat for both organizations, but that would also act as an exploratory vehicle for planning and strategizing the better pursuit of their common ideals.* Under this arrangement, more than just a secretariat would be established, though the principal function of the new entity would be to ensure that the two organizations were well serviced. Rather than a simple management committee, a group would be formed to oversee the functioning of the secretariat and to devise ways in which the two organizations and the whole voluntary sector might best pursue the protection and enhancement of giving and volunteering, and of the worth and impact of the sector.

Responding to Ken's and Bayard's request for candor and a definite recommendation, I bit the bullet and summarized my conclusions:

> Philanthropy and the broader voluntary sector do need to do something better to protect and enhance giving, volunteering, and the tangible and intangible contributions of the sector to our democratic society. . . . CONVO and NCOP should use the coincidence of their current situations, their similar missions, and their shared conviction that something better is needed, to take the first steps toward creating a vehicle for closer organizational cooperation and for fuller pursuit of their common ideals.

To bolster my argument, I said:

> Creating only a secretariat limited to servicing the two organizations would help the two and cut down somewhat on duplication and proliferation, but it would not offer the prospect of setting in place the larger dimension necessary for the greater good. . . . What's needed for now is an entity which can be the secretariat and represent the vehicle for planning and organizing future efforts to strengthen the overall worth and impact of the voluntary sector. Such an arrangement must be extremely flexible, including a back door for withdrawal and a front door for advance.

To be even more specific, I spelled out the essential characteristics of the kind of enterprise I thought was needed for the long haul ("It should exist solely to pursue the commonly held ideal of people contributing their time and money to improve the human condition"), the basic functions (government relations, research, education of the public, and better ongoing communication and connections among the disparate parts of the sector), and even the location of the combined office (Washington, D.C.).

I also dealt with specific functions for each organization over the next year or two, as well as financial arrangements and the actions and timetable necessary to authorize the experiment.

Perhaps more important than anything else, I tried to communicate some of the aspirations and dreams I had been hearing in all of the contacts I had made. For example:

- A public affairs network spinning a web of caring and influential constituents around every member of Congress

- An information source to which the media would turn for information, facts, and background

- Growing impact on public instruction so that, for example, books that students read in history, civics, and public affairs would include information about, and appreciation of, the role and contributions of the voluntary sector

- A research effort that was respected as objective and contributory to sensible public policy

- The ability, based on a reputation for integrity, to set standards and to create mechanisms by which boards and others could measure performance according to those standards

Responding to the highest ideals and aspirations I had heard during all those interviews, I said, "Aside from all the fact finding, alternatives, conclusions, and recommendations, the larger message is that we just might be in on the ground floor and at the threshold of building what John Gardner describes as 'an enterprise . . . encompassing the whole fascinating universe of the voluntary sector and addressing issues infinitely broader and more varied than any organization in the sector has grappled with before.'"

I concluded, "There are decidedly good things about CONVO and NCOP. However, their immediate problems and shortcomings and the coincidence of their staff openings, along with their similar missions and shared desire to build a more effective instrument, suggest that to try to bring off the larger collaboration is the most important thing either organization could ever do."

That was all communicated very early in September, in the report *Feasibility Study of Closer Collaboration Between the Coalition of National Voluntary Organizations (CONVO) and the National Council on Philanthropy (NCOP)*. The reader will understand that when dealing with not one but two voluntary boards, agreements don't come crisply and without a great deal of discussion. There were objections, amendments, and meetings—oh, were there meetings!—and after those discussions were successfully concluded, there was a final four-part dance that was slow and painful to execute. The maneuvers involved three intertwined issues and four participants, and none of the parties wanted to be first on the floor. The issues were: (1) Would I be the interim head of the two organizations and the staff director of the planning stage? (2) Would John Gardner chair the planning stage? (3) Would CONVO and NCOP agree to the report with full understanding that what John and I would be working toward was a new entity, much larger than the sum of the two parts?

I did not want to get involved if we didn't have a real shot at something equal to the needs and dreams of the sector, and John certainly didn't intend to be limited to or preoccupied with a coordinating role between the two players.

For each organization, there was the reality that this was the real moment of truth rather than a postponement of it for a year or so down the line. Granted, if we all couldn't bring it off, the two organizations could retreat, but they had to be in it just as completely as we were, or we wouldn't stand a chance.

To this quadrille, we shuffled rather than glided. Maybe I said first that I'd do it if John would, or maybe he said first he'd do it if I would, or it may have been that Ken said he felt secure about NCOP if John and I would tackle it and if CONVO responded in kind, or maybe it was Bayard who . . . but whatever and whoever, we finally bowed as partners, joined hands and moved out in almost practiced rhythm. For the good times and the rough ones ahead, it was extremely fortunate that we were all responding to the same beat.

CHAPTER THREE

The Organizing Effort

E ven before the next and even more crucial phase of our work, Bayard Ewing and Ken Albrecht rotated out of their top roles with CONVO and NCOP. John and I worried what that might do to solidarity, but it turned out their successors were equally committed and effective.

The new top volunteer officer at NCOP, James Lipscomb, was executive director of the George Gund Foundation in Cleveland, the original home of NCOP; he had served for many years in national and international assignments with the Ford Foundation. Philip Bernstein, CONVO's new principal volunteer, had just retired as executive vice president of the Council of Jewish Federations after a lifetime of leadership roles with that organization. With Ken and Bayard still totally involved and committed, our core team was considerably enhanced.

Our intention to create something larger than the sum of the two parts became all the more obvious when we deliberately labeled the exploratory and planning body the "organizing committee." We realized such labeling would cause discomfort among some who were still tentative, but it was consistent with the degree of commitment we had been assured.

Another important early consideration involved the makeup of the committee. Very deliberately, I had recommended in the feasibility study that the body that would plan for the future would contain a significant proportion of individuals who were not on either board. It had not been an easy condition to sell, but it was essential to the objectivity and credibility of the group finally selected.

I had recommended that the chairman and I would propose the members, and that our nominees would need to be approved by the two top officers of the sponsoring organizations, now Bernstein and Lipscomb. We all had to take a lot of heat, primarily for who wasn't appointed. There were only three official representatives selected from each organization. Though there were a few other board members appointed for other representational considerations, the distinct majority did not have formal affiliation with either group.

Anyone who has ever tried to put together a group representative of a diverse constituency or reflecting a broad cross section of the country will recognize the complexity of our task. At first, there were strong pressures to keep the committee small, but even when we settled on what was interpreted as the unwieldy number of twenty-one, it was excruciating to try to hold to it, and in fact, at the first meeting of the group, the members of the committee insisted we had to go to at least twenty-five to correct weaknesses. We ended up with twenty-seven, and many complaints that we hadn't begun to be representative enough—or on the other side, that we were too big and diverse to get anything done.

Even with the additions, we spent a lot of the first two meetings building additional outreach, including genuine opportunities for many others to influence our decisions.

Because the makeup of the committee was so crucial to everything that transpired and developed, I will list the names and primary affiliations of all the members:

ORGANIZING COMMITTEE

John W. Gardner, chairman	Former U.S. secretary of health, education & welfare; former president of Carnegie Corporation of New York; founding chairman of Common Cause
Brian O'Connell, director	President, NCOP; executive director, CONVO; former national executive director, Mental Health Association

OFFICIAL REPRESENTATIVES OF CONVO

Philip Bernstein — Chairperson, CONVO; former executive vice president, Council of Jewish Federations

Cynthia Wedel — Vice-chairperson, CONVO; president, World Council of Churches; volunteer consultant, American Red Cross

Bayard Ewing — Immediate past chairperson, CONVO; president, National Information Bureau; president, American Federation of Arts

OFFICIAL REPRESENTATIVES OF NCOP

James S. Lipscomb — Chairman, NCOP; executive director, George Gund Foundation

Rosemary Higgins Cass — Vice chairman and counsel, NCOP; coauthor, *Voluntarism at the Crossroads;* partner, Shepard, Cooper, Harris, Dickson, Buermann, Camp & Cass

Kenneth L. Albrecht — Immediate past chairman, NCOP; vice president, Equitable Life Assurance Society of the United States

MEMBERS-AT-LARGE

Ruth Abram — Executive director, Women's Action Alliance

Landrum Bolling — Chairman, Council on Foundations; former president, Lilly Endowment and Earlham College

Leo J. Brennan Jr. — Executive director, Ford Motor Company Fund

Barber Conable — Member of Congress

Jack Conway — Senior vice president, United Way of America; board of directors, Atlantic Richfield Corporation

Joseph Fisher — Member of Congress

Carl Holman — President, National Urban Coalition; executive secretary, Black Leadership Forum

James T. Hosey — Vice president and executive director, U.S. Steel Foundation; chairman, Contributions Council of the Conference Board

Thomas Leavitt	Director, Herbert F. Johnson Museum of Art; board member, American Arts Alliance
Waldemar Nielsen	Waldemar Nielsen, Inc.; author of *The Big Foundations* and *The Endangered Sector*
Manning M. Pattillo Jr.	President, Oglethorpe University; former president, The Foundation Center
Alan Pifer	President, Carnegie Corporation of New York
David Ramage Jr.	Executive vice president and executive director, New World Foundation; former president, Center for Community Change; executive committee member, General Assembly Mission Council, United Presbyterian Church
John J. Schwartz	President, American Association of Fund-Raising Counsel, Inc.
Eleanor Sheldon	Former president, Social Science Research Council; board member, Rockefeller Foundation
Robert H. Thill	Secretary, contributions committee, American Telephone and Telegraph
Glenn Watts	President, Communication Workers of America; board member, Ford Foundation
Sara Alyce Wright	Executive director, YWCA of the USA; president, National Assembly of National Voluntary Health and Social Welfare Organizations
Raul Yzaguirre	President, National Council of La Raza; cochairperson, National Committee for Responsive Philanthropy

The charge to the committee was:

The sponsoring organizations have indicated that it is their hope that the planning process will lead to a new organization encompassing a broad cross section of those concerned with the vitality of the independent sector—social welfare agencies, corporate philanthropy, nonprofit health organizations, private education, cultural groups, public interest organizations, chambers of commerce, foundations, better business bureaus, scientific laboratories, religious groups and many more.

The responsibility of the Organizing Committee is to determine if it is possible to create a mechanism to support and strengthen the efforts of the organizations and individuals comprising the independent sector as they seek to preserve and enhance voluntary initiative and independent action.

The first meeting of the committee would have been a delight to all those who predicted that such a group could never agree on anything. People felt a need to stake out their territory, establish their independence, express their distrust, and insist on adjustments. And that was just in the formal sessions! During the breaks, people wanted to be sure that I knew where they stood, and why the whole undertaking was starting out poorly. John also got a lot of this, but as we sorted it out, we realized we had just experienced a predictable, albeit unusually intense, first meeting of any truly diverse coalition, in which many of the participants need to say what they came to say and to be able to go home and say that they said what needed to be said.

Though we continued to meet and to make some progress, we couldn't seem to make headway on the central issues, especially whether we really—and we meant really—had enough in common as a group and as a sector to make it possible and worthwhile to try to organize around it. We were into the third meeting, and the go-around was bordering on fruitless, when Sara Alyce Wright pointed out that the only way we could determine our commonality or lack of it was to see if we felt that we and our institutions shared important core values. I could tell that some felt such an exercise a little mushy, but everyone agreed to give it a try. When we were finished, we had found our bond and made rapid progress thereafter, even on the difficult questions that had stumped us earlier.

After several rewordings, we stated our common values this way:

The independent sector is so vast and diverse that it reflects an enormous range of values. Using the wide angle lens, we constantly had to remind ourselves that we were dealing with the motivations and values inherent in such different institutions as garden clubs, schools for the blind, scientific laboratories and patients' rights committees. We are also trying to encompass groups that are sharply at odds with one another— the devout and the iconoclastic, those who are pro nuclear energy and those who are anti, and protectionists and free traders. One might argue that in the face of such infinite diversity, the Organizing Committee would do well to pass discreetly over the whole subject of values.

But, without denying the diversity of the sector and without proposing to set limits to that diversity, the committee felt impelled to identify and state certain values that it regards as central to its own efforts—values that the proposed new organization should seek to foster.

The listing has undergone several changes, especially shortening, and now covers:

- commitment beyond self
- worth and dignity of the individual
- individual responsibility
- tolerance
- freedom
- justice
- responsibilities of citizenship

That bonding led us to try to relate those values to the performance and impact of the sector. Essentially, we said that the sector *operating at its best*

- expands the diversity of personal options
- represents a framework and tradition within which individuals can band together to pursue goals of their own choosing: free worship, joint citizen action, and mutual pursuit of an endless number of interests
- represents a seedbed for new ideas, new art forms, and so on
- gives people channels to experiment with activities and solutions
- provides alternatives to government action
- reduces powerlessness and helps promote empowerment
- gives individuals an opportunity for a larger voice in how our society will function
- contributes to a more enlightened electorate
- monitors the responsiveness and effectiveness of government
- encourages wiser use of resources

It seemed and seems important to add:

Although the above represent the highest aims and purposes of the independent sector, we must be very careful not to seem to suggest that everything done in the sector is necessarily good. It is a common fault of supporters of nonprofit initiative to attribute to the sector a role often romanticized and overblown. We need to acknowledge that the very pluralism that provides the freedom for a lot of good things to happen also allows a lot of activity that some might describe as counterproductive or foolish. As long as neither infringes on the rights of others, no one should have official authority to judge which is which, and all in the sector should recognize a responsibility and mutual benefit in protecting the rights of everyone.

We had an easier but not easy time defining the sector, at least as we experienced and wanted to relate to it. Most of us began the process with a view closely determined by personal experience, and some were not altogether comfortable with what we were being asked to embrace. The activists among us wondered why we should have to worry about Harvard and Stanford, and the people interested in dance or opera were not quite sure that public interest lawyers or the Flat Earth Society really represented affinity groups.

We also described two of the sector's most salient characteristics:

Diversity: It encompasses virtually the whole range of human purposes. An extraordinary amount of activity within the sector may be described as "private initiative for the public good"—for example, giving and volunteering. But there are many other purposes, from personal redemption to recreation, that fall within the sector—for example, religions and bird watchers' clubs.

Independence: The activities in the sector are not all independent in the purest meaning of the word, but seen in the whole range of human activities, they are remarkably free of any but self imposed constraints.

It was the point about independence that eventually led to the recommendation of the name, but there were miles and curves to go before we got that far.

Over the next year, there were eight full meetings, scores of subcommittee and task force sessions, and many briefings for various constituencies, all designed to help us address the following questions:

What is the sector's potential for continued and greater impact and service? Is the sector actually in trouble? What are the problems? Can anything be done to address them? Could any type of organized effort be successful? What would the organization actually do? How would such an organization be structured? How would it be governed? How would it be financed? How could it remain committed to the highest ideals of the sector and not fall into a preoccupation with the institutional concerns of the organizations that make it up? How could such an organization be designed so that it would not interfere with the very pluralism it attempts to foster? Can such an organization be put together? Should it be? How would it come into being?

Intertwined with these questions were discussion and debate about almost every conceivable issue in the field: equity, openness, accountability, accessibility, flexibility, empowerment, potential for usefulness, standards, evaluation, regulation, tax policy, motivations for giving, health of volunteering, quasigovernmental organizations, the roles of government, the relationships of the profit and not-for-profit spheres, freedoms of assembly and speech, fraud, waste, and on and on.

In the course of the examination, we became even more aware of the overwhelming obstacles that had stalled or negated all earlier efforts to pull the sector together. It is still sobering to recall even some of them.

There was, first of all, the sheer breadth and complexity of the sector. The broader we stretched, the harder it was to imagine an organization encompassing it all.

We then had to allow for the fierce attachment to independence that exists in so much of the sector. Who could ever get many of those independent individuals and causes working together on anything?

There was also the suspicion—and actual antipathy—that characterizes so many relationships in this disparate, quarrelsome, and competing world. It was the ultimate in presumption and optimism to think we could pull together the consumers and providers, the donors and donees, the prochoice and prolife elements, and many other groups that seemed to be natural antagonists rather than allies.

Furthermore, we faced the danger that any organization seeking to retain the support of so many diverse constituencies would end up serving the lowest common denominator of self-interest and not the highest public interest.

Finally, we would be operating with a scarcity of hard data about the overall sector, which meant that many of our plans would be based largely on guesswork.

As we tackled those questions and realities, we drew on our conviction about our common values and the sector's capacity to advance them, and we kept in clear focus the need to address the obstacles standing in the way of greater impact. We also benefited from our growing commitment to our mission. At that point, we said:

> Despite how very real these problems are and with full respect for them, they are nevertheless constantly countered by an impressively pervasive conviction that if the independent sector is to continue to serve society well, it must—to the extent possible—be mobilized for greater cooperation and impact. Despite all the differences, antipathies and antagonisms that may exist in this quarrelsome, competing and truly independent sector, there are even stronger forces pulling it together. However different all the other beliefs, there is a shared understanding of the sector's capacity to serve human needs and there is a shared stake in the fundamental relationship between the freedom of citizens to organize themselves and the freedom of citizens.
>
> As narrow as those common bonds may be, they are strong enough to justify the possibility that an organization loyal to them and to nothing else might rally the sector around them.

With that possibility in view, we proceeded.

Though the principal story of that crucial year and a half concerns the work and results of the organizing committee, what was happening with the two sponsoring organizations and the common secretariat that had been established had an impact on what a new entity might be like, and whether an even broader coalition could work. Each time a doubter claimed that donors and donees couldn't be joined in the same organization or that the sector was too diverse to decide and pursue common strategies, we had the great advantage of pointing to breakthroughs that had already been achieved within our existing operation.

This was certainly not a period of drifting, but of expanded activity for both organizations and of deliberately shared efforts to achieve cooperation and collaboration.

Almost immediately, NCOP took the gamble of going ahead with its annual national conference, which had been handicapped by lack of staffing and funding. The chair, Helen O'Rourke, had been trying to handle it pretty much without staff and financial support, and cancellation had seemed the prudent course. However, giving up on it would have demoralized an already discouraged organization and hardly sent a message of hope and vitality. So we decided to go forward. With only a couple of months to go, programming, fund-raising, and promotion were put into high gear, with enough progress to assure at least a decent showing. Midway to deadline, all our frantic efforts received a rocket boost when First Lady Rosalynn Carter agreed to participate, and it was suddenly possible to think in terms of a very special meeting. Late registrants, previously undecided speakers, and delayed support decisions suddenly came through, and our anticipated so-so event turned into a new standard for spirit and value.

Right after the conference, we reinstated NCOP's popular quarterly newsletter, *Voice of Philanthropy,* which hadn't been issued for more than a year, expanding its coverage and enlarging its subscriber base. Over the next eighteen months, we published five editions. The outreach helped greatly to hold and build the list of NCOP supporters and to create a sense of curiosity and interest among both funding and grant-seeking organizations.

There was also bolstering news of developments in the International Project headed by Ormsbee Robinson, formerly with the IBM Education Foundation. The primary focus of the effort was to interest U.S. corporations in programs and projects having international significance. Progress included publication of the book *International Business Philanthropy;* cosponsorship of a major conference on international education; a Brookings seminar; and a joint NCOP-Woodrow Wilson Center dialogue on "The Role of Philanthropy in International Affairs in the Years Ahead."

NCOP's board appreciated these clear indications of activity and felt assured and informed by a new and frequent "Board Memo" keeping them briefed on NCOP and the work of the organizing committee.

On the CONVO side, progress was equally impressive.

Initially, CONVO faced a similar need to restore morale and momentum, but once those were developing, our greatest challenge was to try to keep up with expectations, aspirations, and legislative crises and opportunities.

If the annual conference and international program were NCOP's major responsibilities, CONVO's were government relations and research. For both organizations, effective communication with the members, supporters, and board, and with the field in general, were absolute necessities.

For urgent government relations matters, CONVO was enormously fortunate to attract to the staff Bob Smucker, who had handled similar responsibilities when he and I worked together at the Mental Health Association. He was not only experienced in government relations but believed, as I did, in maximum involvement of all constituents. Within the first eighteen months, the government relations issues and involvements exploded.

For example, the organization successfully fought any use of the term and concept *tax expenditures*, which was associated with the argument that because government loses money when people deduct contributions, the government should control how those lost revenues are expended.

CONVO also launched its first judicial test of arbitrary limits on fund-raising costs. The village of Schaumburg had established a limit of 25 percent on fund-raising costs for organizations that were given a permit to solicit support in that community. We recognized that unpopular and newer causes might exceed that limit, at least in initial years of operation, and that therefore communities could use a fund-raising limit to squelch their critics. We argued for full disclosure but not foreclosure.

We were successful in defending the right of voluntary organizations to publish the voting records of legislators on issues of concern to the voluntary groups. We never challenged the legitimacy of the law prohibiting nonprofit organizations from engaging in partisan activity—including telling people who to vote for or against—but we felt it was within an organization's right to reveal what a person's voting record had been.

To mobilize CONVO's members and others to advocate for sensible public policies relating to the sector, we began to develop a vast network of sector representatives who could explain to their elected officials just what the impact of proposed legislation and regulations would be on causes within those officials' own communities.

After government relations, the next most important concern for CONVO—and one also of great interest to NCOP—was research. By early 1978, the research function, including the research committee, became a joint activity of CONVO and NCOP. There were three major research projects during that interim year:

First, we contracted with Martin Feldstein, head of the National Bureau of Economic Research, to determine the current economic significance of the charitable deduction. That important study confirmed that as a result of the ability and practice of individuals to deduct contributions from their taxable income, charitable organizations received far more income than the government lost. This proved that the deduction achieved its intended purpose of stimulating private initiative for the public good.

The second project, which was larger and even more significant than the deduction study and initially put CONVO far out on a financial limb, was a public opinion survey by the Gallup Organization "to determine the giving patterns of Americans." The gamble paid off, as it proved for the first time that "tax incentives are an important determinant of the levels of charitable giving." The hundred-page report also provided important baseline data about the charitable habits of Americans, broken down by age, income, gender, education, and many other factors.

Third, the joint research committee began to report to the members and supporters of both organizations on other research being conducted in and on the sector that could help philanthropic and voluntary organizations to be more effective in their own programming, planning, and fund-raising.

As with NCOP, CONVO sharpened its own communications, including board memos, a new "Memo to Members," outreach to a large range of organizations and individuals in the sector, and use of mass media. In 1979, we took what was then a major step by hiring an experienced communications director to help us strengthen our ability to communicate within the sector and beyond. To our good fortune, that individual was John Thomas, who had worked with Bob Smucker and me at the Mental Health Association. More than seventeen years later, John and Bob are still with IS.

John came just in time to help us with a major opportunity involving a White House tribute to volunteering and private philanthropy. We had kept Rosalynn Carter informed about the work of CONVO and NCOP and of the prospect for an even larger initiative, and she continued to be willing to help. We suggested that one of the most important things that could occur would be for the White House to send a clear signal to the government and the American people that giving and volunteering were activities to be applauded and encouraged. It took a couple of months of planning, but in mid-1979, 250 leaders of the sector, including the leadership of both CONVO and NCOP, came together for a very special celebration at the White

House hosted by the first lady and also attended by the president. It was an important event in our efforts to encourage and educate the public about the importance of personal participation, but it also added timely visibility and credibility to what these two organizations were doing and what the organizing committee was attempting to achieve.

Anticipating that the White House session would be important to share as fully as possible, John Thomas arranged to have a film crew present. He had also gained permission to have the same crew go along on the first lady's visits to some excellent volunteer projects that we had helped to identify. With all that footage, we were able to put together a stunningly good film, *Salute to Volunteering,* which was used by our members and supporters countless times to reach millions of Americans.

One of the decided benefits of the visible expansion of effective activities on the part of NCOP, CONVO, and the combination of the two was that we were able, even during this tenuous period, to significantly expand financial support for both groups.

We were also fortunate that the management committee and secretariat seemed to handle financial and administrative details well. People deeply experienced in the sector will recognize how essential it was that many people toiled invisibly behind the scenes to achieve compatible accounting, personnel policies, reimbursement practices for boards and committees, division of general support contributions, and so many small but vital elements of administration that, if not properly handled, could have caused suspicion, dissension, and withdrawal. The management committee, chaired by Jack Schwartz, deserves everlasting credit for creating and maintaining the machinery that gave everyone assurance about current operations and prospects.

Because of all these advances, when the organizing committee began to firm up its recommendations and clear them with the two sponsoring organizations, there was a good deal of positive experience to convince the two to give the recommendations a fair hearing.

With progress in the first phase of its work and encouragement from the activities of NCOP, CONVO, and the secretariat, the organizing committee turned to some pretty basic considerations, such as who might support a new and large organization, what would it actually do, and how could it be protected from control by larger organizations such as United Way or by parts of the sector such as health and hospitals?

The most important new consideration was what the organization would actually do. After months of subcommittees, discussions, and debates, we decided on the following as the essential functions:

First, *public education* to improve understanding of the sector's role in giving people alternatives and greater opportunities for participation and the creation of a more caring and effective society.

Second, *communication* within the sector so that shared problems and opportunities would be identified and pursued.

Third, *relationships with government* to deal with the infinite interconnections between the two sectors, but particularly to ensure the healthy independence and continued viability of nongovernmental organizations.

Fourth, *research* to provide a body of knowledge about the independent sector and about how to make it most useful to society.

Fifth, *encouragement of effective operations and management of nonprofit institutions* to maximize their capacity to serve individuals and society.

Almost as important as what would be done was the how, and for this we emphasized the creation of a "meeting ground." We saw the new entity as that place where the diverse elements in and related to the independent sector could comfortably come together to discuss common purposes, learn how to perform better, and use their opportunities to contribute to the common pursuits of research, public education, and relationships with government.

We found that the term *meeting ground* helped to convey what we wanted to see developed and also helped indicate what we didn't want. "Any new entity must not diminish the very pluralism which it was created to serve and enhance."

Another principle important to the committee was that any such enterprise could effectively address its mission only by working through a vast network of organizations. Existing independent organizations already involved millions of people and were in touch with every community in the country. To the extent that these organizations were brought into the common tasks, the new organization could accomplish a great deal. To the extent that the new organization tried to overreach these groups and build separately, it would have neither impact nor future.

Another rule that became a lifesaver early and often in the life of INDEPENDENT SECTOR stipulated that the organization had to stay within the narrow core of common interests in preserving and enhancing the impact of the sector. "The more effective the organization becomes, the more tempting it will be for various groups or interests to try to use the organization and its influence for their own purposes, drawing it into issues and battles that do not cut across the broad spectrum of the entire sector."

A pretty basic consideration was how the organization should be funded. Having decided fairly quickly that it should not be dependent on government or even accept government funding, we had to explore and question whether sufficient support would come from private sources. Here too, it won't surprise any reader experienced in these matters that it was one thing to get agreement on what should be done and quite another to go back around the table for fair shares of support.

When I was a young man, my grandfather used to tell a story that in later years came to mind whenever I was involved in dues debates and collections.

Two old Irish friends were into their third jars of stout and had reached the sentimental stage. Pat indicated to Mike that they had been such very dear friends that "if you had two bicycles I'm sure you'd give me one." Mike, caught up in the spirit, responded, "I would in a minute, and it would make me happy to do so." Whereupon, Pat said, "I bet that if you even had two automobiles, you'd still give me one," and Mike assured him it was so. With that, Pat leaned a bit closer and said, "I'll bet that if you had two goats . . . ," but got no further. Mike straightened and looked Pat clear in the eye, and ended the conversation with "I would not, you SOB, you know I've got two goats!"

I wish I had a goat or even a dime for every time I heard someone extol the mission or even the accomplishments of INDEPENDENT SECTOR, only to object to the dues or renege on them.

Most of us had had enough experience in membership organizations to be cautious in the extreme about financial prospects, but in the end, a number of tests and decisions worked in our favor.

During the eighteen months the organizing committee functioned, there had been a four-part fund-raising effort that in several ways was a test of whether the new enterprise could attract private support.

First of all, it had been necessary to maintain and increase support for CONVO and NCOP. CONVO had been concentrating on holding its members and attracting new ones. Despite initial organizational problems and the staff hiatus and change in 1978, the organization held all but one of its forty-four members and had attracted twenty-six new ones. Similarly, NCOP was able to hold its regular supporters and add twenty-two.

Second, we were encouraged by our efforts to secure short-term funding to help sustain the collaboration and, if appropriate, launch the new operation. Our minimum need for short-term funding was $550,000 and our goal was $1 million. By completion of the organizing committee's work, twenty-eight grants had been received, totaling $745,000, a particularly encouraging result considering that we aimed for a broad base of support, both by setting a ceiling of $60,000 from any one source and by reaching out to all regions of the nation for funding.

Third, after long testing and debate, we agreed on a dues structure that spread the load among prospective members, including a sliding scale based on ability to pay. Though any realistic dues arrangements are hard to sell, we successfully made the case that all of us had a stake in the operation and we persuaded members that this could not be another effort that started big on soft money, then zigged and zagged its way—downward—searching for project funds wherever that search might take us.

Lastly, fund-raising and membership development were accepted as high-priority activities for the organization, including the board and president.

Along with the dues, nothing took more of our time than issues related to membership, beginning with Who? Should there be individuals? (At least not at the start.) Did business corporations really fit? (Their philanthropic/public service arms certainly did.) What about local organizations? (At that stage, we were trying to deal with national forces such as Congress and the media, and most of the national organizations that were likely to be involved with us were membership federations involving millions of local groups.) Should and could we seek the membership of an organization that was already an affiliate of one of our umbrella members, such as the Council on Foundations or the National Health Council? (We agreed that a foundation or national health agency should belong first to its natural umbrella group, but that our new organization could not survive simply as an umbrella of umbrella groups. To be effective, we needed some of the major players directly at the table.) Where would we stand on groups primarily funded by government, such as the National Endowment for the Arts? (In many cases, we would need a close working relationship with such groups, but they should not be formal members.) The categories and tough decisions seemed to proliferate endlessly. Even at the end, we emphasized that "the important definition of membership . . . must be viewed as an evolutionary process."

Within that caveat, we proposed that the organization should be a membership association, and the formal members would be organizations with national interests and impact in philanthropy, voluntary action, or other independent activity relating to the educational, scientific, health, welfare, cultural, and religious life of the nation.

Among the reservations the committee had heard repeatedly was whether it was wise or even possible to construct an organization of both grant-making and grant-seeking entities. Many organizations that had to seek funds were understandably concerned that the new operation might be dominated by those who have the money, and some of those who made grants worried that their numerical minority would constantly put them at the mercy of an agenda controlled by the grant seekers. We concluded that the new organization was not that kind of enterprise. The mission and program were deliberately designed to reflect the mutual interests of these and many otherwise different and even competing groups. "All groups in and related to the sector have a stake in its future and they have to work together in some vehicle." We believed that the concept of the meeting ground provided that vehicle without infringing on the separate agendas of the many parts.

We also pointed out that CONVO and NCOP already were examples of cooperative efforts. From the start, CONVO had included both the NCOP and the Council on Foundations, and the NCOP board included a great many representatives of public charities, including the Women's Action Alliance, United Way, the Nature Conservancy, and the National Health Council.

The organizing committee's own experience was a promising indication that when the focus is on the health and future of the sector as a whole, an otherwise very diverse group can discard labels and separate agendas.

We therefore recommended that the new organization include the existing CONVO categories of members (national umbrella groups such as the National Association of Independent Colleges and Universities; nationwide organizations such as the National Urban League; and national organizations without nationwide affiliates, such as the

Population Resources Center), and that it would also include foundations and corporations, such as those represented in NCOP, whose giving programs reflected national and international interests. Among the latter were regional and community foundations, statewide foundations, and major regional voluntary organizations that have national interests and impact.

The organization was also to include national churches, unions, civic groups, cooperatives, and so on, as long as they were joining to participate in the agenda relating to philanthropy and voluntary action.

The emphasis on the members and on spreading the participation was carried over to decisions about governance. We concluded, for instance, that each member organization would have one vote, and that the voting membership body would have broader powers and involvement than usual. As another means of sharing participation and power, it was agreed that the organization should have a board of approximately forty-five persons, and further, to avoid concentrating power in a few people, that we should not have an executive committee. I was told repeatedly that such an arrangement could never work, but it did. It was particularly important that the members felt there was somebody at the table they could count on to represent their point of view.

Consistent with the spirit of involvement and spreading of leadership roles, we agreed that there would be rotation off the board, and that even the chairperson would be limited to three one-year terms in that role. (When the end of John Gardner's three years was approaching, the resolve of many of us was tested, but not John's. It was a wrenching change, but the right move.)

Some people still ask me—with appreciation or disdain—how we chose the title "chairperson." I explain that we left it entirely to the women who served on the committee. They caucused, decided, and that was it.

The rest of the work of the committee and its subsequent report dealt with such essential issues as size, budget, staffing, location, process and timetable for implementation, and much more. It also laid out the increasingly obvious stipulation, but one still very hard for many people to accept, that if the report were approved, both groups would be voting themselves out of existence. It was one thing to agree on most of the other issues, even dues maybe, but all the next steps were made more difficult by the reality and finality of the formal votes to dissolve.

The delicacy of this situation was compounded, excruciatingly, by the fact that we couldn't reach agreement on the name of the new organization. It was awkward enough being asked to go out of business, but doubly hard to accept if one didn't know and was suspicious about what the successor organization would be called.

Long after we had achieved agreement on every other difficult, contentious, and divisive issue, and at a point when we wanted terribly to achieve closure before hard-won agreements unraveled, we couldn't get the two sides to agree on a name. Finally, and in true desperation, we agreed to reject any names, words, and connotations that each side said would be unacceptable. For example, CONVO did not want the term *philanthropy* used, and NCOP did not want the term *voluntary*.

Each had concerns about what the message would be, and perhaps did not want the other to appear to be the survivor. We agreed that we would submit the task to a professional firm, and that the decision would then be made by Phil, Jim, John, and me. If we could not agree, a larger group would be assembled by John and me, with the approval of Phil and Jim.

At that point, we had been through four drafts of the committee's report, reflecting amendments negotiated with both organizations.

We were also getting very close to NCOP's twenty-fifth anniversary conference, which was shaping up as a propitious occasion for cementing the deal. It had already become so much of a mutual enterprise that everyone thought of it as the launching of INDEPENDENT SECTOR. Thanks to the generous spirit of NCOP, CONVO was equally involved in the preparations, the program, and the possible celebration. The cochairs were Edward Van Ness of the National Health Council and Patrick Noonan of the Nature Conservancy, each of whom was then very much identified with both organizations. With the surge toward a new beginning, the theme "The Independent Sector: Reflections and Directions" fit the occasion perfectly.

With spirits high and most of the issues already resolved, the NCOP board met the night before the conference and, with some caveats, approved what turned out to be the next to last edition of the organizing committee report. The CONVO board had already approved in principle a similar draft, also with some caveats, and there was a distinct likelihood that the remaining differences could be resolved at the final CONVO board and membership meetings to occur in December. Though it wasn't over, and anything could happen to set us back, the Denver conference was decidedly upbeat.

Finally, on December 12, 1979, the formalities were concluded—still without a name! The two organizations prepared to phase out, and we all turned to other formalities necessary to bring the new entity into being.

With a clear awareness that the future was still full of uncertainties and difficulties, I couldn't imagine that anything would ever again be as crazy, chaotic, and utterly exhausting as those eighteen months of three simultaneous full-time jobs.

Later in December, with all the votes final and with a little time to reflect and breathe, I went on one of my occasional solitary retreats, which as usual involved walking the deserted Rehoboth Beach for hours and hours to try to clear my head and put the past and future in perspective. For at least the first day, I found myself so preoccupied with the chaos of the past that I went around and around with a rehashing of events. It wasn't until the evening of the second day, on a very cold but moonlit evening, when I had walked perhaps three miles down the beach, all the way from Rehoboth to Dewey, that somehow the thought and words popped into my mind, "The marathon dash is over." I stopped and found myself saying it over and over again, louder and louder, "The marathon dash is over . . . ," until I settled on a dune and cried with the amazement and relief of it.

CHAPTER FOUR

The Birth of INDEPENDENT SECTOR and the Defining First Year

—◦∕∕∿—

It's not easy to dissolve two organizations, even after their boards have finally given authorization. The sensitivities and complications involved in the formal process are hard to handle expeditiously. For example, throughout the prior two years, we had done everything possible to treat the organizations as equals, and we didn't want anything in the transition to suggest otherwise. I assumed we would just dissolve each in exactly the same manner and be done with it. Not so, the lawyer said. For one thing, the organizations were incorporated in states with very different rules, and to make it worse, we were advised not to dissolve CONVO as a District of Columbia corporation if our intent was to immediately form a successor corporation in that jurisdiction. We were advised definitively that we would save time, hassles, and money if we simply merged NCOP into CONVO and changed the name. That probably sounds sensible and simple to most readers, but for anyone who had been at all close to the negotiations over two years, it would be obvious that any hint of a CONVO takeover would bring the sky down.

Fortunately, the NCOP leadership was still technically in place, so I went to Jim, Ken, and a few others, who became coconspirators in

interpreting why we were doing it the way the lawyers had recommended. To anyone who expressed concern, we would say that legal
technicalities to the contrary, the full spirit of mutual dissolution was
being observed, that the lawyers said we had to do it this way, and that
besides it was going to be a lot cheaper!

We also made certain that both boards knew we were protecting
the names of their organizations, which we did and continue to do.
When I asked the lawyers to include those protections in the agreement, they assumed my motivation was to insulate INDEPENDENT
SECTOR from any possibility of dissidents restarting one or both of the
prior groups. I swear on a stack of Bibles that my purpose was only to
add one more comfort for people who felt they were losing their organization, but I also admit it wasn't such a bad idea to avoid someone
else using the name.

The issue of the name went through one more roller-coaster loop
before finally landing. We had been fortunate to enlist the firm of
Ruder and Finn to provide expert study and advice, but after all their
deliberation, they recommended VOLUNTARY SECTOR, even with
awareness that the "V" word was at the top of NCOP's "no" list.
Though the firm argued that their recommendation was sufficiently
strong to be worth the possibility of reopening negotiations with
NCOP, they also agreed that INDEPENDENT SECTOR should be the
backup choice. At that point, there was no way to retreat from our
prior guarantees to NCOP and no logic in taking the risk of reopening negotiations. Also, at a previous point, the organizing committee
as a whole favored the name INDEPENDENT SECTOR on the grounds
that the most important thing this sector represents in American
society is relative independence. For those reasons, the four of us used
our authority to make the choice, and it was finally INDEPENDENT
SECTOR (IS).

Legal issues and the name were just two of the essential matters to
be resolved before the charter meeting scheduled for March 5, 1980,
less than three months after the December decisions. Every bit as complicated and sensitive was the nomination of the initial directors. The
nominating committee was the only bridge between the past and the
future, and for three months it was the only authoritative body to
carry forward the intent of the organizing committee. For the essential assignment of chairing that committee, John and I chose Homer
Wadsworth, head of the Cleveland Foundation and one of the most
respected and knowledgeable people in the sector.

I recently reviewed the nominating committee's voluminous files and was reminded what an almost impossible assignment they faced: ensuring that every possible representation was included so that everybody who cared saw someone on the list they felt would represent their viewpoint. Almost everyone on the list had to be at least a "three-fer" in terms of their affiliations. I recall that as we came down to the wire, we were trying to identify and enlist people who had at least five identifications, such as arts, female, Midwest, volunteer, and donor.

I think it will be of sufficient interest and a good indication of the committee's success in achieving diversity and outreach to list the founding board members. Affiliations are those at the time of nomination and are for identification purposes.

OFFICERS

John Gardner, chairperson	Founding chairman, Common Cause; former U.S. secretary of health, education and welfare
Landrum Bolling, vice chairperson	Research professor of diplomacy, Georgetown University
Kenneth Dayton, vice chairperson	Chairman, executive committee, Dayton Hudson Corporation
Vera Foster, vice chairperson	Board member, VOLUNTEER: The National Center for Citizen Involvement; board member, Common Cause
Cynthia Wedel, vice chairperson	President, World Council of Churches; former president, National Council of Churches; former national chairman of volunteers for the American Red Cross
Raul Yzaguirre, vice chairperson	President, National Council of La Raza; chairperson, National Neighborhood Coalition
Kenneth Albrecht, secretary	Vice president, Equitable Life Assurance Society of the U.S.A.; board member, Council on Foundations
Mary Ripley, treasurer	Former president, VOLUNTEER; past president, National Conference on Social Welfare

John Schwartz, assistant treasurer	President, American Association of Fund Raising Counsel, Inc.
Brian O'Connell, president	Former president, National Council on Philanthropy; former executive director, Coalition of National Voluntary Organizations

OTHER BOARD MEMBERS

Luis Alvarez	President, National Urban Fellows
William Aramony	President, United Way of America
Charles Bannerman	Founder and chairman, Delta Foundation
Philip Bernstein	Former executive vice president, Council of Jewish Federations
Janet Welsh Brown	Executive director, Environmental Defense Fund
Frank Cary	Chairman, IBM
Rosemary Higgins Cass	Partner, Shepard, Cooper, Harris, Dickson, Buermann, Camp & Cass
Carolyn Sue Chin	Marketing manager, American Telephone and Telegraph; Pacific-Asian Coalition
Linda Hawes Clever, M.D.	Chairman, Department of Occupational Health, Presbyterian Hospital of Pacific Medical Center, San Francisco; chairman of the board, KQED, San Francisco
Jill Conway	President, Smith College
Monsignor Lawrence Corcoran	Executive director, National Conference of Catholic Charities
Ada Deer	Native American Rights Fund Lecturer, School of Social Work, University of Wisconsin, Madison
Bayard Ewing	President and board member, National Information Bureau and American Federation of Arts
John Filer	Chairman, Aetna Life and Casualty; former chairman, Commission on Private Philanthropy and Public Needs

Samuel Goddard

Attorney, Goddard and Ahern;
former governor of Arizona

Nancy Hanks

Vice president, Rockefeller Brothers Fund;
former chairman, National Endowment
for the Arts

John Hanley

Chairman of the board, Monsanto Inc.;
director, First National City Bank,
New York

Andrew Heiskell

Former chairman of the board and chief
executive officer, Time Inc.

Carl Holman

President, National Urban Coalition;
executive director, Black Leadership
Forum

Boisfeuillet Jones

Managing director, Lettie Pate Evans
Foundation; president, Emily and Ernest
Woodruff Foundation

Juanita Morris Kreps

Former U.S. secretary of commerce;
trustee, Duke Endowment

Thomas Leavitt

Director, Herbert Johnson Museum
of Art, Cornell University; board member,
American Arts Alliance

James Lipscomb

Executive director, George Gund
Foundation; trustee, Cleveland Council
on World Affairs

Richard Lyman

President, Rockefeller Foundation; former
president, Stanford University

Betty Marcus

American Council for the Arts; board
member, Corporation for Public
Broadcasting

Leon Marion

Executive director, American Council
of Voluntary Agencies for Foreign Service

Walter McNerney

Former national president,
Blue Cross-Blue Shield

Christine Topping Milliken

Vice president and general counsel,
National Association of Independent
Colleges and Universities

Steven Muller	President, Johns Hopkins University and Johns Hopkins Hospital
William Orme	Manager, corporate support and educational relations operation, General Electric; secretary, General Electric Foundation
Martin Paley	Executive director, San Francisco Foundation
Antonia Pantoja	Founder and president, Graduate School for Urban Resources and Social Policy, University of San Diego; founder and executive director, National Puerto Rican Forum; founder, Aspira of America, Inc.
David Ramage	Executive director, New World Foundation
Janet Taylor	Executive director, Associated Grantmakers of Greater Boston
Robert Thill	Secretary, contributions committee, American Telephone and Telegraph
Edward Van Ness	Executive vice president, National Health Council
Homer Wadsworth	Director, Cleveland Foundation
Faye Wattleton	President, Planned Parenthood Federation of America
Harold Wilke	Director, Healing Community; minister, United Church (Congregational)
Sara Alyce Wright	Executive director, YWCA of the U.S.A.; former president, board of directors, National Assembly
Adam Yarmolinsky	Attorney, Kominers, Fort, Schlefer & Boyer; member, Institute of Politics, John F. Kennedy School of Government, Harvard University

Before the charter meeting, recruitment of members and fund-raising went into high gear to take advantage of interest in the new enterprise. Substantial progress was made on both fronts. To our relief and delight, many leadership organizations wanted to be registered as charter members or subscribers.

There was also a great deal of important administrative detail to resolve, or at least get under way, which all came under the dedicated leadership of Steve Muller working with Robert Harlan, who was just finishing up many years as head of the YMCA and who officially became executive vice president of IS early in 1980.

Because there were many carryover program activities from the two organizations, and the organizing committee had spelled out future program directions, it was not necessary to come forward with any major new recommendations right away.

It couldn't have been better timing that shortly before March 5, the Supreme Court ruled in *Village of Schaumburg* v. *Citizens for a Better Environment et al.* that a community may not impose a flat percentage limit on the fund-raising costs of organizations raising money in its territory. As discussed in Chapter Three, INDEPENDENT SECTOR, through the efforts of its predecessor organization CONVO, had played a major role in advocating such a position. This added to the celebration at the charter meeting and to the opportunity to begin helping our members understand and rejoice in the new organization's role in keeping wide open the freedoms of speech and assembly. I explained that, in what was probably one of the most important decisions affecting philanthropy and voluntary organizations, the Court had established that a governmental jurisdiction may not deny a solicitation permit to a charitable organization simply because the organization exceeds the fund-raising and administrative cost ceilings arbitrarily set by the government. The case was particularly significant because it reaffirmed that charitable solicitation is an activity that enjoys constitutional protection as an element of freedom of speech.

It was and is important to note that INDEPENDENT SECTOR does not condone high fund-raising costs and indeed is committed to effective management of voluntary organizations. However, we believe that in special cases such as those relating to emerging organizations, unpopular causes, or new campaigns, administrative and fund-raising costs sometimes do exceed the arbitrary limit of 25 percent set by the Village of Schaumburg. To give government the authority to deny fund-raising privileges on any arbitrary grounds would give the powers that be far too large an opportunity to repress unwelcome or unpopular causes.

The Court indicated that there are already sufficient laws to deal with fraud, and that further efforts of communities and other governmental jurisdictions will be better directed toward disclosure of a charitable organization's activities, including fund-raising costs. In essence, the Court's opinion encouraged disclosure but precluded arbitrary foreclosure.

INDEPENDENT SECTOR's brief was prepared and argued by the legal scholar Adam Yarmolinsky, a member of our new board.

In every way, the charter meeting generated even more interest and participation than we were ready for. We had arranged for what we thought were more than adequate facilities, but realized within ten days of the event that we'd never be able to accommodate all those who planned to attend. It was an acceptable crisis to have to change locations, but we had to be absolutely certain that not one of our new members or prospects lost faith in us because they arrived at the wrong place!

On March 5, at the right place, 239 people participated in the official charter meeting of the voting members. There were already 145 charter members, compared with the total of 86 members and supporters of the two predecessor organizations, and long before the end of the year, we greatly surpassed the ambitious first year's membership goal of 200.

It may have seemed presumptuous that we had arranged to have the event filmed, but it helped us spread the story and excitement throughout the next year and to have at hand a visual record of what has turned out to be a historic occasion.

The agenda included my review of the evolution of INDEPENDENT SECTOR; inaugural remarks by John Gardner; formal signing of the agreements by Phil Bernstein for CONVO and Jim Lipscomb for NCOP; approval of all the legal documents, including bylaws; election of the first officers and board members; celebration of the Supreme Court decision in the *Schaumburg* case; a rallying of the membership for passage of the Charitable Contributions Bill; and a stirring speech by Senator Daniel Patrick Moynihan on the role of the sector in preserving freedom.

For a quick sense of the occasion, here are snippets from the speeches:

GARDNER: INAUGURAL REMARKS

Everyone likes beginnings. But few of us in our lifetimes are lucky enough to be in on a beginning that may prove important for the future of American life. . . .

We want to preserve a great tradition in American life. We want to ensure the vitality of a precious part of our society. But we intend to be honest about ourselves, and we intend to proceed with a regard for the good of the whole society. Not to benefit ourselves at the expense of others, not to pursue a course of self-aggrandizement, not to concentrate on the purposes of a few powerful elements in the sector but to serve all: these are principles we intend to honor.

I believe that, as often happens, those are not only worthy principles but hardheaded, practical sense, because this organization will have nothing but its good name—and it will have to earn that. We do not have an endowment. We do not have the kind of long history that brings acceptance and popular support. We do not have an assured place in the social or political structure. In order to command respect we shall have to deserve respect—which in my view is a healthy requirement.

Ladies and gentlemen, I congratulate all of you on your act of creation. I know that the infant will eventually be a source of great pride to all of us.

MOYNIHAN: ON PLURALISM AND THE INDEPENDENT SECTOR

I am very much here to congratulate you and to toast you—you *did* it. If anything exhibits the energy of the private sector over the past short year and a half, it's that a common sense of purpose and condition has emerged from the most disparate enterprises, from the American Theater Association to the Audubon Society all in one room, all for one purpose. . . .

I think many of you will remember reading Joseph Schumpeter's last great book in 1948 in which he said how this wonderfully creative civilization which we have produced in North America and Western Europe is going to come to an end—not in some great apocalyptic Armageddon in which one class takes over another class and destroys all classes. No. It will come to an end through the slow but steady conquest of the private sector by the public sector.

There is nowhere that this is more in evidence and more advanced than with respect to the non-government enterprises of public concern which you represent. Little by little, you are being squeezed out of existence or slowly absorbed. . . . Your job is to assert that something of the most profound concern to American society is at issue, and that is our tradition of a plural, democratic society. It would be the final irony if, in the name of good purposes, government ended up destroying liberty in the society. But that can happen, and that is what seems to me is your job to make certain does not happen.

O'CONNELL: THE EVOLUTION OF INDEPENDENT SECTOR

The organizing committee began its work with a piercing analysis of whether philanthropy, volunteering, and independent institutions really do make a difference in our society. They went at the task with an almost chilling skepticism, stripping away the myths and shibboleths which so often produce only a romanticized interpretation of the sector's role and goodness. . . .

But even when we viewed the sector in its naked state, there remained both evidence and conviction that individual freedom depends on and flourishes in this independent, albeit imperfect, sector. It provides individuals with allies and outlets and power. It provides society with innovation and experimentation, and with criticism and reform. Even in an imperfect state, these are beautiful qualities. . . .

Along the way of these eighteen months, we have worked with hundreds of organizations to keep them informed and to have the benefit of their views. Despite the enormous variety of groups consulted, we found the same consistent view that we must have a strong independent sector but that we won't have it if we don't work at it. . . .

Having completed all legal steps necessary to implement the organizing committee's report, we are today ready to sign the declaration formally launching INDEPENDENT SECTOR. . . .

"What is past is prologue." We are ready to begin.

The meeting resulted in substantial media coverage, including articles in major dailies such as the *New York Times* and *Washington Post,* wire service summaries that got a good pick-up, and extensive coverage in the trade media, important to creating interest in membership.

Our next major milestone was the first meeting of the new board, which was held May 5 with almost everyone present. The agenda was structured to help people get to know each other and to begin to learn more about their very different pursuits and the commonalities among their problems, operations, and aspirations. From the start, those opportunities for networking, camaraderie, and trust building were so welcomed that they became a regular feature of board meetings.

There was one momentary fright at the first session when I looked up and realized that we had seated Faye Wattleton of Planned Parenthood next to Monsignor Lawrence Corcoran of Catholic Charities. I was afraid we had blown ourselves out of the water. Fortunately, they seemed to get along very well, and thereafter gave every indication of cordial relations.

You won't find it surprising that I considered a highlight of the meeting my formal selection as IS president. Appropriately, there had been a formal selection committee, and at one point, I was told that an impressive and well-connected individual had made known his interest. I can remember thinking that this could be one of those situations where someone works his heart out to bring an organization to a major threshold, only to find that another person is selected to take it from there. I never did hear about the deliberations of the committee but was relieved to learn fairly early that I was their recommendation.

Speaking of executive sessions and presidential matters, a few years later, I was told that when the board was discussing my performance and compensation, the group seemed stymied by wanting to express considerable appreciation without having to extend considerable compensation.

They were concerned, as was I, that the financial remuneration not become a problem for our members, particularly those on the board, whose salaries were less than mine. As I understand it, the board searched for a way to express appreciation, but not too tangibly. Father Corcoran said the board could resolve the matter the same way his institution does. They could make me a monsignor! When I came back into the room, I was baffled by being addressed as "Monsignor," but when I learned the story, I loved it, and for a long time afterwards, certain people routinely referred to me by that honorary title.

There were, you will guess, even greater highlights to the first gathering of such an interesting board, including a fascinating conversation with Barber Conable, ranking Republican on the House Ways and Means Committee, cosponsor of our charitable contributions legislation, and a member of IS's organizing committee. In addition to talking about the status of the legislation and providing advice on increasing support for it, he was wonderfully candid, encouraging, and humorous about how the House viewed our sector. His primary emphasis was on getting key figures in the local affiliates of our member organizations to make sure that their members of Congress knew what was being done by their organizations to improve their communities.

We also had a chance to learn about and discuss program activities already on our plate and to begin to think about future projects.

It was a free-wheeling session, with a good deal of opportunity for people to ask anything they wanted about any facet of our operation. For the most part, that relaxed approach seemed well received, but we could also tell that it was going to lead to some adjustment. For example, at the breaks during that session and in almost every other board meeting for a few years, I would be approached by some directors, generally from cause-oriented voluntary groups, who expressed concern that there wasn't enough time to adequately involve the board in full debates and decisions. I would then be approached by others, usually from the business side, who expressed concern that we were talking the issues to death and should be more action-oriented.

Over the years, it was the corporate people who had to adjust the most, but that didn't mean they got over venting to me some of their frustration over my not simply telling the board what I thought should be done. Suffice it to say that it took a great many meetings before our unique culture began to take hold, and it had a lot of room for differences and differentness.

The first meeting of the board was considerably more civil and cordial than the first meeting of the organizing committee, but the two did have in common an obvious wariness and uncertainty about how much common and uncommon ground they were now plunked down on. What saved the meeting was the inherent goodness of all the people at the table, however different and uncomfortable they may have felt, and the fact that most of the ideas and issues discussed were of common interest and concern. An important part of the commonality was their respect for the person in the chair, John Gardner, so even if they found part of the experience foreign or awkward, they figured he must know what he was doing, and they'd hang in.

Fortunately, we had several relaxed meetings where we got to know and work with one another before very different viewpoints about our roles and priorities almost tore us apart. These disagreements related largely to our responsibility for dealing with proposed federal budget cuts and to the use of our supposed influence to reorder the funding priorities of foundations, federated fund-raising groups such as United Way, and corporate philanthropy. Shortly after newly elected President Reagan had announced his major budget reductions, which represented massive cuts for many voluntary organizations and the people they served, our board meeting was thrown into chaos with angry demands by several directors that IS turn almost all its attention and energy toward defeating the proposals in general and to restoring allocations for specific fields such as health and the arts.

At subsequent meetings, the demands for our intervention escalated, including an expectation and insistence that we cause our funder members to rush to provide financial relief for threatened agencies and people. Though the majority of directors recognized that it was not within our intended mission and capacity to represent each part of the sector to government or to cause our members, whether grant makers or grant seekers, to reorder their priorities, it was still extremely difficult to make clear our limitations to those who were threatened. Our more general roles in government relations and the strengthening of philanthropy seemed distant and pallid in comparison with the help that many people needed right away.

After several clashes and debates, it was generally accepted that we couldn't fulfill the roles expected or demanded of us without destroying our fragile togetherness. However, it was also agreed that we could and had to play a role in explaining to government and the public the consequences of such massive budget adjustments and the reality that private philanthropy and voluntary organizations could not "fill the gap." On an emergency basis, we commissioned Lester Salamon of the Urban Institute to prepare a report on the issues—resulting in the remarkably illuminating and persuasive "The Federal Budget and the NonProfit Sector," which IS published along with related data in a report called "Analysis of the Economic Recovery Programs' Direct Significance for Philanthropic and Voluntary Organizations and the People They Serve." We also hosted scores of sessions for various IS members to learn from these reports and from one another about what could be done to reverse or pare the cuts and how to increase private support.

In each year since, Salamon, in cooperation with Alan Abramson, has done updates to show changes in federal funding since 1980 and from year to year in areas of concern to IS members. We also produced several reports to help government officials, other policy makers, and leaders of the sector to better understand the relative roles and capacities of the governmental and independent sectors.

Those were scary times for a barely born alliance struggling to hold and attract members and trying to serve as a bridge between donors and donees. We lost some important members and were a long time getting over some ill feeling between some directors. Fortunately for the long run, we survived this much too early crisis and in the course of the struggle, gradually achieved a clearer understanding and at least some acceptance of what this confederation could and could not do.

Even during this tumultuous period, there were enough indications of the usefulness and even the impressiveness of the new organization to create a general atmosphere of positiveness and esprit.

As word spread of the significance of the Supreme Court's ruling in the *Schaumburg* case, there was a clearer grasp of how important it was to the achievement of that ruling that the sector had been able to speak collectively and forcefully.

Despite all sorts of congressional opposition, the charitable contributions legislation continued to grow in sponsorship and popularity, including becoming the only one of forty amendments to be accepted for the Senate Finance Committee's tax bill. The testimony we organized involved a wide variety of influential figures, including leaders of foundations, grassroots organizations, environmental groups, universities, civil rights groups, youth-serving agencies, and many others who had probably never rallied together, even around issues of common purpose.

The foundation world was enormously relieved that for the first time, the grant-seeking community came forward to vigorously defend foundations, even to the point of arguing that for the health of the sector, the annual payout requirement for foundations should be reduced. That in itself was a remarkable development given the tough economic times being faced by most voluntary groups.

The sector rallied to the defense of the U.S. Olympic Committee, whose charitable status had been threatened because it was unwilling to support the boycott of the Moscow Olympics.

As plans developed for the 1980 National Conference on Philanthropy, a carryover of NCOP's annual conferences, it was clear that people who previously had never thought about their affinity with so many other types of organizations were eager to come together to explore common needs and share thoughts about research on the sector, government relations, standards, board development, and much more. They also found themselves, many for the first time, willing to call on their members of Congress and delighting in the reality that they could exert influence. About eight hundred people attended the Washington, D.C., conference—more than double any previous attendance—and the evaluations from every side were decidedly positive and enthusiastic.

It was also helpful that the members and directors found, usually to their surprise, that there was a common view of what IS should emphasize. In a major survey of the members and directors to secure thoughts about program priorities, there was striking agreement on the most important things to be done. For example, a distinct majority of both groups rated education of policy makers, the media, and the public the most important area for concentration. A summary of the survey results expressed it: "The most important goal for IS is to raise public, government, and total community understanding of the impact and necessity of the independent sector to American life." Other aspects of government relations were also rated high in importance, and communication within the sector was a clear and important priority.

What we began to hear was that people felt it was high time for various parts of the sector to begin working together; that they liked what they saw in INDEPENDENT SECTOR, in terms of process, participation, and representation; and were impressed with the results. They also responded very positively to our regular communications, particularly the "Memo to Members," which consistently was described as the most important briefing piece about the sector that our members received.

Corporate members in particular, but foundations and voluntary groups too, liked the publication *Corporate Philanthropy.*

It certainly was evidence of interest and growing respect that recruitment of members was far ahead of projections, and that well within our timetable, we exceeded the grant support goal we had set for the three start-up years.

It's fair to say that by the end of our first year, our successes had increased and our reputation had risen dramatically. Obviously, that was to the good, but it was also clear that expectations were rising even faster. Within just a year, we had an almost impossible reputation to live up to, a still very fragile coalition and board, and the certainty of inevitable disappointments. We may have looked awfully good, but I knew very well that critics and mistakes could combine to make us look like a flash in the pan.

We were beginning to learn how essential it was to be impressive with what we did tackle, to do everything possible to recognize what we couldn't take on, and to accept the reality that the more impressive we became, the more critics we would attract, particularly among those who didn't understand or wouldn't accept what we couldn't do.

It had been a good year, both for what we were able to accomplish and what we were able to learn and overcome.

PART TWO

The Power
of Association

The Strength of Coalition
A Quintessential Example

---〜〜〜---

The organizing committee had pointed out that excessive regulation by government was the greatest threat to the independence of nonprofit institutions, and that it was the emerging or unpopular organizations that were particularly at the mercy of all this regulation. The committee elaborated, "Statutes are often unknown to new groups or beyond their capacity to satisfy, and some of the regulations are inherently antagonistic to the kind of activist groups which threaten the status quo. . . . there is no greater danger to the preservation of our liberty than giving the powers that be any great control over what their own reformers might do."

For those reasons, we moved quickly when we saw the advocacy rights of voluntary organizations threatened.

The first excruciating test came out of the Reagan White House in January of 1983, wrapped in the Washington jargon "Amendments to OMB Circular A-122." Later, it was more accurately described as "defund the left." Whatever the source or purpose, I characterized it as "an egregious end run around freedom," but the task of restraining it and eventually rolling it back took nearly two years.

The Office of Management and Budget's (OMB) Circular A-122 governs federal grants and contracts with nonprofit organizations. Without consultation, OMB proposed drastic changes in the treatment of advocacy activities, which eventually would have forced all voluntary organizations that accepted any government funds to forego their right to try to influence legislation or even communicate with government officials. For example, Catholic Charities, which helps to carry out government child care programs and is reimbursed for doing so, would have been prohibited from expressing itself on ways to improve those services. An organization that received only a tiny proportion of its total budget to help evaluate a federal program would have been disenfranchised. And all this was to go into effect in sixty days.

After verifying the accuracy of scary rumors about OMB's actions, I called one of their top officials, who first denied that any such changes were in the making, then minimized their significance, then acknowledged and editorialized that they would indeed stop voluntary organizations from mucking up (not quite his term) the workings of the administration, and finally told me that if I thought anyone in the White House was going to change one G.D. word, I had manure (a euphemism) for brains.

It was by far the most outrageously dishonest, threatening, and profane conversation I ever had with a public official. Not surprisingly, it ended with his obvious eagerness to be sure I understood that if I didn't like what he was telling me, I could go screw myself (or some such word).

Because the network of INDEPENDENT SECTOR was by then in place, we were able to create a firestorm of protest, including many examples of specific and horrendous implications for people and causes in almost every congressional district. There was also extensive media coverage.

For two months, OMB and the White House held firm, but their resolve was being challenged by high-level congressional interventions prompted largely by the local affiliates of our members. For example, Congressman Conable personally called James Baker, White House Chief of Staff, to voice his concerns, and followed up with formal letters to the president and Baker. There was heavy criticism from the media—for example, a *New York Times* editorial headed "OMB Bomb Throwers," written as a result of our meeting with a member of the editorial board.

Our OMB task force, headed by Matthew Ahman of Catholic Charities and including 250 representatives of other prominent organizations, many generally favorable to the Reagan administration, kept building the nationwide outcry.

With all of that, David Stockman, director of OMB, finally announced withdrawal of the regulations. That was a relief and an important battle won, but it soon became obvious that we had only won the first stage of a protracted struggle. OMB treated the event as a temporary setback, figured that our outcry could not be sustained for long, and thought they could come back with more of the same and stick it in our ear. (My OMB contact would have put it differently.)

In November, eight months later, OMB's second draft was released. We had used the long interim to provide fuller evidence of the negative impact their original proposal would have had, but we obviously had not made a sufficient dent. There were improvements, but really only to try to satisfy some secondary concerns expressed by members of Congress about Congress's own responsibility for defining such controls.

Fortunately, our new opening was provided by this emphasis on relationships with Congress, because both houses called for hearings on the overall changes. Those hearings provided us with the best possible opportunity to articulate our concerns and make our recommendations to the committees and to every influential member of Congress. Also, our formal testimony gave us a document to use in restimulating the grass roots.

In testimony before the House Government Affairs Committee, I emphasized that the new recommendations still represented serious infringements on the advocacy rights and responsibilities of voluntary organizations, and I urged that if there was a need to redefine lobbying, the definitions should be consistent with those contained in the tax code governing tax-exempt status.

A point in my testimony that seemed to be particularly persuasive was that "if the definitions, for example, of what constitutes lobbying in the relevant sections of the Tax Code passed by Congress are different from those used by any Administration, then all voluntary organizations will be badly confused about their rights, or worse, in jeopardy of them. Such a dual system is certain to have a chilling effect on a voluntary organization's pursuit of its appropriate advocacy rights and responsibilities."

With pressure mounting, OMB again extended the public comment period as we had recommended and seemed to take more seriously the need for much greater amendment. In part, that was the result of enormous criticism expressed by the House committee, especially its influential chairman, Jack Brooks, and by the fact that in the Senate, David Durenberger introduced legislation that would have overridden the authority and the actions of OMB. We had worked extensively with both legislators, largely through leaders of organizations in their constituencies.

Our case was also helped by two new reports that challenged the OMB recommendations. A Congressional Research Service report questioned the statutory authority of OMB to issue such revisions, and an American Civil Liberties Union report suggested that "the language of the new proposal is unfortunately open to alternative interpretation that would entail substantial abridgments of First Amendment rights."

Finally, in late April 1984, OMB issued a much revised recommendation that went a very long way to respond to our concerns. Also, though the comment period had ended, Congressman Brooks invited our participation in presenting requests for clarification "as to the allowability of the practices described," and our requests were sent to the president by Brooks and the ranking Republican on the Government Affairs Committee, Frank Horton. They and we were assured that our concerns would be accommodated.

Because of the prior behavior of OMB, we felt it necessary to continue our OMB task force, by then grown to an even larger coalition, and for the next year it monitored OMB's administration of A-122. It also helped IS to provide guidance for our members and others on their rights and obligations.

After enough time had passed to be assured that our victory would hold, I began describing that long, harrowing struggle in ways that helped our members realize the significance of it—not just to take pride in the victory, but to achieve greater resolve and confidence in what we could achieve together. I wrote: "During the past almost three years, we have led an all out struggle to force OMB to withdraw and almost totally revise the requirements of voluntary organizations in relation to their advocacy activities. Five years ago, we would have been powerless to protest, and those regulations would now be choking off the sector's most significant public service."

A similar nightmare for IS and our members, also involving challenges to advocacy rights, began in the fall of 1986.

For me and for many in the sector, this chilling episode really started as far back as the early 1970s, when I was national director of the Mental Health Association (MHA). It was not I who brought the issue forward into the life of INDEPENDENT SECTOR, but it was natural that IS should become deeply involved.

In 1972, the MHA celebrated victories in Congress that took the form of greatly increased appropriations for mental health research, training, and community treatment. Over a period of about two years, those new appropriations amounted to approximately $125 million a year, to be awarded by the federal government to state and local mental health authorities, not including the association itself. For an organization that was raising about $25 million a year, those were major accomplishments. After succeeding in getting the legislation passed and then the funds appropriated and authorized, we were horrified that President Nixon "impounded" the money as an early test of what would now be called the principle of "line-item veto." We were absolutely stymied, because Congress, having already given every approval for the funds, had no further role. It was a stand-off between those two branches of government, with only the Supreme Court left as possible arbiter.

Our feisty group, struggling with the unpopular cause of mental illness, sued the president of the United States, and in two separate cases our issues careened their way to the High Court, where eventually we won both, and on lopsided votes. It was one of the greatest victories ever for the MHA.

I hope you'll bear with me for a brief aside that I think will underscore the need for voluntary organizations to be free to battle with government. Shortly after those Court decisions, I was visiting with my counterpart in England, and naturally told her about our stunning victories. She responded not with shared exhilaration, but with alarm. She asked me to promise not to mention these matters while in her country. At first I thought she was kidding, but it became obvious how deadly serious she was. She explained that more than 90 percent of her national annual budget came via one grant from the Ministry of Health, and she was terribly concerned lest there be any interpretation that she had invited me to her country to try to win its mental health community over to our radical and confrontational ways. Because the

MHA in the U.S. was a consumer-oriented advocacy group, I took it for granted that to exercise our independence, we had to avoid any reliance on government funding, but she argued that the services that her organization provided justified its very different approach to government finances and relationships.

For me, that's always been a stunning lesson in what government funding can do to one's independence.

Perhaps I digressed from my story because the next part of the MHA story is so painful.

It wasn't very long after the Court's decisions that some of our MHA state affiliates became subject to financial and program audits. I knew what a financial audit was, but the program side was new. I learned quickly that it entailed an examination of whether we were exceeding the amount of advocacy effort allowed by what was then a very indefinite formula. At that stage, our state affiliates were substantially involved in trying to improve state conditions relating to mental illness, their interests encompassing mental hospitals, rehabilitation programs, and the like. It was pretty obvious that the very best of the affiliates would be heavily involved in influencing public policies and programs. Thus we were highly vulnerable to a claim that we exceeded the "insubstantial" amount of resources that could be expended for advocacy.

At about that time, I was told by both government insiders and informed observers that I was on the so-called "enemies list" of the White House. In truth, I never knew if that was really so, or even if there was in fact any such list, but I soon had no doubt that somebody awfully high up was indeed out to get us, and that the IRS was the principal vehicle. On the personal side, they couldn't do very much because my tax returns were pretty simple. It was the only time in my life I was relieved and grateful I had so little money!

For the organization, the consequences were becoming horrific. One after the other, our state affiliates were reporting that IRS auditing teams were showing up, focusing little attention on financial records but subjecting to total scrutiny minutes, correspondence, and anything else that could provide a sense of interactions with government. Within months, we learned that our enormously effective Maryland division would lose its tax exemption, and the signs were the same for others.

We thought we might get relief by using an old contact with the current IRS commissioner, but the latter angrily rejected any notion of politicization of his organization. Years later, I learned that in fact he was unaware that White House officials had gained considerable leverage over key people in the IRS, particularly with respect to so-called "enemies."

In desperation, we turned to influential members of Congress, who fortunately understood that the administration's arbitrary interpretation of "substantial" or "insubstantial" left us at the mercy of federal officials who might object to our efforts to influence government. Congressman Conable and Senator Edmund Muskie took up our cause, and with their help we were able to enlist impressive cosponsors of legislation that would be more specific about what legislative activity was appropriate for voluntary groups and even declare that advocacy was healthy in the development of sound public policies and programs. The legislators made their displeasure clear to the IRS and the White House and demanded that during consideration of their legislation, foreclosures of tax exemption should be limited to cases of egregious behavior.

After two years of growing support and negotiation, Congress finally passed the law "Lobbying by Public Charities," which clarified and expanded the lobbying rights of nonprofit groups.

With that law on the books and other larger problems facing the White House, the MHA remained generally free of retaliatory efforts, though in certain IRS regions, there were arbitrary interpretations of the law that were somewhat difficult to counter because the definitive regulations stemming from the law were slow in coming.

Actually, "slow in coming" is hardly an accurate description. It was, in fact, ten years before the IRS got around to issuing proposed regulations, and when they finally surfaced, they were brutal in their prohibitions and inhibitions. Contrary to the statute to which they related, which made clear through word and legislative history that advocacy was to be encouraged within broad limits, the regulations treated advocacy as inappropriate and punishable.

I had quite naturally remained interested in the prospective regulations but had not really focused on them until all sorts of people who knew nothing about my MHA background began to tell me of rumors of the awful regulations soon to be issued by the IRS. Déjà vu was never more poignant and painful.

Beginning with an optional session of IS members in late December 1986 to compare information and develop strategy, I was back in the thick of it again, and INDEPENDENT SECTOR was immediately up to its ears in desperate efforts to protect thousands of organizations from perverse IRS interpretation of advocacy rights.

My notes indicate that IS spent considerable time on this issue at every board meeting between January 1987 and September 1990—almost four years!

Every strategy and step described in the previous recounting of the A-122 saga applies in spades to the lobbying regulations struggle, so I won't repeat all of it here. Suffice it to say that the organization and the sector were threatened, angry, aroused, active, tenacious, connected, and when some light showed, willing to be reasonable and judicious.

Lawrence Gibbs, a relatively new IRS commissioner, was at first totally supportive of his staff but couldn't help being bewildered by the sheer number of respected organizations and people, including former commissioners, leaders of Congress, and many others, who argued for reexamination. At our instigation, the majority of the House Ways and Means Committee, the Senate Finance Committee, and the House Appropriations Committee signed letters to Gibbs urging withdrawal. It didn't take him long to compare the original legislation with the regulations and to realize that someone was looking at the two through very different lenses. It would have been awkward for the new commissioner to withdraw the proposed regulations, but he accomplished the same goal by issuing a news release that in essence said that the proposals would be reexamined.

At that point, Commissioner Gibbs asked me to bring a group of leaders to see him so that he could get a firsthand sense of the issues and of those who were leading a campaign upsetting to his leadership and organization. I think he found it unbelievable that we behaved like intelligent, rational human beings who didn't carry placards and spears. I explained our grievances, and with Thomas Troyer of Caplan and Drysdale, presented a comparison of the origins of the 1976 legislation, the legislation itself, and the contradictory regulations. Then, representatives of various parts of the sector, such as arts, human rights, and education, explained why they found the regulations to be so inappropriate and such bad public policy.

Not long after that session, there was a second gathering that brought together a delegation from IS and many of the IRS staffers who had been involved in developing the regulations. Any observer would have concluded that it was not a very successful beginning for efforts to resolve different perceptions and mutual distrust.

At one point, someone on our side pointed out that the regulations were bad enough but would lead to even more exaggerated interpretations by people in the IRS regions and others responsible for compliance. With that, we were taken to task on the grounds that the IRS was above political influence and so rigidly objective and professional that it was an insult to suggest that prejudice or worse could enter into any future reviews.

At that point, I tried as politely as possible to describe my Mental Health Association experience, in order to demonstrate that in my case at least, the IRS had behaved in the worst possible way, leading me not to trust personal assurances that the regulations would be balanced by fair and objective auditors.

Despite my efforts to be reasonably calm and quietly truthful, it was obvious that they were startled, filled with disbelief, and angry. In essence, the session involved our questioning their objectivity, fairness, and—worse—their professionalism. It didn't go well, and except for agreement to meet again, it didn't end well.

Within a couple of days, I received a call from a very key figure in the IRS, who said he had been instructed by even higher echelons to call me to relay the service's chagrin, acknowledgment, and apologies for what the records clearly revealed was grossly inappropriate behavior in the case involving the MHA's Maryland affiliate, and perhaps others. It was obviously a painful call for him to make, but he did it with dignity and kindness.

Shortly afterwards, Commissioner Gibbs accepted a suggestion we had made to establish an Exempt Organizations Advisory Group, made up primarily of leaders from our sector and legal and tax experts on philanthropic and voluntary organizations. For the next two years, discussions proceeded on two and then three levels, leading to resolution of the immediate issue of the advocacy regulations and to exploration of many other important matters relating to the IRS and nonprofits. The advisory group met regularly to learn of the progress of a working group on regulations and, where necessary, to form new working groups on other matters. Gradually, there developed regular consultation between IS and teams within the IRS to try to resolve some of the stickiest issues of the regulations. As you might imagine, this required mutual respect and the ability to compromise and disagree.

We had moved from absolute adversaries to wary negotiators to cooperative professionals earning and depending on each other's respect.

Even with all of that, it took two years to achieve regulations that were consistent with the original law and had sufficient safeguards to satisfy both sides that the law would be administered properly.

In my last report on this subject to the board, in January 1991, I concluded:

> It took a full 14 years for the Internal Revenue Service to issue final regulations under the 1976 Lobby Law and the initial proposed regulations went in the exact opposite direction of the legislation they were supposed to replace. It was at that point that IS organized a firestorm of protest that led to four years of negotiation. The regulations are worth the effort. The final version, issued August 30, 1990, is faithful to the 1976 Law that extended greatly the lobbying rights of nonprofits.

Since that time, the IRS and IS have worked particularly well together on many sensitive matters, including cooperation on ways to achieve fuller compliance by voluntary and philanthropic organizations with laws and regulations governing such required behavior as openness and accountability. There is also very close collaboration between the IS research program and the IRS on efforts to more effectively collect, analyze, and report information about the sector, including the number, types, income, and expenditures of exempt organizations.

It fits under the subject of cooperation with former adversaries to tell you about a joint research project with the IRS that at the time struck many people as the antithesis of our "appropriate" adversarial relationship with government. From the start of our research program, we saw and pursued a need to prod and later assist government in collecting as complete information on the voluntary sector as it does on business. It was important to know far more accurately how many organizations there were, their finances, staffing patterns, program emphases, birth rates and death rates, and much more. The Bureau of Labor Statistics, the IRS, and others already collected some of this data, but it was incomplete, neglected, and inaccurately reported.

When CONVO was still functioning, we had cooperated in efforts to markedly improve Form 990 (on which exempt organizations are required to report annually to the federal government) and to get states to accept that form or something close to it so that reporting obligations could be simplified and made more uniform. Much later, and after three or four years of major collaboration with IRS, as well as extensive pulling and pushing with others in the executive branch and Congress, IS finally convinced all the essential players to commit more resources toward adequate collection, analysis, and reporting of the information necessary for a full understanding of the makeup, functions, governance, and trends of the sector. Even if it had ended there, that accomplishment, in its own almost invisible way, would have deserved to be known as one of our "big ones." Unfortunately, it didn't end there, and several more years of struggle and investment would be required before we could see light again.

At the worst possible moment, major budget cutbacks at the IRS slashed the new commitment, and we were almost back to zero. Some figured we would just have to wait for better circumstances, but a few stalwart believers within IS (led by Virginia Hodgkinson) and an unexpected funder wouldn't let the opportunity pass. They determined what it would take to keep the project viable, what part of the analysis could be handled by IS on a crash basis for two or even three years, and whether the IRS could and would accept money from a private source to enable it to improve collection of the data, test our analyses, and begin fuller dissemination of the information to the sector and to the public. With all those complicated arrangements miraculously resolved, the funder—whose board, at that stage, would have been horrified to think that any of its money was going in any way, shape, or form to support the IRS—committed itself to three years of grants to IS to carry on the project.

The story is made even better by the fact that an earlier head of that foundation had declined membership in IS because his board suspected we would be too liberal. He did, however, provide a "president's grant" to be applied to some assuredly neutral project. He acknowledged with a knowing twinkle that in the end, their money would end up helping our general fund because, as he put it, "all money is fungible." I think he would have applauded when, a few years later, we took fungibility to creative new heights!

There are many other events in our relations with government that are described in later chapters, but the principal message here is that we had developed the courage and capacity both to *fight* government whenever that was necessary and to *cooperate* with government when that was called for. Both approaches were necessary to the constructive pursuit of our mission.

Battles and Cooperation with Government

T he organizing committee had the advantage of CONVO's prior consideration of its mission, goals, and activities in relation to government, and we benefited greatly from the active participation of Congressmen Barber Conable and Joseph Fisher on the organizing committee and its government subcommittee. With those advantages, the committee proposed the following role for IS in its relationship with government: "to deal with the infinite interconnections between the two sectors, but particularly to ensure the healthy independence and continued viability of nonprofit organizations. This may include efforts to influence public policy where the welfare of the entire independent sector is concerned. Such attention must not be limited to the Federal government but relate as well to state and local government."

In developing this role, the committee drew on several assumptions. First, it assumed both that government participation in the nonprofit world was likely to increase and that some of this involvement could inadvertently be destructive.

It saw four primary means through which government affects the sector: (1) constitutional protections such as freedoms of speech and assembly and separation of church and state; (2) the tax structure; (3) funding mechanisms (contracts, grants, and so on); and (4) oversight and regulation.

Another assumption was that the concept and values of pluralism had to be understood and accepted by government if there was to be a positive climate for strengthening rather than inhibiting the capacity of the independent sector to be of public service. Government should have an explicit and coherent policy of enhancing the vitality of the sector. (Because of the importance of an informed electorate, this assumption related also to the public education program.)

It was also assumed that if the new organization approached government only through institutional self-interest, its impact would be minimal.

Finally, the committee believed that the organization should relate to government agencies and officials in positive ways in seeking solutions to common problems and in the basic relationships of the two sectors.

When I began to assemble resource materials for this chapter, I realized that to squeeze in just the highlights of the government relations story would be impossible, but I was nevertheless gratified by how very much there is to celebrate. Looking over minutes, notes, reports, testimonies, and each year's "Highlights," a special document sent out to members, suggests that the whole book could legitimately be given over to hopes fulfilled in government relations. Selecting a short list of them unfortunately leaves out many high points and people deserving attention.

It isn't quite sufficient to the story to describe the accomplishments without emphasizing also some of the unique elements in our approach that helped achieve success. Without repeating what I've said before about process, involvement, and other aspects of our operations, it might help to provide two summaries, one my own and one much more impressively objective.

In my "Highlights" for 1985, I described several successes in government relations activities, and to explain how and why we had prevailed in several uphill struggles, I stated: "In the past, the organizations of the sector have only been able to express themselves on such issues in disorganized fashion. This time we were able to focus the passion, provide the facts, and organize ourselves in the congressional districts. That combination of passion, facts, and organization achieved far greater results than anyone ever thought possible."

As far back as the spring of 1981, when against everyone's prediction and all odds we succeeded in getting the Senate Finance Committee to include the charitable deduction for all taxpayers in its tax bill, Senator Bob Packwood, a cosponsor of our legislation and a high-ranking member of the Finance Committee, told our board: "INDEPENDENT SECTOR has proved to be one of the most organized, efficient and knowledgeable networks I have had the pleasure to work with. I place major responsibility for the success of this bill on the efforts of your organization in getting the support of so many people and organizations from all over the United States. It is one of the few times that I have seen a bill lobbied so well."

When the charitable contributions legislation (CCL) was enacted four months later, I issued a congratulatory memo to IS members in which I said: "Ours was a peoples' bill. Nobody took it seriously except you and your constituents—the people. *You* generated the outpouring that Senator Dole reported 'couldn't be stopped.' It's a beautiful demonstration of the responsiveness of elected officials to their constituents. Along the way there have been discouraging obstacles and setbacks but these have been more than matched with tenacity and organization. The result is glorious. It's a special occasion."

Victory was not achieved without a great deal of internal turmoil and difficult negotiation among many of our members and an excruciating decision that Jack Moskowitz, head of our CCL Coalition, and I had to make in half a minute, just before the full Senate was finally to vote on our issue. For about two years, we had said we could not accept a compromise that would have set a limit on how much of a contribution a nonitemizing taxpayer could deduct. Many of our members, including most of the religious community, were adamant that if we agreed to a *floor*—meaning that the taxpayer who used the short form could deduct a limited percentage of charitable contributions—this would also quickly become the standard for the higher-income tax payers who used the long form to itemize and deduct the full amount of all their contributions. We knew that if all taxpayers lost the full deduction, the consequences would be terrible. Many organizations heavily involved in our coalition had declared firmly that if a floor or other limit were imposed, they would turn around and oppose our own CCL bill.

With the full Senate in session and barreling toward summer recess within an hour, we were presented a take-it-or-leave-it compromise that our key sponsors urged us to accept. When we begged for time,

Pat Moynihan gave us thirty seconds before he and Bob Packwood would go back before the full Senate to call for a vote or withdrawal of our cherished proposal.

As a group of us huddled in the shadow of the towering Moynihan, we saw the possibility that going along might not split our teetering alliance. Though the dreaded floor was called for, it was to be phased out over five years, resulting in full deduction of everyone's contributions in 1986. Some in our tense circle shouted against compromise; some walked away saying they would let other people decide but couldn't be identified with any decision involving a floor; and the rest, in varying degrees of horror at the consequences for their organizations, agreed that we probably had to grab what was being offered. Packwood and Moynihan, who certainly understood compromise but didn't quite grasp how tough it is to make a snap decision in a true coalition, wouldn't listen to any of the *ifs, ands,* and *buts* we were required to try to negotiate, and faced with those constraints Jack and I gave our "OK." They rushed back in, and within fifteen minutes we had a victory that in another fifteen a lot of our group were afraid they couldn't live with. For several days, our largest role was to put ourselves squarely on the line in explanation and celebration of a real breakthrough, however imperfect.

In a special memo to IS members, I said:

This phase-in was necessary to accept in order to keep early year costs within the ceilings set by the administration and Congress. Our object was to get the legislation on the books—and to do so without accepting the permanent *floor* being pushed hard by Treasury. (The *floor* would have meant that for both non-itemizers and later almost certainly for itemizers people would only be able to deduct contributions above a certain figure such as $200.) That would have totally contradicted our commitment to broadening the base of giving.

From the start, our long-term purpose in pushing the legislation has been to encourage all Americans to give to the causes of their choice. We knew that this legislation would do that directly but also that it represented an indirect and symbolic way by which our government would again be encouraging this kind of charitable behavior on the part of all citizens. Thus getting the Charitable Contributions legislation on the books—and without a *floor*—was our goal. We had to accept a phase-in or lose and then wait at least two years to start to push the legislation again. We're not happy with the modest amounts in the first years, but frankly we would have gone with a zero allowance in the first couple of years to get into the law now. We knew from the experience of the six months that if we had lost and began gearing up for passage when the next serious tax bill is before Congress—likely two or even three years away—that at that point we would again be faced with such a phase-in—or more likely the dreaded permanent *floor*. Taking this disappointing phase-in and getting a commitment now to 50 percent in 1985 and 100 percent in 1986 was the obvious course.

The legislation in 1986 will reach a cost to the government of approximately $2.5 billion. *Business Week* reports that our willingness to compromise on the early years of the phase-in caused Treasury to accept "a time bomb" for the out years. . . .

The reactions from the administration, Members of Congress, their staffs, the press who follow tax matters and everyone who knows anything about such legislation is uniformly amazement. A year ago, six months ago, and even one month ago, none of them took us seriously. Now they want to know how in the world it happened.

We know—and we're willing to talk. The organizations of the sector and more importantly their constituents proved once again that in a democracy numbers are the eventual name of the game. You're great.

It was pivotal that as early as 1980 we had begun to organize our government relations efforts in all key congressional districts and to do so through involvement of *local* leaders of our members' *local* affiliates, who could make clear the local significance of federal actions.

Many times, people who were impressed with our results would ask me who our extraordinary lobbyist was or what well-connected law firm represented us with government. Without slighting the impressive role of Bob Smucker, vice president for government relations, or the various law firms we used—usually pro bono—when special skills such as regulatory drafting were needed, I would emphasize the primary role of our nationwide network and the supporting role of staff and counsel. I was often disappointed that groups needing and deserving greater influence in Washington would view the task of building their own outreach as too cumbersome or time-consuming and would go the route of engaging a firm of professional lobbyists, then wonder why that firm couldn't produce results. They didn't grasp that the same firm succeeded with its commercial clients largely because those clients could provide political action committee (PAC) funds to the campaigns of key legislators, which provided the lobbyist with access and leverage. Such political activities were not appropriate for nonprofit organizations.

Obviously, among the most significant examples of our shared achievements were the Supreme Court cases involving freedom of speech, and efforts to preserve advocacy rights, covered respectively in Chapters Four and Five. These required continued vigilance. For example, for several years we had a Schaumburg subcommittee, which was involved in many other court cases to preserve and extend the free speech principles articulated in the Schaumburg decision and to make certain that federal and other courts throughout the country observed the law of the land as interpreted by Schaumburg.

Tax issues were obviously a continuing priority, especially in proposals that would have weakened the opportunity for people to deduct the full amount of their charitable contributions. I'll leave to Bob Smucker the eventual authorship of a full volume on those battles, but a few references here may give a sense of them.

Some short-term victories have to be measured by how much you didn't lose that you might have, and some long-term gains are a matter of how much you later win back. Examples of both occurred during at least a dozen years of bitterly fought proposals to reduce the impact of the charitable deduction. The good news is that we defeated or greatly minimized many of the most damaging proposals and later won back many of the temporary losses we did sustain. The bad news is that a succession of administrations and congresses were so preoccupied with the government's financial needs that they tried to transfer some of the fiscal burden to voluntary organizations while at the same time attempting to undercut the income of the very organizations to which they were turning.

In the tax area, threats to our income came in the form not only of challenges to the deduction of charitable contributions but of recommendations to tax the interest income, fees received from clients, and endowment income of nonprofit organizations. At one point, in the midst of the absolutely crazy contradiction of being asked to provide more service while having every source of existing income attacked, I exploded in a memo to our members:

> The government pushed the workload on us and we accepted. The government asked us to set an example of restraint in the face of national deficits, and we accepted. Three years later, after being the ones to carry forward the voluntary spirit heralded by the Administration

and Congress, we are the very same ones being asked to transfer five percent of our income to provide the government with a supplement of a tiny fraction of one percent of theirs. We are rather proud to be known as soft-hearted, but rather angered to be treated as soft-headed.

Later, after several more "revenue enhancers" or indirect taxes were proposed to ease the government's financial problems at the expense of philanthropic and voluntary groups, I was slightly more temperate but every bit as angry:

Now, along comes a Joint Committee report that serves up the idea of a new excise tax on exempt organizations, which it says could raise $3.5 billion in 1988, of which at least $1.5 billion would come out of the program and granting capacity of voluntary organizations and foundations. On top of that $1.5 billion loss, the Joint Committee proposes that the deduction for itemized deductions should be allowed only against the fifteen percent tax rate. This proposal alone would reduce charitable giving by $6.7 billion annually, according to research by Professor Lawrence Linsey of Harvard. For the Federal government to consider slashing another $8 to $9 billion, or ten percent, or any substantial proportion of it, from the income of the sector to which it is transferring so much of the service burden is absurd and cruel.

Through a succession of massive campaigns to rally our members, their affiliates, and many, many others, we were able to defeat the excise tax; the tax on interest, earned income, and endowment income; the lowered ceiling on how much an individual could contribute and deduct; and the idea that itemized deductions would be allowed only against the 15 percent tax rate. In addition, we succeeded in preserving most of the existing benefits of tax exemption and contributions deduction that had been "on the table"—a euphemism for "Let's see how much opposition we get."

On the other hand, during those awful periods, we lost the charitable deduction for nonitemizers and the deduction of gifts of appreciated property at market value. We also incurred a modest but potentially ominous new floor that limited deductions of contributions for people with incomes over $100,000.

In subsequent years, there were some vitally important "win backs." These included the first phase, restoration of full deduction of gifts of tangible personal property, such as art objects; the second phase, full deduction of all gifts of appreciated property at market value; and restoration of full deduction of gifts to establish and supplement foundations.

For the sake of the tale and the lesson, I'll describe one excruciatingly awkward moment in the battle to avoid any limitation on deduction of contributions. There was a proposal to impose a 5 percent floor on deductions, meaning that a wealthy person could deduct only contributions above 5 percent of adjusted gross income. We were aware that the proposal was favored by President Bush's key people in the Office of Management and Budget (OMB). This was regrettable, but understandable because of their total preoccupation with ways to raise revenue without violating the president's "no new taxes" pledge. On several occasions, the president let it be known that he had instructed OMB officials to back off from support of this provision. This, after all, was the president who was calling for greatly increased participation by volunteers and their organizations.

We were dismayed, therefore, to hear that the president's key budget negotiators were willing to support that dreaded floor. At about that time, the president's Points of Light Foundation was scheduled to have a planning retreat with the president at Camp David, and I struggled with a real conflict of interest. Did my membership on the foundation's board make it inappropriate to use this extraordinary opportunity to discuss with the president what I viewed as a contradiction between his support for the sector and his aides' support of the floor? To test myself, I talked it over with Jim Joseph, who also had been asked by the president to be a founding member of the board. We agreed that responsibility to our organizations and to the president required us to find a way to introduce the topic.

It took a lot of pressing to arrange this side conversation with the president during an otherwise extremely pleasant and successful day at his home away from home. Our case was also tough to pursue in that absolutely magical setting where one is so easily disarmed.

To the obvious upset of his aides, our time finally arrived, and Jim and I found ourselves maneuvered into a corner with the president, where I presented a very carefully rehearsed summary of our concerns and alarm, with just enough reference to the contradiction the issue represented for his administration to make the point. President Bush was not happy but remained reasonably cordial. He reaffirmed his full backing of the financial and other needs of our organizations. He seemed surprised that any such compromises could be taking place and said it was hard to know just what would finally come out of the terribly difficult process of give-and-take in the final showdown with Congress. He ended by saying he didn't think we would have to worry, because he certainly didn't want to be party to anything that would hurt those he was trying so much to advance.

With all conversations at Camp David off the record, it was hard for Jim and me to use this session as fully as we would have liked to try to get the floor removed from consideration. Through indirection, we certainly tried, but we had to count primarily on the president and his top aides to get his sentiments communicated to their negotiators. Alas, the final results on this issue went against us. I don't report this to suggest that the president was disingenuous. With distance, my reaction is more, "So much for my power as an insider!" The episode reinforced my belief that our influence was largely through the army of believers in our networks.

A bit more needs to be said about the agonizing effort to win back the full deduction of gifts of appreciated property. Not only was the outcome finally favorable, but we reversed an almost total history of "once lost, forever lost," which meant that once the government had taken away rights and privileges of voluntary organizations, it was almost a given that they could never be regained. That axiom has finally been exploded, and our tenacious pursuit of gifts of appreciated property helped do it. A big part of the reason and of the lesson learned is a sustained and growing nationwide crusade over more than seven years. It was chaired by Sharon Cranford of the Association of American Universities.

The first "win back" came in 1991, when we recovered a piece of the deduction. Though we were disappointed, it was nevertheless important and encouraging that Congress made a one-year exception by allowing market value deduction of gifts of tangible personal property. In 1992, that exception was extended for another year, which may sound automatic, but it came at a time when a great many people within the administration, Congress, the IRS, and Treasury Department were determined to kill it.

Finally, in 1993, we won back full and permanent deduction of all gifts of appreciated property, including stocks and land.

In my bulletin to the membership, I wrote:

TENACITY PAYS OFF!

Since the 1986 Tax Act, gifts of appreciated property have been restricted for many donors and many types of gifts including stocks and land. Through the tenacious efforts of an extended coalition that has operated in the intervening seven years, those limitations have now been removed, and already there is a wonderful surge of major gifts to museums, colleges, church-building campaigns, and others. When the victory was finally achieved, the head of the coalition responded, "It was a victory of the whole community, and IS is the means by which the community works together."

Such bulldog determination and record-setting longevity for an ad hoc coalition was the secret for reversing other bitter losses. With each uphill victory, we gained three advantages for future progress: (1) the victories themselves; (2) the inspiration we gained from the evidence that we could win; (3) greater respect from government, including greater reluctance to take us on. All of those advantages will be needed to gain back the deduction for nonitemizers and remove the floor that still limits deduction of some contributions. They will also be needed to counter future ill-advised efforts to limit our roles and income.

Two other long-running struggles where real progress has been made but where no end is in sight involve the dreaded terms *U.B.I.T.* and *Competition*. Many of these battles were fought at the regulatory level, but in most cases our big victories came either through congressional action or through the involvement of congressional leaders with legislative authority over the regulatory bodies that had to be dissuaded from inappropriate positions.

U.B.I.T. stands for Unrelated Business Income Tax. The law is clear that income received by voluntary organizations is only tax-exempt to the extent it is related to the mission of the organization. The law became necessary, and was certainly appropriate, when it was revealed that New York University (NYU) had inherited the Mueller Spaghetti Company and was running it as a tax-free corporation. Other spaghetti companies and the IRS quite naturally objected, and despite pleas by NYU that the profits were used to further the university's educational purposes, the tax code was revised to say that income that is unrelated to the program mission of a tax-exempt organization has to be taxed. On that basis, NYU could continue to sell spaghetti, but it would have to do so through a taxable profit-making entity. In today's terms, if an art museum sells replicas of its paintings, the income is tax-exempt, but if it rents one of its parking lots to a business next door, that income is taxable.

During the 1980s, at a time when many nonprofit institutions were struggling to maintain or increase income and were being pushed, particularly by corporate donors, to be more entrepreneurial and marketing-oriented, there was a scramble for earned income. Much of this was healthy, but there were some downsides, including forays into *unrelated* business ventures. Quite rightly, the IRS began to look carefully at the taxable nature of these activities, and quite naturally, the institutions tried to interpret them as mission-related.

From my point of view, the government was going much too far in efforts to tax nonprofits, but many voluntary groups were trying to stretch the law to absurd lengths to avoid taxation. Both sides put us to severe tests. Many of our members insisted that we should defend them even if we seemed to be arguing for a return to the tax-exempt sale of spaghetti, and the Treasury Department would have had us support tightening of the regulations and law to the point that any earned income would be taxed. We made neither side happy.

After more than a year of careful study, consultation, and deliberation, we took the position that there was really little need to change either the existing legislation or regulations. The law was very clear, and the problems were out at the edges where many of our groups were flaunting the law. We did work closely with the Oversight Subcommittee of the House Ways and Means Committee, the Treasury Department, and the IRS to clear up ambiguities that clouded compliance and enforcement, but beyond that we argued that the primary need was to enforce the law. That infuriated some of our members and certainly infuriated many in government, including the powerful chairman of the Oversight Subcommittee, J. J. Pickle of Texas. He had proposed rather major changes in the law that we thought were unnecessary and inappropriate, and he really took us on in hearing rooms and once even at the corner of Independence and South Capitol streets. We had bumped into each other, and I tried to get off with a polite greeting but instead got the brunt of his pent-up fury. He shouted that we were obstructing his ability to get support from even his own party members on his subcommittee.

That was what it was like for more than another year, with Congressman Pickle punishing us for obstructing him by telling our story to key members of Congress through the voices of local agencies. Finally, the issue ever so slowly moved out of the crisis stage.

After four years of almost regular reference to the issue in our various briefing memos, I was able to report that the U.B.I.T. proposal had generated little support in the Oversight Subcommittee, and that there was no evidence that the interest of the majority of the subcommittee members was to go beyond making very minor modifications in present U.B.I.T. law. I added that throughout this period, affiliates of IS members who were constituents of congressmen on the subcommittee had been in regular contact with those House members, giving them information on the negative impact the changes would have on services they provided. Those grassroots contacts clearly were pivotal in convincing committee members that major U.B.I.T. modifications were not needed.

U.B.I.T. was very much linked to the competition issue. Some businesses claimed that nonprofits were unfairly competing with them. Their classic example was that YMCAs ran health clubs that were identical to for-profit health clubs. Other nonprofits were also under the gun, including colleges that rented out their facilities during the summer for business conventions, and health organizations that sold hearing aids, prostheses, and clothes. Even the Girl Scouts were attacked for selling cookies.

The issue was taken seriously enough that some states began to question the tax exemption of organizations that seemed to be selling more services than those provided free to people in need.

In many cases, including hospitals and other health care facilities, the issue came down to whether these tax-exempt institutions were indeed doing a reasonable proportion of "charity work." The federal government also became involved, and finally at all levels of government, there were efforts to redefine the parameters of tax exemption. The question was usually looked at in terms of whether an organization was engaged in serving those most in need. However, that measurement was difficult to apply to research institutes, groups focused on peace, or even museums. In many ways, the issue was even harder than U.B.I.T. to get a handle on and resolve.

One thing that helped us was that the very definition of exemption makes clear that the intent was not simply to serve those least advantaged—though that, of course, is a focus of many voluntary groups—but also to support scientific, cultural, religious, recreational, safety, library, and many other pursuits not defined as social welfare.

Through several years of effort, we were able to work with the parties involved to bring some understanding and reduce the heat. We found that most businesses, or even business trade groups, were not much concerned about the issue. For example, in a 1986 survey by the Institute of Enterprise Advancement, the issue of competition with nonprofits ranked seventieth out of seventy-five items of concern.

However, in certain industries, such as health clubs, the issue was extremely tense. Part of the difficulty was that the profit-making side tended quite naturally to want to concentrate on clients who could pay for the service. Their opposites called this "skimming," saying non-profit groups were left to provide services for those who couldn't pay. Some nonprofits believe that the better course for them is to have a fee schedule based on ability to pay, with any profits used to help spread the services to those who can't cover the costs. This approach achieved *some* better understanding among legislators, who are now not so quick to question the exemption of the Y, as long as the Y is clearly serving the total community and not just those who can pay.

These issues raised other contentious differences involving such charged subjects as property taxes and user fees. They also led to reconsideration of the definition of exemption and a need for clearer understanding of its rationale. IS put together an important book, *Why Tax Exemption? The Public Service Role of America's Independent Sector,* which includes the overall explanation and examples of the public service role of nonprofit organizations in fields such as public policy, human rights, human services, arts, culture and humanities, education, the environment, grant making, health, and religion.

That report was just one of the major studies with which we were involved to help communicate the importance and legitimacy of this third sector of our society and its need for exemption from taxes, and in most cases, the need for donors to deduct their contributions from their income taxes. Increasingly, we have articulated the case and prepared exempt organizations to explain this reasoning to policy makers.

My standard argument to policy makers was that if we believed pluralism was important in our society, we had to search for every possible way to encourage voluntary activity. Certainly, we should not adopt measures that would shrink that increasingly important part of our national life. Whatever occurred as the result of tax reform, I would say, must not eliminate or reduce government encouragement of the voluntary sector.

Like related issues, regulatory matters, especially those that would have limited the necessary degree of independence for philanthropic and voluntary organizations, were never far from our top priorities. Over the fifteen years, there were eleven very serious proposals to limit the rights of organizations in our sector, and they came at us from many different directions. Two of the more excruciating struggles to preserve advocacy rights are described in Chapter Five.

In 1993 alone, there were seven serious legislative and regulatory proposals that would have dangerously limited the advocacy rights of voluntary organizations and their funders. These included (1) legislation that almost passed in Congress to deny use of the nonprofit postal rate for any mailings that relate to education of the public or to advocacy for improved public services or policies; and (2) a recommendation defeated only at the eleventh hour that would have denied placement of National Service Volunteers in organizations that engage in any advocacy roles.

Successful efforts to defeat all of those threats took every speck of effort by every part of the organization, but in the end we were able to prevail, and the results acknowledge and encourage the sector's quintessential role in providing the organizational vehicles through which citizens can express their concerns and ideas. Beyond the significance of the outcomes was an awareness of what the organizations of the sector could accomplish when we pooled our concerns and power, and a new respect within government that the sector was impressively able to defend itself.

There was another frightening close call that began in 1986 and was complicated greatly by our previous disagreements with Congressman Pickle on the U.B.I.T. revisions. For quite some time, Pickle had also been interested in clearer definitions and closer monitoring of the political activities of tax-exempt organizations. As most readers will know, engaging in electioneering is just about the most egregious violation an exempt organization can commit. On this issue, Jake Pickle had reason to be very angry. We shared every ounce of his distress, but unfortunately we couldn't agree with key parts of his proposed solution, and as you can imagine, it was hard to negotiate with him or his loyal staff.

His fury went far beyond his upset with us. The situation he faced, and therefore that we faced, involved the despicable behavior of a nonprofit organization that violated all the rules by playing an open role in opposing him for reelection. And the true story gets worse, much worse, with connections to two of the most explosive and illegal undercover operations of our times: the sale of arms to Iran and the use of some of the profits in covert support of Nicaraguan rebels. Some of those profits even went to a U.S. nonprofit organization, the National Endowment for the Preservation of Liberty, led by Carl "Spitz" Channel, which served as a vehicle for political efforts to defeat certain Democratic congressmen who were staunch opponents of President Reagan's Nicaragua policies. Jake Pickle was one of them.

It was one thing for nonprofits to oppose Congressman Pickle on unrelated business income. It was of unimaginably greater consequence that a nonprofit should be caught financing his defeat.

All we could do was publicly share his astonishment and anger, and to argue, as we had in the face of other terrible transgressions, that any such act should be punished to the fullest extent of the law. But to Pickle's rage, we said the law did not need to be changed to make patently clear how illegal the behavior already was. That was not very persuasive to someone who was the target of such gross misuse of nonprofit status and who was already white-hot angry with the covert operations supporting various political factions.

In a way, we were fortunate that Channel and his foundation were as far beyond the bounds of legitimate behavior as they were. It was also to our advantage that justice moved swiftly, with the earliest possible indictment and conviction. Even those who initially wanted to punish any organization engaged in an uncomfortable degree of advocacy cooled off or found themselves unable to mount an all-encompassing challenge to laws and regulations governing nonprofit activity.

We were able to use our government relations and media networks to again demonstrate our repugnance for disgraceful actions perpetrated in the name of charity and our full support of efforts to pursue those who cheated under the cover of charitable status. We also drew attention to all the worthy activities of exempt organizations, making clear that these had to be taken into account when sweeping changes of laws and regulations were being considered. Despite some continuing differences, regulatory bodies recognized that we had become their most important partner in helping to educate nonprofit organizations about their obligations, and that we had consistently called for punishment of those who were not in compliance.

Against that background, we were able to get government officials to convey to Congressman Pickle and others that we were not the enemy and indeed had a remarkable record of leadership on the very issues for which Pickle stood. We got to see some of his top aides, with whom we had had a very positive relationship prior to the U.B.I.T. standoff. In those sessions, I reviewed in detail the leadership efforts IS had already made in the areas of compliance, openness, standards, accountability, and especially obedience to the laws relating to electioneering.

We found every possible point in Pickle's proposed legislation with which we could agree and lined up many of our members in support of those provisions. We also were wide open in explaining our differences and in working with a large and impressive network of Pickle's constituents and those of other key members of his committee.

For the strategists among the readers, it might be interesting to review the positives going for us in what was otherwise a very scary crossroads of nonprofit regulation. We had a good record on the issues, a vast array of constituents supporting us in Pickle's congressional district, and a prior history of good relationships with his office. We had a sensible case, the support of many of his key subcommittee members, and access to his staff. We could also rely on what I'll call "character references" from the Treasury Department and the IRS. Without trying to be judge or jury, we had been the first to indicate publicly that if the charges were true that Channel and the foundation had illegally engaged in efforts to defeat Pickle, they should be punished to the full extent of the law. And finally, though we had stated that we would go all out in support of the bill if changes were made, the chairman knew that we had a great deal of strength—likely sufficient to defeat his legislation if we remained dissatisfied with it.

Gradually, the negotiations for amendment proceeded, and the atmosphere improved. Though both sides still had some problems, the improvements were sufficient to help get passage by the subcommittee. Then, in what could be described as friendly candor, we advised Pickle that we would continue to seek further amendments in the Ways and Means Committee, and subsequently in the Senate. He didn't like it, but he wasn't sufficiently upset to scuttle the process or give us a chance to.

Eventually, with the particular help of Senators Alan Cranston and Pat Moynihan and Congressmen Charles Rangle and Richard Schulze, most of our amendments were made, including a final and cliff-hanging end-of-the-year conference between the Senate and House that removed the last of our major objections.

We may have seemed stubborn right to the end, but the very last issue would have changed existing language that allowed a charity to respond to a candidate's request for a study, paper, or the like without opening itself to charges of political activity. The change would have made such activity subject to very vague interpretation and an enormous penalty. To have given that broad and clearly arbitrary power to future political leaders would have been just too dangerous, and we could not back away.

Among the provisions with which we had agreed from the start was closer oversight to ensure that existing laws on political activity were obeyed. To that end, and consistent with past efforts, we issued the latest in our series of compliance guides: *Tax-Exempt Organizations' Lobbying and Political Activities Accountability Act of 1987: A Guide for Volunteers and Staff of Nonprofit Organizations.*

An even more helpful book with broader implications, but one also designed to educate and encourage our members and others, is Bob Smucker's *The Nonprofit Lobbying Guide: Advocating Your Cause and Getting Results.* For years, I had been encouraging Bob to write about his rare experience and ability in advocacy efforts. Even when I thought he was convinced, he would back off with the legitimate excuse of more immediate, action-oriented priorities. Finally, on one of our planning retreats, I did the uncharacteristic thing of telling him what his top priority was, and that it wasn't negotiable. I also told him that he had to be out of the office for the equivalent of two months, and that his review at the end of the year would be determined largely by whether he'd gotten the book finished. I added that if he didn't get it done, I didn't want to discuss the possibility of his writing a book ever again, because it was obvious he just wasn't up to it.

That's the only thing I think really got to him. Whatever it was, the book has been out for five years and is the best thing I've seen or ever expect to see on the subject. The most able practitioner I've ever watched puts it on the line, providing the best possible guide for the many people and organizations who continue to neglect their advocacy opportunities because the "why" and "how" have never been properly explained to them.

Another never-ending priority was the project begun at that stormy early board meeting on major changes in federal spending. Since 1981, we have provided annual reports that cover the most recent actions of Congress and proposals advanced by the current administration. These are prepared by Lester Salamon and Alan Abramson and now constitute almost a longitudinal study of the changing financial relationships between government and the nonprofit sector.

One of our very earliest projects in the area of financial relationships with government grew out of a different concern, expressed by our members almost from the start, related to contractual relationships. CONVO had already encountered growing problems between voluntary organizations and their partners in government, such as increasingly late payments for services rendered. It was often six months or more after work had been completed that payments were finally made, requiring the nonprofits to borrow money at what was sky-high interest in the 1980s.

The board called for a major study of financial relationships, and former Governor Samuel Goddard of Arizona, a member of the board, agreed to head it. From the start, the task force struggled with an attitude of "Take it or leave it" on the part of many branches and levels of government, and an attitude of "Get them to provide more dollars for our services, but get them off our backs" from too many voluntary organizations.

Between these extremes, the task force on organizational and financial relationships with government struggled to achieve its own understanding of the problems and needs, with emphasis on the causes and clients served, and then sought to develop some ground rules for both sides. An additional year was involved in testing its ideas with government representatives.

What finally emerged was the report *Accountability with Independence—Toward a Balance in Government/Independent Sector Financial Partnerships.* At the heart of it is a series of agreements that should be incorporated into any formal contract between the two sides, a suggested set of obligations of each, and importantly, some guidelines as to the degree of independence a voluntary partner should expect, given the advantages it offers government in terms of flexibility and proximity to the people. Rarely a month went by when I didn't pull out that report and give it to people on one side or the other who were concerned about a breakdown in relationships or trying to strengthen them.

One of the stickiest projects we ever had to negotiate between government and a great many of our bitterly divided members involved the Combined Federal Campaign, which is the annual charitable solicitation among government employees. Almost every health and social welfare organization wanted to be involved in the campaign, and even many groups beyond human services hoped to gain access.

I think it was 1982 when bitter feelings erupted at a board meeting. Many were angry that United Way seemed to dominate the campaign and have undue influence over it with whatever administration was in power. This, it was felt, led to an exclusion or low priority for members not under the umbrella of United Way, including grassroots and advocacy groups. As usual during those early years, there was a demand that INDEPENDENT SECTOR step into the crisis and solve it.

The most we could take on, which turned out to be substantial, was to bring all the parties, including government officials, together to clarify the issues and facts, mark out the substantial areas of agreement, and identify issues of honest disagreement among our members.

It was significant how much misinformation and how many false accusations were flying about. We were able to quiet these significantly by simply providing opportunities for full and open discussion and by involving individuals who were clearly in possession of the facts.

It was also helpful that we identified a great many areas of substantial agreement and were able to follow up on these with key government decision makers. Some immediate and encouraging changes were made in the way the campaign was organized and conducted. The areas of agreement we had uncovered enabled us to work constructively with government over the next several years.

One of the areas of major disagreement, initially involving many of our members and later government representatives and ourselves, related to whether the campaign should include advocacy organizations or even service agencies that engage in advocacy. Because of our stance on advocacy matters in other situations, we felt it essential to weigh in on the side of inclusion.

United Way in particular was pretty upset with us, as were many of the large health and welfare organizations, but they eventually accepted our decision, or at least didn't openly fight it. We had an even tougher time with the government people and eventually joined in a suit that fortunately determined that the government's position to exclude organizations engaging in "litigation and advocacy" was unconstitutional.

Many years later, there are still a lot of disagreements and feelings about who is in and who is not, but I think we helped create a process for sorting out the facts and the issues and determining how they can be dealt with constructively.

Though this was by no means the most far-reaching or successful activity we undertook in government relations, it is the one I recall getting the most heat on, but it was also the one that later drew the most praise for effective use of the meeting ground to resolve an otherwise viciously divisive set of issues.

Among the most significant examples of our shared achievements were the Supreme Court cases involving the freedoms of speech and assembly. The organizing committee had made it clear that the highest of all the many priorities was to address "the fundamental relationship between the freedom of citizens to organize themselves and the freedom of citizens."

That was our orientation and motivation for diving into the Supreme Court case *Village of Schaumburg* v. *Citizens for a Better Environment et al.,* even before IS was fully formed and before we had anything like the resources or experience to justify an all-out defense of associational freedoms.

Also in our early years, we were deeply involved with two other Supreme Court cases, *Riley* and *Munson,* that could have weakened essential freedoms. Fortunately they did not, and indeed both helped establish that voluntary organizations are often the means by which citizens organize themselves to express and exercise collective will.

Writing in celebration of these judicial successes, I emphasized both the rights that had been protected and our responsibilities to be worthy of those rights:

> Organizations of this sector operate with funds voluntarily contributed and therefore have the highest moral responsibility to be absolutely certain that we fulfill the public's trust. We also enjoy the advantages of tax exemption and therefore have particular responsibility to cooperate with government in developing sound oversight laws and compliance with them. There is nothing less attractive in our society than people who cheat and defraud in the name of charity. . . . We and government have a mutual responsibility to establish appropriate expectations. In doing so, however, neither of us should ever be allowed to become so judgmental that we obscure the quintessential role of this sector to protect and encourage maximum citizen interest and participation. In that regard, we are right to rejoice in and celebrate this additional Supreme Court protection of freedom of speech.

Even though it seems inadequate to just list a number of other diverse and important projects, doing so might lead interested people to the archives:

• We provided assistance to the Council on Foundations in the long, uphill road to establish the Foundation Investment Fund, which now allows small and midsize foundations to pool their investments for maximum return.

• We gave cooperation and encouragement to the Treasury Department and the IRS in developing and obtaining approval of *intermediate sanctions,* by which the IRS can give fair warning and impose certain penalties on organizations that are not living up to the responsibilities associated with their exempt status. In the past, there had been only one action that could be taken—namely, total revocation of tax exemption.

• We successfully challenged the redefinition of religion, which had the potential of undermining the essential separation of church and state.

• We mounted successful defenses of the rights of corporations to deduct contributions to charitable activities and organizations abroad and to fully deduct contributions within the new minimum tax.

• Almost annually, we protected nonprofit postal rates, or at least ensured only minimal increases in them, and finally obtained a longer-term compromise that provided for periodic increments far below what had been proposed.

• We helped defeat the proposal to "sunset" the deduction of charitable contributions, meaning that the issue would have had to be reconsidered every three or four years.

• We actively participated in many important efforts to achieve uniform reporting requirements, including the Solicitation Law Project and the Model Solicitation Law Project.

• Every four years, we developed and rigorously promulgated a "Guide for the New Administration and Congress," setting forth requests for specific commitments from each candidate on issues important to the sector.

• We successfully pursued many other important court cases, including: (1) *Taxation With Representation* v. *Donald T. Regan,* which determined that greater restrictions on lobbying by public charities than on lobbying by other groups (for example, trade associations and veterans organizations) violated constitutional rights to freedom of speech and equal protection; (2) *Golsbrough Christian Schools* v. *United States of America* and *Bob Jones University* v. *United States of America,* which continued denial of tax-exempt status to schools discriminating on the basis of race or racial minorities, but which did so in a way that would have given government greater control over tax-exempt organizations, including greater application of the concept of "tax expenditures."

• We supported the government's position—which eventually prevailed—that Social Security participation should be required of nonprofit organizations.

- We gave active support to several governmental actions encouraging community service by young people, including the National and Community Services Act of 1988.
- We actively supported the emergence of state associations of nonprofits, among other things helping in the development and initial publishing of *State Tax Trends*. (This publication has now been turned over to the National Council of Nonprofit Associations, a body we helped to establish.)
- We organized many White House receptions and other opportunities for leaders of the sector to meet with presidents and other top federal officials.

When I used to draft my "Highlights" at the end of each year, I went through tougher guilt pangs than I'll bet any newspaper editor ever does. There were always so many people and events deserving mention, but I knew that nobody would read the summaries if they were properly inclusive. Now my problem is compounded by the seventeen years I've tried to cover, particularly in government relations, where we were so busy for so long. There's a great deal more that should be recorded and many more people who should be acknowledged. I wish somehow it could all be put down, not just to be fair and representative but for the guidance of future leaders, who will be responsible for an unbelievable array of challenges and might profit from knowing what we dealt with in the formative years, and how. Maybe every founder feels that way, and maybe no one would end up reading it all, but I can't help wishing.

CHAPTER SEVEN

Telling the Sector's Story

The organizing committee had framed separate external and internal goals for the proposed information and education program. Under external, they placed "public education," which was designed "to improve public understanding of the sector's role and function in giving people alternatives, greater opportunities for participation, and for creating a more caring and effective society."

Among the internal goals was "communication within the sector so that shared problems and opportunities may be identified and pursued" and "a regular flow of relevant information about the sector and activities within it which encourage giving, volunteering and not-for-profit initiative."

Even before we could begin planning for an extensive program, we were deep into communication efforts within the membership and among the broader public.

At the most internal level, we were involved with the practical and important consideration of how INDEPENDENT SECTOR presented itself, which began, of course, with the name. The firm that assisted us with the name, Ruder and Finn, provided advice on a logo and prepared a forty-page booklet on how the name and logo should be presented. It also offered guidance on many other aspects of public appearance and presentation.

At about the same time, we developed our first brochure in support of a program effort. Not surprisingly, this related to the charitable contributions legislation and was headed, "A Proposal to Encourage Charitable Giving and Citizen Involvement." The brochure featured pictures and statements of a broad range of congressional and sector leaders who were in favor of allowing all taxpayers to deduct their charitable contributions.

From the start, we strengthened our communications with members, building on efforts begun with CONVO and NCOP. Our major new initiative took the form of the biweekly "Memo to Members."

Essentially, I had brought forward a model developed for the vast network of the Mental Health Association, where the interests were also diverse and the readers overwhelmed by their in-boxes. The "Memo to Members" included brief sentences or very short paragraphs on matters of likely interest to most of our members, along with attachments for those who wanted fuller information. In an attempt to ensure that most people would at least look at the memo, I was always on the lookout for bits of humor related to our unique world.

I figured later that there had been about five hundred such memos, and for almost every one, I had hid away for a while to think hard about what I was seeing and hearing that I thought the members might want to read about.

There was also a regular flow of other briefing pieces, issues of *Corporate Philanthropy,* a news service series, sample columns for use in the members' own publications, and many other written materials.

From the day the announcement of our formation appeared in the *New York Times* and wire service stories throughout the country, we were up to our necks getting the message out, capitalizing on attention received, and responding to hundreds of questions, both from those who were just curious and those who were serious membership prospects. Fortunately, John Thomas was absolutely the right person to get on top of all these responsibilities and opportunities.

Later in our first year, we put together a process and a team for the thorough planning of our overall public information and education (PI&E) program. It was clear from our survey of the charter members that PI&E was perceived as our primary long-term responsibility. We were fortunate to attract Landrum Bolling as the head of the PI&E committee. At that time, he was chairman of the Council on Foundations.

He had formerly been president of both Lilly Endowment and Earlham College and had an extensive journalism background.

After reviewing the organizing committee's discussions, the PI&E committee divided its planning into three areas: (1) mass media; (2) the educational system of the country, especially schools; and (3) IS members who already represented vast constituencies.

The committee then set out to define the "case" for encouraging, giving, and voluntary initiative; to obtain the creative cooperation of the mass media in helping to spread the word; to utilize the enormous communications capacity of IS member organizations to tell the story to their millions of members; and to enlist the participation of educational organizations so that students might learn about the sector as part of the formal education process.

From the start, the committee wanted to capitalize on the extraordinary outreach of our own member organizations. We realized that there were many things we would need to do with media, but that we should not be so preoccupied with media that we failed to use the communication mechanisms of our existing and growing roster of members. We also knew that we had to keep those groups well informed if we were to succeed in anything.

As early as 1981, the committee and staff began planning for a major film that would present visually and dramatically what the sector is and does. The film could be used by our members to help millions of participants understand the context of their contributions of time and money. We hoped this would both reinforce the habits of participation and extend them to other people. The film would also be appropriate for service clubs and other civic groups, and for classroom use. And it could find outlets in the broader media, beginning with public television.

Landrum's committee placed special emphasis on the film, and the board quickly picked up the excitement and priority of it. Our only problem was that to do it well would cost a minimum of $300,000.

From prior discussions with Jack Scott and his successor as head of the Gannett Foundation, Gene Dorsey, I thought they might be willing to consider a major contribution to the film's production costs and was encouraged that Gene and his people were at least open to my coming to Rochester, New York, to talk about it. The journey there was filled with traumas well beyond those relating to a major request. That's a kind of fun tale in itself, now a little less scary.

The only time we could all get together was an early morning about a week after my call. Unfortunately, I had an unbreakable commitment to give an after-dinner presentation in Hartford, Connecticut, the night before. After examining every possible transportation option, I concluded that the only way to do both was to charter a plane for a late-night flight. Obviously, it couldn't be anything fancy, but even at that, I wondered how it would look to the board and our members if it ever became known that I was flying around in chartered planes.

If they could have seen the plane and experienced the night, their largest worry would have been about my sanity. The plane was about as old as the pilot, which was not reassuring. It was also tiny, which the pilot said would allow me to sit in the copilot's seat with a good view of things; this turned out to be the opposite of pleasant. The flight was to take about an hour and a half, but because of head winds that seemed to be pushing us backwards and detours that drew us away from our destination, it took closer to three hours—a nightmare of precipitous drops, mountainous bumps, and gyrating instrument dials (and passenger). During this ordeal, my pilot's efforts at reassurance never got better than "Don't worry, I do this all the time." Double jeopardy was never more poignant. I had little doubt that I was going to die, and it would be all over the papers that it happened in a chartered plane!

Though I survived, the experience shortened my life expectancy considerably. At least, however, my lavishness wasn't found out. For those members who might now worry about the extravagance and what it said about my regular travel arrangements, I can offer assurances that that's as close as I ever got to being a Concorde high flyer.

The good news is that the appointment went wonderfully. The foundation took a keen interest in the project and subsequently invested more than $300,000 in the film's production, promotion, and distribution. In early 1983, we released *To Care: America's Voluntary Spirit*, with premieres in thirteen metropolitan areas and extensive initial promotion to our members. The promotion quickly broadened to emphasize schools, service clubs, and television.

The film was produced by Oscar-winning documentary filmmaker Francis Thompson, whose IMAX film *To Fly* opened the Air and Space Museum in Washington and today is the most widely seen documentary worldwide. The writer-director was Bayley Silleck, who coproduced the IMAX film *Cosmic Voyage* for the museum's twentieth anniversary.

To Care is still regularly used in orientation of volunteer leaders, in schools, and for special TV features about the sector. The film was the most important and tangible step we took toward providing a common articulation of the sector's roles and impact.

Of course, *To Care* was a major part of our broader media efforts, which from the start also included a regular flow of news releases, story ideas, briefings, interviews, sample columns, and other materials. In a remarkably short period, we became a respected source for reporters, editors, feature writers, and others who were trying to produce stories about aspects of voluntary effort. There were three immediate ways I could tell how dramatically coverage was growing. An increasing part of my time was involved with communications, including all kinds of interviews, ranging from telephone calls for facts to special media features. Second, John Thomas kept displaying enormous piles of press clippings. And third, I was becoming concerned about the cost of our clipping service!

To sustain the coverage depended on our ability to keep the information flowing and to find new ways to tell the stories. We were able to create a steady stream of regular and special features drawing on our various reports, such as those on giving and volunteering, the relationship of religion and generosity, and the motivations of the most generous. We also provided up-to-date information about contributions and tax policy, trends and levels of giving, and on and on.

One of the great benefits of our research and publication efforts was our ability to penetrate the mass media with a regular flow of positive information about the impact of the sector. Within a year of our founding, we were able to tell parts of the story on major TV shows such as *Today* and *The MacNeil-Lehrer Report* (as it then was). The Associated Press found our releases of regular interest and used us as an active resource for wire service stories. Kitty Teltsch of the *New York Times* began to place enough stories on the sector that she was assigned to it as a full-time beat and, by her own account, began to look to us as her principal source of ideas and contacts. We were assisted greatly by the growth of electronic databases, which enabled any reporter, editor, or feature writer to locate us and to draw on stories that we had already filed or in which we were quoted. At the same time, we were feeding to our members every compelling fact and story we could find, and increasingly these showed up in their own publications to help spread the word.

Out of sheer necessity, IS also began to produce books to enlarge the depository of published information. From my earliest days with the National Council on Philanthropy and the Coalition of National Voluntary Organizations, I had been trying to communicate the role and impact of philanthropy and voluntarism in America. When INDEPENDENT SECTOR was formed, I found that role accentuated. One of our basic functions was to help the American people understand and take pride in our country's tradition of participation so that it would be reinforced and passed along.

One of my immediate difficulties was that the case was hard to document. People within the sector felt passionately about its impact, but rarely could cite substantiating literature. During a discussion of this dilemma at an early IS board meeting, Nancy Hanks, former director of the National Endowment for the Arts, Rockefeller family adviser, and volunteer leader extraordinaire, lamented that the only authority ever quoted was de Tocqueville. In deference to the person in the chair, someone countered that we now had John Gardner to quote, but Nancy topped that by noting, "But John just quotes Tocqueville all the time."

The absolutely essential issue of getting the sector's story out was such a major matter that John Gardner and I found ourselves concentrating on it at one of our early retreat-like sessions. I told him that out of desperation for persuasive testimony, briefings, and interviews, I had gradually been pulling together some of the best literature I could find that set forth the philosophy and usefulness of pluralism, voluntarism, and citizen participation. I said I was doing this to create a resource for myself and to build credibility for my arguments, but had begun to think it might be worthwhile to pull these writings together into a book. I expressed doubts about whether I was the right person to do that job or would have time for it, but John was adamant that I should take it on—and get to it.

Not long after that conversation, I found myself talking with Tom Buckman, president of the Foundation Center, about the need to make the case for philanthropy and bring it to the attention of leaders within the sector and beyond. Because the center was thinking about broadening its publication efforts, he showed particular interest in the project, and with the prospect of that outlet and the obvious need for such a resource, I set out to pull together what became *America's Voluntary Spirit*.

With the extraordinary assistance of Ann Brown O'Connell, I located close to one thousand possibilities, but with almost every one, additional leads surfaced. The project could have been endless, but fully acknowledging that we had not turned over every stone, we finally went ahead with forty-five selections.

I wanted the volume as a whole to provide a good overview of what the sector means to the American experience and to be a valuable resource for speakers and writers. I was particularly determined that the book represent a balanced view. If it turned out to be too glowing or self-congratulatory, it would not be accurate or useful. At the same time, I wanted it to be a manageable volume rather than an all-inclusive tome.

The following examples of chapter titles and their authors might help to convey the scope of the book:

- *Our Religious Heritage*
- *Altruism: Self-Sacrifice for Others* (Lewis Thomas)
- *Man the Reformer* (Ralph Waldo Emerson)
- *Of the Use Which the Americans Make of Public Associations in Civil Life* (Alexis de Tocqueville)
- *The Gospel of Wealth* (Andrew Carnegie)
- *The Difficult Art of Giving* (John D. Rockefeller)
- *Principles of Public Giving* (Julius Rosenwald)
- *Private Initiative for the Public Good* (John W. Gardner)
- *The Third Sector* (John D. Rockefeller 3rd)
- *The Third Sector: Keystone of a Caring Society* (Waldemar Nielsen)
- *The Social Goals of a Corporation* (John H. Filer)
- *We Cannot Live for Ourselves Alone* (Vernon E. Jordan Jr.)

To make the book more valuable to scholars and others looking for additional documentation and good literature, the bibliography that Ann did the most to prepare covered more than six hundred references.

The book seemed to fill a need, but it made it all the more obvious that we needed vivid tales of ways that specific grants, voluntary organizations, and individuals made a difference in the health of communities and the country. To try to fill some of that need, Ann and I created the books *Philanthropy in Action* and *Volunteers in Action,* which included more than five hundred examples of very different ways that money, volunteers, and voluntary organizations address all kinds of critical problems.

Over its first fifteen years, INDEPENDENT SECTOR produced fourteen books, largely to try to move in quickly where major voids existed but always with the goal of stimulating others to become the major resources of the future.

We were also becoming better able to provide our members and media with quite specific information about the sector, and to advise members on how they could put such information to use to increase support and effectiveness. Here's a very brief and random sampling of titles:

- *Care and Community in Modern Society: Passing on the Tradition of Service to Future Generations*

- *Senior Citizens as Volunteers*

- *America's Teenagers as Volunteers*

- *A Portrait of the Independent Sector: The Activities and Finances of Charitable Organizations*

- *Why Tax Exemption? The Public Service Role of America's Independent Sector*

- *Everyday Ethics: Key Ethical Questions for Grantmakers and Grantseekers*

- *Financial Compensation in Nonprofit Organizations*

- *Effective Leadership in Voluntary Organizations*

- *Faith and Philanthropy in America*

- *The Future of the Nonprofit Sector*

- *Governing, Leading, and Managing Nonprofit Organizations*

- *Nonprofit News Coverage—A Guide for Journalists*

- *Compendium of Resources for Teaching About the Nonprofit Sector, Voluntarism and Philanthropy*

- *Resource Raising: The Role of Non-Cash Assistance in Corporate Philanthropy*

- *Youth Service: A Guidebook for Developing and Operating Effective Programs*

- *Profiles of Effective Corporate Giving Programs*
- *Aiming High on a Small Budget: Executive Searches and the Nonprofit Sector*

One aspect of our strategy for a comprehensive communications plan involved what we referred to as the "trade press," which included publications that specialized in philanthropy or the nonprofit sector—for example, *Foundation News, Nonprofit Times, Chronicle of Philanthropy,* and *Fundraising Management.* We applied the term also to specialist publications in fields such as religion, education, arts, and the environment, working hard to keep all of them informed and supplied. They, like the publications of our members, were natural channels for getting the story out to people who already had an interest and were inclined to pass along news and information to others.

The primary stimulus for trade and mass media coverage was our "Giving and Volunteering" reports. These biennial studies and releases usually led to major wire service stories, which were used throughout the country, and appearances on such shows as *Good Morning America.*

We were very fortunate that the attention was not limited to the few weeks surrounding the release of our biennial reports. With each feature and story, the word spread and the interest grew. Later, we scheduled news conferences and interviews on various parts of the reports, such as support for the arts, volunteering by blacks, or the growing philanthropy of women.

John Thomas was particularly careful to cultivate relationships with key people from both the trade press and the mass media. In our quarterly reviews each year, he and I would take time to think about what news we might have that would be of particular interest to people on our various media lists. Just stopping to think awhile would always produce ideas that we had not thought about in the busy intervening months. We were also able to open doors with the help of some of our board members and top representatives of our member organizations. These helpers included foundations working in the field of communications and board and committee members who were well connected in media circles. We rarely had to go begging. Increasingly, we were a source of information of interest to the public, and our task was to package it in such a way that even skeptical reporters and writers would recognize that it was worth consideration.

Our increased visibility and credibility were also factors that helped us crack the Advertising Council, which, early in our life, agreed to produce a campaign on individual giving and volunteering—fortunately assigned to the prestigious and effective firm of Ogilvy and Mather. The first campaign was labeled "Lend a Hand" and was specifically designed to celebrate the breadth and depth of giving and volunteering in the United States and to motivate Americans to keep that special part of our country alive and well.

Later, the campaign was more sharply focused to emphasize the encouragement to "Give Five"—five hours a week and 5 percent of income to voluntary efforts. This gave us an extraordinary head start in getting that message to the public and in producing related materials for use in the newsletters, fund-raising materials, reports, and other publications of our members and their affiliates.

Important lessons were learned along the way. When the initial "Lend a Hand" campaign was drafted, it was previewed with great fanfare at the 1982 annual meeting and assembly of members. The results were not what we had hoped for. Though many found the ideas appealing and persuasive, a significant number raised valid concerns—for example, about the symbolism of a barn raising in which women were portrayed largely in supportive roles, such as serving meals. On the basis of this feedback, Ogilvy went back to the drawing board and at the next meeting of members, the finished product was greeted with great enthusiasm. We learned from that experience the wisdom of listening carefully to our membership.

One very focused part of our education effort was to raise the levels of giving and volunteering. At the very first IS annual meeting of members, representatives of the Dayton Hudson Corporation proposed that we amend the program goals set forth by the organizing committee and contained in the initial draft of our first five-year program plan. They applauded the five program emphases, including government relations and public information and education, but said that the only way we could really fulfill our overall mission was to measurably increase volunteering and giving. The amendment passed, and eventually the program mission and goal were described as "measurable growth in support of the sector as manifested by increased giving and volunteering."

It was appropriate to turn to Ken Dayton, former CEO of Dayton Hudson, to lead the task force that would develop our specific plan for implementing that goal. He and others on the task force represented extensive and successful marketing experience, which proved absolutely critical to achieving a sound plan. They knew how to get at

some of the research questions necessary to determine what was most
likely to succeed.

At first, they hoped we could take advantage of the universally understood practice of tithing, but the task force found that level of
giving too great a stretch from existing levels and beyond what people surveyed felt was doable, at least for the foreseeable future. In the
course of that research, however, we discovered that people did want to
know what others contributed in time and money and what generally
was expected of them. We also learned that approximately 13 percent
of the public, or twenty million people, were already giving 5 percent or more of their income annually to the causes of their choice,
and that 14 percent, or twenty-three million people, were volunteering five or more hours a week. With that many people already at that
level, and with the average American giving approximately two percent of income and two or more hours of volunteering per week, we
believed that the public could identify with the standard of "fiving."
Furthermore, the research showed that people admired those who
were generous and aspired to match their performance. Through other
studies, we found that the capacity for greater generosity was significant. On that basis, the task force recommended that we develop the
program that subsequently became known as "Give Five."

The task force's report and recommended program were approved
by the board and membership in 1985, and we began a three-pronged
implementation through (1) national media, (2) members and their
affiliates, and (3) state and local coalitions designed to increase
regional media coverage and involvement of local organizations.

We knew from the start that this would be a long-term effort, but
that at a certain point people would recognize the message and the
standard, and that with recognition would come increased generosity.
Indeed, where there were coalitions that functioned two years or more,
the levels of recognition grew from an initial 15 percent to 40–50 percent, and levels of participation began to climb.

We were fortunate that the Advertising Council adopted the "Give
Five" campaign as one of its principal public service efforts; that support continues. With our dependence on donated time and space and
on the voluntary participation of our members, it was not possible to
achieve what we now know would be doable if we were able to purchase time and space, but even with that limitation, "Give Five" is
growing in recognition and practice. Ken Dayton was ably followed
as head of the effort by Gene Dorsey and Ted Taylor, and over the

years, staff leadership was provided by Meg Graham, Brian Foss, Sandra Gray, and John Thomas.

One of the most important and promising of our efforts with the mass media was our Project with Journalism Schools. In 1993, we conducted a pilot project at Louisiana State University that involved an extensive survey of journalists; a two-day seminar for journalists and nonprofit leaders; a guidebook for journalism schools, working journalists, and nonprofit organizations; and a strategy for adapting and replicating this experience in other journalism schools throughout the country.

By 1994, we had succeeded in persuading three other major journalism schools to replicate the Louisiana experience. Our object was to try to bring the model to key schools in each of the regions and gradually to bring the topic of our sector into the regular curriculum for graduate students and working journalists.

From the mid-1980s, there was increasing media attention on problems in the sector, particularly regular reports of fund-raising scams, high fund-raising costs, and gross mismanagement. INDEPENDENT SECTOR had already been deeply involved in efforts to promote openness, accountability, and effectiveness, but we were faced with the prospect that the public could lose faith in voluntary organizations in general. With materials already at hand, such as the values and ethics report and a companion report on performance and accountability, we were at least somewhat equipped to help communicate to media representatives, and through them, the public, that the overwhelming majority of voluntary organizations perform remarkably well; that most of the problems being exposed involved fraudulent behavior that was already against the law and should be exposed and prosecuted; and that the media could help in informing donors, volunteers, and board members of existing guidelines about board responsibility, standards, ethics, and compliance with the law.

Initially, there were many sessions with skeptical or cynical reporters who thought we were trying to defend the sector, including the scoundrels, at all costs. (Later, they would be won over by evidence that we had been striving for some time to make clear what kind of behavior was expected of voluntary organizations and what was totally unacceptable.) One such session was with reporters Gilbert M. Gaul and Neill A. Borowski of the *Philadelphia Inquirer,* who had done a series and a subsequent book titled *Free Ride,* both sweepingly critical of voluntary agency effectiveness.

On the chance that the *Inquirer* series might lead to a sudden escalation of exposés about the sector that would repeat some of the reported misinformation, we organized an extensive two-pronged effort to counter the distortions and use the media's interest to better educate boards and the public about the sector, including the ethics and standards expected of it. We organized a group of national and regional spokespersons and provided briefing kits to them. For about six months, everything and everyone was at the ready, but fortunately they were barely needed. Some felt let down that they didn't get to play their roles, but in the long run the exercise was very useful. It made sector leaders aware of our vulnerabilities, showed them what we could do to improve performance, and encouraged them to work with media to communicate positive things about the sector's ethical behavior. The exercise also underlined what the public should know about organizations that asked for time and money.

From the start, the PI&E committee gave special attention to educational institutions—initially kindergarten through high school, but later all levels—to prepare young people for a lifetime of active citizenship and personal community service. A major subcommittee led for several years by Steve Minter, director of the Cleveland Foundation and former U.S. deputy secretary of education, identified about fifteen national organizations that had tremendous influence on school curricula, teaching materials, and the like. Working with these groups, we were able to identify schools, school districts, and even states that were light years ahead of others in devoting attention to citizenship and community service. These front-runners provided both classroom instruction on the importance of such service and actual opportunities to contribute to the community.

The subcommittee also identified the dozen or so textbook publishers who produced most of the books used in civics, social studies, and other subjects where citizenship and service were most likely to be taught.

As early as 1984, the board approved a pilot phase for the project then labeled "School Curricula and Student Community Service." By 1985, we had commissioned and approved an initial guidebook for schools and had laid plans for a major forum on student community service and for meetings with the major textbook publishers.

The forum took place in 1986 and included sessions on improving the guidebook. By gaining the participation of many of the national groups that influenced state and community school systems, we secured a ready market for the guidebook and for a film we made of forum highlights. We also had involved many textbook publishers and applauded them for the significant growth in their attention to these subjects.

Our work with educational institutions attracted the attention of Russ Edgerton, head of the American Association of Higher Education (AAHE), who shared our concern and was able to make education in voluntarism a topic of high priority to his group. In 1985, I was invited to give the keynote address at AAHE's national conference on higher education and deliberately titled my address "Citizenship and Community Service: Are They a Concern and Responsibility of Higher Education?"

I began by pointing out that our American democracy, the longest-lived in the history of the world, had provided almost all of us with greater freedom and opportunity than any nation had ever known, and that among the crucial factors that fostered and preserved that liberating democracy were active citizenship and personal community service. I spoke of clear signs that such service might not be as vital a part of our society for the current younger generations and those who would come after them, and urged educators and educational institutions to take on the task of fostering active citizenship, because others could not be relied on to do so.

There is no way of knowing how much our efforts and those of our members and their affiliates influenced subsequent events, but my distinct impression is that we, along with many groups, helped to bring the issue of student involvement to the forefront of public attention. Happily, it is now a true wave of the times, which bodes well for the future health of the sector and of the country.

On top of all of these communication and public education activities, John Thomas and his tiny staff were heavily involved in all of our efforts to help others use internal and external communications to achieve their goals—for example, by educating the media on the relationship between tax policy and charitable contributions. The department was also very active in publicizing research reports and making the most of research activities, including research forums. It worked with all of us to develop a comprehensive and coordinated publications program and to improve and sharpen individual publications and their promotion.

One of the newer but highly significant undertakings of the communications department has been to educate IS members in new technologies such as the Internet. Member organizations need to see the relevance of these technologies to their own activities and to play a part in ensuring that the philanthropic and voluntary sector fully benefits from them—for example, when special cable TV channels and Internet chat-rooms are assigned for subjects such as conservation and health education.

Our communication achievements were often the envy of our members—even very large organizations with appealing causes and substantial public relations staffs. But with each success, most people just expected more. If we could get on the *CBS Evening News*, why didn't we make it onto NBC? Or if we got an op-ed piece in the *New York Times*, why couldn't we use those pages regularly for other worthy messages?

Through it all, our accomplishments were given high ratings by our members in their regular evaluations of our performance, which made it easier to live with the inevitable expectation that we could turn on a media blitz at will.

CHAPTER EIGHT

Fostering Research on the Sector

The organizing committee had been fairly crisp and definite about the research program. The purpose of the program was "to provide a body of knowledge about the independent sector and about how to make it most useful to society."

The IS research committee and board added a few clarifications, so the charge became "To develop an identifiable and growing research effort that produces the body of knowledge necessary to accurately define, describe, chart and understand the sector and the ways it can be of greater service to society."

The organizing committee had stipulated that the primary purpose, at least for the initial years, should be to develop a comprehensive body of knowledge about the independent sector itself. The committee stated, "We need to bring into focus and clarify the factors and facts which define the sector and its usefulness to individuals and society and we need to understand better how to preserve those characteristics of American life."

The secondary purpose was "to stimulate lively exploration of the wider ranging questions which might relate to our understanding and improvement of philanthropy, voluntary action and not-for-profit enterprise."

To pursue these research purposes, the committee proposed that the organization work with and through others. For example, "Almost invariably the role will not be to do the research or even try to be a significant funder of it. The role will be to facilitate, encourage and stimulate. The organization will need enough staff research sophistication to carry out these facilitating tasks, but a large research group should not be anticipated."

Important guidance on research was provided to the organizing committee and IS through the agenda-setting efforts of the Center for a Voluntary Society, the Filer Commission, Yale's pioneering Program on NonProfit Organizations (PONPO), and the Association of Voluntary Action Scholars. John Simon of Yale provided particularly helpful guidance to the organizing committee, including a wonderfully cogent briefing at the 1979 National Conference on Philanthropy, in Denver.

We also had the indispensable support of the research committee of the Coalition of National Voluntary Organizations, which had quickly become a joint committee with the National Council on Philanthropy. That committee planned and oversaw the initial research activities, including the first surveys performed for us by the Gallup Organization and our efforts to gain a better understanding of the relationship between tax policy and charitable contributions.

A particularly important crossroads was faced as far back as 1979, when the CONVO research committee discussed the first IS/Gallup survey of the public's knowledge of and attitudes toward giving and volunteering. A prominent fund-raiser foresaw that many of the questions could elicit negative comments that might be better left unreported. He wanted assurances that CONVO's reports would be presented in such a way that the public would think even more positively about giving time and money to voluntary organizations. He even wanted mechanisms established to be sure that negative findings in the survey would not be leaked. This was a defining moment. He was not alone, but fortunately the majority expressed the firm position that if our own research projects and those we wanted to encourage were tainted by subjectivity, bias, or propaganda, we would contradict and defeat our purposes right from the beginning.

All of these early decisions and efforts set the stage for the explosion of IS's research program beginning in early 1982. Five factors contributed to those giant steps. First, a plan was in place. Second, we realized at almost every turn how much more we needed to know if we were really to understand the sector and make a case for it. Third, income from memberships and a special solicitation gave us enough funds to support a research director and the first three years of programming. The fourth factor was that we were able to recruit Virginia Hodgkinson as our first vice president for research from a similar role with the National Institute of Independent Colleges and Universities. And finally, Robert Payton, head of the Exxon Education Foundation, became head of the research committee and quickly helped to pull together an extraordinary group. The momentum was later maintained by his successors Stan Katz and Julian Wolpert.

A sense of our progress over the next dozen or so years may be obtained from a few examples:

- We moved from the first edition of *Americans Volunteer,* based on the 1980 IS/Gallup survey, to an enormous variety of studies and reports based on trend-line data drawn from five successive biennial surveys.
- By 1989, we were able to produce separate analyses of the giving and volunteering levels, patterns, motivations, and much more, of various segments of the population, including the elderly, single women, Hispanics, and teens.
- By 1995, we could provide trend-line data and targeted information for groups concerned specifically with health, environment, arts, and scores of other categories.
- With all the data available by 1995, IS was able to produce on very short notice a study of one hundred organizations, which assessed the likely impact on them and the people they served of proposed cutbacks in federal funding.
- For our first research forum in 1983, we scoured the country for people with any interest in our subjects, and by 1995 there were several separate organizations of researchers encouraged and assisted by IS, including the International Society for Third-Sector Research.

A major factor in our direct and indirect impact was the research forums, begun in 1983. They were designed with a number of purposes in mind: to reveal who was already studying what; to provide an outlet for those researchers' work and build a network among them; to provide a bridge between scholars and practitioners; to encourage academics and their disciplines and institutions to recognize the attractiveness and legitimacy of this research field; to suggest ideas for research, including dissertations; to build interest among publishers; and to prompt funding sources to recognize the importance of such research.

From the beginning, these purposes were remarkably well served. For years, people would indicate that it was at a particular forum, or through participation in several, that they found a supportive network, met a future collaborator, got the idea for an academic course or program, learned about funding sources, identified possible publishers, got ideas for new studies, learned about data sources, teaching materials, bibliographies, and the like, and a great deal more. Just the three hundred or so pages of advance reading for each forum provided a major resource for learning and outreach. Later, the books published annually by Jossey-Bass with the best of the papers from each forum helped build the foundations of future scholarship. The themes of the spring research forums included "The Constitution and the Independent Sector," "Philanthropy and the Religious Tradition," "Leadership and Management," and "Transmitting the Tradition of a Caring Society to Future Generations."

All of our hopes for what might be possible in a full-blown research effort came together in those forums. Each was special, but it was the series as a whole that built the network and generated the attention, confidence, support, and stimulation. In an unbelievably short time, a new, identifiable, and legitimate field of research had been created.

With the dramatic growth of the field—including forums and conferences sponsored by other organizations—several of us at IS, including Virginia, recognized that our initiating and demonstrating purposes had largely been served, and as in earlier phases, it was time to move on to areas where we might again make a unique contribution.

We were surprised that this recommendation became so controversial, even among many of the very people and groups who had been developing their own parallel activities, and among some of those who regularly criticized us when they felt we were doing something that others should have a chance to do. The research committee's compromise, approved by the board, was to hold our forums every other year for at least a while, until it was felt that our withdrawal would not be viewed as creating more of a problem than an opportunity.

I suspect that someday, when IS has moved out of many of the areas where it made a remarkable early contribution, all but those who remember the history will wonder what it was we did that the old-timers considered so terribly important. That will hurt, but if what our successors are doing is so much bigger and better as to obscure our early efforts—and I hope and expect it will be—I'll be delighted with the outcome.

Virginia and the research committee also turned their energies to stimulating the interest of various academic disciplines. We knew from the start that our greatest impact would be achieved by encouraging existing disciplines to recognize the validity and attractiveness of research relating to our sector.

Our initial foray in this direction almost came a cropper. With great pushing and pulling, we were able to organize a full day's seminar on philanthropy with a prominent group of social philosophers. For the first part of the day, four of us—Bob Payton, Michael Novak, Peter Dobkin Hall, and myself—attempted to present information and viewpoints designed to generate interest among these distinguished philosophers, but the reception was just barely polite. I think it's fair to say that they couldn't figure out what in the world we were saying that would hold the slightest interest for them.

Finally, but without design, one of us pointed up the sector's role in advancing pluralism in a democratic society, and suddenly the philosophers took over what became an enormously animated discussion. Philanthropy was an impossible sell, but pluralism was easy, and the related discussion of current and prospective research was wonderfully rich. What had started as an absolute dud of a session even produced a book: *Philanthropy: Four Views*, published by Transaction Books and the Social Philosophy and Policy Center of Bowling Green State University.

We also expanded our efforts to interest selected academic institutions in establishing formal centers that would include research, teaching, graduate degrees, continuing education, and other functions. For example, through early discussions with Joel Fleishman, then provost at Duke, I knew of his interest in philanthropic studies and of the sympathetic view of Duke's president at that time, former Governor Terry Sanford. One of the university's star faculty members, Charles Clotfelter, was beginning to produce some important economic analyses relating to the sector. Around that same time, I made an approach to the Duke Endowment about possible support of IS's research efforts but was reminded that its benefactions were restricted to the Carolinas. We had invited the endowment's president, John Day, to our research forums, and through those contacts were aware of his interest in the research side of our operation. When we just couldn't find any basis for the endowment to support our own efforts, I explored with him the possibility of talking to Joel and others at Duke about the establishment of a center there. The idea took hold, and a first-rate center was established, initially with a focus on economics but later expanded significantly.

There was a similar pattern in discussions with people at Lilly Endowment and later at Indiana University. Thomas Erlich, IU's president, and his wife Ellen had a keen interest in philanthropy and voluntarism. The idea of a center was substantially carried along by Charles Johnson at Lilly, who involved me in discussions with his top leadership and then in joint conversations with university officials. I attended a meeting that included the heads of eight or nine schools within the university, and I recall worrying whether the ambitions might have gotten out of hand. They hadn't, and the idea indeed blossomed into the most comprehensive of the academic centers, with major initial funding from Lilly. A fellow conspirator, Bob Payton, was enticed to become the center's first director, which couldn't have been a more fortuitous break for everyone who wanted to see more across-the-board involvement with our issues on the part of academia.

Our goal was not to try to achieve a center in every major institution but to have a sufficient number of centers with regional and national significance to provide visibility for the sector and respect for an academic role in its study and development. Similarly, our aim was not to try to establish a new academic discipline but rather to create a credible and respected field of interest reaching into and crossing all academic disciplines.

In my "Highlights of 1987," I mentioned the informal and sometimes more direct encouragement we had given to a "number of academic institutions and academicians to begin to pay overdue attention to this sector as a legitimate and attractive area for research, education and training, and the establishment within IS of a 'meeting ground' for these people and centers." I added, "This almost invisible activity of IS may turn out to be our most important long-term contribution to building an understanding of the role of the sector and the ways by which it fulfills its public services."

It's interesting that the very next item in that 1987 report called attention to our role in "development and publication of a classification system for the sector and surprisingly swift progress in gaining the cooperation of the federal government, state governments, standard setting bodies, researchers and others for this uniform way of collecting and reporting information on the sector." And I added, "This too is almost invisible, even to our members, but will have extraordinary long-term influence on a better understanding of the sector, including its roles and impact."

Given the number of studies and reports developed by IS as resource materials for researchers and practitioners, it may seem strange to refer to our work in this area as somewhat invisible, but I was always worried that the early direct benefits of these activities involved a relatively small group of researchers, and that therefore, despite the degree of our investment, our members might see little immediate relevance. We were constantly engaged in discussions, among ourselves and with members, about the need for "practical" or "applied" research, such as surveys and reports of salaries and benefits, but the conviction of our organizing and research committees held us on course, and the long-term benefits to members and the sector will turn out to be the greater.

Among the research surveys and reports were the following:

- *The Classification of 501(c)(3) Organizations According to the National Taxonomy of Exempt Entities*

- The fourth edition of what we had previously called *Dimensions of the Independent Sector: A Statistical Profile,* retitled *NonProfit Almanac* and three times longer than previous editions, which provided much fuller information about specific parts of the sector, such as international and civil rights

- *National Summary: Not-for-Profit Employment from the 1990 Census of Population and Housing*

- *Compendium of Resources for Teaching About the NonProfit Sector, Volunteerism, and Philanthropy*

- *Academic Centers and Programs: Focusing on the Study of Philanthropy, Volunteerism, and Not-for-Profit Activity*

- *From Belief to Commitment: The Community Service Activities and Finances of Religious Congregations in the United States*

- *The Impact of Federal Budget Proposals upon the Activities of Charitable Organizations and the People They Serve, 1996–2002: The 100 Nonprofit Organizations Study*

Many of these projects came within the scope of the National Center for Charitable Statistics (NCCS), which initially had been a joint project of the Council on Foundations, United Way, the American Association of Fund-Raising Counsel, and IS. In 1983, the other participants asked us to take full responsibility, and though enthusiastic about the work of NCCS, we saw severe obstacles to our taking it on. The first was expectations of great expansion in the center's programming, and the second was our research committee's worry that these immediate responsibilities would take us away from longer-term investments in building the larger field of research.

A third consideration was that our approach in such matters was to look to someone else to take on such functions and to assume them only if they were essential and no one else was ready to step in.

In the end, our other NCCS partners accepted a less ambitious effort if we would agree to take it over. Our research committee continued to be wary but agreed that many of the functions were absolutely necessary—for example, producing the kind of statistics essential to building a larger research capacity—and that no one else seemed to be equipped to move readily and effectively into the breach. We worked out an arrangement by which the research committee would continue to focus almost exclusively on the longer-range and broader goals, leaving NCCS as a separate committee. The research committee also would have preferred separate staffing, but that wasn't a possibility, and Virginia was convinced she could handle both, which proved decidedly accurate. Even at that, we set up the operation on a trial basis, with IS providing the secretariat for two years in an arrangement either side could cancel. Two years later, in 1985, we agreed to assimilate the center, but not as a corporation in its own right. We didn't change the name, but essentially NCCS became one of our programming committees.

There was another financial lesson that related to NCCS. A number of our funders who were eager to see us take it on assured us that they would continue or initiate separate annual support for NCCS. I predicted, on the basis of past experience, that it wouldn't be long before they, or more likely their successors in those jobs, questioned why they were making two grants to the same organization, but I was assured that the commitments were long-term. Even while the operation was still in its secretariat phase, almost all of those funders withdrew on the grounds that they were already providing support to IS. I end this aside with a little philosophy. Even successful membership organizations get into trouble when they become overly dependent on grant income, even if it's the funders who are pushing them in new directions!

Another possibly useful aside: one of IS's major problems, then and later, was that many people assumed we could raise a great deal more money than was really possible or practical. There was also a fairly pervasive assumption that once IS had proved itself, many related functions would be put under our umbrella. I even had a call one day from one of our board members, telling me that an organization he chaired had been given the good news that a major foundation was willing to approve a $2 million program-related investment if IS would become a partner and accept responsibility for repayment of the loan. No one had ever bothered to ask us if we might be willing. My board member was furious when I said I'd have to recommend against it, and his organization subsequently dropped membership in IS.

I've come away from this and so many other funding experiences with an absolute conviction about the necessity to stay one's own course without letting even friends and funders decide what I should take on.

Another tough decision about research priorities involved religion. It was not an area where many on our research committee and board wanted us to go. There was a fairly pervasive view that religious institutions were different from the rest of the sector and therefore not really appropriate for us to pay much attention to. (This didn't include religiously affiliated services such as hospitals and schools.)

It had been my own experience as a community organizer that religious congregations played an enormous role in motivating and guiding people to serve, as well as in providing services to neighborhoods and raising the conscience of communities.

Fortunately, Bob Payton, Virginia, and I constituted a stubborn core, and it was determined that religion, including religious congregations, would be prominent in any definition of our research interests.

Fortunately, too, Lilly Endowment applauded this stance and was willing to support us in it. In 1986, we undertook the first major national survey on the sources and uses of contributions in religious congregations, which was designed to provide clearer understanding of the relationships between philanthropy and religion. By 1989, our research forum focused on "Philanthropy and Religion" and produced an important book, *Faith and Philanthropy in America.*

In 1993, we completed our second study and report, *From Belief to Commitment: The Community Service Activities and Finances of Religious Congregations in the United States.* It made clearer than ever how much American communities rely on their religious congregations, not just for the practice of faith but for community service.

By the early 1990s, we hoped we had made the case irrefutably that religion and the sector were totally intertwined, but alas, the research then being undertaken was not following this lead. The main reason was that adequate statistics about religious institutions were difficult to obtain, largely because of the separation of church and state: the government could not require filing of information about the functions and finances of congregations.

In addition, many researchers found that advocacy and mutual assistance organizations were generally so small that they were not even counted in government reports.

On the other hand, three parts of our sector—education, health, and arts—constituted most of the employment and expenditures (not counting religion), and so it seemed practical to take a look at the sector through the lens of those bigger institutions. These researchers would argue that that's where the critical mass was and where figures were generally available. The problem was that these researchers would look at colleges, hospitals, and art museums, and draw conclusions from them about the sector as a whole. They justified leaving out advocacy and mutual assistance organizations because in essence they were *de minimus,* and they left out the whole half of the sector affiliated with religion because those institutions were different, and information on them was not available anyway.

Gradually, the best of these researchers recognized that it was important to make clear what was being counted, and that their conclusions related only to those in the count. Unfortunately, it's still the norm that people read such reports and assume the conclusions apply to the entire sector.

One of our longest-running research projects, begun in 1989 and ongoing in 1996, started out as a supposedly quick review of the literature that would certainly be accomplished in less than six months!

One day, in an almost idle conversation that Virginia will no doubt regret eternally, we agreed that too little was really known about motivations for giving and volunteering, but that each of us fairly regularly came across germane references in such diverse fields as theology, psychology, economics, and even geography. We thought it would be interesting to have someone search the literature in various disciplines

for reliable findings about the motivations behind altruistic or charitable behavior. We even thought the literature might provide indications of successful applications of those motivations, and if that was
the case, we could provide our members and others with guidelines
for valuable new approaches to fund-raising and recruitment.

The project got larger and larger. In my naive way, I would tell Virginia to cut it off and simply report on what had been found, however
inadequate, and leave the rest to someone else who might be stimu-
lated by our not immodest beginnings. She would remind me that it
was I who got her hooked, and she was determined to at least leave it
in a suitable state, which was always at least another year away.

Having left my active role with IS toward the end of 1994, I don't
have at hand the "Highlights" of that year, but I do remember that in
the plan for the year, we anticipated that one of the highlights would
be "completion of the four-year project and publication of the related
book on motivations that influence altruistic, caring, and charitable
behavior." On the way toward that report and a much fuller contribution than I ever envisioned, the 1993 research forum addressed the
question of how the American tradition of caring could be perpetu-
ated. Again, a book resulted: *Care and Community in Modern Society:
Passing on the Tradition of Service to Future Generations.*

An early concern, later allayed, about the giving patterns among
baby boomers, turned us to a special study to determine the attitudes
and practices of younger people. In 1990, we published *Giving and
Volunteering Among Teenagers, 14–17 Years of Age,* a report that provided wonderfully encouraging indicators of future generosity. We
advised our members and others that if we could nurture already
favorable attitudes and behaviors, the future pool of generous people
would be very great.

On the basis of that initial pilot effort among younger people, we
were able to produce an even larger study of their participation in charitable activities, and published a related report, *American Teenagers as
Volunteers.* This study reinforced the good news that teenagers want to
be involved, that they usually say yes when asked, are pleased to be
treated as having something to contribute, and feel good about themselves when they do play a part. The report also showed how readily
such participation can be expanded by the organized efforts of congregations, schools, and youth-serving organizations.

At times our research efforts had to become pretty tightly focused,
such as when we were trying to analyze the impact of proposed government policies on charitable giving. In 1983, for example, we found

it necessary to develop a new capacity to design, produce, analyze, and publish research relating to tax policy and contributions. In the following year, we paid for the development of an econometric model, and during 1984 alone spent more than $100,000 for data on and analysis of various tax reform proposals, such as the possible 2 percent floor on all charitable deductions. That ability to generate facts brought us far greater credibility and influence with Congress and others.

When we developed the Measurable Growth in Giving and Volunteering program ("Give Five"), we relied heavily on Virginia and others to whom she turned to get accurate information on what seemed to have worked and not worked in attempts to stimulate charitable behavior.

Along the way, our research capacity and networks became crucial in all kinds of necessary and promising endeavors.

We worked closely with Lester Salamon and others to more accurately predict and clarify the impact on individuals and programs of cutbacks in federal social spending.

In 1989, we found ourselves far more involved than intended in consultation with and assistance to other countries eager to learn more about pluralism and voluntarism in America. Among other things, I organized and chaired a Salzburg seminar, "The Role of Non-Profit Organizations: Comparisons of Functions, Operations, and Trends." In the following year, our research forum dealt with "The NonProfit Sector in the United States and Abroad: Cross-Cultural Perspectives" and resulted in the book *The Nonprofit Sector in the Global Community.*

At times, we became involved in analyzing such specific issues as characteristics of successful corporate philanthropic programs and even the relative staffing strengths of private foundations and corporate programs with comparable budgets.

In the early 1990s, under the supervision of Sandra Gray and her Leadership and Management program, IS began taking a keen, active interest in the study of effective evaluation of philanthropic and voluntary organizations and programs.

We also commissioned a researcher (selected after a competition supervised by the research committee) to produce a volume on the Filer Commission.

Though several additional chapters could be written about just the initial years of the research program, I know I'll wear out my welcome if I go on much longer. There is, though, one last episode that was fun as it unfolded and valuable in its results.

At a Council on Foundations meeting, Alex Plinio, then director of contributions for Prudential, gave a paper with a title something like "Fourteen Ways That Companies Provide Noncash Assistance to Voluntary Organizations." I urged him to expand it into a more formal article and told him that INDEPENDENT SECTOR would be pleased to publish it as part of a series of occasional papers. About a year later, I asked Alex how it was coming, and he said he had run into the interesting problem that he kept finding new examples that should be included. By then, he was up to "Twenty-Nine Ways . . ." He had also been promoted to vice president for public service and president of the Prudential Foundation, so he would have even less time to work on the paper. Finding the idea more interesting than ever and sharing his frustration with the time constraints he faced, I said we would provide him with some research and editorial assistance. Another year went by, and I commented to him that we really should be getting something published. This time, Alex said that between his own efforts and those of Joanne Scanlon, the part-time research assistant, he was coming across all kinds of new information that really should be included. By then, he was up to "Forty-One Ways . . ."

Six months later, out of eagerness to have this important resource document published, and seeing that my offer of modest help had produced not-so-modest results, I said we absolutely had to go with what we had. The result was Plinio and Scanlon's excellent *Resource Raising: The Role Of Non-Cash Assistance In Corporate Philanthropy*, which in six categories contains forty-nine types of assistance and more than one hundred examples. Even with that, Alex still says, "You know, Brian, I wish we hadn't rushed into print, because it's still very incomplete."

Creativity and tenacity characterized much of our research program, but despite all its dramatic and visible contributions over such an extended period, the largest results of our research program came from less obvious efforts to encourage others to study and report on the sector. Our goal was to make research in and on the sector a legitimate and attractive field of scholarship. We wanted to help achieve a clear understanding of everything relating to the sector, including its limitations and faults. Our unchanging priority was to build a field of research that would have credibility and influence.

CHAPTER NINE

Promoting Effectiveness, Openness, and Accountability

T here was never any doubt within the organizing committee that among the responsibilities of the new organization would be the effectiveness of the sector. We also knew it would not be right to try to achieve awareness of the sector and its usefulness to society without seeking certainty that philanthropic and voluntary organizations use every contributed hour and dollar to the maximum benefit of people and causes. The committee summarized the responsibility this way: "Encouragement of effective operation and management of philanthropic and voluntary organizations to maximize their capacity to serve individuals and society as a whole. This includes appropriate measures of board accountability and efficient administration."

As illustrations of possible work, the committee suggested a good many activities, such as encouraging standard setting and evaluation; promoting operational principles such as access, accountability, openness, and full disclosure; leadership efforts to prevent fraud and other abuses; the collection and distribution of information about existing efforts at self-regulation; board training and program evaluation; and encouragement of high-quality training programs for volunteer and staff leaders.

As early as the second meeting of the IS board, several short-term projects were recommended, including meetings of interested members on such topics as use of electronic data processing; marketing for nonprofit organizations; planning; evaluation; board development; and, in light of the energy crisis of those years, energy conservation by IS members.

The board also initiated exchanges among members on standard setting, evaluation, and board and staff development.

After successful efforts to secure start-up funding for the program for the first few years, Roger Heyns, head of the Hewlett Foundation, agreed to lead the initial leadership and management committee, and Brenda Wilson joined the staff as vice president for leadership and management. Within a year, Brenda was lured away to the first of a succession of major leadership roles in her specialty field of higher education. She was replaced by Sandra Trice Gray, who has provided her own good model of leadership over more than a dozen years. In those many years, Sandra and the organization have perhaps been most helpful to the mission by constantly and aggressively seeking good examples of effectiveness and passing them along.

We also had at hand one of the country's and the sector's most effective leaders, who was able to devote a good part of the next seven years to this side of our program. Shortly after John Gardner stepped out of the chair, he undertook our Studies in Leadership project.

It had been John's dream to devote a good deal of attention to reflection and writing about the leadership lessons he had learned in many different settings. I couldn't have been more enthusiastic and encouraging, but when we first talked about it, I didn't grasp that this might be accomplished under IS's aegis. Later, I learned indirectly that he didn't feel right about raising money for his own projects and therefore planned to work almost full-time for at least three years without remuneration or reimbursement. Even though he was ready to make these further sacrifices to continue his service to society, I felt that this towering public servant deserved better. The point I made to him flat-out was that he was one of the nation's greatest assets, and that if he intended to remain active in public service, many funders would be eager to encourage and support that work. I was adamant, and he was stubborn. I told him he was no longer the chairperson, and I was going to raise the money anyway. After more words, he backed up halfway, but tried to compromise by saying he would accept specially raised funds as long as they were to cover only direct expenses and no salary or fee. I fudged and told him I would report that compromise to prospective funders but would abide by the conditions of their grants. It was the easiest fund-raising task I ever undertook, even with John's additional condition that he didn't want any one funder to be asked for more than a modest amount. It took only about ten visits to gain ten commitments, which all just happened to include conditions that some compensation be paid for the work involved. Even then, what John would accept was woefully short of any reasonable estimate of his worth, but that was as far as he would be pushed.

With the enthusiastic approval of the board, John's work became a project of INDEPENDENT SECTOR, and we had the additional advantage of having him in our midst several more years.

In the next two years, John produced twelve "leadership papers," which are still in circulation and have been distributed in numbers well exceeding a quarter of a million. Examples are *The Nature of Leadership, The Tasks of Leadership, Leadership and Power, The Moral Aspect of Leadership,* and *Constituents and Followers.*

On reading the very first paper, I told him, "Reads to me like the first chapter of a book!" He scowled and said he had no intention of producing a book and certainly didn't want to be tied to that goal, but with each issue I would at least hint that it sure looked like the makings of a book, and I finally dropped all pretense and began to refer to later issues as "chapter eight" or "chapter nine."

John had labeled each of the pieces "in discussion stage" and took seriously the comments, including criticisms, he received. With those and some considerable additional other writings, he headed toward a book that in 1990 became *On Leadership,* probably the most important book for which IS has played a part. I felt forgiven and rewarded for my badgering and pushing when I discovered he had dedicated it to me.

Fortunately, the Leadership Studies program continued for many years, focusing later on community leadership and community building, and including several wonderfully insightful papers such as *Building Community,* which I've told him "sound like chapters!"

One additional reference to him belongs here, and that involves the creation of the John W. Gardner Leadership Award, established by the board and membership in 1984 in recognition of his service as the founding chairperson. It honors outstanding Americans "who in their own way exemplify the leadership and the ideals of John W. Gardner."

It has been awarded to seventeen people, all of whom have spent at least a good part of their career, and achieved recognition, through service in our sector.

This book provides the opportunity for a disclosure that I've wanted to make for at least a dozen years. One of the first persons selected for the award was Kenneth Dayton, former CEO of Dayton Hudson and now head of the Oakleaf Foundation. Ken turned down the award on the grounds that the Dayton brothers do not accept any forms of recognition; they want their good deeds to speak for themselves. Ken deserved the Gardner Award for his extraordinary leadership of corporate public service and for so many other contributions to society. I know I'll get a call and a letter from Ken protesting this "outing," but I'm delighted to expose him for the supreme leader he is.

Throughout our first fifteen years, IS focused a good deal on efforts to make the organizations of the sector even more effective than they were. That included such essential matters as openness and accountability, but also a large sense of moral responsibility and stewardship.

To help people be aware of and better equipped to fulfill their basic responsibilities, we produced scores of pamphlets, such as *It's the Law: Disclosure of Information by Tax-Exempt Organizations,* a ten-part "Nonprofit Management Series," and a number of books, including *The Board Member's Book* and *A Vision of Evaluation.*

One of our most timely and consequential endeavors to provide leadership and guidance at a time of crisis was our study on values and ethics headed by Ira Hirschfield and the related book, *Ethics and the Nation's Voluntary and Philanthropic Community.* The project had two primary origins. A number of board members who had agreed entirely with our position in the three Supreme Court cases that threatened arbitrary government regulation of voluntary organizations felt that we had equal responsibility to articulate what the sector and its individual organizations must stand for. The other impetus was several media exposés calling attention to deceitful and illegal behavior by voluntary organizations.

Almost as soon as the report was completed, the United Way scandal screeched through the country, and we were fortunately ready with a message for boards of all voluntary organizations and for all their contributors about the standards to which the sector and its organizations are bound. We also made clear that we were more critical than anyone else of organizations that failed those standards.

The report of the committee on values and ethics stated that concerns about lapses in ethical conduct arose in every part of society, but that the public expected the highest values and ethics to be practiced habitually in the institutions of the charitable, nonprofit sector. Because these institutions, fundamentally, were dedicated to enhancing basic human values, expectations of them were particularly high.

The title of the report included the phrase "obedience to the unenforceable," quoted from England's Lord Justice of Appeal John Fletcher Moulton more than sixty-five years earlier. The true test of greatness, said Moulton, "is the extent to which the individuals composing the nation can be trusted to obey self-imposed law." The committee added: "In the independent sector, public trust stems from our willingness to go beyond the law or even the spirit of the law. We act ethically because it is the right thing to do."

The committee made a particular point that "when our institutions do not reflect high standards of openness, honesty and public service, our contributors and clients are ill-served. This sector depends upon public goodwill and participation. If public support is eroded, so is our capacity for public service."

We went on to underscore certain ethical behaviors that nonprofit organizations should stand for, including *commitment beyond self,* which is at the core of a civil society; *obedience to the laws,* a fundamental responsibility of stewardship; *commitment beyond the law* to obedience to the unenforceable; and *commitment to the public good,* which requires those who presume to serve the public good to assume a public trust.

One of the largest, and I think most successful, projects in our Leadership and Management program grew out of a desire to learn more about what was already working well and then pass that knowledge along to our members. As with research, we were handicapped by limited literature even about what constitutes excellence in nonprofit endeavor. The closest thing to a consensus was the view of many businesspeople that voluntary organizations were generally poorly managed.

One of the frustrations for businesspeople serving on voluntary boards is that it is so hard to define and measure success. Nonprofits just don't have the simple measure of bottom-line profits. Many individuals from the commercial sector so desperately want voluntary organizations to mirror the best practices of business that they are extremely impatient with their nonprofit counterparts. It became routine to hear such observations as "These do-gooders and bleeding hearts just don't know how to manage" or "If we could just get more management discipline into these cause-oriented organizations, they would be far more effective."

It's my own observation that these perceptions are usually inaccurate and unfair. Voluntary organizations, like businesses and other human institutions, vary in their effectiveness. About one-third are models of excellence—beautiful examples of caring, innovation, and efficiency. One-third are good to fair. And one-third are poorly managed and generally ineffective.

With publication of our four-year study *Profiles of Excellence: Achieving Success in the Nonprofit Sector,* we took our largest step toward clarifying the characteristics of successful voluntary operations. The efforts of Burt Knauft, Renee Berger, and Sandra Trice Gray, along with the dedicated participation of committee members led by Ed Weaver and Astrid Merget, produced a remarkably useful combination of evidence, examples, guidelines, and references. Their book is a long-term contribution to a still sparse literature and an immediate help to conscientious board and staff members.

One of the most important parts of the study was the definition of certain "hallmarks of excellence" that characterize the best of non-profit organizations. To determine these standards, we asked our members, community foundations, United Ways, and others to nominate models of effectiveness. We didn't try to stipulate what constituted excellence, because that would have produced a self-fulfilling prophecy. We just asked them to name two or three voluntary organizations that they considered stunningly good, with some indication of why each was chosen. Several hundred organizations were brought to our attention. We then reduced that list to a manageable number, making sure that it still included arts, social welfare, environment, and so on. After securing a good deal of information from these groups, we made more eliminations and then arranged field visits to interview clients, funders, board members, staff, and others associated with each of the remaining organizations. We were trying to find out whether these organizations really did measure up to their billing, and if so, what seemed to be the characteristics that made them so special. *Profiles of Excellence* summarized the common denominators that were found, described each of the organizations in some depth, and summarized how other organizations might replicate their performance.

The four hallmarks of excellence that we identified were primacy of mission, effective leadership, a dynamic board, and strong development efforts.

Another book that seemed helpful in identifying and articulating what constitutes effectiveness, if not excellence, was *The Board Member's Book,* which I put together initially in 1985 (with a second edition in 1993) to summarize a lot of lessons I had learned about what constituted good boards and how to develop them. It's still one of the "best sellers," not because it's that stellar but because the hunger is so great among conscientious leaders for practical guidance about board development, fund-raising, budgeting, evaluation, and recruiting and monitoring the chief staff officer. And because I sympathize so much with board and committee chairs who don't understand parliamentary procedure and are intimidated by it, I even included a chapter titled "Robert's Rules of Order—Demystified."

That book provided much of the basic material for a "Nonprofit Management Series" that included twelve booklets. We realized that the book was more than most people would want to bother with or spend money on, and thought the series would make the information more accessible.

We also tried to reach volunteer and staff leaders with humorous lessons, believing that some people learn best with a lighter approach, which might even spoof common mistakes of voluntary organizations. Later, those spoofs were collected into a book, *Board Overboard: Laughs and Lessons for All but the Perfect Nonprofit*. The chapters cover many of the same subjects as appear in *The Board Member's Book* but approach them with examples of how not to run things. It's an indication that we would do just about anything to get the messages across!

A much more serious and difficult project evolved out of the committee's desire—very much supported by the board—for methods of evaluation that could provide funders and others with indisputable evidence of an organization's effectiveness. In an episode in *Board Overboard,* the evaluation committee reports after two years of effort, "Any group as bright as we are which has worked as long and hard as we have must have done a great deal of good." Though an exaggeration, it isn't too far off the mark as a depiction of many assessments.

We were particularly eager to get a handle on an organization's effectiveness in hard-to-measure categories—for example, the results of advocacy initiatives designed to influence government practices. We thought we should start with some of our own activities and try to study our results in ways that might be replicable by our members and others. Unfortunately, even after a year of very serious search, we couldn't find anyone who had ever developed and implemented such an exacting evaluation scheme.

In the course of our search, we did come across a distinguished sociologist, Linda Fisher of Chicago, some of whose experience was relevant to our concerns and who was interested in working with us to develop and test a likely model. It doesn't do her or the committee justice to be so brief, but in essence, she concluded that though we might not achieve absolutely definitive answers, we could get pretty close to them via a four-pronged approach. She developed and tested a set of objective questions, then sought out and interviewed four categories of informed people. For example, when the objective was to learn if IS had *really* had a significant influence in the passing or blocking of legislation, she would interview (1) key legislators and staff from the committees in which the legislation was considered; (2) reporters who had considerable experience in covering that beat and were doing so when the specific legislation was under consideration; (3) people likely to have an informed opinion who were recommended by the first two groups; and (4) IS members who worked in the pertinent areas.

Linda pointed out that if we wanted to appear more scientific, we could put a numerical ranking on answers to multiple-choice questions and provide a score. But we decided, with her agreement, simply to ask knowledgeable people whether they felt that INDEPENDENT SECTOR had been singularly influential, very effective, effective, somewhat effective, or useless. The interviews were also designed to elicit what it was that seemed to make us effective or ineffective and what we could have done to be more effective.

The process helped sharpen our planning so that we could be even more specific about what we were trying to achieve and evaluate.

For at least a year, Linda and her firm evaluated various projects relating to our influence with government, our ability to help develop greater research activity in and on the sector, and our effectiveness in helping people recognize and understand our "Give Five" symbol and message.

For several years after that important process, we presented Linda's interview model and the results to special sessions at annual and regional meetings of our members and before other umbrella groups in areas such as health and arts.

My impression is that this extremely valuable and valid approach has not taken hold, and I believe the principal reason is that evaluation always seems to drain time and money from more urgent pursuits. Also, our approach was expensive. We tried to make the point that in the long run, it had the potential to save a great deal of time and money and would increase an organization's ability to demonstrate its effectiveness to funders. The model stands out there, at the ready, when organizations realize they can't get away with "Any group as bright as we are . . ."

All of our various prior efforts to help our members become more effective, understand what was expected of them as exempt organizations, grasp the values and ethics they should uphold, or build boards, led us in more recent years to give special emphasis to evaluation. Our members kept telling us that even in organizations committed to evaluation, there were mountainous obstacles, including an antipathy to having someone look over one's shoulder.

By 1993, Sandra and the committee had developed, field tested, and released our report and guide, *A Vision of Evaluation.* Subsequently, other special guides have been developed, and a continuing series of forums has been conducted for IS members and for major parts of the sector such as education and youth service.

In the mid-1980s, an unexpected opportunity came along that thankfully we were ready for. It was a perfect illustration of the principle that if you know where you want to go, you're likely to be ready when opportunity knocks.

Hank Zuker, a prominent professional in the field of Jewish philanthropy and an adviser to Cleveland's Mandel family and their Premier Industrial Corporation, visited me, among many others, to try to determine what we thought might be particularly important causes for future support by the Mandels. At that point, they were considering a colossal jump in their annual support from an already wonderfully generous level.

Hank mentioned various possibilities, including new targets and ventures in areas the family was already interested in. Among these were Jewish education and culture, Cleveland area social services, the Council of Jewish Federations, and assistance to Israel.

I had known that Mort Mandel, with the assistance of his brothers, had used an extraordinary management style to develop Premier into a major economic force. Putting that together with IS's desire to get some significant funders interested in research and leadership relating to the sector in general, I brainstormed with Hank about ways of improving the effectiveness of voluntary organizations, including attracting and nurturing capable young staff who could serve the sector in the long term. We discussed the idea that because of the Mandels' wide-ranging philanthropic interests, they might be naturals for investing in the expansion of the sector as a whole.

Hank was sufficiently interested to ask me to summarize my thoughts in writing, and after further consideration, I wrote a long memo to Hank and Mort that became the skeletal plan for what evolved into the comprehensive Mandel Center for Nonprofit Organizations.

Many of the thoughts were not original to me. They were the product of prior discussions with many individuals about what INDEPENDENT SECTOR and others could do to further the sector's unique roles. There were also some existing models of academic centers, though nothing quite so comprehensive as I was proposing. The Yale Program on NonProfit Organizations (PONPO) and the Lincoln Filene Center for Citizenship and Public Affairs at Tufts University had provided evidence that academic involvement and investment in these matters was not out of the question.

My memo led to further conversations with Hank, with others involved in Premier and Mandel philanthropies, and then with a broader group of Cleveland institutions, including the Cleveland and George Gund foundations. These in turn led to exploratory discussions with the president, provost, selected deans, and others at Case Western University. Top leadership of the university was interested, but understandably had a hard time selling this as a new priority when so many other needs and hopes existed in almost every part of the institution. Even the deans who were supportive found it hard to convince important faculty members that this was an important new endeavor, and that it was sensible to take advantage of the interest of the Mandels and other potential funders.

Finally, after more than two years of discussion, consultation, and negotiation, all parties agreed to participate in the formation of the Mandel Center. The center was formally launched in 1985 as a joint activity of the schools of management, law, and applied social studies. It quickly became an enormous resource for the development of new and strengthened leadership for agencies in the region, and a major force for research and its application in the development of more effective nonprofit organizations, both nationally and internationally.

There were many players involved in the development of the center, but Hank and Mort recall, as I do, that the initial flicker of the idea and the beginning blueprint and negotiations grew out of a concept at the ready within INDEPENDENT SECTOR.

Included in our leadership and management endeavors were several editions of the *Directory of Educational and Training Programs Relating to Nonprofit Leadership and Management* and an ongoing series of forums for the leaders of those programs. Sandra was masterful in setting up an extensive network of all those who showed some interest in her topics. She also produced a regular publication, *Leadership IS,* which kept this group networked and informed.

Among the great many relevant books, reports, and other publications written to assist our members and the sector in general were *Governing, Leading and Managing Nonprofit Organizations,* by Dennis Young, Virginia Hodgkinson, Robert Hollister, and Associates; *Profiles of Effective Corporate Giving Programs,* by E. B. Knauft; *Aiming High on a Small Budget: Executive Searches and the Nonprofit Sector; Governance Is Governance* by Ken Dayton (which illustrates that trusteeship responsibility is the same in all three sectors); *Financial Compensation in Nonprofit Organizations; For Organizations in Trouble—Or Don't Want to Be* (a guide for organizations trying to figure out what went wrong or most likely will); and a series of columns on leadership and management subjects for placement in members' publications.

There was one pamphlet that caused quite a stir, both positive and negative: *The Common Sense of Sabbaticals or Project Leaves.* Staff leaders loved it, but some board members thought I was trying to start an insurrection. I believe it was reprinted (obviously by staff!) as often as anything else we produced. I thought the proposal rather modest—for example, three months of leave after ten years of service for heads of organizations who had been through a pretty driving decade—but many volunteer leaders who came from business felt it was just further evidence that nonprofit leaders don't work as hard as business executives. I concluded a later draft: "I hope that the awarding of opportunities for renewal becomes a wave of the future for philanthropic and voluntary organizations. It will be a sign of our maturity when we recognize that fulfillment of trusteeship includes just such investment in the future of our institutions."

In addition to evaluation and sabbaticals, there were other important subjects that I thought were seriously neglected—for example, the almost routine failure to attend to the vulnerability of relationships between the chief volunteer and chief staff officers and all the negative things that follow if those relationships sour. Another example is recruitment of the chief staff officer, which is often described as the board's most important responsibility but which is far too often handled terribly and with dreadful consequences. A third example is the board's role in fund-raising, usually dealt with by delegation or lip service.

From our earliest days, we worked closely with the Association of Governing Boards for Colleges and Universities (AGB) to translate their successful experience into similar results for other parts of the sector. In 1987, after a year's consideration, we jointly launched the National Center for Nonprofit Boards (NCNB), which later became an independent body active throughout the country and even internationally.

There was an interesting point at which AGB wanted us to establish the center permanently within IS, but we thought it more logical that the center be an extension of AGB. The funders didn't care which, but they didn't want a new organization established. We knew that if we took on that kind of major operating responsibility, everything else we were trying to do would be subordinated, and AGB was fearful that they would lose ability to focus on their basic mission with universities. In the end, interested funders recognized the need to look toward a new entity, as long as the initial years involved a pilot effort with dual controls.

A similar quandary that might have swamped us arose from a proposal by a couple of funders that we establish a subsidiary insurance company to provide liability coverage to thousands of organizations that were having trouble retaining or getting it. With the help of other carriers—and with the encouragement of what is now known as First Nonprofit Companies—we were able to identify sources of liability coverage for voluntary groups, and the crisis was thereby averted without our having to take on massive responsibility in an area where we would have had absolutely no experience.

Similarly, but more through our own devices, we were drawn into a study of pooling the sector's purchasing power. We had been considering setting up contractual relationships with various corporate groups, who would provide our members with rental cars, hotel bookings, computers, office equipment, and numerous other goods and services at substantial discounts. The idea sounded so good, both in terms of interest to members and an additional and perhaps substantial income stream for IS, that several people thought we ought to jump in before somebody got there first. Fortunately, we proceeded more carefully, and to the distress of an available funder, decided to start with the proverbial study.

At least we went at it with urgency, and the result, though not what we expected, proved in the long run to be even more valuable to our members and the overall sector. In essence, what we found was that someone had indeed already beaten us to it—and had been there a long while. Several regional purchasing networks were in existence, some related to consortia of large organizations, a few run as extensions of an individual hospital's or university's own purchasing efforts. The YMCA and certain other national organizations already had such an arrangement for their local members. We found that many of these programs were amenable to extending their benefits to others as a means of increasing volume, lowering prices, and producing additional income for the administering group. Thus, to both our regret and delight, the service was already available, or potentially so, to most of our members. For IS to try to deal with the balance would have been a small service at great expense.

Since that time, many of the state associations of nonprofits have moved into this arena by forging relationships with larger programs or establishing their own.

Beyond our direct activities, we tried to operate in ways that might serve as a good example to the field. This goal applied to the way we communicated with members, our approach to planning and evaluation, the organization of our government relations network, and the quality of our publications, news releases, research surveys, and so on. On the evidence of their evaluations of us, our members seemed to feel that our goal was fulfilled.

On one occasion, the board's view of us as a model got me into hot water. After many years of very favorable balance sheets, including dogged and successful efforts to build up a modest reserve, we ran into a year-end deficit. I had warned that this might occur but had pointed out that it would be more than covered by the budget surpluses of the prior three years. I wasn't at all worried and was somewhat surprised that many management committee and board members seemed to feel it would send the wrong signal to the membership. But my explanation was accepted, and the matter was not pursued.

The following year, we had a second deficit, having in the interim transferred the accumulated budget surpluses to the reserve fund. I had argued for leaving some of the surplus available for what I unfortunately called the "inevitable" occasional deficit, but the committee thought it would be safer not to have a cushion to fall back on. Though the second deficit was modest, it required us to call on our reserves for the very first time, and with that, the management committee reacted as though we were headed for bankruptcy. I understood and shared their concern about a possible trend that could get serious, but I assured them the trend would not continue. As I probed the inordinate degree of concern, it wasn't so much that the signs portended anything horrendous for us, but rather that we were being looked to as a model, and deficits were unpalatable. I've often wondered why businesses and even foundations can have deficits, but a voluntary organization that has one is held up to reprimand, even in the face of otherwise very strong financial statements. My question notwithstanding, it was the end of my deficits at IS.

Perhaps the best vehicle we had for raising up models of good leadership and management practices was our annual meetings, where those topics took up 50–60 percent of the program. Sandra would have made it 75 percent, except that she would have had to organize even more of each meeting's sessions. That was a brutally busy time for her each year, but the illustrations in this chapter (standing for many others that deserve to be included) provide evidence that we were true to the organizing committee's belief that any group dedicated to preserving and strengthening this unique side of America has to devote a considerable part of its effort to the "encouragement and effective leadership and management of philanthropic and voluntary organizations to maximize their capacity to serve society."

CHAPTER TEN

Making the Most
of the Meeting Ground

A couple of days before our 1985 annual meeting in New Orleans, John Thomas met with Nan Perndes, a *Times-Picayune* reporter who was trying to get a handle on just what this convention was all about. To describe our unusual collection of members, John indicated that some were philanthropists who were generous donors, some were philanthropoids who were executives of foundations, and some were philanthropees who spent the money. The opening line in the reporter's story the next day was "Today more than 750 pists, poids, and pees descend on our city."

It was not a bad way of capturing the diversity of our membership and the unusual experience of bringing them together on what the organizing committee called "the meeting ground." The committee had anticipated quite accurately that once these organizations were even loosely confederated, there would be many useful interchanges and pursuits well beyond the defined program concentrations, such as research and government relations. At one point, they predicted the development of "a greater sense of community among the organizations of the sector."

The yearly get-togethers were even called the Annual Meeting *and* Assembly of Members, and though the business aspects provided the legal and practical reasons for coming together, the larger attraction by far was the chance to swap ideas and information, expand one's network, and gain some encouragement and maybe even inspiration to take back to difficult tasks. We tried to achieve these results also in regional meetings and briefings, which included an even greater number of our members. In addition, we organized councils relating to our major program pursuits such as leadership and management; each council included those representatives of our members who had a particular interest in that area of concentration. We attempted to provide written briefings at least quarterly to keep council members in the know, and there were often meetings of the councils at the annual meeting. Though it was quite natural that some councils included people in similar jobs—for example, research director—most had a disparate membership, and from time to time we would organize special sessions so that individuals who had responsibilities in common had a chance to learn from each other. We learned early that however different the missions of their organizations, the people responsible for communications or government relations found a great deal to share.

Many of our members also discovered, in some cases to our absolute surprise, that leaders and organizations could learn a good deal from the most unlikely sources. I recall a session on marketing at an early annual meeting where one of the resource people was the marketing professional at the Salvation Army. In advance, some attendees told me they couldn't imagine how museums or universities could learn much on that topic from him, but the colonel was the hit of the day, demonstrating a sophistication as useful as it was surprising.

At most of our meetings, we worked hard to get the participants to mix, and we even spent a good deal of time organizing roundtables and small discussion groups with assigned seating so that there could be a much richer sharing of experiences and contacts. Whenever we saw a table or room that included individuals from community foundations, corporate philanthropy, housing, women's issues, opera, preservation, and international understanding, we knew we could leave them absolutely to themselves and the session would be wonderfully rich. That was the meeting ground.

We made an early mistake that was hard to correct. We had thought it would be an important courtesy, and provide a benefit both to our members and to organizations in the geographic area of the meeting, to have the local arrangements committee extend an open invitation to leaders of community agencies. That proved so popular that at our third annual meeting and assembly of members, in the Twin Cities, we had close to five hundred local registrants—more than half the total attendance.

The problem was that the numbers got in the way of achieving the kind of camaraderie and networking we were trying to achieve among our members, and the sessions quickly focused on what could and should be done in the surrounding community rather than on what the attending national leaders could achieve nationwide. Also, most of the one-time attendees from the local community didn't understand or observe the ground rule forbidding solicitations, and our grant-making members felt besieged. For those reasons, future meetings were restricted to members, prospective members, and other individuals important to the subjects being covered.

With the meeting ground at hand and a growing acceptance of our commonality, there developed a greater interest in topics that previously would not have seemed pertinent, as well as a greater awareness of the relationship of each part of the sector to the whole. That made our written communications more widely relevant. For example, though the "Memo to Members" rarely contained specific information about developments in fields such as international exchange or health research, leaders of organizations in those fields appreciated being informed about regulatory problems faced by others, the development of academic centers, changing national demographics, and trends in the creation of private organizations in other countries.

The existence of the network also proved advantageous when totally unanticipated needs or interests emerged. For example, at one point, many members asked us to study benefits programs such as retirement plans. (One key concern was the portability of benefits when a person moved from one organization or field to another.) The problem was obviously greatest in small organizations, but even in the 1990s, inadequate benefits were discouragingly pervasive. An activist serving in a neighborhood agency is still not likely to have such benefits. A person in a regional theater may have some, but at such a low level as to contradict the intent. An employee of a large health agency is likely to find that his or her benefits cannot be carried to another job, even when the move is to a similar agency. At root, the problems are caused by lack of money, concern on the part of boards about overhead, and the dispersion of the sector, which has made it hard for insurance carriers to get a handle on how to provide benefits to people in very small groups, or those moving from one agency or community to another.

An even newer IS project concentrates on ways to open far more opportunities in the sector to idealistic, able young people who will be the leaders of tomorrow and often are ready for leadership responsibilities today.

A very different project looked for ways in which IS and its members could be more responsive to inquiries from other nations about how to develop voluntary organizations, funding sources, and even something like an independent sector. By the late 1980s, and certainly by the early 1990s, many of us were seeing people from a great variety of nations who had begun to realize that voluntary initiative and citizen influence were essential to their liberation and to the release of human potential.

In 1990 and 1991, there were discussions in Europe and the United States about the need for an international network to assist the growing number of people and groups eager to increase citizen participation and influence in their countries. The Council on Foundations and IS were asked to work with the European Foundation Centre to determine what might be done. This led to the establishment of a formal exploratory committee in late 1991, and subsequently to an organizing committee that worked in 1992 and 1993 and which I chaired. The committees concluded that "effective societies exist in direct proportion to their degree of citizen participation and influence" and that "there is a need to bring together private donors and other nongovernmental organizations to strengthen citizen action and influence."

Reflecting the difficulties involved in these deliberations but also the positive outcomes, the final report stated: "Most of us had not met when we became involved in this consideration, and most of us were skeptical at the very least that anything could be accomplished. We have moved from the condition of unallied doubters to a unified body embracing a shared vision. Despite all of our differences and differentness, we are agreed that something very significant may be unfolding in the world and that the moment should be seized."

From those beginnings, CIVICUS: World Alliance for Citizen Participation was launched in Barcelona in mid-1993, and in the ensuing years, its progress and impact have been significant. Just seeing the several hundred delegates at the first world assembly in Mexico City in 1995 sparking and learning from one another provided the clearest possible indication that something very special was indeed unfolding, and that the moment was in fact being seized.

Sandra Trice Gray staffed the organizing committee and then the search committee, which recommended to the new board that Miklós Marschall of Hungary be appointed the first executive director of CIVICUS. The encouragement of the IS membership and board, including the major commitments by Sandra and me, were very much an outgrowth of the unique advantages of the meeting ground.

This service of IS may turn out to be one of its most significant accomplishments, but even if that still fragile and always difficult international coalition fails or does not achieve the impact so many people hope for it, the lessons learned and the contributions made during its development and early years will be important building blocks.

As large as CIVICUS and other projects spawned by the meeting ground were, most of what we did within this general category of "meeting ground" could never be adequately described, and even if it could, would not seem nearly as significant and useful as was really the case. But because there was a network that spread even far beyond our members, there developed a "switchboard" (to use a buzzword) that was lit up all the time. There were phone calls, faxes, letters, and personal approaches requesting information and guidance on our program concentrations and every possible tangent of them, as well as subjects that had nothing to do with them. Because we were gaining in visibility and credibility, our members and a great many others turned to us regularly for things that might only remotely relate to our mission and often did not even meet that criterion. This responsibility became such a large part of our life that we were constantly trying to figure out how to organize it. On several occasions, we sought to determine if it really was as great a load as we estimated, and those analyses indicated that approximately 15–20 percent of total staff time was taken up in responding to inquiries beyond our five program areas. These included requests for credible contacts or consultants to help with organizational problems or development; speakers and speech material; staff searches (and sometimes searches for board members); advice on fund-raising; sources of help on bylaws and policies; financial guidelines, such as recommended levels of reserves; briefings on compensation, including benefits; and examples of awards programs.

One particular subject on which we received a stream of requests for help was coalition building. More thoughts about that are included in the next chapter, but the longer this extraordinary federation lasted, the more people turned to us for information about how we did it and advice for their own examinations of mergers, ad hoc coalitions, federations, new national organizations, and even international needs and possibilities.

Certainly among the "hopes fulfilled" was our success in attracting members and obtaining support for the various new program areas and special projects. Membership grew to approximately nine hundred out of what we determined was a likely maximum of around eleven hundred, and our regular appeals and special campaigns for project support and investment in our future were generally oversubscribed. In most of these appeals for members and supporters, it was the members themselves who presented our case, and in large part, their own enthusiastic support and their willingness to convey it to their peers were what made these development efforts so successful. For example, in the membership drive to celebrate our tenth anniversary, it was the members, under the leadership of Ted Taylor, who organized themselves into regions and specialty areas—such as health and arts—who communicated why the mission was still so vital and so applicable to every part of the sector.

Also contributing to our success was our ability to document IS's increasing program impact. At that point, we were able to say: "In 1980, INDEPENDENT SECTOR represented only great needs and high hopes. Now, the evidence is clear that by working together the organizations of the sector can have enormous impact on the health of the sector and on our ability to be of public service."

It was somewhat disconcerting that when board members would talk about taking on some major new project and I would try to relate it to what we were already doing and our internal capacity to support it, there was rarely recognition of how much of our resources was already absorbed in ongoing obligations. These included the annual meeting, the "Memo to Members," routine publications and communication responsibilities, the fielding of requests for information and guidance within our program areas, and all the other things that an organization at the hub of a federation or coalition inescapably has to do. I would try to point out that there were very good organizations, including some large umbrella groups, that *only* did an annual conference and maybe one publication such as a journal or newsletter; their registrations and subscriptions covered all their organizational costs, and their members expected nothing more of them. I wasn't proposing that for us, but just using it as evidence that some of the functions we were taking for granted and didn't really count as parts of our "program" were in fact the total program of other very respected and successful enterprises. Sometimes I would think I had made my point, only to be brought down in fact and spirit by the rejoinder that "those activities are important and good, but we've got to give evidence of a great deal more that is really tangible!" There were times when the meeting ground seemed more like an amphitheater where the lions were never satisfied with what or whom they had for lunch.

In fairness though, the stadium most often cheered us as winning gladiators, and the occasional wounds healed quickly. We were complimented by our members' wanting more, and my resistance to expansion was motivated only by fear that overstretching would spoil our ability to do the most important things well, including maintaining an effective meeting ground.

PART THREE

Lessons and Afterthoughts

Building, Energizing, and Maintaining Large and Diverse Coalitions

lmost from the start of INDEPENDENT SECTOR, we began to receive inquiries about coalition building, and over the years the interest escalated. This was not the result of idle curiosity but reflected a pervasive and growing need to figure out how to create collaborations, federations, and other partnerships necessary to deal with the increasing complexity of human needs and of our communities. More and more people were finding that their causes were linked to those of others, and that solutions were not possible without allies. School dropouts and failures are related to inadequate nutrition, teen pregnancy, illiteracy, gangs, drugs, and so much more. International harmony is linked to control of nuclear power, reduction of hunger and famine, youth exchange, language training, and many other factors. Leaders of single issue causes, trying to improve schools or transportation systems or access to health care, realize they've got to join with others to have enough leverage to make a difference.

Alarmingly, this overwhelming need for collaboration is up against inadequate experience in forming and maintaining intricate alliances. It was because we seemed to be achieving some success that we were besieged for information about how we had done it and guidance on how they might go at it.

Though both John Gardner and I had considerable experience with complex human institutions, I don't believe either of us thought of ourselves as students of the topic. We had proceeded not from any well-worn textbooks or checklists but more from a random collection of well-learned *musts* and *mustn'ts* when dealing with people who have to work together but who don't know it or don't want to.

John had founded Common Cause, built the Urban Coalition, and achieved rare unity among the myriad fiefdoms of the U.S. Department of Health, Education and Welfare. I had been by far the longest-serving head of the enormously diverse and fractious Mental Health Association, had been chairman of the organizing committee of the National Assembly of Health and Social Welfare Organizations, and had served as first chairman of the National Committee on Patients' Rights. To the extent that these experiences blended into the development of IS, they are part of what I'll try to cover here. I don't pretend that what follows is anything like a definitive discourse on collaboration, but it might help explain what caused one excruciatingly complex model to work.

In many ways, this whole book is necessary to the explanation, but I know from experience that most people who are interested in IS will sooner or later want to know what I think really caused it to succeed (and they don't want a book-length answer). Alternatively, they will give me their own interpretation, which is usually so simplistic that it causes me to wish they would read the whole book!

This chapter is my compromise. Perhaps a larger number of people will at least understand more of the reasons for IS's success as an organization, and they *might* be sufficiently interested to move on to other parts of the book.

For now, here are ten possible lessons growing out of the IS experience. The first four of them have already been addressed in considerable detail, so no elaboration is provided here:

1.   The problems were very real and growing, and the consequences of not addressing them became harder for conscientious people to ignore.

2.   We made good use of the head starts and lessons provided by such groups as the Filer Commission, CONVO, and NCOP, and we were

informed by the thinking and even the potential competition of other groups, such as ACTION, Committee for the Third Sector, and Alliance for Volunteerism. Even shipwrecks of the past help produce better navigation charts.

3. The plan was visible enough to catch people's attention, bold enough to stir their passions, and potentially powerful enough to really make the difference.

4. We went for and achieved major early successes and communicated them in ways that built momentum for membership and support, and for moving to even higher levels of achievement.

The remaining six lessons need some additional comment.

5. We stretched inclusiveness to the point of bewilderment, despite concerns about being too broad, diverse, and unmanageable.

In responding to inquiries and doubts about broad-based coalitions, I would almost always fall back on one of John's many apt phrases, in this case, "a wide-angle lens." Though questioners were interested in our diversity, they almost always wanted to think of their own efforts as less complex. Many, for example, wondered why we hadn't just stopped at the combination of NCOP and CONVO. I would explain that it was enormously useful to have them as an initial base, but that they were not representative of the breadth of the sector, and we were not going to succeed unless we went far beyond them. Then folks would question whether that approach wouldn't, for them, become cumbersome and unmanageable, and perhaps end up requiring too much time for the placation of all the different players. It was fascinating but frustrating that even though most of these groups approached us because of our perceived success in one of the broadest-based coalitions they had ever heard of, they would sit there and pile up their doubts.

Another fairly simple concept was also terribly difficult for people to accept. It involved another of John's phrases, "wholeness that transcends diversity." My listeners would nod at the sagacity of it but quickly fall into worries about having people with too much differentness in the circle.

One of the hardest things to do is to reach out to those you actively dislike or with whom you've had prior battles. It's hard enough to be open to those you don't know, but when the challenge extends to those you do know and wish you didn't, it's easier to argue for a smaller or at least different group of partners.

One of the hardest lessons about inclusiveness I ever learned or hope to learn involved the National Committee on Patients' Rights. It will certainly demonstrate that the necessary partners can sometimes view each other with hostility. To succeed in establishing the principle of patients' rights, achieving the articulation of those rights, and fostering the practice of them, we needed to have at the table the full range of providers and consumers. That included psychiatrists, psychologists, social workers, mental hospital administrators, and state mental health commissioners, and an equally varied group of patients, former patients, parents, and other advocates.

The Mental Health Association and I had been asked to call the first exploratory session—not because we were necessarily trusted by all sides, but because we were at least not viewed by anyone as an enemy. It took a great deal of work to get most of these groups to send key representatives to the session (itself a lesson in coalition building), but out of respect for the role I'd been asked to play, or curiosity, or a desire to protect their own interests, almost all of the parties showed up.

Initially, I was curious about the fact that many of the patient-related representatives arrived quite early, and I thought they might have misunderstood the starting time. They said they hadn't, and I figured they just wanted a little advance time to prepare. The next arrival, unfortunately, was the key representative of the American Psychiatric Association, who went into the room and immediately stormed into my office with an almost hysterical protest. By the time I got him calmed down, a number of others had arrived, and when we all got to the room, it was obvious we had a problem. Screaming at us from the blackboard was the message "PSYCHIATRY KILLS!" Around the room, the message was repeated, along with other pungent summaries of what the patients thought of providers and provider groups.

My first thought was to try to meet with the patients as a group and then separately with the providers, but I decided that what needed to be said and worked through required the participation of everyone. I even started with the deliberate but almost absurd banalities of introducing ourselves and indicating what we hoped might come out of the session and possible further collaboration. Fortunately, that round robin produced a sense of some common ground and shared hopes, and by staying with those and building on them, we gradually increased enough trust around the relatively narrow areas of concentration to keep the process going.

One of the lessons about inclusiveness is enormous forbearance and a sustained effort to understand where people are coming from and why.

Even within relatively civil alliances, there will often be times when many of the partners will get tired of hearing different voices and viewpoints. Most of the participants will be preoccupied with their own full-time, stressful responsibilities, and it will require all their forbearance to sit around listening to a lot of people who see things quite differently. One of John Gardner's apt admonitions was a help to us in this area, and might help others, too: "To survive and succeed requires an infinite regard for differences among good people."

Inclusiveness and civility need to be abundant even in ongoing federations such as the American Heart Association. Though IS was not a federation made up of formally affiliated chapters, I was able to draw on a good deal of experience I had gained with the heart and mental health associations. In *The Board Member's Book,* when discussing the role of the national office in such a federation, I tried to pass along some of my experience:

> It is important to say something about the national board of an association with local chapters. It doesn't matter whether the national operation is organized as a corporate headquarters or the hub of a federation; it will still be the central entity and as such must provide dynamic leadership for the total organization. This includes responsibility for the organization's spirit, direction, thrust, policies, and guidelines.
>
> One basic way to reduce built-in tensions and to keep the national level attuned to local needs is to be sure that the national board of directors is composed overwhelmingly of people who come from the affiliates. Even if your organization operates as a tight national corporation, there can't be correct decision-making and follow-through without local leaders having a substantial part in making the decisions. On the national level, the organization should be very largely peopled and run by individuals who have current or at least recent experience on the firing line. The local affiliates must feel it's their national association, or, regardless of how dynamic the leadership, there won't be followership.

Even if you achieve the ultimate in representation, don't expect that harmony will automatically follow. You will still have to work hard at it. Remember Pogo's discovery: "We have met the enemy and he is us."

The object of all the lessons to minimize friction and create unity is to use the wonderful volunteer energy and time to fight for the cause and not against one another.

That's a pretty good rule for the role of all boards and board members.

6.   We stayed with and made the most of the common ground where we belonged, and we resisted every fierce effort to move us onto ground and into battles where we didn't belong.

In the case of the first few meetings of the National Committee on Patients' Rights, the only thing that made it possible to proceed was to stay with the tiny strip of common ground until enough trust was built to widen the path a little. Gradually, we were even able to have some mixed subcommittees, carefully chosen to utilize representatives who had credibility with their groups and who were most likely to struggle to produce something constructive. In the end, we produced the Code of Patients' Rights, which today is likely to be found visibly displayed in any inpatient mental care facility and even many outpatient ones.

After leaving the mental health field, I learned that the group had tried to stay together, at least for periodic sessions or other projects, but it didn't work. That's another important lesson about collaborations: many of them are and can only be ad hoc. However, even when disbanded, they leave a legacy of broader networks and understanding.

One of the most discouraging realities of coalitions is that people find it hard to accept the limitations of such a group, and the stronger the coalition, the more likely the frustration. This doesn't mean that people have to compromise at the absolutely lowest common denominator. The more successful the partnership, the more certain it is to be pushed awfully hard to overextend itself. For IS, this was always the greatest threat to stability—and sometimes to survival. Even after the harsh clashes and bitter disappointments of our first few years, we never went very long without having to deal, perhaps to the point of confrontation, with new participants who hadn't gone through the process of learning our limitations or with more seasoned members who knew the ground rules but felt that their crisis merited an exception.

Because the expectations of IS, even within the common denominator of our members' interests, were always so much greater than resources, we had to find ways to establish what we could and couldn't do. To make such distinctions stick, we had to involve the members in decision making. That required a time-consuming and very convoluted process, but it often made the difference in heading off all the inevitable "bright ideas" and extravagant expectations.

In each of our five-year plans, I said something similar to the following:

> The disciplined development of INDEPENDENT SECTOR's original program plan for 1980–1986 provided the membership with a process for mutual agreement and action on priority goals and objectives. In a federation as informal as INDEPENDENT SECTOR, which involves organizations of enormous diversity and for which there are more urgent tasks than can be accommodated, even in areas of common interest, there is particular need for participatory agenda setting. Loyalty to the process and agenda kept us focused on what we all agreed was most important to accomplish together. It was important both as our green light to go ahead on agreed-upon activities and as our red light to say no to many other good ideas subsequently urged upon us. Obviously flexibility and adjustments were necessary, but at least we could evaluate new directions and detours against an existing course. We subscribe to the planning notion that if you don't know where you're going, you'll end up someplace else.
>
> We also subscribe to the evaluation maxim that if you don't know where you've been, you can't be sure you've been there. During the five years there were two evaluations of the organization, with emphasis on the fulfillment of the program plan. But even good programs get outdated. The people who develop them move on, and the newcomers don't feel a sense of ownership of what others decided should excite them. So the cycle has to be repeated.

We studiously avoided trying to meddle in issues that were the clear province of the Arts Alliance or the National Assembly of Health and Social Welfare Organizations, and in one of the toughest tests of our resolve, we stood absolutely firm when several foundations proposed that we establish specialist IS councils on health, arts, environment, social welfare, and so on. It was understandable that funders would find it easier to support just one umbrella organization rather than several, but we wouldn't have survived if we had moved in on those territories, and we certainly would never have had the experience to deal knowledgeably with any of their subjects.

Sometimes, the most daring thing you can do is not to be daring. There were several times when I was cornered by one or more members who would appeal to what they knew were my own passions and convictions about certain issues, such as support for children's services, research on cancer, or greater investment in international understanding. With their own attractive passion, they would browbeat the hell out of me because I would not turn the organization loose on their urgent priorities. They would try to persuade me that it was illogical, after so much success, for me not to have a right to a few of my own deeply felt causes.

Sometimes, members would argue that the cause they were advocating was an overriding priority, self-evidently essential to everything else on the public agenda. I can't tell you how many times people pounded the table to convince me that quality of public schools was the overarching priority of our times, on which everything else depended, or that all would be lost if we didn't solve the problem of drug abuse, or that AIDS was *the* epidemic of our times around which a moral society had to rally.

Invariably, they would try to corner me by asking what other cause could possibly be as overarching as theirs. It was obvious that I could never convert any of these wonderfully motivated leaders to anything less than their demands, but at least I could send them away understanding why I couldn't accede. I would tell them of the many similar sessions I had weathered with all the same arguments, except that in each case the cause was different. Other delegations could make every bit as good an argument for peace, control of nuclear fission, the struggle against racism, or dozens of other excruciating issues of our times.

When they would leave, I would find myself repeating Pat Moynihan's observation, "It's a world of competing sorrows."

I would also take some slight comfort from the fact that I resisted my own activist instincts to jump headlong into any of those great crusades, recognizing that to do so in the name of INDEPENDENT SECTOR would have been the beginning of the end of our fragile coalition and its ability to pursue its own important mission. Those folks would leave wondering where my heart and courage had gone, and for solace

I would return to the thought that not being daring is sometimes the most daring thing you can do.

7.   From the start, we invested heavily in identifying, enlisting, and utilizing the right leadership for the mission and for the signal their participation conveyed.

Obviously, leadership started with and spotlighted John Gardner, but he would be the first to point to the breadth and depth of allies, including the extraordinary lineup of successors in the chair: Richard Lyman, John Filer, Gene Dorsey, Raul Yzaguirre, and Barbara Finberg.

On the staff side, the listing begins with those enormously able and loyal stalwarts—in order of seniority—Bob Smucker, John Thomas, Virginia Hodgkinson, and Sandra Trice Gray. It is indicative of the value of long-term staff leadership that the five of us represented more than seventy-five years of service in what was still a very young organization. We also benefited hugely from the leadership of Bob Harlan and Burt Knauft, who served successively as executive vice president. (At this point in the IS story, I particularly wish I had not lost the argument with the editors about filling the book with the names of people who helped build the organization. On the other hand, the editors' point comes home when I think of just the staff people I should list. If I were to enumerate all who deserve credit, the list would be as lengthy as the 'begats,' and such a listing of names wouldn't even begin to adequately express credit and appreciation.)

Every human institution depends on good leadership, but coalitions and collaborations require particular investment. They are usually pretty fragile operations, and the leaders and other partners are usually preoccupied with external full-time obligations, which compounds the tenuousness. The ad hoc nature of the enterprise, and the urgency of it, may help hold things together in the short run, but a longer-term effort will almost certainly require realistic degrees of investment in holding the partners together and maintaining their level of commitment.

It is particularly important in a collaborative enterprise that leadership reflect the strengths and diversity of the group. That was the case at IS, and was a major reason for the rapid rise in the number of people who were willing to be involved. From the start, people like Phil Bernstein, Ken Albrecht, Bayard Ewing, Jim Lipscomb, Homer

Wadsworth, and many, many others represented steadiness, credibility with their peers, capacity to stay with the enterprise even during the storms, and so very much more. These qualities grew in importance as the cast of characters grew. The membership needed to know that people they trusted were centrally involved and would keep them informed of progress *and* problems. Such leaders are absolutely necessary to counter the inevitable destructive elements who may be on the fringe or closer, and who through their egos, backbiting, or rigid adherence to their own agendas can undermine an organization's prospects or make success infinitely more difficult. As John put it, "As good as we were, we would never have survived the [blanks] and [blanks] and [blanketyblanks] if it hadn't been for those who shared leadership and responsibility with us." (In this case, the editors might have been delighted to have me include some of the names John actually used, but though that might enliven the book, it wouldn't contribute to coalition building!)

There was one aspect of criticism that I do recall discussing with him early and often, and that was the fact that it's a great deal easier to be a critic than a builder. We had far more than our fair share of both, but one builder is worth dozens of critics, so therefore the odds were with us.

Another older lesson that we drew on led us to exclude from deliberations people who had just too little record of cooperation and mutual respect. We bent over backwards to accommodate strong-willed, passionate champions of their causes, and we didn't exclude dissenters and mavericks who had shown they could occasionally make peace with people of differing views. But we drew the line at those who couldn't or wouldn't see beyond their own boundaries or tolerate priorities other than their own.

We were always on the lookout for a reasonable smattering of people notable for their broad perspective. As important as it is to make the group representative of the coalition's essential constituencies, it is equally important to have individuals who possess those human qualities that lend themselves to collaborative efforts.

After the initial exhilarating years, we would sometimes forget that new participants would not fully understand or feel connected to the excitement of those early times, and we had to return over and over again to the obvious but too often neglected principles of renewal. The longer the enterprise lasts and struggles, the more essential it is to remember that one of the leader's most important responsibilities is to keep the dream alive.

8.   There was absolute commitment to process, including openness, team building, and infinite regard for differences of opinion among good people.

Beginning with our earliest discussions with members of the CONVO and NCOP boards, stretching through the struggles of the organizing committee and into the first years of IS, we had to work awfully hard to build trust, step by step, until people knew that they could rely on us to do what we said we would do—or explain openly and completely why we couldn't. They gradually accepted that there would be no surprises, no hidden agendas, and no back room meetings when their interests were at stake.

As the networks grew, we continued building a shared leadership, so that when people beyond our reach expressed curiosity, concerns, doubt, or upset, there was someone to whom they could turn who would be able to say, "Don't worry. Mary is in the thick of it, and you know you can trust her." It was equally important that those who wanted the organization to do their bidding learned from people they respected that we would not bow to demands and pressure no matter the source. That helped build trust, especially among those who feared we would be subject to control by United Way, or the Ford Foundation, or other major institutions or groups of them.

Throughout the work of the coalition, but particularly in the initial stages, it was essential to invest time in building camaraderie and in opening up communications sufficient to uncover upset, suspicions, and loss of trust. I spent a significant amount of time talking to members in person, checking in with them by phone, and sending regular written updates, to minimize any sense of isolation and to learn when things might be turning sour. When I realized that an individual felt left out, or just plain disagreed with the way we were going, I listened hard and, where appropriate, tried to make adjustments. Equally important, I did not mask real differences. I knew it was a lot better to explain honest differences than to be vague or to make promises that could not be kept.

When I could tell that an individual needed more convincing than I could provide, I encouraged John or others to help explain our situation. Usually, those efforts were sufficient to persuade the person that we might be right, or at least that we had arrived at our conclusion with careful consideration of all the nuances and consequences. We did a lot of agreeing to disagree, but people knew we were trying desperately to be fair. We heard regularly that members believed they could count on us for candor and a willingness to be clear on where we stood.

Whenever I was tempted toward obfuscation, if only to avoid awkwardness or ruffled feelings, I'd remember with amusement the story about President Franklin D. Roosevelt and his dealings with the constantly quarreling Henry Wallace, secretary of agriculture, and Harold Ickes, secretary of the interior. Wallace came to the White House one day and typically derided Ickes for some recent action, insisting that the president overrule him. Roosevelt, feigning sympathy and support, replied, "Henry, I'm inclined to agree with you." Within hours, Ickes showed up and typically complained of Wallace's efforts to undercut the Department of the Interior in budget negotiations. He insisted that the president call Wallace to task. Roosevelt gave every indication of concern and support, and concluded, "Harold, I'm inclined to agree with you." Mrs. Roosevelt heard all of this from the other end of the room, and as soon as Ickes left, berated the president for his duplicity and disingenuousness. The president looked contrite and said, "Eleanor, I'm inclined to agree with you."

Our approach to and style of communication was central to our process. People felt informed, comfortable that they were in the loop, alerted to problems, and on top of the issues.

There's another point that we stressed in the early days, and that involved a paper record. Not only did we want to be certain to keep everybody abreast of what was going on, but we found it essential during those early explorations and struggles to do a summary of almost every meeting, including subcommittees and task forces. We needed to get in writing what agreements had been made, what the follow-up should be, and what were the next points or topics to be addressed. On the surface, that may seem terribly obvious or unduly compulsive, but I learned long ago that you need to capitalize on areas of agreement and, wherever possible, stretch them. When an agreement is summarized in writing, the next session is more likely to start from that point rather than rehash the previous discussion. If people do want to reopen prior agreements, it's better to do it early than to proceed on the assumption that all the building blocks are solid.

For us and for most collaborations, federations, or alliances, communications also meant very careful work with the trade and general media, and that wasn't limited to trying to get coverage. Much of the time, we were just involved in briefings to be sure key communicators felt they were in the know.

One aspect of process that turned out to be an absolute lifesaver involved the identification of different levels of commitment. We had found in the beginning that every time we agreed to take an interest in something, there was an expectation that it meant we were ready to go all out. There were many times when we wanted to lend our support but did not have the resources to go full bore or did not consider the issue as urgent as others. Sometimes, the most we could—or felt obliged to—do was send a letter indicating our support of the efforts of others, rather than try to get all of our members galvanized for action.

In every program plan, we repeated: "In analyzing the various projects in which the organization is asked to assist or take responsibility, we will establish different levels of commitment and intensity, and define our criteria for each. Some projects will obviously have to be decided on the basis of whether we can give them the all-out attention they deserve. When that is not possible, we must develop the discipline to say no. We'll also need to assess whether we can be helpful through some means requiring less commitment and outlay."

The following levels of commitment or intensity were described:

1. A letter of encouragement for an activity carried entirely by others

2. Agreement to let our members know about someone else's activity or about a request for their optional participation in it

3. Written encouragement to IS members to consider participating in an ad hoc session or similar activity to be called and handled by the originating organization

4. Agreement that IS would call an ad hoc session for interested members on a subject suggested by one or more members and likely to be of interest to many others

5. Agreement to organize and chair an ad hoc group exploring a somewhat complex subject or activity that needed sustained examination and that could result in a proposal for continuing or special IS attention

6. Adoption of a position statement or other formal expression of organizational support for a particular bill, program, or initiative

7. Agreement to pursue a topic or project through an existing IS function—for example, making it a topic at the National Conference on Philanthropy

8. Assignment to an existing committee, or establishment of an ad hoc committee

9. An all-out effort, including possible utilization of our congressional network

10. The securing of funding for special projects, including those requiring assignment of IS staff

I need to add one last lesson about the process, and that is to beware of two types of process extremists.

The first is known as the process freak, who carries procedural concerns to such absurd extremes that substance gets subordinated or even lost. I am always on guard when someone urges me to adopt some new process, such as zero-based budgeting, total quality management, or even management by objectives. My caution reflects not a lack of respect for such processes, but repeated experiences with individuals who elevated those planning devices to such levels of preoccupation and priority that an organization lost its zeal and momentum. I worked with a person who had, and maybe still has, a stellar reputation as a visionary planner but who required so intense a level of engagement in planning by everyone, including top leadership, that the organization had little time for action.

The other dangerous process type, often harder to recognize but equally damaging, is the person who seems to be devoted to democratic involvement but who really is a master manipulator. People will tell me even today that some of these folks are absolutely committed to hearing fully from every possible stakeholder and have a remarkable record of achieving consensus. However, I've watched these types exercise uncanny cleverness and inexhaustible energy to wear everybody down to agree with them.

Such "experts" would actually be more open and honest if they started the process the absurd way I heard one chairman do: "Thank you all for coming. After being selected as your leader, I have given our topic a great deal of study and have consulted with those considered best informed. I am passing around a paper summarizing my thoughts, and in the interest of getting this job done quickly, I do very much hope you will agree with me that my summary constitutes the right position to adopt."

9.   A very real part of our success is attributable to our original and ongoing commitment to building the membership and other sources of financial support.

In my swan song to IS, I said: "In putting it together, everything was the membership. We knew from the start it had to be an independent organization. In fact, we knew that this organization had to be truly independent if we were going to be anything like a model of the independent sector. And that had to begin with the membership. The membership, the membership—that's what this organization is all about. Everything we've been able to accomplish relates to the quality, the conviction, and the participation of the membership."

Despite all of our important program pursuits and the enormous pressures to take on more of them, we did not swerve from our resolve not to become dependent on soft money or accept government funding. The dues structure was designed to cover our core budget, spread the financial load as evenly as possible, and keep us free of control from either the donor side of our membership or very large members. There were several major calls for reducing the dues, increasing the share carried by large donor organizations, and accepting government support, all for the understandable purposes of reducing the financial burdens on existing members and attracting new ones. Several of us had seen too many examples of organizations zigging and zagging in the direction of available funding and trying to hold together a membership that had not demonstrated a willingness to get behind the enterprise. The sliding scale payment of dues allowed many small organizations to participate with equal votes, but nobody got a free ride, and nobody could throw their weight around.

If INDEPENDENT SECTOR is any one thing, it is a membership coalition, with every emphasis, including financial, on the ownership and responsibility of the members.

The importance of that sense of ownership and responsibility had been underscored for me in a tragic reorganization of the old National Assembly of Health and Social Welfare Organizations. The assembly had been around for many years, consisting primarily of major national organizations such as the American Red Cross, the YWCA, the American Lung Association, the Mental Health Association, the Child Welfare League, and perhaps fifty others. Each organization appointed an official delegate to the assembly, and the board was drawn largely from those representatives. The organization was funded primarily by dues, supplemented by some grant income.

In the early 1970s, someone came up with the idea that the organization would have greater visibility, fund-raising capacity, and clout if the delegate body were replaced with a committee of one hundred prominent citizens, most with name recognition and some prior interest in health and welfare. This was done, and the board was then drawn from the new group. There was also a council of staff representatives from participating national organizations.

I can't remember how much time and money went into the reorganization, but both were staggering. All of us hoped it would work for the good of our mutual interests and individual causes, but many of us worried about the consequences if this untried idea flopped. It didn't take long to find out. Within a couple of years, the experiment came tumbling down, and the whole mess was dropped back into the laps of the prior stakeholders, the national organizations.

The problems were multiple and obvious. First, the committee was chosen largely for name recognition, without regard to any real commitment to participation or fund-raising. Little such commitment was shown. Second, the member organizations no longer felt really connected or responsible, so many drifted away, and others ceased or reduced their financial support. Third, the exploratory and start-up grants ran out, leaving the enlarged operation bankrupt.

As a revealing aside, when I recently looked back at the list of one hundred, I was surprised to see that I was on it, which says something about how seriously it was taken, and I had not remembered that John Gardner was also on it, which says something about the connectedness.

It was left to the council of staff to sort through the wreckage and decide if anything was salvageable. I was asked to chair that effort, and the first decision—the only easy one—was that if any part of the organization was to be resurrected, it would have to be tied to its members. That certainly didn't preclude maximum possible participation by others, but there had to be some essential connection between those who were providing financial support and the program and operations.

Some of the decisions were excruciating. For example, during the two years of the failed experiment, the size of the staff had increased greatly, and compensation, including salaries and retirement arrangements, had jumped alarmingly. It would have been easier to put the organization to bed, but many of the functions still needed to be performed, and at least there was something to build from. It took a couple of years to get it all sorted through and back on track.

At IS, there was naturally pressure from the membership to lower the dues, and the pressure from inside the board to avoid undue dependence on soft money. Fortunately, there was rarely any debate about the use of government funds. Our policy prohibiting it was reinforced by every clash we had with government officials and agencies.

We regularly sought short-term grants to help us start up program areas or pursue essential program projects, and we did receive some earned income, such as registration fees and publication revenues, but the emphasis was always on the dues to sustain our ongoing responsibilities. Despite our resolve and a strict policy requiring an annual audit of our performance by the management committee, there were two occasions when we became too dependent on soft money, such as short-term grants, for the support of ongoing staff positions and related expenses. Both slides were corrected at the expense of discouraging cutbacks, but the discouragements and other adverse consequences would have been far greater had we let the situation worsen.

I've learned from all of my mistakes and scars that the three basic questions that have to be addressed when forming a new organization are: Who will pay for it? Can that support be sustained? And will the support compromise the organization's ability to really accomplish its mission?

10. Luck.

We benefited a great deal from the kind of luck that occurs when you are prepared for it, and we also experienced the accidental kind of luck that happens when everything doesn't go wrong all at once, or when great things happen that you couldn't ever have anticipated. We had our share of every kind, and must never be so smug as to think we did it all ourselves.

CHAPTER TWELVE

Hopes Not Realized and Other Regrets

For the most part, this book has concentrated on things that went well, and on balance, most did.

Along the way, I've mentioned some of the downsides, which I was obliged to do for reality's sake. I was tempted to leave it at that, but I find that a fairly common inquiry concerns "what didn't work." On the chance that some enumeration of the disappointments might add to the candor and the lessons, I'll review some of them here. This also gives me an opening to try to stir some of the dreams that haven't come true, at least not yet. I'll start with those.

I had really hoped that by now we would have achieved a far higher level of public awareness and understanding of what the sector is and does, and how much it means to the American experience. My fantasy was, and I guess still is, that someday a very large part of the population will *really* understand and take pride in this independent sector, but I am now much more aware of how difficult that goal is to achieve. Obviously, there's great pride in the progress made. We've contributed to the quantity and quality of news coverage, and the topic is much more in evidence throughout the media, but we have not yet reached the point at which people recognize how much the work of the voluntary sector is threatened. Maybe all I can hope for is much more coverage and an alert understanding among a larger percentage of the millions of our neighborhood, community, regional, and national leaders.

I confess to falling short of what I thought was an even more practical goal within the dream. I envisioned a number of popular books that would help alter public perceptions. As ubiquitous and important as all voluntary participation is, there hasn't been a book to accomplish what Rachel Carson did for the environment with *Silent Spring*. One of my personal frustrations and failures was that I knew from so many speeches to community groups that ours was a subject that really fascinated and encouraged people, but I couldn't find a single publisher interested in a book I had tried to put together, or even interested in encouraging someone in their own stable of writers to try such a book. With some good leads and door openings, we also tried to interest syndicators in a regular column, but they, like the book publishers, just didn't think the topic was popular enough. Some day, someone is going to crack that barrier, and it will represent a giant leap.

A different dream I've clung to is of breaking through a mindset of the sector's leaders and funders that stands in the way of adequate investment in the sector's larger potential. At a time when many leaders of voluntary organizations criticize their counterparts in business for being so fixated on quarterly results that they can't see the future, we overlook the fact that our own long-term scopes seem rusted on "today." The nonprofit sector is the most labor-intensive of the three sectors, but invests by far the least in its paid workforce, and it recoils from spending more for fear of being criticized for high overhead. We worry about the effectiveness of our organizations, agree on the need to attract more bright young people, shudder at the implications of high staff turnover, talk endlessly about expanding the base of financial and volunteer support, and cringe at the paltry levels of investment in planning and evaluation, but we turn our backs on all this common sense with the rationalization that we are too busy doing good, and that no one will give us money to invest in these extras anyway.

When I try to talk about how much businesses spend on human resource development (HRD) and research and development (R&D), leaders of voluntary organizations turn me off as though the comparisons were specious. I generate some attention when I indicate how much money even small and medium-size community governments spend on finding and nurturing young leaders, but the curiosity is mostly grounded in envy. Even leaders who come from business will only stay with me through the part of the conversation that relates to applying their investment practices, but their interest founders on more immediate obligations.

That contradiction among business leaders exists also in corporate philanthropy, which usually fails to practice what corporations do best. One of the pitfalls many companies fall into is to model their philanthropy after private foundations, especially in emphasizing program support and de-emphasizing or prohibiting support for financial and organizational development. I keep urging corporate leaders to ask, "What is it that we and the corporation know and do well that, if applied to voluntary organizations and the nonprofit sector generally, might produce the greatest results?" I believe the priority of corporations should be to strengthen the structure of the organizations they care about rather than to fund those organizations' programs; by making such a shift, they help lay foundations for the work of the future.

Within this dream of investment, I also have a practical and what I believe is a realistic intermediate goal. I've been trying to get a visible and substantial grant maker, or a group of grant makers, to establish what I call "The Growth Fund: A Program for Nonprofit Effectiveness and Growth," which would encourage the application to nonprofit organizations of *building* strategies like those practiced routinely by successful businesses. My growth fund would have four responsibilities:

1. To build into the sector's orientation and practice the idea that investment in capacity building is an essential and seriously neglected function of philanthropic and voluntary organizations.

2. To assist the sector in identifying significant impediments to growth, such as inadequate recruitment and retention of able staff, and to develop strategies for dealing with those impediments.

3. To provide matching funds for diverse, competitively selected projects that have the greatest likelihood of demonstrating that investment in growth pays off.

4. To publicize investment activities of philanthropic and voluntary organizations that are considered models of capacity building.

Possibly related to a growth fund, I also dream about an institution similar to what the military calls a command and general staff college.

Here, the top leaders of our sector would finally have a place to gather to consider the larger issues relating to the sector's growth and future, with the emphasis on the leadership responsibilities that would be entailed in dealing with those issues. There is already an encouraging growth in the number of academic and other centers focused on our sector, and related work is done by the Council on Foundations, IS, and others. Nevertheless, it is still not the practice of very top leaders—those who can make the greatest difference—to come together for large enough blocks of time to *really* explore how the quantum leaps I think are possible for the sector could be achieved.

I also find myself wondering why we could not have made more progress in reaching into the nation's campuses to recruit young people and build pathways for them into and up through our sector. Though labor-intensive, the sector is dispersed, and many of its organizations are small to midsize, which is an impediment to coordinated recruitment efforts. But there is a rich lode of able, motivated, and interested young people that we are failing to tap. That's absolutely crazy. Every time I've tried to organize recruitment experiments, I've been confronted with all the reasons it would be difficult, expensive, or impossible. Until it happens, though, we have no chance of achieving those bigger leaps.

I mentioned earlier my great disappointment that we've not achieved reasonable degrees of public awareness and support, even among the leaders of our society. By now, we should have been farther along in orienting policy makers to what the sector is and does. I'm particularly discouraged that such a goal seems so elusive. Maybe in the long run it will be achieved through the efforts of constituents who press these messages with their elected officials. Maybe, too, we'll see fuller fruits of our work with schools and departments of public administration so that staffs of elected officials will at least have some understanding of our role, in contrast to the fairly pervasive indifference and even suspicion that confronts us now.

The chapter on government relations contains plentiful evidence of our progress, but while acknowledging and taking pride in that, I know we're not going to see much light until there is a more realistic understanding among government officials of the role that philanthropic and voluntary organizations play in the public business of this country. If that's pie in the sky, I will settle, for now, for a Congress that truly understands the relationship between tax policy and levels of charitable contributions, and for state and local legislators who recognize that tax exemption encourages expansion of voluntary initiative, thereby making communities healthier. These legislators must be helped to see that removal of such stimulants as the property tax exemption will cost the community far more dollars than government would gain.

As I look back, I find it terribly, terribly disheartening to note how many of the same battles we have had to fight over and over again. For example, it's heartbreaking that so many people in government, in different administrations and parties, challenge the advocacy role and rights of our organizations. They just don't seem to understand that advocacy is often our best service. When they reflect on the great accomplishments of the sector, such as civil rights, child welfare, changes in attitudes and laws relating to smoking, even they tend to cite the results of our advocacy activities. Perhaps the opposition is due to a belief that advocacy implies criticism. Whatever the cause, these negative attitudes are real and discouraging.

John Gardner was even able to put a positive spin on these never-ending battles. At one point, I was expressing my frustration about the fact that we were struggling with many of the very same issues we had battled time and time again—advocacy rights, tax incentives, postal rates, competition with small businesses, and on and on, ad infinitum. As the litany escalated, John began to nod and smile, seeming to enjoy it all. I asked him if he had *really* been listening and *really* understood what I was saying. "Oh yes," he responded, "but look at it this way, Brian—the members will surely know they need us!"

The economist Joseph Schumpeter helps explain the continuity of these struggles with his observation that inexorably, government will try to centralize power in itself.

I was disappointed that even closer to home than Congress we had achieved relatively little awareness among the country's volunteer leaders of the positive information that we had generated from research and from our leadership and management studies. I think it's fair to say that this awareness is now gradually increasing, but it is still far from widespread.

It was one of my greatest disappointments and deepest blows when we lost the nonitemizer deduction for charitable contributions in the Tax Reform Act of 1986. Fortunately, by that point, we were winning on many other fronts, but IS didn't hide or minimize the loss, and the organization is committed to eventual reversal.

For the sake of completeness, I'll repeat here what I stated in Chapter Seven: that we didn't get as far as I had hoped and expected with our continuing effort to help Americans understand the concept and follow the practice of "giving five," which still is a right goal. We'll get there.

One of the regular causes of grief was the gross misbehavior of some voluntary organizations. I knew from so many years in the field that those awful situations involved only a tiny percentage of all organizations; nevertheless, when someone cheats or misbehaves in the name of charity, it's pretty disheartening and tends to raise questions about the performance of the sector as a whole. I'm proud that IS devoted so much time to helping organizations understand what's expected of them ethically.

Whenever those exposés hit, they at least provided us with the occasion to articulate again, within and outside the organization, the legal and moral obligations we must meet in order to be worthy of the public trust.

There were naturally some criticisms of us that caused distress and regret. For example, to this day, I wish we could have found some way to counter the impression that we were not inclusive, or that we didn't seem interested in the issues of grassroots organizations. Without real success, we tried to explain that many of our member organizations represented grassroots causes and groups, and we would point out constantly that our major advances involved protection of the freedoms of speech and assembly, of which grassroots groups were the primary beneficiaries. Approximately one in six of our members was a very small group, often without any staff, but the organizing committee had felt that at least for the foreseeable future, we had to concentrate on national legislation and regulations, national media, and other national institutions, and that we had to keep the operation manageable. We stretched all those requirements almost to the breaking point, but to have opened the organization to every interested local organization would have totally swamped us in numbers and focus. We established an associate's program to spread the network and the service, but that didn't solve the problem. I'm not sure there was a solution, but I regret I couldn't find one.

Similarly, we did not find the right solution to satisfy those who were establishing state associations of nonprofits and wanted to be our formal affiliates.

Many government relations issues, such as challenges to tax exemption, became particularly pressing at the state and local levels. To address those matters and others, such as pooled purchasing and leadership training, an increasing number of groups were organizing state alliances of voluntary organizations. It was hard for them to collect enough money in dues to establish and maintain much of an operation, and also difficult to get start-up money from very many funders. The latter suggested, among other things, that the state groups affiliate with IS, which sounded fine except that the resulting financial obligations we would have faced would have been at least five or six times our total income. We had already reached out to many of the leaders who were putting these new state groups together so that they were at least in our network, but that wasn't a very satisfying affiliation, particularly when they needed money and other resources to meet needs in their states and the expectations of their members.

Reluctantly and with much criticism from the groups and their prospective funders, we had to decide not to become their official hub. We did everything short of that to help, however. We promoted their funding requests to grant makers, advised on organizational and program development, participated in their national and regional meetings, provided initial funding for their national office, and established, paid for, and eventually transferred to them the important publication *State Tax Trends*.

There were always other groups who thought we didn't do enough for them. We listened hard and adjusted often, but not to everyone's satisfaction. Disappointments are part of the territory, but I wish there had been ways to be even more responsive or at least to explain better why we could not be.

I can't end this litany of regrets without expressing apologies once again for failing to acknowledge in these pages the thousands of wonderful people who made all the good things happen. But had I done so, this would have been a book of names only. These individuals do indeed deserve such a tribute, but a judgment was made—and I have to live with it—that my limited space be devoted to the story of events rather than people. It is a shortcoming and a regret because people, and lots of them, made the difference.

I am unable to think about our low points without experiencing and expressing the personal sorrow involved in the loss of some of the very best of our partners and friends. Three of the original six principals, Phil Bernstein, Bayard Ewing, and Jim Lipscomb, are gone, as is Homer Wadsworth, to whom we entrusted everything between the dissolution of the two founding organizations and the charter meeting of IS. John Filer, a founding board member and third chairperson, has passed. Bob Harlan, our first executive vice president and a very special friend and partner, is gone, too. And we've lost one of our earliest and longest-serving staff members, Skip Helsing. Their departures dwarf all other regrets and sadness.

CHAPTER THIRTEEN

A Personal View of the Future

This book has been about the history of INDEPENDENT SECTOR and the possible lessons to be learned from it. What follows is a personal view of the future. It is certainly not any effort to steer IS's next stage; Sara Meléndez is now in my place and will size things up her own way. New board members will soon be in the majority, and they, too, will look at things afresh. It's a guess (not a recommendation or prescription) that at least for the foreseeable future, they are likely to concentrate in the same areas as those favored in the past. I'm hardly capable of objectivity, but when I review the organizing committee report and think about the most fundamental problems still facing the sector, it is clear to me that the organization will have to continue to address relationships with government—to tell the sector's story, to foster research, and to stand for effectiveness, openness, and account-ability. As John Gardner has said on several occasions, "If we hadn't already created IS, we'd be scrambling to put it together."

In my swan song, after covering many specific examples of our impact to date, I concluded: "If I had to sum it up under one accom-plishment, it would probably be most accurate to indicate that we have proved that this disparate sector can be rallied to the original mission, to create a national forum capable of encouraging the giving, volunteering, and not-for-profit initiative that help all of us to serve people, communities, and causes better." As I look back on my years with IS, and on almost all of my experience with citizen organizations, my quintessential belief is in the absolute need and benefit of citizen involvement and influence in public matters. There is throughout the country and the world a sense of exhilaration when people can have influence over their own destinies. There is a universal yearning to be free. Of all our tasks that remain undone, the fuller pursuit and achievement of such freedom is foremost. In this country we still have a very long way to go to put into awareness and practice John Gardner's axiom:

> Liberty and duty.
> Freedom and responsibility.
> That's the deal.

For my final annual report at IS, I was asked to summarize my predictions for the sector over the next fifteen years. My immediate response was "Bigger and better." I pointed out that the importance of active citizenship and personal community service was being more and more appreciated, and that there was a new commitment to trusteeship, stewardship, and the development of future volunteer and staff leaders. These developments will make our organizations even more effective. With each exhilarating example of impact, other organizations are inclined to feel that they too can make a difference in their communities and causes. As long as INDEPENDENT SECTOR and others can counter the tendency of government to try to restrict the rights of citizens to organize themselves, things will definitely become bigger and better.

As I consider whether the sector will be as vibrant and important twenty-five and even fifty years from now, I find myself equally confident. But it would be irresponsible to leave this hopeful view of the future too generalized and unsubstantiated. For the twenty-fifth anniversary of *Fund Raising Management* I wrote a piece called "The Future Looks Good—For Those Who Invest in It." My assignment was to identify some of the "big issues" that will almost certainly influence the future of voluntary institutions.

Capacity for Giving and Volunteering

- Perhaps the most positive point is that the wellspring of generosity is demonstrably deep and far from tapped out.

- Even in these tough economic times, there are repeated reports of staggering successes in campaigns that reach for hundreds of millions, and even billions.

- IS's surveys continue to indicate that the proportion of income contributed by middle- and even low-income givers is greater than that provided by all but the upper categories of the well-to-do.

- In all categories of income, there is a growing proportion of tithers and fivers, as well as increasing evidence that when people recognize and understand the symbol and standard of "Give Five," they move toward that standard.

- Less than 10 percent of the givers with annual incomes over a quarter of a million dollars account for more than 50 percent of all that is given by people at that income level.

- The largest single reason people give is that they are asked, and the more personal the request, the more likely the gift.

Public Attitudes and Behavior

- IS's studies continue to indicate that public confidence in nonprofit organizations is very high. Obviously, nothing in this observation should cause complacency, but at least the public thinks well of what we do and assumes that we do our work more efficiently than government and with greater concern for individuals than either government or business. It believes that we work toward our goals in an honorable and humane way, with continuing regard for the rights and needs of individuals.

- The public is forgiving if an organization acknowledges its difficulties and works openly to correct them. Covenant House has already returned to the level of support it enjoyed prior to a leadership scandal, and most United Ways have recovered their upward trend after slumping when the president of the national organization was charged with wrong doing.

- It should also be viewed as good news rather than bad that in the face of recent transgressions and negative publicity, the public is becoming increasingly discerning. To merit support, organizations have to be seen as open, accountable, and able to prove their effectiveness. Good performance is by far the best way to vindicate public trust.

- Individual organizations and the sector as a whole should help the public distinguish between effective and ineffective performance. The public should know what questions to ask, where to get information, how to interpret reports—all those skills that enable people to make more informed decisions about appeals for their time and money.

- Ninety percent of the American people contribute money, and more than 50 percent are active volunteers. People want to be involved. Asking, with a clear case, is still the best way to obtain support.

Making the Most of the Positive Trends

- IS's studies in recent years make clear that baby boomers are becoming generous with their time and money, and that teens are even more inclined to accept responsibility for service to community. Given the enormous size of these age groups, the future can be very bright, as long as the favorable dispositions are nurtured and built on.

- Giving of time and money involves a broadening spectrum of Americans, including more older people, men, low-income families, and people with major problems of their own.

- The generosity of persons of color is expanding dramatically. Growing diversity throughout the sector is a particular strength.

- People feel good about being involved and knowing they can make a difference. Even those who are not yet involved admire and envy those who are active and generous.

- Organizations that continue to invest in the quality of their asking continue to set the trend for growth.

Evidence of Impact

- Increasingly, we hear the lament that Americans don't really have a civic spirit anymore. There is a pervasive view that in earlier times, we were far more willing than we are today to help one another and to become involved in causes and public issues.

Actually, the past was not as good as remembered and the present is far better than perceived.

- A far larger proportion and many more parts of our population are involved in community service today than at any time in our history.

- Whether our interest is wildflowers or civil rights, arthritis or clean air, Oriental art or literacy, the dying or the unborn, organizations are already at work, and if they don't suit our passion, it is still possible to start our own.

- We organize to serve every conceivable aspect of the human condition and are willing to stand up and be counted on almost any public issue. We organize to fight zoning changes, approve bond issues, improve garbage collection, expose overpricing, enforce equal rights, and protest wars.

- In very recent times, we have successfully organized to deal with the rights of women, conservation and preservation, learning disabilities, conflict resolution, Hispanic culture and rights, education on the free enterprise system, the aged, voter registration, the environment, Native Americans, the dying, experimental theater, international understanding, population control, neighborhood empowerment, control of nuclear power, consumerism, and on and on. Our interests and impact extend from neighborhoods to the ozone layer and beyond.

Governmental Oversight

- Next to the possible loss of public confidence, the greatest danger involves governmental encroachments on the independence that is the sector's most important and beneficial characteristic. Of course, nothing should deny or impede the government's absolutely appropriate responsibility to be certain that voluntary organizations are worthy of the special privileges provided by tax exemption.

- The full range and intensity of current problems cannot be covered here, but examples include negative interpretations of the very definition of what an exempt organization is and can do; the pervasive misconception that exemption is deserved only by organizations that serve the poorest in our society; revenue shortfalls at all levels of government that are overriding the need to support and sustain voluntary initiative; destructive confusion about the relative roles of the three sectors; serious incursions on the freedoms of speech, assembly, and association, often taking the form of challenges to the advocacy role of voluntary groups; and the raising of serious questions about whether certain institutions, or even whole parts of the sector, are still worthy of tax exemption. (Health-care institutions, particularly, are being challenged to prove their charitable or public purpose.)

- Though the problems are outstripping our ability to deal with them effectively, at least we are much better organized than we were ten or twenty-five years ago, thanks in part to the presence and impact of such groups as IS and the state associations of nonprofits.

Research into Our Role in Society

- There is a fairly urgent need to more clearly understand and articulate the roles *and* the limitations of voluntary organizations.

- There is also an urgent need to understand the changing roles and relationships of the three sectors, including the problems of overlap and competition.

- If we are going to convince the public of our worth, we need to understand and articulate far better than we do at present the impact of philanthropic and voluntary organizations, as well as public attitudes toward us.

- Applied research in fund-raising effectiveness is obviously the order of the day.

- Similarly, we have to devote a good deal more research to marketing, planning, evaluation, collaboration, and many other key aspects of our operations.

Obviously, the news is not all good, but in my view, the outlook for the sector is decidedly positive. For the individual organization that has a worthy cause, is open and accountable, is able to demonstrate its effectiveness, and invests in its development, the outlook is very bright.

A final few words about my own future, which also involves an interesting tale—in fact, something like a fairy tale come true. When I advised the IS board that I would be stepping down at age sixty-five, I knew that I wanted to remain active, but without running anything ever again. I also knew that though many individuals assume that when they retire, the world will beat a path to their door to offer them interesting and remunerative things to do, for most people the phone rarely rings. As I was pondering and exploring how to establish more promising connections, I was approached by Emmett Carson, then of the Ford Foundation, who wanted to know if I planned to continue to be active in areas of mutual interest. I assured him I did and indicated some particular issues I very much welcomed a chance to spend more time on. Emmett then encouraged me to outline those interests in a memo that he could share with the foundation's leaders. He also asked me to seek out an exempt organization with which I could become affiliated and to which Ford could make a grant.

That gloriously encouraging conversation led me to be much more specific about my goals. Above all, I wanted to continue to work on strengthening the capacity of the independent sector here and abroad so that it can be of greatest possible service to society. Second, I hoped to improve understanding of the roles and values of the sector among policy makers and the public. Third, I intended to increase my efforts to promote active citizenship and community service and to help establish a clear understanding of the fundamental relationship between such citizenship and effective communities and societies. And finally, I wanted to help achieve a clearer understanding of the relative public service roles of the governmental and independent sectors and to build bridges between leaders of both sectors for greater cooperation and coordination.

I looked for a comfortable affiliation that would be compatible with these goals and would allow me to concentrate on them without expectations of other heavy responsibilities. The organization that best fit that bill turned out to be the Lincoln Filene Center for Citizenship and Public Affairs at Tufts University.

After three-way discussions and clarifications, there was agreement that all of us wanted to advance work in the areas I'd chosen, and that Emmett and the Ford leadership would be willing to provide three years of support, with the possibility of two additional years. All of this was subject to formal application by Tufts and approval by Ford. Subsequently, the application was approved, and I was appointed professor of public service.

The degree of concentration and the horizons of my work were extended when the Kellogg Foundation joined Ford as a primary sponsor and the Mott and Hearst foundations added their encouragement and support.

And thus it has turned out that there is indeed life after INDEPENDENT SECTOR!

Fortunately, I'm able to continue my identification with IS under the title founding president, but with no intention of being under foot or of looking over Sara's shoulder.

I said in my last "Memo to Members": "By the time you get this, Sara Meléndez will have taken over as president and will begin to put her own good stamp on future Memos and much else. This will be about my 500th Memo. That's about 17 years of one person's slant, leaving you ready if not gasping for a fresh voice."

I ended that memo with the indication that because of my dual identification with IS and the Filene Center, they weren't rid of me altogether. I concluded: "So this is hardly 'farewell.' But it does give me an additional opportunity to express thanks to the Membership and acknowledge how much you have contributed to heartening developments, with more to come."

Together, we demonstrated the power of association.

Appendixes

M y quandary throughout this project has been whether to write exclusively for future leaders of INDEPENDENT SECTOR and for researchers and historians, or also for audiences interested in a broader view of philanthropy and voluntary action and in the specific topic of coalition building.

To try to be of interest and service to all three groups has required some compromises, one of which was not to pile into the appendices many documents that would have appealed only to serious students of the organization or sector. However, for this small but important group, we have established the IS archives at Indiana University. I encourage interested readers to make use of this facility. They should write to Indiana University Archives, 755 West Michigan Street, Room 0133, Indianapolis, IN 46202, or call (317) 274–0464.

The archives already contain many documents relating at least to the first ten years of IS, including board and committee agenda packets, minutes, and other materials. The organization's commitment is to ensure that the archives reflect a full and accurate history. For example, all the records and resource materials that I've assembled for this book will be transferred there.

The appendixes that follow are now limited to items likely to be of interest to a cross-section of readers who share a curiosity about the types of people and organizations involved in our broad coalition.

Roster of Charter Members

CHARTER ASSOCIATE MEMBERS

This was a membership category for eligible organizations that paid full dues but preferred not to become full members.

Allied Chemical Corporation
Caterpillar Tractor Company
Celanese Corporation
Consolidated Natural Gas
  Company
Crocker National Bank
  Foundation
East Ohio Gas Company
Essick Foundation, Inc.

General Mills Foundation
International Paper Company
  Foundation
Olin Corporation
PPG Industries
Price Waterhouse Foundation
Sears Roebuck and Company
Security Pacific Charitable
  Foundation

VOTING MEMBERS

Aetna Life and Casualty Company
Agudath Israel of America
Alcoa Foundation
Alliance for Volunteerism

American Arts Alliance
American Association of
  Community and Junior
  Colleges

American Association
of Fund-Raising Counsel, Inc.
American Association
of Homes for the Aging
American Association
of Museums
American Cancer Society
American Council for the Arts
American Federation of Arts
American Heart Association
American Hospital Association
American Lung Association
American Red Cross
American Social Health
Association
American Telephone and
Telegraph
American Theatre Association
Appalachian Mountain Club
Arrow, Inc.
Association for International
Practical Training
Association of Black Foundation
Executives, Inc.
Association of Governing Board
of Universities and Colleges
Association of Jesuit Colleges
and Universities
Association of Junior Leagues,
Inc.
Atlantic Richfield Foundation
Mary Reynolds Babcock Foun-
dation
BankAmerica Foundation
Bethlehem Steel Corporation
Borden Foundation
Bristol-Myers Fund
Camp Fire, Inc.
Carnegie Corporation of New
York
Carter Hawley Hale Stores, Inc.

CBS, Inc.
Center for Responsive
Governance
Chase Manhattan Bank, N.A.
Chevron U.S.A., Inc.
Children's Aid International
Cleveland Foundation
Conoco, Inc.
Continental Group Foundation,
Inc.
Council for the Advancement
and Support of Education
Council for the Advancement
of Small Colleges
Council for American Private
Education
Council for Financial Aid to
Education
Council of Better Business
Bureaus/Philanthropic
Advisory Service Division
Council of Jewish Federations
Council on Foundations
CPC International, Inc.
Charles A. Dana Foundation,
Inc.
Dart Industries
Dayton Hudson Foundation
Deere and Company
Geraldine R. Dodge Foundation
Gaylord Donnelly Foundation
E. I. du Pont de Nemours
and Company
Durfee Foundation
Eastman Kodak Company
Eaton Corporation
Epilepsy Foundation of America
Equitable Life Assurance Society
of the United States
Family Service Association
of America

Ford Motor Company Fund
Foremost-McKesson
  Foundation, Inc.
Foundation Center
Fresh Air Fund
Gannett Newspaper Foundation
General Conference of Seventh
  Day Adventists
General Electric Company
General Motors Corporation
Girl Scouts of the U.S.A.
Grace Foundation, Inc.
Grotto Foundation
Gulf + Western Foundation
George Gund Foundation
Hawaiian Foundation
Edward W. Hazen Foundation
Hewlett-Packard Company
  Foundation
Hogg Foundation for Mental
  Health
Hospital Research and
  Educational Trust
IBM Corporation
Independent College Funds
  of America, Inc.
Independent Research Libraries
  Association
International Service Agencies
International Telephone and
  Telegraph
James Irvine Foundation
Jerome Foundation
Johnson and Johnson
Joint Action in Community
  Service
Henry J. Kaiser Family
  Foundation
Charles F. Kettering Foundation
Leukemia Society of America,
  Inc.

Levi Strauss Foundation
Lilly Endowment, Inc.
Lutheran Council in the U.S.A.
Lutheran Resources
  Commission—Washington
March of Dimes Birth Defects
  Foundation
Merck Company Foundation
Joyce Mertz-Gilmore
  Foundation
Metropolitan Life Foundation
John Milton Society for the
  Blind
Philip Morris, Inc.
Charles Stewart Mott
  Foundation
National Assembly of
  Community Arts Agencies
National Assembly of National
  Voluntary Health and Social
  Welfare Organizations, Inc.
National Assembly of State Arts
  Agencies
National Association for
  Hospital Development
National Association of
  Independent Colleges
  and Universities
National Association of Schools
  of Art
National Association of Schools
  of Music
National Audubon Society
National Black Media Coalition
National Board of Young Men's
  Christian Associations
National Board of Young
  Women's Christian
  Association of the U.S.A.
National Catholic Development
  Conference, Inc.

National Coalition of Hispanic
  Mental Health and Human
  Services Organizations
National Community Education
  Association
National Concilio of America
National Conference of Catholic
  Charities
National Council of the
  Churches of Christ in
  the U.S.A.
National Council of La Raza
National Council of Women
  of the United States, Inc.
National Executive Service Corps
National Health Council, Inc.
National Information Bureau,
  Inc.
National Mental Health
  Association
National School Volunteer
  Program, Inc.
National Self-Help
  Clearinghouse
National Society for Autistic
  Children
National Society of Fund Raising
  Executives
National Trust for Historic
  Preservation
National Urban Coalition
National Urban Fellows, Inc.
National Urban League, Inc.
National Wildlife Federation
Nature Conservancy
New World Foundation
New York Community Trust
New York Life Foundation
Nordson Foundation
Northwest Area Foundation

Opera America
Overseas Development Council
Owens-Illinois, Inc.
Parents Without Partners
J. C. Penney Company, Inc.
People-to-People International
Pepsico Foundation, Inc.
Pfizer Foundation, Inc.
Planned Parenthood Federation
  of America, Inc.
Population Resource Center
Procter and Gamble Fund
Prudential Foundation
RCA Corporation
Reading Is Fundamental, Inc.
Republic Steel Corporation
Rosenberg Foundation
Safeco Insurance Companies
Salvation Army
San Francisco Foundation
Schering-Plough Corporation
Dr. Scholl Foundation
Shell Companies Foundation,
  Inc.
Sherwin-Williams Company
Lois and Samuel Silberman
  Fund
Alfred P. Sloan Foundation
Spencer Foundation
Standard Oil Company (Ohio)
Student Conservation
  Association, Inc.
Support Center
Synagogue Council of America
Syntex (U.S.A.), Inc.
Teachers Insurance and Annuity
  Association of America/
  College Retirement Equities
  Fund (TIAA-CREF)
3M Company

Time Inc.
Times Mirror Foundation
Trebor Foundation
Trust for Public Land
Union Carbide Foundation
Union of Independent Colleges
 of Art
United Negro College Fund
United States Catholic
 Conference
United States Committee
 for UNICEF
United States Olympic
 Committee
United States Steel Foundation,
 Inc.
United Way of America
VOLUNTEER: The National
 Center for Citizen
 Involvement
Volunteers of America
Izaak Walton League of America
Westinghouse Electric Fund
Women and Foundations/
 Corporate Philanthropy
Xerox Corporation
Zero Population Growth

The Start-Up Funders

Atlantic Richfield Foundation
Mary Reynolds Babcock
  Foundation, Inc.
Bush Foundation
Carnegie Corporation
  of New York
Chase Manhattan Bank, N.A.
Cleveland Foundation
Commonwealth Fund
Charles A. Dana Foundation, Inc.
Dayton Hudson Foundation
Francis Drown Foundation
Educational Foundation of
  America and The Ettinger
  Foundation
Equitable Life Assurance Society
  of the United States
Fluor Corporation

Ford Foundation
Gannett Newspaper
  Foundation, Inc.
George Gund Foundation
William and Flora Hewlett
  Foundation
James Irvine Foundation
Ittleson Foundation, Inc.
Robert Wood Johnson
  Foundation
Henry J. Kaiser Family
  Foundation
Lilly Endowment, Inc.
John and Mary R. Markle
  Foundation
Andrew W. Mellon
  Foundation
Philip Morris, Inc.

Charles Stewart Mott
  Foundation
Nordson Foundation
Northwest Area Foundation
Rockefeller Foundation

Russell Sage Foundation
Alfred P. Sloan Foundation
Spencer Foundation
Times Mirror
Trebor Foundation, Inc.

1995 Membership Roster

AAFRC Trust for Philanthropy
AASK America Adopt a Special
 Kid
Access Video Fund
ACCESS: Networking
 in the Public Interest
Accountants for the Public
 Interest
Advertising Council
Advocacy Institute
Aetna Foundation
Affiliated Leadership League
 of and for the Blind of
 America
Africa Fund
Aga Khan Foundation U.S.A.
Agricultural Educational
 Foundation
Aid Association for Lutherans

Aid to Artisans
Alcoa Foundation
Horatio Alger Association
 of Distinguished Americans
Alliance for International
 Education and Cultural
 Exchange
Allied-Signal Foundation
Alzheimer's Association
America's Charities
America's Development
 Foundation
American Arts Alliance
American Association
 for Higher Education
American Association for the
 Advancement of Science
American Association of
 Community Colleges

American Association
of Fund-Raising Counsel
American Association
of Museums
American Association
of Retired Persons
American Association
of University Women
American Autoimmune Related
Diseases Association
American Cancer Society
American Chemical Society
American Council for the Arts
American Council of Learned
Societies
American Council
on Education
American Craft Council
American Diabetes Association
American Ditchley Foundation
American Express Foundation
American Farmland Trust
American Fisheries Society
American Foundation for AIDS
Research
American Foundation
for the Blind
American Heart Association
American Humane Association
American Humanics
American Indian College Fund
American Indian Graduate
Center
American Institute for Cancer
Research
American Institute
of Philanthropy
American Leadership Forum
American Library Association

American Medical Association
American Museum of Natural
History
American Red Cross National
Headquarters
American Social Health
Association
American Solar Energy Society
American Stock Exchange
American Symphony Orchestra
League
American Tinnitus Association
American Women Composers
Americans for Indian
Opportunity
Americans for Medical Progress
Educational Foundation
Amigos de las Americas
Amoco Foundation
Apple Computer
Applied Research and
Development Institute
Arc of the United States
Arca Foundation
ARCO Foundation
Arizona Community
Foundation
ARROW
Arthritis Foundation
Arts & Business Council
Asian Pacific American Legal
Consortium
Aspen Institute
ASPIRA Association
Associated Grantmakers
of Massachusetts
Association for Healthcare
Philanthropy
Association for Research

on Nonprofit Organizations & Voluntary Action

Association for Volunteer Administration

Association of Advanced Rabbinical & Talmudic Schools

Association of America's Public Television Stations

Association of American Universities

Association of American University Presses

Association of Art Museum Directors

Association of Black Foundation Executives

Association of Catholic Colleges and Universities

Association of Episcopal Colleges

Association of Governing Boards of Universities and Colleges

Association of Jesuit Colleges and Universities

Association of Jewish Family and Children's Agencies

Association of Junior Leagues International

Association of Lutheran Development Executives

Association of Performing Arts Presenters

Association of Science-Technology Centers

Association of Theological Schools

AT&T Foundation

Atlantic Foundation of New York

Mary Reynolds Babcock Foundation

Bainbridge Educational Foundation

Ball Brothers Foundation

Association of Baltimore Area Grantmakers

Battle Creek Community Foundation

Bauman Foundation

BellSouth Corporation

Benton Foundation

Beverly Foundation

Big Brothers/Big Sisters of America

Bing Fund Corporation

Blandin Foundation

Blanton-Peale/Institutes of Religion and Health

H&R Block Foundation

Blue Cross of California, Public Benefit Programs

Borden Foundation

Boston Foundation

Boy Scouts of America

Boys and Girls Clubs of America

Brain Trauma Foundation

Otto Bremer Foundation

Bristol-Myers Squibb Foundation

Brunswick Foundation

Burnett Foundation

Edyth Bush Charitable Foundation

Bush Foundation

Patrick and Aimee Butler Foundation

California Association of Nonprofits

California Community
Foundation
California Wellness Foundation
Camp Fire Boys and Girls
Cancer Care
CARE
Carnegie Corporation
of New York
Annie E. Casey Foundation
Catalyst
Caterpillar Foundation
Catholic Charities USA
CBS Foundation
Center for Applied Linguistics
Center for Corporate Public
Involvement
Center for Creative Leadership
Center for Creative Management
Center for Media Education
Center for Non-Profit
Corporations
Center for Nonprofit
Management, University
of St. Thomas
Center for Policy Alternatives
Center for Public Service, Seton
Hall University
Center for Research in
Ambulatory Health Care
Administration
Center for the Study
of Philanthropy-City
University of NY
Center for the Study
of the Presidency
Center for Women's Policy
Studies
Centre on Philanthropy
Challenger Center for Space
Science Education

Champion International
Corporation
Chase Manhattan Bank, N.A.
Chevron Companies
Chicago Community Trust
Chicago Tribune Foundation
Child Care Action Campaign
Child Health Foundation
Child Welfare League of America
Children's Aid International
Children's Fund of Connecticut
Chorus America (APVE)
Christian Church Foundation
Christmas in April USA
Chrysler Corporation Fund
Church Women United
Citibank
Citizens' Scholarship
Foundation of America
City Cares of America
City Innovation
City of Hope National Medical
Center
Edna McConnell Clark
Foundation
Cleveland Foundation
Van Cliburn Foundation
Clorox Company Foundation
Close Up Foundation
Coca-Cola Company
College and University Personnel
Association
College Board
Colonial Williamsburg
Foundation
Colorado Association
of Nonprofit Organizations
Colorado Trust
Columbia Foundation
Columbus Foundation

Combined Health Appeal
of America
Comerica Incorporated
Committee for a Responsible
Federal Budget
Commonwealth Community
Foundations
Commonwealth Fund
Communications Consortium
Community Anti-Drug
Coalitions of America
Community Foundation
of Greater Flint
Community Foundation
for Greater New Haven
Community Foundation
for Palm Beach & Martin
Counties
Community Foundation
for Southeastern Michigan
Community Foundation
of Greater Memphis
Community Foundation
of Metropolitan Tarrant
County
Compeer, Inc.
Compton Foundation
Conference of National Park
Cooperating Associations
Conference of Southwest
Foundations
Congress of National Black
Churches
Conservation Fund
Consortium of Endowed
Episcopal Parishes
Continental Corporation
Foundation
Cooperative Development
Foundation

Coordinating Council
for Foundations
Corning Incorporated
Foundation
Coro/Eastern Center
Corporation for Enterprise
Development
Council for Advancement
and Support of Education
Council for American Private
Education
Council of Better Business
Bureaus/Philanthropic
Advisory Service
Council of Energy Resource
Tribes
Council of Independent Colleges
Council of Jewish Federations
Council of Michigan
Foundations
Council on Economic
Priorities
Council on Foundations
Council on International
and Public Affairs
Counterpart Foundation
Cowles Media Company/Cowles
Media Foundation
CPC International
Cystic Fibrosis Foundation
Dade Community Foundation
Charles A. Dana Foundation
Dance/USA
Danforth Foundation
Dayton Hudson Foundation
Deafness Research Foundation
Delaware Association of
Nonprofit Agencies
Direct Relief International
Geraldine R. Dodge Foundation

Dole Foundation for
  Employment of People
  with Disabilities
Gaylord and Dorothy Donnelley
  Foundation
R. R. Donnelley & Sons Co.
Donors Forum of Chicago
Donors Forum of Ohio
Donors Forum of Wisconsin
Dow Chemical Company
Joseph Drown Foundation
Peter F. Drucker Foundation
  for Nonprofit Management
Drug Policy Foundation
Duke Endowment
DuPont
Durfee Foundation
Dyson Foundation
Earth Share
Eastman Kodak Company
Ecolab Foundation
Ecumenical Center for
  Stewardship Studies
Educational Testing Service
El Pomar Foundation
Elderhostel
Elderworks
Enterprise Foundation
Environmental Defense Fund
Environmental Media Services
Environmental Support Center
Epilepsy Foundation of America
Equitable Foundation
Eureka Communities
Evangelical Council for Financial
  Accountability
Evangelical Lutheran Church
  in America
Exxon Corporation

Fairfield County Community
  Foundation
Maurice Falk Medical Fund
Families International
Fannie Mae Foundation
Fel-Pro/Mecklenburger
First Interstate Bank
  of California Foundation
First Nations Development
  Institute
First Nonprofit Companies
Father Flanagan's Boys' Home
Florida Association of Nonprofit
  Organizations
Food Research and Action
  Center
Ford Foundation
Ford Motor Company Fund
Henry Ford Museum
  and Greenfield Village
Foreign Policy Association
Foundation Center
Foundation for Advancements
  in Science and Education
Foundation for Independent
  Higher Education
Foundation for the Carolinas
Foundation for the National
  Capital Region
Freedom Forum
Fresh Air Fund
Frey Foundation
Friends of the National Library
  of Medicine
Lloyd A. Fry Foundation
H. B. Fuller Company
Fund for New Jersey
Fund for Theological Education
GE Fund

General Board of Global
Ministries, United Methodist
Church
General Conference
of Seventh-Day Adventists
General Mills Foundation
General Service Foundation
Wallace Alexander Gerbode
Foundation
J. Paul Getty Trust
Gifts in Kind America
Giraffe Project
Girl Scouts of the U.S.A.
Girls Incorporated
Global Fund for Women
Richard & Rhonda Goldman
Fund
Morris Goldseker Foundation
of Maryland
Goodwill Industries
International
Goodyear Tire & Rubber
Company
Edwin Gould Foundation
for Children
Graco Foundation
Grand Rapids Foundation
Grantmakers in Health
Grantmakers of Western
Pennsylvania
Greater Bridgeport Area
Foundation
Greater Worcester Community
Foundation
Lucile & Robert H. Gries Charity
Fund
George Bird Grinnell American
Indian Children's Fund
Grotto Foundation

GTE Foundation
George Gund Foundation
Alan Guttmacher Institute
Miriam and Peter Haas Fund
Walter and Elise Haas Fund
Evelyn and Walter Haas, Jr. Fund
Walter A. Haas School
of Business, Public and
Nonprofit Management,
University of California
Habitat for Humanity
International
Hallmark Corporate Foundation
Luke B. Hancock Foundation
Mary W. Harriman Foundation
Harris Trust & Savings Bank
Hartford Foundation for Public
Giving
Hawaii Community Foundation
Charles Hayden Foundation
Hazelden Foundation
Edward W. Hazen Foundation
Healing Community
William Randolph Hearst
Foundations
William and Flora Hewlett
Foundation
High/Scope Educational
Research Foundation
Hispanic Association of Colleges
and Universities
Hispanic Association
on Corporate Responsibility
Hispanic Policy Development
Project
Hispanics in Philanthropy
Hitachi Foundation
Hoblitzelle Foundation
Hoffman-La Roche Foundation

Hogg Foundation for Mental
Health
Hole in the Wall Gang Fund
Honeywell Foundation
Hospital for Special Surgery
Hostelling International-
American Youth Hostels
Housing Assistance Council
Hudson-Webber Foundation
Huffy Foundation
Human Life International
Humboldt Area Foundation
Hubert H. Humphrey Institute,
Public Policy, Philanthropy
and the Nonprofit Sector
Roy A. Hunt Foundation
Huntington's Disease Society
of America
IBM Corporation
Illinois Association of Nonprofit
Organization
IMPACT II
Independent Charities
of America
Indiana Donors Alliance
Indiana University Center
on Philanthropy
Innovation Network
Institute for Educational
Leadership
Institute for Women's Policy
Research
Intel Foundation
InterAction-American Council
for Voluntary International
Action
Interlochen Center for the Arts
International Center for the
Disabled

International Center
for Journalists
International Development
Conference
International Executive Service
Corps
International Primate Protection
League
International Service Agencies
International Society for Third
Sector Research
James Irvine Foundation
Ittleson Foundation
Jacksonville Community
Foundation
JCC Association of North
America
Jerome Foundation
Jewett Foundation
JM Foundation
Johnson & Johnson
Johnson Foundation
Walter S. Johnson Foundation
Christian A. Johnson Endeavor
Foundation
Robert Wood Johnson
Foundation
Joint Action in Community
Service
Joint Center for Political
and Economic Studies
Josephson Institute of Ethics
Jostens Foundation
Joyce Foundation
JSJ Foundation
Alexander Julian Foundation
Junior Achievement
Henry J. Kaiser Family
Foundation

Kaman Corporation
Greater Kanawha Valley Foundation
Ewing Marion Kauffman Foundation
W. K. Kellogg Foundation
James S. Kemper Foundation
Harris and Eliza Kempner Fund
Kerr Foundation
Charles F. Kettering Foundation
Kids Voting USA
Carl B. & Florence E. King Foundation
Esther & Joseph Klingenstein Fund
John S. and James L. Knight Foundation
Kosciuszko Foundation
KPMG Peat Marwick Foundation
Kresge Foundation
Samuel H. Kress Foundation
Albert Kunstadter Family Foundation
Land Stewardship Project
Land Trust Alliance
Laubach Literacy Action
Laurel Foundation
Lawyers' Committee for Civil Rights Under Law
League of Women Voters of the United States
Sara Lee Foundation
Leukemia Society of America
Levi Strauss & Co.
The Lighthouse, Inc.
Eli Lilly and Company
Lilly Endowment

Lincoln Filene Center, Tufts University
Literacy Volunteers of America
Local Initiatives Support Corporation
George Lucas Educational Foundation
Lupus Foundation of America
Lutheran Brotherhood Foundation
John D. and Catherine T. MacArthur Foundation
Mallinckrodt Group
MANA, A National Latina Organization
Mandel Center for Nonprofit Organizations, Case Western Reserve University
March for Life Education & Defense Fund
March of Dimes Birth Defects Foundation
Marin Community Foundation
John and Mary R. Markle Foundation
Marsh & McLennan Companies
Maryland Association of Nonprofit Organizations
MATHCOUNTS
Matsushita Electric Corporation of America
Mayo Foundation
McConnell Foundation
Robert R. McCormick Tribune Foundation
McGregor Fund
McKesson Foundation
McKnight Foundation
Meadows Foundation

Medical Education for South African Blacks

Medtronic

Richard King Mellon Foundation

Memorial Sloan-Kettering Cancer Center

Menninger Foundation

John Merck Fund

Mercy Medical Airlift

Merrill Lynch & Company Foundation

Metropolitan Association for Philanthropy

Metropolitan Atlanta Community Foundation

Metropolitan Life Foundation

Metropolitan Museum of Art

Mexican American Legal Defense and Educational Fund

Eugene and Agnes E. Meyer Foundation

Michigan Nonprofit Forum

Midwest Center for Nonprofit Leadership, L. P. Cookingham Institute

John Milton Society for the Blind

Milwaukee Foundation

Minneapolis Foundation

Minnesota Council of Nonprofits

Minnesota Mutual Foundation

Mississippi Center for Nonprofits

Mobil Foundation

Monsanto Fund

Moore Foundation

Stewart R. Mott Charitable Trust

Charles Stewart Mott Foundation

Muscular Dystrophy Association

Museum Trustee Association

Muskegon Country Community Foundation

Mutual of New York

NAACP Legal Defense and Educational Fund

National ABLE Network

National Academy of Public Administration

National Action Council for Minorities in Engineering

National AIDS Fund

National Alliance for Choice in Giving

National Alliance for the Mentally Ill

National Alliance of Breast Cancer Organizations

National Alliance of Business

National Assembly of Local Arts Agencies

National Assembly of National Voluntary Health and Social Welfare Organizations

National Assembly of State Arts Agencies

National Assistance League

National Association for Bilingual Education

National Association for Community Leadership

National Association for Visually Handicapped

National Association of Community Action Agencies

National Association of Homes and Services for Children

National Association of Independent Colleges and Universities

National Association of Independent Schools

National Association of Schools of Art and Design

National Association of Schools of Dance

National Association of Schools of Music

National Association of Schools of Public Affairs and Administration

National Association of Schools of Theatre

National Association of Service & Conservation Corps

National Association of Student Personnel Administrators

National Association of United Methodist Foundations

National Association on Drug Abuse Problems

National Associations in Colorado Springs

National Audubon Society

National Board for Professional Teaching Standards

National Catholic Development Conference

National Catholic Educational Association

National Center for Learning Disabilities

National Center for Nonprofit Boards

National Charities Information Bureau

National Civic League

National College Access Network

National Committee for Responsive Philanthropy

National Committee to Prevent Child Abuse

National Community Reinvestment Coalition

National Concilio of America

National Conference

National Congress for Community Economic Development

National Consumers League

National Council for Adoption

National Council for International Visitors

National Council for Research on Women

National Council of Educational Opportunity Associations

National Council of La Raza

National Council of Nonprofit Associations

National Council of Private Agencies for the Blind and Visually Impaired

National Council of the Churches of Christ in the USA

National Council on Child Abuse & Family Violence

National Council on Economic Education

National Cultural Alliance

National Down Syndrome Society

National Easter Seal Society

National Executive Service Corps
National FFA Foundation
National Foundation for Cancer Research
National Foundation for the Centers for Disease Control and Prevention
National Fund for Medical Education
National Geographic Society Education Foundation
National Headache Foundation
National Health Council
National Health Foundation
National Hispana Leadership Institute
National Hispanic Scholarship Fund
National Home Library Foundation
National Hospice Organization
National Humanities Alliance
National Institute for Dispute Resolution
National Institute for the Conservation of Cultural Property
National Interfaith Hospitality Networks
National Lekotek Center
National Medical Fellowships
National Military Family Association
National Multiple Sclerosis Society
National Neighborhood Coalition
National Network for Youth
National Network of Women's Funds

National Park Foundation
National Parkinson Foundation
National Peace Corps Association
National Press Foundation
National Public Radio
National Puerto Rican Coalition
National Retiree Volunteer Coalition
National Society for Experiential Education
National Society of Fund Raising Executives
National Stroke Association
National Trust for Historic Preservation
National Urban Fellows, Inc.
National Urban League
National Victim Center
National Wildlife Federation
National Youth Employment Coalition
Native American Rights Fund
Native Americans in Philanthropy
Natural Resources Defense Council
Nature Conservancy
Neighborhood Reinvestment Corporation
New Hampshire Charitable Foundation
New York Botanical Garden
New York Community Trust
New York Life Insurance Company
New York Public Library
New York Regional Association of Grantmakers

New York Times Company
   Foundation
Nokomis Foundation
Nonprofit Academic Centers
   Council
Nonprofit Coordinating
   Committee of New York
Nonprofit Management
   Association
Nonprofit Management
   Program, New School
   for Social Research
Nonprofit Resource Center
Nord Family Foundation
Nordson Corporation
   Foundation
North American Association
   for Environmental Education
North Carolina Center
   or Nonprofit Organizations
Northern California
   Grantmakers
Northwest Area Foundation
NOW Legal Defense
   and Education Fund
NYNEX Foundation
Oakleaf Foundation
OICs of America
Older Women's League
OPERA America
Operation Smile International
Oral Health America
Outward Bound USA
Pacific Telesis Foundation
David and Lucile Packard
   Foundation
Paget Foundation
Parish of Trinity Church
   in the City of New York
Parents Anonymous

Park Ridge Center for the Study
   of Health, Faith and Ethics
Partners of the Americas
Pax World Service
Peninsula Community
   Foundation
J. C. Penney Company
People-to-People Health
   Foundation
Pew Charitable Trusts
Pfizer Foundation
Philanthropic Group
Philip Morris Companies
Piton Foundation
Pittsburgh Foundation
Planetary Society
Points of Light Foundation
Population Council
Population Resource Center
Premier Industrial Foundation
Presbyterian Health
   Foundation
Presbyterian Women
Presidential Classroom
   for Young Americans
Prince Charitable Trusts
Princeton Project 55
Private Agencies Collaborating
   Together
Private Sector Initiatives
   Foundation
Pro Choice Resource Center
Procter & Gamble Fund
Project Hope
Project SEED
Prudential Foundation
Public Affairs Council
Public Agenda Foundation
Public Allies
Public Education Fund Network

Public Leadership Education
  Network
Public Radio International
Puerto Rican Legal Defense and
  Education Fund
Quest International
Radio and Television News
  Directors Foundation
Rainbow Research
Raychem Corporation
Raytheon Company
Reader's Digest Foundation
Reading is Fundamental
Recording for the Blind and
  Dyslexic
Reinberger Foundation
Religion in American Life
Replication and Program
  Strategies
Research! America
Resourceful Women
Retirement Research Foundation
Charles H. Revson Foundation
Rhone-Poulenc, Inc.
Sid W. Richardson Foundation
Mabel Louise Riley Foundation
Fannie E. Rippel Foundation
Rochester Area Foundation
Rockefeller Brothers Fund
Rockefeller Family Fund
Rockefeller Financial Services
Rockefeller Foundation
Rohm and Haas Company
Rosenberg Foundation
SAFECO Insurance Companies
Saint Paul Companies
Saint Paul Foundation
Salk Institute for Biological
  Studies
Salvation Army

San Antonio Area Foundation
San Francisco Foundation
Sarkeys Foundation
Save the Children Federation
Dr. Scholl Foundation
School Food Service Foundation
School for Field Studies
Sears Merchandise Group
Seattle Foundation
Second Harvest
Shepherd's Centers of America
Sherwin-Williams Company
Sierra Club
Sierra Health Foundation
Harry Singer Foundation
Sister Fund
Skillbuilders Fund
Skillman Foundation
Alfred P. Sloan Foundation
Smithsonian Institution
John Ben Snow Foundation
Social Welfare Research Institute,
  Boston College
Society for Values in Higher
  Education
South-North News Service
Southeastern Council
  of Foundations
Southern California Association
  for Philanthropy
Southern Education Foundation
Spencer Foundation
Spunk Fund
W. Clement & Jessie V. Stone
  Foundation
Stronghold Foundation
Student Conservation
  Association
Student Pugwash USA
Studio Museum in Harlem

Subaru of America Foundation
Support Centers of America
Synergos Institute
Taconic Foundation
Taft Institute
Tandy Corporation
TechnoServe
Tenet Healthcare Corporation
Tenneco
Texaco Foundation
Theatre Communications Group
3M
Time Warner
Travelers Aid International
Trilateral Commission
Trust for Public Land
TV-Free America
Union Institute Center
   for Public Policy
United Cerebral Palsy
   Associations
United Leukodystrophy
   Foundation
United Negro College Fund
United Scleroderma Foundation
United States Catholic
   Conference
United States Committee
   for UNICEF
United States-China Educational
   Institute
United Way International
United Way of America
University of Pennsylvania
   Center for Community
   Partnerships
University of San Francisco-
   Institute for Nonprofit
   Organization Management
UPS Foundation

U.S. Trust Company Foundation
US West Foundation
Vellore Christian Medical
   College Board (USA)
Very Special Arts
Vesper Society
Visiting Nurse Associations
   of America
Volunteers of America
Volvo North America
   Corporation
Izaak Walton League of America
Washington Center
Washington Council of Agencies
Washington Mutual Savings
   Bank
Washington Regional
   Association of Grantmakers
WAVE
Wege Foundation
Weingart Foundation
Weyerhauser Family Foundation
Whirlpool Foundation
Mrs. Giles Whiting Foundation
Amherst H. Wilder Foundation
Woodrow Wilson National
   Fellowship Foundation
Winston-Salem Foundation
Wisconsin Energy Corporation
   Foundation
Women and Philanthropy
Women in Communications
Women's College Coalition
Women's Funding Network
Women's Philharmonic
Women's Research & Education
   Institute
Robert W. Woodruff
   Foundation
Woods Fund of Chicago

World Federation for Mental
  Health
World Institute on Disability
World Resources Institute
World Vision
Wyman Youth Trust

Xerox Corporation
YMCA of the USA
Young Audiences
Youth Service America
YWCA of the USA
Zellerbach Family Fund

Board Members
1980–1995

Affiliations are as of the time of election to the board.

Rebecca Adamson, First Nations Development Institute
Kenneth L. Albrecht, The Equitable Life Assurance Society
   of the U.S.A.
Luis Alvarez, National Urban Fellows
William Aramony, United Way of America
Tomas Arciniega, California State College, Bakersfield
Robert H. Atwell, American Council on Education
Nancy R. Axelrod, National Center for Nonprofit Boards
Gwendolyn Calvert Baker, YWCA of the USA
Charles Bannerman, Delta Foundation
Judy Barker, Borden Foundation, Inc.
James J. Bausch, Save the Children
Thomas F. Beech, Burnett-Tandy Foundation
Judy Belk, Levi Strauss & Co.
Douglas J. Bennet, National Public Radio
Philip Bernstein, Council of Jewish Federations
Landrum R. Bolling, Council on Foundations

William L. Bondurant, Mary Reynolds Babcock Foundation
Arie R. Brouwer, National Council of Churches of Christ in the USA
Janet Welsh Brown, Environmental Defense Fund
Michael H. Brown, City Year
Norman A. Brown, W. K. Kellogg Foundation
Anne L. Bryant, American Association of University Women
Peter McE. Buchanan, Council for Advancement and Support
   of Education
Joan Brown Campbell, National Council of Churches of Christ
   in the USA
Lisle Carter, United Way of America
Frank T. Cary, IBM Corporation
Rosemary Higgins Cass, National Council on Philanthropy
Emelda M. Cathcart, Time Warner Inc.
Elaine L. Chao, United Way of America
Carolyn Chin, AT&T
Linda Hawes Clever, Presbyterian Hospital of Pacific Medical Center
Sanford Cloud Jr., Aetna Life and Casualty Company
David Cohen, Advocacy Institute
Dennis A. Collins, James Irvine Foundation
The Honorable Barber Conable Jr., Congressman,
   New York
Jill K. Conway, Smith College
Kinshasha Holman Conwill, The Studio Museum in Harlem
Alison G. Coolbrith, Aetna Life & Casualty
John E. Corbally, John D. and Catherine T. MacArthur Foundation
Msgr. Lawrence J. Corcoran, National Conference of Catholic
   Charities
Charles A. Corry, USX Corporation
Jane A. Couch, National Trust for Historic Preservation
Peter J. Davies, InterAction
Kenneth N. Dayton, Dayton Hudson Corporation
Ada E. Deer, Native American Rights Fund
Anne Cohn Donnelly, National Committee for Prevention
   of Child Abuse
Eugene C. Dorsey, Gannett Foundation
John E. Echohawk, Native American Rights Fund
Lucille A. Echohawk, Council of Energy Resource Tribes
Walter D. Eichner, ARCO
Sara L. Engelhardt, The Foundation Center

Carl Holman, National Urban Coalition
Rev. M. William Howard Jr., National Council of Churches
John E. Jacob, National Urban League, Inc.
Sibyl C. Jacobson, Metropolitan Life Foundation
Dorothy A. Johnson, Council of Michigan Foundations
Geneva B. Johnson, Family Service America
Anna Faith Jones, The Boston Foundation
Boisfeuillet Jones, The Woodruff Foundation
James A. Joseph, Council on Foundations
Stanley N. Katz, American Council of Learned Societies
John D. Kemp, United Cerebral Palsy Associations
Vanessa Kirsch, Public Allies
Honorable Juanita Morris Kreps, Former Secretary, Department
   of Commerce
Thomas W. Leavitt, Herbert F. Johnson Museum of Art,
   Cornell University
Reynold Levy, AT&T Foundation
Valerie S. Lies, Donors Forum of Chicago
James S. Lipscomb, The George Fund Foundation
Richard W. Lyman, Rockefeller Foundation
Felicia B. Lynch, Hitachi Foundation
Margaret E. Mahoney, Commonwealth Fund
Barbara Mandel, National Council of Jewish Women
Wilma P. Mankiller, Cherokee Nation of Oklahoma
Mrs. Edward S. Marcus, American Council for the Arts
Leon O. Marion, American Council of Voluntary Agencies
   for Foreign Service
Elizabeth Martinez, American Library Association
David Mathews, Charles F. Kettering Foundation
Cynthia Mayeda, Dayton Hudson Foundation
J. Michael McCloskey, Sierra Club
J. Oscar McCloud, The Fund for Theological Education
Catherine E. McDermott, Grantmakers in Health
Walter J. McNerney, Blue Cross-Blue Shield
Wayne Meisel, The Corella & Bertram F. Bonner Foundation
Sara E. Meléndez, INDEPENDENT SECTOR
Astrid E. Merget, Ohio State University
Christine Topping Milliken, National Association of Independent
   Colleges and Universities
Steven A. Minter, The Cleveland Foundation

Rita Moya, National Health Foundation
Steven Muller, Johns Hopkins University
Anne Firth Murray, The Global Fund for Women
Waldemar A. Nielsen, Aspen Institute
Bruce L. Newman, The Chicago Community Trust
Patrick F. Noonan, Conservation Fund
Roger H. Nozaki, Hitachi Foundation
Louis Nunez, National Puerto Rican Coalition, Inc.
Brian O'Connell, INDEPENDENT SECTOR
Doris J. O'Connor, Shell Companies Foundation
William A. Orme, General Electric Foundation
Martin Paley, San Francisco Foundation
Antonia Pantoja, ASPIRA Association and National Puerto Rican
   Forum
Robert L. Payton, Exxon Education Foundation
Janice Petrovich, ASPIRA Association
Alicia A. Philipp, Metropolitan Atlanta Community Foundation
Alex J. Plinio, The Prudential Foundation
Fern C. Portnoy, Piton Foundation
Gary H. Quehl, Council for Advancement and Support
   of Education
David Ramage Jr., The New World Foundation
Albert Rees, Alfred P. Sloan Foundation
William S. Reese, Partners of the Americas, Inc.
Milton Rhodes, American Council for the Arts
Dorothy S. Ridings, The Bradenton Herald
Rebecca W. Rimel, Pew Charitable Trusts
Mary R. Ripley, National Conference on Social Welfare
Robert B. Rogers, Ewing Marion Kauffman Foundation
Charles R. Rooks, Meyer Memorial Trust
Juan Rosario, ASPIRA Association
Terry T. Saario, Northwest Area Foundation
Ann Mitchell Sackey, National Council of Nonprofit Associations
Steven A. Schroeder, Robert Wood Johnson Foundation
Felice N. Schwartz, Catalyst Inc.
John J. Schwartz, American Association of Fund-Raising
   Counsel, Inc.
Deborah Seidel, Association of Junior Leagues
Albert Shanker, American Federation of Teachers
James P. Shannon, General Mills Foundation

James P. Shannon, General Mills Foundation
Yvonne Shepard, AT&T
Paul H. Sherry, United Church of Christ
Fred Silverman, Apple Computer
Clifford V. Smith Jr., GE Fund
Cecile M. Springer, Westinghouse Electric Corporation
Bishop Joseph Sullivan, U. S. Catholic Conference
Eric Swanson, Radio and Television News Directors Foundation
Howard Swearer, Brown University
Ross O. Swimmer, Cherokee Nation
Joe A. Taller, The Boeing Company
Linda Tarr-Whelan, Center for Policy Alternatives
Alfred H. Taylor Jr., The Kresge Foundation
Janet C. Taylor, Associated Grantmakers of Greater Boston
Robert H. Thill, AT&T
Carol Truesdell, Pillsbury Company
Jeff K. Trujillo, El Pomar Foundation
Roberta van der Voort, United Way of America
Edward H. Van Ness, National Health Council, Inc.
Homer C. Wadsworth, The Cleveland Foundation
Faye Wattleton, Planned Parenthood Federation of America
Edward T. Weaver, Gulf + Western Foundation
Cynthia C. Wedel, World Council of Churches
William S. White, Charles Stewart Mott Foundation
Harold H. Wilke, Healing Community
Eddie N. Williams, Joint Center for Political and Economic Studies
Patricia L. Willis, BellSouth Corporation
Eugene R. Wilson, ARCO Foundation
J. Richard Wilson, National Society of Fund-Raising Executives, Inc.
Kirke P. Wilson, Rosenberg Foundation
Sara Alyce Wright, YWCA of the U.S.A.
David K. Yamakawa Jr., National Mental Health Association
Adam Yarmolinsky, John F. Kennedy School of Government,
   Harvard
Jerry Yoshitomi, Japanese/American Cultural and Community
   Center
Raul Yzaguirre, National Council of La Raza

Staff Members
1980–1996

(Five Years' Service or More)

Joseph M. Aguayo
Darryl L. Barnes
Mindy Berry
Jeanne L. Bohlen
Alice H. Brown
Barbara A. Bruno
Corthelia E. Bumbry
Myra Cook
Mark W. Cullinane
Colleen A. Darling
Yvonne D. H. Dock
Hector Ericksen-Méndoza
Brian E. Foss
Heather A. Gorski
Margaret M. Graham
Sandra T. Gray
Keith A. Greenidge
Robert W. Harlan
Harold R. Helsing

Virginia A. Hodgkinson
Linda G. Johnson
E. B. Knauft
Brenda J. Lee
Susan M. McConaghy
Richard M. Michaud
Char Mollison
Sharon Fitzgerald Noga
Stephen M. Noga
Brian O'Connell
Nancy Patterson
Thomas Pollak
Sandra L. Pruitt
Lori R. Pujol
Lillie S. Saunders
Darlene M. Siska
Jennette Smith
Robert M. Smucker
Sandy Solomon

Sharon L. Stewart
Joy A. Terrell
Jeanne Thomas
John H. Thomas
Trish Thomas
David Tobin

Christopher Toppe
Murray Weitzman
John C. Welch
Lisa M. Wellman
Beverly C. With

⟆ Bibliography

Bellah, R., and others. *The Good Society.* New York: Knopf, 1991.

Booth, J.D.L. "A Global View of Philanthropy." Speech given to INDEPENDENT SECTOR, Washington, D.C., October 20, 1986.

Bremner, R. H. *American Philanthropy.* Chicago: University of Chicago Press, 1960.

Carter, R. *The Gentle Legions.* Garden City, N.Y.: Doubleday, 1961.

Cass, R. H., and Manser, G. *Voluntarism at the Crossroads.* New York: Family Service Association of America, 1976.

Commission on Foundations and Private Philanthropy. *Foundations, Private Giving, and Public Policy.* Chicago, Ill.: University of Chicago Press, 1970.

Commission on Private Philanthropy and Public Needs. *Giving in America: Toward a Stronger Voluntary Sector.* Washington, D.C.: Commission on Private Philanthropy and Public Needs, 1975.

Cornuelle, R. C. *Reclaiming the American Dream.* New York: Random House, 1965.

Curti, M. E. "American Philanthropy and the National Character." *American Quarterly,* 1958, *10*(4), 420–437.

Dayton, K. N. *Governance Is Governance.* Washington, D. C.: INDEPENDENT SECTOR, 1987.

Dewey, J. "The Ethics of Democracy." In R. B. Westbrook, *Dewey and American Democracy.* Ithaca, N.Y.: Cornell University Press, 1991.

Donee Group. *Private Philanthropy: Vital and Innovative? or Passive and Irrelevant?* Washington, D.C.: National Committee for Responsive Philanthropy, 1975.

Eells, R. (ed.), and National Council on Philanthropy. *International Business Philanthropy.* Old Tappan, N.J.: Macmillan, 1979.

Gardner, J. W. *The Collaboration of CONVO and NCOP.* Washington, D.C.: Coalition of National Voluntary Organizations, 1978.

Gardner, J. W. *The Heart of the Matter.* Leadership paper no. 3. Washington, D.C.: INDEPENDENT SECTOR, 1986.

Gardner, J. W. *Leadership and Power.* Leadership paper no. 4. Washington,
    D.C.: INDEPENDENT SECTOR, 1986.
Gardner, J. W. *The Nature of Leadership.* Leadership paper no. 1.
    Washington, D.C.: INDEPENDENT SECTOR, 1986.
Gardner, J. W. *The Tasks of Leadership.* Leadership paper no. 2. Washington,
    D.C.: INDEPENDENT SECTOR, 1986.
Gardner, J. W. *Attributes and Context.* Leadership paper no. 6. Washington,
    D.C.: INDEPENDENT SECTOR, 1987.
Gardner, J. W. *Constituents and Followers.* Leadership paper no. 8.
    Washington, D.C.: INDEPENDENT SECTOR, 1987.
Gardner, J. W. *Leadership Development.* Leadership paper no. 7.
    Washington, D.C.: INDEPENDENT SECTOR, 1987.
Gardner, J. W. *The Moral Aspect of Leadership.* Leadership paper no. 5.
    Washington, D.C.: INDEPENDENT SECTOR, 1987.
Gardner, J. W. *The Changing Nature of Leadership.* Leadership paper no. 11.
    Washington, D.C.: INDEPENDENT SECTOR, 1988.
Gardner, J. W. *Leadership: An Overview.* Leadership paper no. 12.
    Washington, D.C.: INDEPENDENT SECTOR, 1988.
Gardner, J. W. *Renewing: The Leader's Creative Task.* Leadership paper no.
    10. Washington, D.C.: INDEPENDENT SECTOR, 1988.
Gardner, J. W. *The Task of Motivating.* Leadership paper no. 9. Washington,
    D.C.: INDEPENDENT SECTOR, 1988.
Gardner, J. W. *On Leadership.* New York: Free Press/Macmillan, 1990.
Gray, S. T. (ed.). *A Vision of Evaluation.* Washington, D.C.: INDEPENDENT
    SECTOR, 1993.
INDEPENDENT SECTOR. *Analysis of the Economic Recovery Program's Direct
    Significance for Philanthropic and Voluntary Organizations and the
    People They Serve.* Washington, D.C.: INDEPENDENT SECTOR, 1982.
INDEPENDENT SECTOR. *Accountability with Independence—Toward
    a Balance in Government/Independent Sector Financial Partnerships.*
    Washington, D.C.: INDEPENDENT SECTOR, 1983.
INDEPENDENT SECTOR. *It's the Law: Disclosure of Information by Tax-
    Exempt Organizations.* Washington, D.C.: INDEPENDENT SECTOR,
    1986.
INDEPENDENT SECTOR. *Americans Volunteer.* Washington, D.C.:
    INDEPENDENT SECTOR, 1988.
INDEPENDENT SECTOR. *Nonprofit Management Series.* Washington, D.C.:
    INDEPENDENT SECTOR, 1988.
INDEPENDENT SECTOR. *Tax-Exempt Organizations' Lobbying and Political
    Activities Accountability Act of 1987: A Guide for Volunteers and Staff*

of Nonprofit Organizations. Washington, D.C.: INDEPENDENT
SECTOR, 1988.

INDEPENDENT SECTOR. *Aiming High on a Small Budget: Executive Searches
and the Nonprofit Sector.* Washington, D.C.: INDEPENDENT SECTOR,
1990.

INDEPENDENT SECTOR. *Ethics and the Nation's Voluntary and Philanthropic
Community.* Washington, D.C.: INDEPENDENT SECTOR, 1991.

INDEPENDENT SECTOR. *Giving and Volunteering Among Teenagers, 14–17
Years of Age.* Washington, D.C.: INDEPENDENT SECTOR, 1991.

INDEPENDENT SECTOR. *American Teenagers as Volunteers.* Washington,
D.C.: INDEPENDENT SECTOR, 1992.

INDEPENDENT SECTOR. *Directory of Educational and Training Programs
Relating to Nonprofit Leadership and Management.* Washington,
D.C.: INDEPENDENT SECTOR, 1992.

INDEPENDENT SECTOR. *From Belief to Commitment: The Community
Service Activities and Finances of Religious Congregations in the
United States.* Washington, D.C.: INDEPENDENT SECTOR, 1993.

INDEPENDENT SECTOR. *Why Tax Exemption? The Public Service Role of
America's Independent Sector.* Washington, D.C.: INDEPENDENT
SECTOR, 1993.

Irwin, I. H. *The Story of Alice Paul and the National Women's Party.*
Fairfax, Va.: Denlingers, 1964.

Knauft, E. B. *Profiles of Effective Corporate Giving Programs.* Washington,
D.C.: INDEPENDENT SECTOR, 1985.

Knauft, E. B., Berger, R. A., and Gray, S. T. *Profiles of Excellence: Achieving
Success in the Nonprofit Sector.* San Francisco: Jossey-Bass, 1991.

Lyman, R. W. *What Kind of Society Shall We Have?* Occasional Papers
Series. Washington, D.C.: INDEPENDENT SECTOR, 1980.

McCarthy, K. D., Hodgkinson, V. A., Sumari Walla, R. D., and Associates.
The Nonprofit Sector in the Global Community. San Francisco:
Jossey-Bass, 1990.

Nielsen, W. A. *The Big Foundations.* New York: Columbia University Press,
1972.

Nielsen, W. A. *The Endangered Sector.* New York: NAL/Dutton, 1979.

Nielsen, W. A. *The Golden Donors.* New York: Truman Talley Books/
E. P. Dutton, 1985.

O'Connell, B. *Feasibility Study of Closer Collaboration Between the Coalition
of National Voluntary Organizations (CONVO) and the National
Council on Philanthropy (NCOP).* Washington, D.C.: Coalition
of National Voluntary Organizations, 1978.

O'Connell, B. (ed.). *America's Voluntary Spirit: A Book of Readings.*
    New York: Foundation Center, 1983.
O'Connell, B. *Philanthropy in Action.* New York: Foundation Center, 1987.
O'Connell, B. *The Common Sense of Sabbaticals or Project Leaves.*
    Washington, D.C.: INDEPENDENT SECTOR, 1988.
O'Connell, B. *The Board Member's Book.* (2nd ed.) New York: Foundation
    Center, 1993.
O'Connell, B. *Financial Compensation in Nonprofit Organizations.*
    Washington, D.C.: INDEPENDENT SECTOR, 1993.
O'Connell, B. *For Organizations in Trouble—Or Don't Want to Be.*
    Washington, D.C.: INDEPENDENT SECTOR, 1993.
O'Connell, B. "The Future Looks Good—For Those Who Invest in It."
    Fund Raising Management, March 1994.
O'Connell, B. *Board Overboard: Laughs and Lessons for All but the Perfect
    Nonprofit.* San Francisco: Jossey-Bass, 1996.
O'Connell, B., and O'Connell, A. B. *Volunteers in Action.* New York:
    Foundation Center, 1989.
Payton, R., Novak, M., O'Connell, B., and Hall, P. D. *Philanthropy:
    Four Views.* New Brunswick, N.J.: Social Philosophy and Policy
    Center/Transaction Books, 1988.
Plinio, A., and Scanlon, J. *Resource Raising: The Role of Non-Cash Assistance
    in Corporate Philanthropy.* Washington, D.C.: INDEPENDENT
    SECTOR, 1986.
Salamon, L. M., and Abramson, A. J. *The Federal Budget and the Nonprofit
    Sector.* Washington, D.C.: Urban Institute, 1982.
Schervish, P. G., Hodgkinson, V. A., Gates, M., and Associates. *Care and
    Community in Modern Society: Passing on the Tradition of Service
    to Future Generations.* San Francisco: Jossey-Bass, 1993.
Schwartz, J. J. *Modern American Philanthropy: A Personal Account.*
    New York: Wiley, 1994.
Smucker, R. *The Nonprofit Lobbying Guide.* San Francisco: Jossey-Bass,
    1991.
U.S. Treasury Department's Report on Private Foundations. Washington,
    D.C.: U.S. Treasury Department, 1965.
Wuthnow, R., Hodgkinson, V. A., and Associates. *Faith and Philanthropy
    in America.* San Francisco: Jossey-Bass, 1989.
Young, D. R., Hodgkinson, V. A., Hollister, R. M., and Associates.
    *Governing, Leading and Managing Nonprofit Organizations: New
    Insights from Research and Practice.* San Francisco: Jossey-Bass, 1992.

‑‑‑ Index

A

Abram, R., 37
Abramson, A., 67, 100
Accountability, promoting, 134–147
ACTION, 159; Office of Voluntary
    Citizen Participation of, 28, 30
Advertising Council, 114–116
Advocacy rights: coalition for, 74–83;
    and government proposals, 97;
    guide on, 100; issues of, 178
Aetna Life and Casualty, 58
Ahman, M., 75
Albrecht, K. L., 22–23, 32, 34, 35, 37,
    55–56, 57, 165–166
Alliance for Volunteerism, 27, 31, 159
Alvarez, L., 58
American Arts Alliance, 38, 59
American Association of Fund-Raising
    Counsel (AAFRC), 26, 27, 38, 58,
    128
American Association of Higher
    Education, 8, 119
American Cancer Society, 14
American Civil Liberties Union, 76
American Council for the Arts, 59
American Council of Voluntary
    Agencies for Foreign Service, 59
American Enterprise Institute, 28
American Federation of Arts, 37, 58
American Heart Association, 161
American Lung Association, 172
American Psychiatric Association, 160
American Red Cross, 37, 171–172
American Telephone and Telegraph, 38,
    58, 60
Aramony, W., 58

Aspen Institute, 28
Aspira of America, 60
Associated Grantmakers of Greater
    Boston, 60
Associated Press, 110
Association of Governing Boards for
    Colleges and Universities, 145
Association of Voluntary Action
    Scholars, 28, 122
Atlantic Richfield Corporation, 37

B

Baker, J., 74
Bannerman, C., 58
Bellah, R., 7
Benefits issue, 150–151
Berger, R., 139
Bernstein, P., 35–37, 53, 58, 62,
    165–166, 180
Black Leadership Forum, 37, 59
Boards: for coalitions, 161–162;
    effectiveness of, 140
Bob Jones University v. United States
    of America, 104
Bolling, L., 37, 57, 107–108
Booth, J.D.L., 4
Borowski, N. A., 117
Bowling Green State University, Social
    Philosophy and Policy Center of,
    125
Bremmer, R., 5
Brennan, L. J., Jr., 37
Brewster, K., 28
Brookings Institution, 28, 44
Brooks, J., 76
Brown, J. W., 58

Buckman, T., 111
Burke, E., 6
Bush, G.H.W., 91–92

C

Carnegie, A., 112
Carnegie Corporation of New York, 38
Carson, E., 188
Carson, R., 175
Carter, J. E., 21, 28, 30, 47
Carter, R., 14
Carter, R. S., 21, 28, 44, 46–47
Cary, F., 58
Case Western University, Mandel
    Center at, 143–144
Cass, R. H., 37, 58
Center for a Voluntary Society, 28, 122
Channel, C. "S.," 97–99
Charitable contributions legislation, 62,
    86–88, 107
Child Welfare League, 172
Chin, C. S., 58
Citizens for a Better Environment case,
    45, 61–62, 68, 89, 103
Civic engagement, and voluntary sector,
    7–8, 13–14
CIVICUS: World Alliance for Citizen
    Participation, 7–8, 151–152
Civil rights movement, and volun-
    tarism, 13
Cleveland Council on World Affairs, 59
Cleveland Foundation, 60, 143
Clever, L. H., 58
Clotfelter, C., 125
Coalition for the Public Good, 26, 27,
    29
Coalition of National Voluntary Orga-
    nizations (CONVO): collaboration
    sought by, 21, 22–23, 26, 29–34, 158,
    159, 167; dissolving, 55–56, 62; and
    government funding, 100–101; and
    organizing effort, 35, 37, 44–47,
    49–54; and research, 122; roles of,
    3, 27, 61, 82, 111
Coalitions: for advocacy rights, 73–83;
    building and maintaining, 157–173
Combined Federal Campaign, 101–102

Commission on Foundation and
    Private Philanthropy (Peterson
    Commission), 24–25, 26
Commission on Private Philanthropy
    and Public Needs. *See* Filer Com-
    mission
Committee for the Third Sector, 27, 159
Commitment, levels of, 169–170
Common Cause, 36, 57, 158
Common ground, for coalitions, 68–69;
    162–165
Communication Workers of America,
    38
Competition, and tax exemptions,
    95–96
Conable, B., 37, 65, 74, 79, 84
Conference Board, 31; Contributions
    Council of, 37
Congressional Research Service, 76
Conway, J., 37
Conway, J. K., 58
Corcoran, L., 58, 64, 65
Cornell University, art museum at, 38,
    59
Cornuelle, R. C., 17–18
Corporation for Public Broadcasting,
    59
Council on Foundations: and birth of
    IS, 57; and coalitions, 27, 28, 31; and
    independence, 9; and international
    network, 151; and investments, 103;
    and organizing effort, 37, 51; and
    research, 128, 133, 177
Covenant House, 184
Cox Committee, 15
Cranford, S., 92
Cranston, A., 99
Curti, M., 3

D

Day, J., 125–126
Dayton, K., 57, 115–116, 137, 144
Dayton Hudson Corporation, 57, 115
Deer, A., 58
Delta Foundation, 58
Dewey, J., 7
Diversity, in voluntary sector, 41

Dix, D., 14
Dole, R., 86
Donee Group, 17, 25, 27
Dorsey, G., 108, 116, 165
Dues issues, 49–50, 171–173
Duke Endowment, 59, 125–126
Duke University, research center at,
    125–126
Durenberger, D., 76

E

Edgerton, R., 119
Effectiveness: and accountability,
    134–147; measuring, 138–141
Emerson, R. W., 112
Emily and Ernest Woodruff Founda-
    tion, 59
Environmental Defense Fund, 58
Equitable Life Assurance Society of the
    U.S.A., 37, 57
Erlich, E., 126
Erlich, T., 126
Ethics, and accountability, 137–138, 179
European Foundation Centre, 151
Evaluation, and accountability, 141–143
Ewing, B., 22–23, 26, 32, 34, 35, 37, 58,
    165–166, 180
Excellence, hallmarks of, 139–140
Exempt Organizations Advisory Group,
    81

F

Feldstein, M., 26, 45–46
Filer, J. H., 24, 58, 112, 165, 180
Filer Commission: and coalitions, 158;
    criticism of, 17; findings of, 24, 25,
    26, 27, 30; and research, 122, 132
Finberg, B., 165
First National City Bank, 59
First Nonprofit Companies, 145
Fisher, J., 37, 84
Fisher, L., 141
501(C)(3) Group, 26, 27
Fleishman, J., 125–126
Ford Foundation, 19, 38, 167, 188–189
Ford Motor Company Fund, 37
Foss, B., 117

Foster, V., 57
Foundation Center, 111
Foundation Investment Fund, 103
Foundations, criticisms of, 15–17
France, flexibility in, 6
Funding: for coalitions, 171–173; for IS,
    128–129, 146–147

G

Gallup Organization, 46, 122, 123
Gannett Foundation, 108–109
Gardner, J. W., 2, 9, 18, 21, 33–34,
    35–36, 39, 52–53, 56–57, 62–63, 66,
    111–112, 135–136, 158–159, 161,
    165–168, 172, 178, 182–183
Gaul, G. M., 117
General Electric, 60
General Electric Foundation, 60
George Gund Foundation, 35, 37, 59,
    143
Georgetown University, 57
Gibbs, L., 80, 81
Girl Scouts, 95
Give Five campaign, 115–116, 132, 141,
    179, 184
Goddard, S., 59, 101
Goddard and Ahern, 59
Golsbrough Christian Schools v. United
    States of America, 104
Government: advocacy rights regulated
    by, 73–83; battles and cooperation
    with, 84–105; control by, 14–15;
    funding by, 66–67, 100–102; over-
    sight by, 186–187; relations with,
    45, 177–178
Graham, M., 117
Gray, S. T., 117, 132, 135, 139, 142, 144,
    147, 152, 165
Growth fund proposed, 176

H

Hall, P. D., 125
Hanks, N., 59, 111
Hanley, J., 59
Harlan, R., 61, 165, 180–181
Harvard University, Institute of Politics
    at, 60

Havel, V., 8

Healing Community, 60

Hearst Foundations, 189

Heiskel, A., 59

Helsing, H. R. "S.," 181

Herbert F. Johnson Museum of Art, 38, 59

Heyns, R., 135

Hirschfield, I., 137

Hodgkinson, V., 83, 123–125, 128–132, 144, 165

Hollister, R., 144

Holman, C., 37, 59

Horton, F., 76

Hosey, J. T., 37

House Appropriations Committee, 80

House Government Affairs Committee, 75–76

House Select Committee on Small Business, 16

House Ways and Means Committee, 16, 65, 80, 94, 99

I

IBM, 58

Ickes, H., 168

Inclusiveness, for coalitions, 159–162

Independence: and government relations, 77–78, 96, 101; for voluntary sector, 9, 41–42

INDEPENDENT SECTOR (IS): and academic research centers, 125–127, 143; and advocacy rights, 73–83; annual meeting and assembly of, 149–150; archives of, 191; associational power of, 71–154; beginnings of, 11–69; birth and first year of, 55–69; board meetings for, 64–66; board members of, 217–222; charter meeting of, 62–64; charter members of, 193–197; and coalition building, 157–173; commonalities in, 68–69; communication by, 106–120; criticisms of, 179; and effectiveness and accountability issues, 134–147; founding board of, 57–61; funders of, 199–200; funding for, 128–129,

146–147; future for, 182–189; government relations of, 84–105; Leadership and Management program of, 132, 138; lessons from, 155–189; and media coverage, 108–110, 114–118; as meeting ground, 148–154; membership of, 153, 201–216; naming, 53, 56, 106–107; public information and education (PI&E) program of, 107–108, 118; publications by, 69, 105, 107, 111–114, 144, 153; regrets about, 174–181; requests for information from, 152–153; research by, 121–133; research forums of, 123–124, 132; roles of, 3, 7, 84–85; staff members of, 223–224; and strength of coalition, 73–83; Studies in Leadership project of, 135–136; surveys and reports by, 127–128. *See also* Voluntary sector

Indiana University: IS archives at, 191; research center at, 126

Indians, goodness of, 5

Institute for Voluntary Organizations, 28

Institute of Enterprise Advancement, 95

Insurance issues, 145

Internal Revenue Service (IRS), 17, 78–83, 92–94, 99, 103–104

International Society for Third-Sector Research, 123

Involvement, Inc., 28

Irwin, I. H., 4

J

Jefferson, T., 6

John W. Gardner Leadership Award, 136–137

Johns Hopkins University and Hospital, 60

Johnson, C., 126

Jones, B., 59

Jordan, V. E., Jr., 112

Joseph, J., 91–92

Jossey-Bass, 124

K

Katz, S., 123
Keenan, T., 15
Kellogg Foundation, 189
Knauft, E. B., 139, 144, 165
Kominers, Fort, Schlefer & Boyer, 60
KQED, 58
Kreps, J. M., 59

L

Leadership: award for, 136–137; for coalitions, 165–167; IS programs on, 132, 135–136, 138
Leavitt, T., 38, 59
Lend a Hand campaign, 115
Lerner, M., 6
Lettie Pate Evans Foundation, 59
Lilly Endowment, 126, 129
Linsey, L., 90
Lipscomb, J., 35–37, 53, 55–56, 59, 62, 165–166, 180
Lobbying. *See* Advocacy rights
Lobbying by Public Charities Law of 1976, 79, 82
Louisiana State University, and journalism project, 117
Luck, for coalitions, 142–144, 173
Lyman, R. W., 6, 59, 165

M

Mandel, M., 142–144
Mandel Center for Nonprofit Organizations, 143–144
March of Dimes, 14
Marcus, B., 59
Marion, L., 59
Marschall, M., 7, 152
Maryland, advocacy rights in, 78, 81
McNerney, W., 59
Media coverage, 108–110, 114–118
Meeting ground: function of, 48; IS as, 148–154
Meléndez, S., 182, 189
Membership: for coalitions, 50–52, 171–173; for IS, 153, 201–216
Mental Health Association (MHA): and advocacy rights, 77–79, 81; and

coalitions, 158, 160, 172; and communication, 107; experience with, 21, 45, 46
Mental Health Commission, 21–22
Merget, A., 139
Milliken, C. T., 59
Minter, S., 118
Model Solicitation Law Project, 104
Monsanto Inc., 59
Moskowitz, J., 86–87
Motivations, research on, 130–131
Mott Foundation, 189
Moulton, J. F., 138
Moynihan, D. P., 63–64, 87, 99, 164
Mueller Spaghetti Company, 93
Muller, S., 60, 61
Munson case, 103
Muskie, E., 79
Mutual dependence, in voluntary sector, 5–7

N

National and Community Services Act of 1988, 105
National Assembly of National Voluntary Health and Social Welfare Organizations, 38, 158, 171–172
National Association for Retarded Children, 14
National Association of Independent Colleges and Universities, 51, 59
National Bureau of Economic Research, 45
National Center for Charitable Statistics, 128
National Center for Nonprofit Boards, 145
National Center for Voluntary Action (NCVA), 27, 31
National Committee for Responsive Philanthropy, 27–28, 38
National Committee on Patients' Rights, 158, 160, 162
National Conference of Catholic Charities, 58, 64, 74
National Conference on Philanthropy, 68, 122

National Council of La Raza, 38, 57
National Council of Nonprofit
    Associations, 105
National Council on Philanthropy
    (NCOP): and coalitions, 158, 159,
    167; collaboration sought by, 21,
    22–23, 26, 27, 29–34; dissolving,
    55–56, 62; and organizing effort, 35,
    37, 43–47, 49–51, 53–54; and
    research, 122; roles of, 3, 68, 111
National Endowment for the Arts, 51
National Endowment for the Preserva-
    tion of Liberty, 97–99
National Health Council, 51, 60
National Information Bureau, 37, 58
National Information Center on
    Volunteerism, 27
National Mental Health Association, 14
National Neighborhood Coalition, 57
National Organization for Women, 19
National Puerto Rican Forum, 60
National Service Volunteers, 97
National Urban Coalition, 37, 59.
    See Urban Coalition
National Urban Fellows, 58
National Urban League, 51
Nature Conservancy, 51
New World Foundation, 38, 60
New York University, and unrelated
    business income, 93
Nielsen, W. A., 14–15, 17, 38, 112
Nixon, R. M., 77
Nonprofit organizations. See Voluntary
    sector
Noonan, P., 53
Novak, M., 125

O

O'Connell, A. B., 3, 112–113
O'Connell, B., 36, 58, 64
Office of Management and Budget
    (OMB), 73–76, 91
Ogilvy and Mather, 115
Oglethorpe University, 38
Orme, W., 60
O'Rourke, H., 43–44
Oversight Subcommittee, 94–95

P

Pacific-Asian Coalition, 58
Packwood, B., 86, 87
Palatine Fathers, 23
Paley, M., 60
Pantoja, A., 60
Patman, W., 16
Pattillo, M. M., Jr., 38
Payton, R., 123, 125, 126, 129
Perndes, N., 148
Peterson, P. G., 24
Peterson Commission, 24–25, 26
Pickle, J. J., 94, 97–99
Pifer, A., 38
Planned Parenthood Foundation
    of America, 60, 64
Plinio, A., 133
Points of Light Foundation, 91–92
Population Resources Center, 52
Premier Industrial Corporation,
    142–143
Presbyterian Hospital of Pacific Medical
    Center, Department of Occupa-
    tional Health at, 58
Process, for coalitions, 167–171
Project with Journalism Schools, 117
Purchasing networks, 145–146

R

Ramage, D., Jr., 38, 60
Rangle, C., 99
Reagan, R., 66, 73, 75, 97
Recruitment issues, 177
Reece Committee, 15
Regan, D. T., 104
Religious congregations: research on,
    129–130; and voluntary sector, 4–5
Riley case, 103
Ripley, M., 57
Robinson, O., 44
Rockefeller, J. D., 112
Rockefeller Brothers Fund, 59
Rockefeller Foundation, 15, 38, 59
Roosevelt, E., 168
Roosevelt, F. D., 168
Rosenwald, J., 112
Ruder and Finn, 56, 106–107

S

Sabbaticals issue, 144
Salamon, L., 67, 100, 132
Salvation Army, 149
San Diego, University of, Graduate
School for Urban Resources and
Social Policy at, 60
San Francisco Foundation, 60
Sanford, T., 125
Scanlon, J., 133
Schaumburg case, 45, 61–62, 68, 89, 103
Schools: projects with, 117, 118–119;
research centers in, 125–127, 143,
177
Schulze, R., 99
Schumpeter, J., 63, 178
Schwartz, J. J., 26, 38, 47, 58
Scott, J., 108
Senate Finance Committee, 16, 68, 80,
86
Sheldon, E., 38
Shepard, Cooper, Harris, Dickson,
Buermann, Camp & Cass, 37, 58
Sierra Club, 19
Silleck, B., 109
Simon, J., 28, 122
Smith College, 58
Smucker, B., 45, 46, 88, 89, 100, 165
Social Security, 104
Solicitation Law Project, 104
Staff development issues, 175–176
State alliances, 179–180
Stockman, D., 75

T

Tax-Exempt Organization's Lobbying
and Political Activities Accountability Act of 1987, 100
Tax policies: and advocacy rights, 75,
78–83; on exempt organizations,
89–90, 100; on floor for contributions, 86–88, 90–92; on gifts of
appreciated property, 92–93;
research on, 132; on unrelated
business income, 93–95
Tax Reform Act of 1969, 15, 17
Tax Reform Act of 1986, 92–93, 178

Taxation With Representation
v. Donald T. Regan, 104
Taylor, J., 60
Taylor, T., 116, 153
Technologies, for communication, 120
Teltsch, K., 110
Thill, R. H., 38, 60
Thomas, J., 46–47, 107, 110, 114, 117,
119, 148, 165
Thomas, L., 112
Thompson, F., 109
Tocqueville, A. de, 5, 111, 112
Transaction Books, 125
Troyer, T., 80
Trust, for coalitions, 167–171
Tufts University, Lincoln Filene Center
for Citizenship and Public Affairs
at, 143, 188–189

U

United Kingdom: ethics in, 138;
Ministry of Health in, 77–78
United Presbyterian Church, General
Assembly Mission Council of, 38
U.S. Bureau of Labor Statistics, 82
U.S. Department of Health, Education
and Welfare, 158
U.S. Department of Treasury: Advisory
Committee on Private Philanthropy
and Public Needs in, 26; and philanthropy, 16–17, 19; and tax policies,
87–88, 92, 94, 99, 103–104
U.S. Olympic Committee, 68
U.S. Steel Foundation, 37
U.S. Supreme Court: and advocacy
rights, 77, 89; and government
regulation, 137; and limits on costs,
61–62, 68; and speech and assembly
freedoms, 102–103
United Way of America: and coalitions,
26, 27; and effectiveness, 139; and
federal campaign, 101, 102; and
monopoly, 19, 167; and organizing
effort, 37, 51, 58; and research, 128;
and scandal, 137, 184
Unrelated Business Income Tax
(U.B.I.T.), 93–95, 97–98

Urban Coalition, 158. *See* National Urban Coalition

V

Van Ness, E., 53, 60
Village of Schaumburg v. Citizens for a Better Environment et al., 45, 61–62, 68, 89, 103
Voluntary sector: American history of, 4–7; associational power of, 71–154; awareness of, 174–175, 177–178, 184–185; challenges to, 13–20; characteristics of, 41–42; coalition in, 55–69; collaboration sought in, 21–34; commission findings on, 24–25; communicating about, 106–120; criticisms of, 17–19, 117–118; dues issue in, 49–50; effectiveness and accountability in, 134–147; functions in, 48–49; future for, 182–189; governance issues in, 52; groups in, 25–29; impact of, 2–3, 185–186; independence for, 9, 41–42, 77–78, 96, 101; international network for, 151–152; management in, 47; membership issues in, 50–52; needs of, 25, 32–33; obstacles to organizing, 42–43; options for, 30–32; organizing committee in, 36–40; organizing effort in, 35–54; positive trends for, 185; research on, 45–46, 82–83, 121–133; significance of, 1–10, 187; values in, 39–41. *See also* INDEPENDENT SECTOR
VOLUNTEER : The National Center for Citizen Involvement, 57

Volunteering: capacity for, 184; motivations for, 130–131

W

Wadsworth, H., 56, 60, 165–166, 180
Waldemar Nielsen, Inc., 38
Wallace, H., 168
Walsh Committee, 15
Wattleton, F., 60, 64–65
Watts, G., 38
Weaver, E., 139
Wedel, C., 37, 57
Westbrook, R., 7
Wilke, H., 60
Wilson, B., 135
Wisconsin at Madison, University of, School of Social Work at, 58
Wolpert, J., 123
Women's Action Alliance, 37, 51
Women's suffrage, and voluntarism, 4
Woodrow Wilson Center, 44
World Council of Churches, 37, 57
Wright, S. A., 38, 39, 60

Y

Yale University: Program on NonProfit Organizations at, 122, 143; and third sector, 28
Yarmolinsky, A., 60, 62
YMCA, 61, 95–96, 146
Young, D., 144
YWCA of the USA, 38, 60, 171
Yzaguirre, R., 38, 57, 165

Z

Zuker, H., 142–144

Praise for *Box of Butterflies*

"With *Box of Butterflies*, Roma Downey has created a beautiful and personal testimony to the presence of God in our lives and in our world. Her book is filled with stories and poems and quotations that give us hope in God's healing power and love. Roma talks personally about her own sorrows and struggles, and her book will offer consolation to others, helping them face their troubles with renewed courage and trust in God."

—Most Reverend José H. Gomez, Archbishop of Los Angeles

"I have known my 'Angel friend,' Roma, for decades. We met when I guest-starred on her TV show, *Touched by an Angel*. We became friends then and we still are, today, because Roma is the REAL THING. She loves Jesus with a rare purity, and His love radiates from within her. You will love her new book. It will touch you and move you and strengthen you."

—Kathie Lee Gifford, *TODAY* show

"I've long said that the happiest people don't have the best of everything, they just make the best of everything. In *Box of Butterflies*, Roma shares personal struggles and the perspectives that have helped her overcome. Roma will help you find the strength within to go to heights you never imagined."

—Tony Robbins, *New York Times* bestselling author of *Unshakeable*

"Roma Downey is one of the most generous, compassionate, and all-around amazing people I have ever met. She's never too busy or too important to care about the person in front of her. I can't think of a clearer indicator of greatness than that. Somehow, she has managed to capture her humanness, empathy, and humility in the pages of her book *Box of Butterflies*. Reading this book is like having a face-to-face chat with Roma herself. You'll come away refreshed, comforted, and inspired to live with deeper peace and greater faith. I hope you enjoy it as much as I do!"

—Judah Smith, pastor and *New York Times* bestselling
author of *Jesus Is _____*.

"This book gladdens the heart, nudges the memory, and lightly touches the soul with inspiration. *Box of Butterflies* is an invitation to hope, joy, and insight in the tradition of the Irish bards."

—Cardinal Donald Wuerl, Archbishop of Washington

"God promises us in His Word that we will not be overcome, but rather that we are overcomers. My friend, Roma, embodies that truth. Despite loss and heartache, she chooses to make God's goodness greater than her circumstances. Her personal story and the Scriptures she shares in *Box of Butterflies* will encourage you with reminders of God's love and presence in your everyday life."

—Christine Caine, founder, A21 and Propel Women

"Like an opened box of butterflies, Roma Downey's stories flew off the page and filled my heart with hope. Find a quiet spot and journey with Roma from the war-torn streets of Northern Ireland to the shores of sunny Malibu. As you do, you just might see the exquisite design in your own life. God is at work! *Box of Butterflies* is proof."

—Karen Kingsbury, #1 *New York Times* bestselling author

"The moment I read the first word, I was instantly connected and inspired. This book brings inspiration and clarity to life's journey. Dive in and swim in the wisdom. 💯 "

—LL COOL J

"When someone gives you hope in your life, it is priceless! *Box of Butterflies* is a profound collection of God's great promises that are overflowing with hope! As you learn them, share them with the world!"

—Dr. Ronnie Floyd, president, National Day of Prayer, senior pastor, Cross Church, and immediate past president, Southern Baptist Convention

"This inspiring book reveals how our struggles generate new strength, and even become the means by which we grow in the Spirit. Read Roma Downey's text slowly, savor it—let it sink into your heart. I warmly recommend it to anyone weighed down by the difficulties of life."

—Bishop Robert Barron, Auxiliary Bishop of Los Angeles

"It's said that tears cleanse the windows of the soul, and you'll find several refreshingly soul-cleansing moments within the pages of this book. You'll also find it a deeply inspiring and motivating read, authored not by an 'angel' but by a faithful overcomer who's willing to honestly share her life's tragedies and triumphs. A beautiful book written by a beautiful person."

—Laurie Crouch, Trinity Broadcasting Network

For my beautiful daughter,
Reilly . . .
the little girl who grew
up to be my best friend

Box *of* Butterflies

Discovering the Unexpected Blessings All Around Us

ROMA DOWNEY

HOWARD BOOKS
AN IMPRINT OF SIMON & SCHUSTER, INC.

New York   London   Toronto   Sydney   New Delhi

Howard Books
An Imprint of Simon & Schuster, Inc.
1230 Avenue of the Americas
New York, NY 10020

First Howard Books hardcover edition March 2018

HOWARD and colophon are trademarks of Simon & Schuster, Inc.

For information about special discounts for bulk purchases, please contact Simon & Schuster Special Sales at 1-866-506-1949 or business@simonandschuster.com.

The Simon & Schuster Speakers Bureau can bring authors to your live event. For more information or to book an event, contact the Simon & Schuster Speakers Bureau at 1-866-248-3049 or visit our website at www .simonspeakers.com.

Manufactured in China

10 9 8 7 6 5 4 3 2 1

Library of Congress Cataloging-in-Publication Data has been applied for.

ISBN 978-1-5011-5093-7
ISBN 978-1-5011-5096-8 (ebook)

CONTENTS

1

INTRODUCTION

13

ONE: STRENGTH

53

TWO: KINDNESS

83

THREE: COURAGE

113

FOUR: LOVE

153

FIVE: STILLNESS

183

SIX: GRATITUDE

205

SEVEN: HOME

228

CONCLUSION: YOU NEVER WALK ALONE

Dear Readers,

    My darling Roma has written this very special book, called *Box of Butterflies*. I couldn't be more proud of her, and I delight in sharing it with you. Whether you bought this book as a beautiful gift for yourself or for someone you love, I know you will be truly touched by the Spirit that exudes from its pages as Roma shares the beauty of her soul and the sweetness of her spirit. You'll find great warmth and wisdom within.

    I feel so fortunate to have had Roma in my life for all these years. If you don't already know it, God was the one who brought us together many years ago, when we played angels on our beloved television show *Touched by an Angel*. The relationship between the angels Tess and Monica was much like the one that developed between Roma and me off camera—authentic, caring, loving, protective, and true. We are soul sisters, and it is as if we have known each other forever. As you will learn in these pages, she has become my daughter, and I am her mama. I've loved seeing her grow into the beautiful mother, wife, producer, author, and extraordinary woman she is today.

    Like many of us, Roma has experienced terrible loss and struggle in her life. But like the caterpillar that uses the darkness of the cocoon to transform into a butterfly, Roma has taken the darkness of life's challenges and, with God's help and grace, used those same trials to bring light to our world. Roma has, indeed, earned her wings.

Roma came to America from Ireland with nothing but a prayerful heart full of hope and a mind full of dreams. She has had a wonderful career in Hollywood but has remained strong in her faith and continues to glorify God by creating projects for Him. In this book, Roma shares stories about her journey, the trials and the triumphs, the joys and the sorrows. I am certain that her story, combined with the beautiful poetry and Scripture she has selected, will inspire hope, restore broken faith, and remind us all that God loves us. That we are never alone. We are all connected, and our loving God and His angels are always standing by, watching over us.

May this *Box of Butterflies* be a blessing to all of you, as Roma has been to me.

God bless you,
Della Reese

I Have Decided

I have decided to find myself a home
in the mountains, somewhere high up
where one learns to live peacefully in
the cold and silence. It's said that
in such a place certain revelations may
be discovered. That what the spirit
reaches for may be eventually felt, if not
exactly understood. Slowly, no doubt. I'm
not talking about a vacation.

Of course at the same time I mean to
stay exactly where I am.

Are you following me?

Mary Oliver

INTRODUCTION

I love the poems of Mary Oliver—like the one you just read—and you'll find a few scattered throughout these pages. There is something about the beauty and honesty of her poems that echoes the prayers of my heart. She reminds me of the simplicity of faith, of how God's image is reflected in nature all around us, and that when we are quiet, when we connect to the stillness within ourselves, we can hear Him speak.

I hope that within the pages of this book you'll find moments like that. Moments when your heart flutters as it makes a connection, like finally being able to recall a distant memory, moments when you are filled with the relief of remembering that you are not alone and that God's loving presence is all around you.

I've been a person of faith my whole life. I was raised in a household where it was always the right time for a prayer, where gratitude to God for His blessings was part of the everyday fabric of our lives. I lost my mother suddenly when I was only ten, and our faith became even more essential as my family leaned on each other and God to get us through that difficult and painful time.

I remember the first time I went with my father to visit my mother's gravesite, not long after she passed. We'd brought some pansies to plant by her gravestone. My mother loved pansies. She used to say she thought they looked like little butterflies.

As we stood there on the breezy hillside praying, a butterfly flew right in front of us, dancing on the wind. And my dad said, "Would you look at that! That wee butterfly could be your mother's spirit right there."

As a young girl of ten, the idea that a beautiful butterfly could represent my precious mom gave me great comfort. I have always felt that that butterfly was a gift from God, a reminder of His loving presence. Since that day, butterflies have appeared to me throughout my life, bringing with them peace and reassurance. I always see them as a remembrance of my mother and a sign from God that even though we may feel so incredibly alone sometimes, He is always there.

Now, some people tell me, "Well, Roma, you live in California; it's sunny and your garden is full of flowers, so of course you see butterflies all the time!" And while yes, that is true, I don't see only physical butterflies. Over the course of my life I have

> *We delight in the beauty of the butterfly, but rarely admit the changes it has gone through to achieve that beauty.*
>
> MAYA ANGELOU

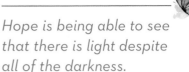

seen butterflies appear in all sorts of unexpected places. A truck will drive by on a rainy city street with a butterfly painted on the side; or in the

Hope is being able to see that there is light despite all of the darkness.

DESMOND TUTU

midst of a long mountain drive, a butterfly will show up on a billboard, on a piece of jewelry in a store, or as a tattoo on a waitress's neck as we stop for some food. I can't explain it, but throughout my life at the precise moments I need a sign of hope, I see a butterfly, and it always serves as a reminder of God's love and reassurance that I am not alone.

If you visit my home, you'll see paintings of butterflies, butterflies on mugs and napkins and pillows and more. Butterflies and angels with wings to fly. Because to me, the butterfly is not just a sign of God's presence but also a symbol of the promise that we all hold within. A butterfly begins its life as a simple caterpillar, creeping and crawling along the ground. And yet that is just its beginning. Through the process of metamorphosis, through the patience and darkness of the cocoon, this little caterpillar emerges on the other side as a stunning butterfly, a creature with wings and the ability to fly.

I once heard a story of a little boy who saw a cocoon and was so anxious to help the butterfly emerge that he got a small pair of manicure scissors so that he could help cut the butterfly out. What he didn't know was that it is through the process of emerging from the cocoon on its own that the butterfly gains the power to fly. It's the very struggle to push out of the cocoon that gives its wings their strength. Without that process, without the struggle, the butterfly isn't ready to fly. To soar.

I know that this life can be filled with sorrow. We all experience loss and heartbreak. But oh, if we can just remember that in the struggle our wings become stronger. We can get through even the hardest times, and one day we will fly.

We sometimes forget this. We think we will always be caterpillars crawling along the ground or bound in a cocoon. But we all hold the potential to become something else. There is always the chance for rebirth.

One year, for Valentine's Day, my husband, Mark, took me out to our patio, which overlooks the Pacific Ocean in Malibu, where we live. He handed me a large, exquisitely designed box with a fragrant gardenia on top. I was surprised by how light it was, and I must have looked puzzled. Mark smiled and told me to just open it carefully. So I took the lid off gently, and out flew fifty butterflies. I gasped as I watched them ascend into the sky. My heart filled with joy and delight and my eyes filled with tears. I turned to look at Mark, my heart overflowing with gratitude. My lovely husband had given me a box of butterflies, knowing that for me, the butterfly is a sign of God's grace, God's presence.

It was the dearest gift I could have received.

It reminded me of the blessings of my life and the little lessons I have learned along the way, and so I decided to call this book *Box of Butterflies*. It is my prayer that each page of this book is a butterfly for you. A reminder that God is with you. That He will never leave you or forsake you. And that no matter how dark the cocoon may sometimes seem, there is always light on the other side. The struggle means your wings are growing and being strengthened. Have faith. There are angels watching over you.

Back in 1994, I was an out-of-work actress looking for a job. I had been in Los Angeles for just over a year and was still waiting for my big break. To be honest, I had never really intended to come to L.A. and try to make it as a TV actress. I was classically trained in London and had moved to New York with my heart set on Broadway. My dream came true in the early 1990s, when I was cast on Broadway alongside Sir Rex Harrison in a revival of Somerset Maugham's *The Circle*. Yet much to my surprise, some television producers saw my performance and called me in to read for an NBC miniseries called *A Woman Named Jackie*, a six-hour film about the life of Jackie Kennedy.

My agency sent me the script, and I read the first of six episodes. The material

> He who is not courageous enough to take risks will accomplish nothing in life.
>
> MUHAMMAD ALI

was compelling, but I didn't know what character they were thinking of for me. I called my agent to ask. He said with a laugh, "Well, the title role, of course."

My jaw dropped. It was hard to imagine me, an Irish woman, playing this iconic American beauty. And yet I booked the role, and the series went on to win the Emmy for best miniseries that year. On the heels of its success, I decided to pack my bags again and move to Hollywood to see what other TV or film opportunities might arise.

The idea of moving to Los Angeles filled me with trepidation. I hardly knew anyone on the West Coast, and I did not even know how to drive a car. But I prayed and felt certain I should go. I decided I would try it out; if I did not like it, I could always go back to New York. I felt strongly that if I didn't give it a chance, I would always regret not having tried. So in spite of being afraid of what lay ahead and with no certainty of outcome, I got on a plane at JFK and flew west.

It was pilot season—that time of year when the hope that keeps all actors in this challenging profession rises, when you think that your next big break might just be around the corner. When you hope that the perfect, special script with the perfect, special role might just show up and change your life.

Courage is being scared to death but saddling up anyway.

JOHN WAYNE

I read through a number of scripts that my agent wanted me to consider, but none was terribly appealing. And then I picked up one with the working title *Angel's Attic* (later to be retitled *Touched by an Angel*). I felt a fluttering in my stomach. I knew immediately that this was something different.

As I opened the packet and began to read, tears came to my eyes. This was the kind of material I had been looking for. The series told the story of angels who show up at crossroads in people's lives with a message of faith and love. The angels come to earth to remind people that God loves them and hasn't forgotten them.

I called my agent and told him that I wanted to come in to read for one of the roles. We booked a meeting, and a few days later they called me in to be considered for the role of Monica, one of the lead angels.

As I began preparing for the audition, I couldn't believe that this script presented me with an opportunity to play an angel and bring to life so many elements of the faith that I held dear. In addition, the two lead angels were women who shared an empathetic and loving relationship. Most of the scripts I was reading were about women in conflict, fighting over something or in competition with one another. But here were two women, two angels, who had so much love for each other. The story was inspirational and told of God's grace, not something that Hollywood or network television was necessarily known for.

As I prepared for my audition, I realized that playing the role of Monica would require a compassionate heart. And I felt deep in my soul that I had been prepared for this role by the loss I had experienced in my own life. I knew that I could relate to the very people Monica was coming to visit, that I could meet those people in their places of loss and hurt because

I had felt loss and hurt so intensely myself at such a young age. I understood then that God had been preparing me, and I'd now been given the chance to turn my pain into purpose.

When I went in to read for the part, I felt torn about how to approach my portrayal of Monica. I had, of course, worked on my American accent during the rehearsals for playing Jackie, but there was something within me that felt like the lyricism and musicality of my native Irish accent might be right for this special part of an angel. I knew it would be risky. It might cause me to lose the role. Once people hear my accent, it's often all they can hear, even when I'm speaking in an American accent. But I couldn't ignore this feeling.

> The wound is the place where the Light enters you.
>
> RUMI

I walked into the room and read my lines, as I'm sure every other actress had read them, in an American accent. It seemed to go well. But then, before I left the room, I turned around and cautiously asked if I could read it again. The producers nodded, perhaps a bit confused. And then I read Monica's lines in my native Irish brogue.

The energy in the room changed immediately. Everyone in the room could feel it. Something clicked.

As I left the audition, I thanked God for guiding me to listen to my instincts. Sure enough, I was called back for a screen test, and they requested that I read it again in my Irish accent.

A few days later, I received a call from my agent. "I have good news and bad news," he said.

"Good news first," I said.

"You booked the show!"

"That's amazing," I said. "What's the bad news?"

"If the pilot gets picked up, you have to move to Utah," he said.

I laughed and said I thought I could handle that! I had never been to Utah but had heard it was beautiful. I was so thrilled with this opportunity, the chance to play Monica, and knew that my life was going to change in huge ways.

Obviously that pilot was an answer to prayer. It was a breakout moment for me and resulted in almost a decade of creating a beautiful show and being part of a cast and crew who truly became my family.

But it became so much more than just my profession. Playing an angel for almost ten years truly changed me. It touched my heart deeply, and strengthened my faith as well.

My favorite part of each episode was filming the scene we called the "angel revelation." It came about forty minutes into the show. Monica was an undercover angel pretending to be a nurse or a doctor or a police officer, but she was truly there to help someone at an emotional crossroads. The moment always came when they broke down, feeling lost in the midst of their painful circumstances, before finally fully surrendering to God. They would cry out: "I cannot do this by myself. God help me." This was the central, emotional heart of each episode. Monica would then reveal her true identity as an angel from Almighty God. She was a messenger, and the message was this: "There is a God, He loves you, and He has a plan for your life." Before filming this scene, I would close my eyes, open my heart, and pray.

It was an emotional moment to film, but it also filled me up—so much so that I would leave the set feeling as if God had just touched me personally. This was the moment that person opened his or her eyes and felt the truth he or she had forgotten: That he or she was a special child of a loving God—a child who was loved unconditionally. That God was always there. That he or she had never been alone, despite desperate feelings of loneliness.

It was a moment of remembering.

When we are caught up in the busyness of our lives, we forget our true role in this life. When we are wrapped up in worrying about the future or are stressed about something we did in the past, we do not feel God's peace. But if we can simply stop and be in the *now*, we can remember Him. In remembering Him we come to a point of stillness and surrender. And it is in our stillness that God comes in. It is in the silence that we hear the whisper of His voice.

Be still, and know that I am God.

PSALM 46:10 (NIV)

It was such a privilege to bring that message of unconditional love to a nation full of viewers for so many years.

And in some ways, that is what I am trying to do in this book. I pray this book is a moment of remembering for *you*. A remembering of who you really are, how much God loves you, and that you are never, ever truly alone.

Before we would film each scene of revelation, we would pray as a cast and crew. My personal prayer was always, "Less of me, more of You." I pray that for this book as well. This is not about me or my life or even my faith. This is about how God has shown up in my life—and how He can show up in yours.

In these pages I'll share songs and prayers and poems that have kept me going in both the sunshine and shadows of my life. I'll share glimpses of God that I have found in the written word or in a particular image. And I pray that as you read these words, you may remember, you may awaken, you may feel God's gentle presence. And that you then may go forward, knowing that the greatest Shepherd, Companion, and Father is always by your side.

For I am the Lord your God
who takes hold of your right hand
and says to you, Do not fear;
I will help you.

ISAIAH 41:13 (NIV)

He did not say "You shall not be tormented, you shall not be troubled, you shall not be grieved," but he said, "You shall not be overcome."

JULIAN OF NORWICH

He heals the brokenhearted, and binds up their wounds.

PSALM 147:3 (NIV)

STRENGTH

one

STRENGTH

*Our wounds are often the openings into the best
and most beautiful part of us.*

DAVID RICHO

ALL MY LIFE I have been drawn to the ocean. I love the sound of the waves. The natural rhythm of the ebb and flow is like a massage for my mind and my spirit. I have always done my best thinking by the sea. And I often take my worries to the ocean's edge and quietly pray while I walk on the sand.

There is something about the vast expanse of water that helps to put my troubles in proper perspective. In the grand scheme of things, all the concerns I have or deadlines I need to meet suddenly don't seem so critical. The scale of the ocean serves as a reminder of the magnificence of God and the smallness of the things I may be worrying about. As the waves wash in and out, they remind me that this, too, shall pass. It calms me and restores me. Sometimes I stand alone on the shore and sing at the top of my voice and see my footprints on the sand. With each wave that races to the beach, I watch them gently wash away.

I did not grow up by the seaside, but Ireland is a small island surrounded on all sides by water. I grew up in the North West, and many of my childhood summers were spent in Donegal. The ocean there is wilder than the Pacific, but even when it was cold—and it was often cold—I loved being near it and found it energizing.

> I need the sea because it teaches me.
>
> PABLO NERUDA

We would go to the little seaside town of Moville on day trips or family outings, and after a full day of playing on the beach or walking along the shore toward Greencastle, we'd end up having our evening meal at a nice family-run hotel. It felt so swanky to eat out and have a waiter serve us. I now have the good fortune to eat out regularly, but back then this was a total luxury. My brother Lawrence and I would order steak and chips, and they would serve our ketchup in these little silver bowls. And as a special treat, we were allowed to order a bottle of Coca-Cola or Fanta Orange. We'd go home tired from all the sea air and meat and potatoes.

When I look back on my childhood, I know it was a happy one. We lived in a tiny row house, in a neighborhood filled with other children. It was a time when kids went out onto the streets to play. Boys had their own games, primarily soccer, while the girls would pass the time with hopscotch using an old shoe polish tin as the marker, or throwing tennis balls against the drugstore wall to the beat of a variety of rhyming songs that all the girls would sing. When wet weather drove us indoors, we'd play paper dolls and put on talent shows and play dress-up—all the games of imagination that ignited in me dreams of being an actress and living a different life.

My mother loved the theater. In another life she may have loved pursuing a career on the stage herself. It was from her that I developed my love of and passion for performing. With her encouragement, I took dance classes and music classes and singing classes and elocution classes. Yes, elocution! She would come with me and sit off to the side of the classroom, urging me on with her love and her laughter and her enthusiasm. I adored her. She was warm, gregarious, and very funny. She would have made an excellent comic actress, like an Irish Lucille Ball.

At bedtime she would lie on top of the covers on my bed, as the night slowly ushered in the darkness, singing show tunes to me as I fell asleep. Then one week shy of my eleventh birthday, my mother died of a heart attack. Her young, vibrant life was cut unexpectedly short, and my happy childhood abruptly ended.

It happened on an ordinary day. My mother, brother, and I were walking from our row house to the library nearby. Without warning, my mother collapsed in the street. She was able to get back up and sit on the side of the road while my brother ran to a neighbor's house for help. They got their car and drove us home and helped my mother to her bed.

Mom, not wanting her children to worry, kept trying to reassure us. "Oh, I've just got a wee tummy ache. Don't worry, I'll be fine with a bit of rest."

My father was summoned, as well as the doctor, and it was decided that she would go to the hospital for some tests. An ambulance arrived, but because our row house was so narrow, they couldn't fit a stretcher up the staircase to fetch her, so instead, my mother was carried down in a chair by four men. I remember her making jokes as they strapped her in and hoisted the chair, her humor making the men who carried her laugh. It is one of the last memories I have of her alive.

My brother, father, and I were standing in the doorway of what we called "the good room," and as she passed by she looked at us, smiling, and said, "Don't worry, I'll see you soon. Lawrence, you take care of your sister until I get back. Roma, you take care of your da."

We never saw her again.

The next morning, a hush descended on the household as news spread that our mother was ill, and various adults whispered as they entered and exited the house. The phone's constant ringing was the soundtrack to the tense morning. It was clear that something bad was going on.

Pretty soon my brother and I were packed up to go to the hospital with my father. I was hopeful that we were going there to bring our mother home. We entered a waiting room, a room that I remember being defined by the loud tick-tock of the clock echoing in the stressful silence.

There we sat, my father, my brother, my mother's sister Ruby, and her best friend, Maureen, who shared the same name as my mom. Eventually a doctor came in and asked my father to step outside.

And when my dad came back in, he was crying. I had never seen him cry before.

"She's gone," he said, with a quiet sob.

Be strong and courageous. Do not be afraid or terrified because of them, for the Lord your God goes with you; he will never leave you nor forsake you.

DEUTERONOMY 31:6 (NIV)

At first, I didn't understand. There is always a part of you that doesn't want to believe in the face of tragedy. But as I watched my father cry, I knew there was only one thing that could make him cry. My mother was dead.

For me, it was like the lights had been turned out and all the color of life removed.

She had been the joy in our home. She was the warm fire on a cold night; she was the cheerful word on a gloomy day. She was the center of my world, and then suddenly, in an instant, she was gone.

No more Mom sitting in the corner waiting for me, no more songs as I fell asleep, no more holding hands and running in the rain.

I often say that my father was sadness in a suit after the loss of my mother. I know he felt her absence deeply. She had been so gregarious and joyful, and laughter came very easily to her, while my father was more reserved and even a little shy. Our entire household had to recalibrate after she was gone, and for a while, we stumbled around in the dark, all of us grieving, unsure of the way forward.

This was the second tragedy for my father. He had been married before, and his first wife had died, leaving him with four children under the age of twelve to raise on his own. He met and married my mother many years later, when his four children were grown, and he had built another happy family. Yet once again, he found himself wearing the heavy mantle of widower, this time with two children under the age of twelve. His now grown children did what they could to help, but they had lives and families of their own. Because of our age differences, they were more like aunts and uncles to me, but they tried to help us feel a sense of family in the wake of another tragic loss. They, too, knew what it was to grow up without a mother.

I took my troubles to the Lord; I cried out to him, and he answered my prayer.

PSALM 120:1 (NLT)

My dad did his best to be not only a father but a mother to us as well. He didn't sing me to sleep, but every night he would lie down beside me and read poetry to me before I went to sleep. And then he would turn out the lights and make the sound of the ocean to calm me into slumber.

I look back on this painful time and remember being so confused. How could my mother be so healthy and by my side one day and then gone the next? I worried that perhaps it was my fault—if I had somehow been *more*, she would have stayed. I strove to be a good girl, so scared that if I did something wrong, my dad would be taken as well.

I remember riding home from the hospital in a taxi that horrible morning she died. I sat in the backseat with my brother, and my mother's best friend, whom we called Auntie Maureen, sat up front with the driver. It was a rainy, bleak day. I stared out the rain-flecked window, feeling so alone. And then I heard my aunt say quietly to the driver, "My best friend, Maureen O'Reilly, just died. Those are her w'anes back there." It was the first time I had heard those words spoken out loud. Without looking at each other, my brother and I reached out across the backseat of the taxi and clasped each other's hands, knowing that our lives had been changed forever.

That memory has stuck with me all these years. And, to me, that moment embodies the instinct we all have during difficult times. To reach out for someone's hand, to be reassured that no matter how painful life is, there is always someone to reach out to. A brother, a sister, a friend, or God.

Because the truth is, though we may feel so alone, we are never truly alone.

What I sometimes find astonishing is that the song my mother sang to me every night before I went to sleep is a song from the Rodgers and Hammerstein musical *Carousel*. It is called "You'll Never Walk Alone." When I was a child, listening to my mother's beautiful voice sing me to sleep, it reminded me that even after she put me to bed and closed the door and went down to the living room to be with my father, she was somehow still with me. And, of course, after her death, that song came to symbolize so much more. That no matter where I am, she will always be with me.

You'll Never Walk Alone

When you walk through a storm
Hold your head up high
And don't be afraid of the dark.
At the end of the storm is a golden sky
And the sweet silver song of a lark.

Walk on through the wind,
Walk on through the rain,
Tho' your dreams be tossed and blown.
Walk on, walk on, with hope in your heart
And you'll never walk alone,
You'll never walk alone.

Richard Rodgers and Oscar Hammerstein II

Even today, as I read those words, my eyes fill with tears. What truth lies in those lyrics. Dark and stormy times will come, but when they do, we must keep walking through the wind and the rain, our eyes fixed on where we pray the golden sky will appear.

This is the essence of faith, isn't it? To keep hold of the knowledge that this isn't the end, that there is a promise of heaven, that God can redeem even the most difficult circumstances.

Shortly after my mother died, my father shared the poem "Footprints" with me. I have carried that poem in my wallet

ever since. It talks about a person of faith looking back on her life and seeing two sets of footprints on the sand, representing that God has been by her side her entire life. But as the person looks closer, she notices that during the darkest times in her life, there is just one set of footprints. At first she reaches out to God in anger—*How could you abandon me when I needed you most?* But God gently says, *No, my dear child. For it is then that I was carrying you.*

Throughout my life, I've found that it is in those very moments of darkness that God can come in. In the dark is when His light can shine the brightest. For when we are struggling, unable to hold it all together, is when we surrender. And that is when He can finally pick us up and carry us.

Our glory is hidden in our pain, if we allow God to bring the gift of himself in our experience of it.

HENRI NOUWEN

The Lord is my shepherd, I lack nothing.

He makes me lie down in green pastures,

he leads me beside quiet waters,

he refreshes my soul.

He guides me along the right paths

for his name's sake.

Even though I walk

through the darkest valley,

I will fear no evil,

for you are with me;

your rod and your staff,

they comfort me.

You prepare a table before me

in the presence of my enemies.

You anoint my head with oil;

my cup overflows.

Surely your goodness and love will follow me

all the days of my life,

and I will dwell in the house of the Lord

forever.

Psalm 23 (NIV)

A MESSAGE IN
THE MOON

When you walk to the edge of all the light you have,
And take that first step into the darkness of the unknown,
You must believe one of two things will happen:
There will be something solid for you to stand upon,
Or, you will be taught how to fly.

PATRICK OVERTON

When I think of my father, I can see that throughout my life, he was always trying to give me wings so that I could go anywhere I wanted. He said over and over that my education would be my passport out and that I needed to work hard in school so I could go to college. He was always supportive and encouraging of my artistic desires, and when the time came to interview for college, he went with me and sat in the waiting area!

As I was preparing to leave Ireland for school in England, I began to feel anxious. This was before the Internet and cell phones, and to be so far away from my father, with no way of immediately reaching him, made me extremely nervous.

One night, just a few days before I was scheduled to leave, he took me outside to the backyard. It was a clear night with a full moon. And he said, "Roma, wherever you are in the world, that moon will be shining on you. So whenever you feel alone, always look into the night sky, and you'll be reminded of how much I love you. I'll leave a message for you in the moon."

I hugged him, so grateful for his sweet gentleness and his constant care and attention.

And as that first full moon

Education is not the filling of a pail, but the lighting of a fire.

WILLIAM BUTLER YEATS

ascended after I had settled in England, I went outside and looked up at the moon. And I felt my dad's love. It was a great comfort.

Since my mother had passed away, I had lived in fear that something might happen to Dad. If he was late coming home from work or I came home to an empty house when I expected him to be there, I would get worried, so frightened that he, too, was gone.

My father tried to reassure me in those moments, but also to strengthen me. I'll never forget something he said to me at a very young age: "Roma, remember that if you can bury your da, you can do anything. There won't be anything you can't do if you can bury your da." He knew that his death was my greatest fear. He also knew that day would come, and he wanted to strengthen me so that I would not fall apart in that moment, but be able to gather myself. To find the resources of strength within. And to know that he was by my side, always.

Unfortunately that day came sooner than I expected; my father died during my final year in drama school. In my deep grief, I was so worried that since his spirit had now gone from this earth, I would not be able to feel his love in the moon. That he would no longer be able to send messages. That I would see the moon and not feel his presence, as I always had before.

I was almost afraid to go outside and see.

But I finally walked out to the very backyard where he had

promised his moon messages. I looked up at the big, bright moon. And, sure enough, I felt him—his quiet love, so silent yet strong. I picked up his message: *Wherever you go in the world, Roma, the same moon will always be shining down on you. So never forget, no matter where you are, I will always be there, loving you.* Tears streamed down my face as I felt his love so powerfully.

The moon has been a beautiful comfort to me all these years. And I've now shared this message with my children. Even though we have the technology to be literally at each other's fingertips no matter how many miles may be between us, I sometimes text them when we are apart and say: *Go look at the moon! I left a message for you there.*

he will cover you with his
feathers, and under his
wings you will find refuge;
his faithfulness will be your
shield and rampart. PSALM 91:4

The moon, though it can shine so brightly, has no true light source of its own; it simply reflects the sun. I love the idea that when we send messages of love to the moon, the moon in return does what it does best . . . it reflects those messages to our loved ones. I like to imagine that the moonlight becomes love light.

Throughout the journey of my life, these symbols have helped me feel close to my parents despite their early deaths. Butterflies for my mother, the moon for my father. Both by extension have always reminded me that though I sometimes feel alone, they are still with me in spirit. And, of course, they remind me that I have another Father who has also never left my side: my Heavenly Father.

I've carried a longing for my parents in my heart for many years now. No matter how much I've grown, I still long for the touch of my mom's hand on my brow, the special cadence of her laugh, or my dad's quiet strength. I greatly miss their physical presence.

There are moments when I think it's just so sad and unfair that I haven't been able to share the joys of my life with my parents. I know without a doubt that the course of my career would have delighted my mother, who loved the theater. And I know both my parents would have adored meeting my beautiful daughter, Reilly; they would have been there for her birth and would have held their precious granddaughter in their arms and in their hearts. I know they would have loved meeting my husband, Mark, and the two fine sons, James and Cameron, whom he brought into my life. Of course I have missed my parents every single day since their deaths, but my faith allows me to believe that one day, all will be restored. Someday, there will be a heavenly reunion. Someday, I will see them again, and we will all walk hand in hand, like we did all those years ago.

For the truth is, we never walk alone.

You can do the impossible, because you have been through the unimaginable.

CHRISTINA RASMUSSEN

Remember

Remember me when I am gone away,
    Gone far away into the silent land;
    When you can no more hold me by the hand,
Nor I half turn to go yet turning stay.
Remember me when no more day by day
    You tell me of our future that you plann'd:
    Only remember me; you understand
It will be late to counsel then or pray.
Yet if you should forget me for a while
    And afterwards remember, do not grieve:
    For if the darkness and corruption leave
    A vestige of the thoughts that once I had,
Better by far you should forget and smile
    Than that you should remember and be sad.

Christina Georgina Rossetti

Death is nothing at all.

It does not count.

I have only slipped away into the next room.

Nothing has happened.

Everything remains exactly as it was.

I am I, and you are you,

and the old life that we lived so fondly together

is untouched, unchanged.

Whatever we were to each other, that we are still.

Call me by the old familiar name.

Speak of me in the easy way which you always used.

Put no difference into your tone.

Wear no forced air of solemnity or sorrow.

Laugh as we always laughed at the little jokes

that we enjoyed together.

Play, smile, think of me, pray for me.

Let my name be ever the household word that it always was.

Let it be spoken without an effort,

    without the ghost of a shadow upon it.

Life means all that it ever meant.

It is the same as it ever was.

There is absolute and unbroken continuity.

What is this death but a negligible accident?

Why should I be out of mind because I am out of sight?

I am but waiting for you, for an interval,

somewhere very near,

just round the corner.

All is well.

Nothing is hurt; nothing is lost.

One brief moment and all will be as it was before.

How we shall laugh at the trouble of parting

    when we meet again!

Henry Scott Holland

MY SURROGATE MOTHER

It is not flesh and blood, but heart which
makes us fathers and sons.

FRIEDRICH SCHILLER

I first met Della Reese on the set in Wilmington, North Carolina, where we were filming the pilot for *Touched by an Angel*. I had already gone through hair and makeup and even filmed a few scenes. But I was eager to meet this woman, this other angel who would be my counterpart on the show. As I wrapped a scene, I heard that Miss Della Reese had arrived and was getting made up. I went back to the makeup trailer to finally meet her—and there she was, wearing bright and colorful clothing that was nothing compared to the luminous smile she wore on her face. She *radiated* love and warmth and joy.

I walked up quietly, politely reaching out my hand and saying, "I just wanted to introduce myself."

Della stood up and said, "Oh, baby, I don't shake hands, I hug." And she wrapped me in the biggest, most loving embrace I had ever experienced.

It was love at first sight.

We are an unlikely duo when you think of it—a tough-talking black singer from Detroit, Michigan, and a small, soft-spoken white woman from Ireland. But we hit it off right away, talking about our lives, the challenges we had faced, and our strong faith, which we both knew kept us going and definitely brought us together on this project. The chemistry that we so easily shared offscreen was very present in our relationship on-screen, and I know it enhanced the experience for the viewers. Della, like Tess, was the older, wiser, tougher angel—feisty and formidable and fiercely protective of those she loves.

And in the protective way that Tess loved Monica, Della came to love me.

Now, deep within me, there lives a little girl still longing for a mother. Since the age of nearly eleven, I have been searching for that kind of tender, unconditional love that only a mother can give. And I found that in Della Reese.

Soon, we were always together on set. There is a lot of waiting between rehearsals and actual filming on a film set, so Della and I would meet in our trailers and play backgammon, share books, drink tea, and talk.

When my daughter, Reilly, was born, I chose Della to be her godmother, and at Reilly's christening, Della lifted my precious baby girl heavenward and said, "As long as there is breath in my body, I will always stand up for this child."

I can honestly say that there is absolutely no safer place in the world than in the arms of Della Reese.

Della and I share a love that is deeper than friendship. She became my family that very first day. I truly felt as if I had known her all my life. She has become the first person I call when I need wisdom, and she is a loving teacher and instructor.

A few years later, I was on the *Touched by an Angel* set in Salt Lake City, rehearsing the angel revelation scene, when I heard a commotion offstage. And then someone rushed up to me and said, "Roma, you must go see Della immediately. She needs you."

I quickly ran to Della's trailer, where I found her crying and incoherent, struggling to take off her angel costume and get changed into her regular clothes. I tried to calm her down and get a sense of what was going on. Della was clearly distraught and overwhelmed with grief. Something terrible had happened. "She's gone, she's gone," she cried out as she collapsed into my arms.

I managed to piece together that Della's only daughter had died.

I hardly knew what to do, but I did know that Della needed to get home to Los Angeles. I helped get her dressed and then we rushed into a waiting car to head to the Salt Lake City airport. As we were pulling away, I rolled down the window and called out to an assistant: "Please have someone grab my purse and some shoes and bring them to the airport!" I'd hardly even noticed that I was still in my white angel costume, with no shoes on my feet.

Della looked at me and said, "No, baby, you need to stay, Reilly needs you here." But I brushed aside her concern, now being the strong one in the relationship. "No, I'm coming with you," I said firmly.

Della looked at me sadly and took my hand in hers. "I don't want to talk," she said quietly as she turned to gaze out the window.

There is a holiness about your tears. Each one is a prayer that only God can understand.

KATHE WUNNENBURG

"That's okay," I said. "I won't say a word. I'll just be here with you the whole way, holding your hand."

When we got to the airport, I purchased tickets for the flight back to L.A. and met my assistant, Linda, who had brought me my purse, my ID, and a pair of shoes. We somehow made it through security and onto the plane without too much fuss. Della is such a recognizable person, but I knew that now was not the time to deal with requests for autographs. I was a guard dog, protecting my mama. No one would bother her. I would keep her safe until I got her home and into the loving arms of her husband, Franklin.

There was a moment during the flight when Della finally fell asleep, and I could feel the tension leave her body. I silently prayed that she could rest a bit before having to wake up and deal with the reality of this heartbreak. But after only a few moments, she jolted and awoke, and I could feel the remembering take place in her body. I squeezed her hand. My heart was breaking for her, and I silently prayed that God would give her strength and comfort.

When we arrived in L.A., I walked Della down the jetway to the gate, where Franklin was waiting. "Daddy," she said, which was what she called him, and she was enveloped in his embrace. I sat down in a nearby chair, wanting to give them privacy in this deep moment of grief, knowing that my job was done. I hadn't wanted her to be alone in her pain, and now she was with her beloved, and she could go home and begin the grieving process.

I didn't have anywhere to stay and hadn't packed anything for the trip, and I had planned to fly back home to Utah to be with my Reilly. But the last flight back had already left. I sat down, unsure what to do, and then I saw a familiar face. It was Martha Williamson, the executive producer of *Touched by an Angel*. She walked up to me and said, "Is it just you here by yourself?"

And I said, "Yes, Della has gone home with Franklin."

Martha smiled. "Well, I just had a feeling I needed to come and be here for one of my angels. I thought it was Della I came for. But now I guess I am here for you!" So I went home with her and flew back to Utah the next day.

A few months later, Della and I were back in Los Angeles, taking a walk on the beach together. Looking out on the beauty of the ocean, Della said, "God is wonderful, isn't He?" I nodded in agreement, grateful that she could still feel His goodness in this dark time in her life. "But really, baby," she continued, "I did not know until now just how wonderful He is. You see, He brought me into your life because you needed a mama, didn't He?" she said quietly. Again I nodded, now holding her hand as she gazed out at the grand expanse of the sea. "But, baby," she said softly, "I didn't know He was bringing you into my life because I was gonna need a baby girl . . ." Her voice caught with emotion, and I put my arms around her, tears rolling down my face as well. She wiped her eyes and turned to face me. "Will you be my baby girl, Roma?" she asked me.

"Yes," I said, my heart welling with emotion.

"Well," she said lovingly and with strength, "then I am your mama. I am your mama."

Now, in that moment, I was longing for my real mama and Della for her real baby girl. But we were also overflowing with gratitude to God for giving us each other to fill the holes in our aching hearts. God had a plan for us. We didn't know the comfort we would find from loving each other, but God knew.

The redemption of our losses doesn't make the pain go away; it doesn't mean the loss didn't happen. But it does mean that, in even the darkest moment, there can be light again.

The real hope is not in something we think we can do,
but in God, who is making something good out of it
in some way we cannot see.

THOMAS MERTON

There is an appointed time for everything.

And there is a time for every event under heaven.

A time to give birth, and a time to die;

A time to plant, and a time to uproot what is planted.

A time to kill, and a time to heal;

A time to tear down, and a time to build up.

A time to weep, and a time to laugh;

A time to mourn, and a time to dance.

A time to throw stones, and a time to gather stones;

A time to embrace, and a time to shun embracing.

A time to search, and a time to give up as lost;

A time to keep, and a time to throw away.

A time to tear apart, and a time to sew together;

A time to be silent, and a time to speak.

A time to love, and a time to hate;

A time for war, and a time for peace.

What profit is there to the worker from that in which he

toils?

I have seen the task which God has given

the sons of men with which to occupy themselves.

He has made everything appropriate in its time.

He has also set eternity in their heart,

yet so that man will not find out the work

which God has done from the beginning even to the end.

I know that there is nothing better for them

than to rejoice and to do good in one's lifetime;

moreover, that every man who eats and drinks

sees good in all his labor—it is the gift of God.

I know that everything God does will remain forever;

there is nothing to add to it and there is nothing

to take from it,

for God has so worked that men should fear Him.

That which is has been already

and that which will be has already been,

for God seeks what has passed by.

Ecclesiastes 3:1–15 (NASB)

Let me not pray to be sheltered from dangers
but to be fearless in facing them.

Let me not beg for the stilling of my pain
but for the heart to conquer it.

RABINDRANATH TAGORE

STRUGGLES MAKE
YOU STRONGER

Just when the caterpillar thought the world
was over, it became a butterfly.

ENGLISH PROVERB

Mark and I had the privilege of bringing the epic story of Ben-Hur back to the big screen, a huge undertaking that involved lots of talented people, much travel, and a big crew for special effects.

But there is a small moment in the film, probably one that most people won't even notice, that has come to mean so much to me.

It comes toward the end of the film, as Judah Ben-Hur has just accomplished what he was striving to achieve for the entire film—revenge. He, along with his mother and sister, had been wrongfully imprisoned for the attempted assassination of the governor. He has just won the epic chariot race that led to the demise of his longtime nemesis, Messala. But as he stumbles out of the arena and looks around, he is surprised to find that instead of being filled with triumph from his victory, he feels profoundly empty. This driving force had been his mission for his entire life. Now, having achieved what he thought he so desperately needed, he realizes that his victory delivers no fulfillment.

As Judah begins to walk down the street, he sees a man being forced to carry a heavy wooden cross. The man is surrounded on either side by Roman guards, and Judah can see how deeply the man is suffering. Remembering his many years as a slave, forced to walk long distances with no water or rest, he rushes up to this poor man to offer some water. But the Romans kick him away. "No water for him!" they yell.

In anger, Judah grabs a rock to defend the man carrying the cross. But the man looks him in the eye and says: "I give my life of my own free will."

Judah stops in shock and watches the procession continue. He follows along silently as the group walks to the place where this man is crucified. Judah can't look away. As the man takes his last breaths, Judah hears Him say: "Father, forgive them, for they know not what they do."

The man on the cross is of course Jesus, and Judah is so overcome with emotion that he drops to his knees. He finally understands and knows what he needs to do. Revenge didn't quench his thirst. But forgiveness will.

Judah looks down at his hands. He's still clutching the rock that he grabbed back on the street to defend Jesus.

And as forgiveness fills his heart, he is able at last to let it go. The rock drops to the ground.

And he is finally free.

To me, that scene represents the need we all have to let go, to surrender. To hand our burdens over to God. Sometimes, like Judah, we don't realize how much we are carrying and how much it is weighing us down. Sometimes we carry anger, like Judah. Other times, disappointment or sadness or regret. Usually the burden we carry stems from the struggles in our lives.

Ring the bells that still can ring

Forget your perfect offering

There is a crack, a crack in everything

That's how the light gets in.

LEONARD COHEN

We all have the opportunity to kneel before God and lay our stuff down.

He will always take it.

And therein lies such freedom.

What is weighing you down? What loss have you experienced that you haven't been able to truly grieve or let go of?

Could you, like Judah, drop that rock and finally open your hands to receive what God wants to bestow?

God is always looking to redeem, restore, renew, and forgive.

Loss is a part of our lives, but it is in those times of darkness that God forges a new person. Just as the caterpillar must go into the darkness of the cocoon to become a butterfly, we often find that God's loving redemption is strongest in our most painful suffering. God is always looking for ways to transform us through our circumstances if we will just let Him in. We must remember that through the struggle, God is building our wings so that we can soon emerge a new creation, stronger than before, and able to fly.

God is the ultimate creator and miracle worker. He can make anything from our lives—no matter what they look like. He can make beauty from ashes, winged creatures from creepy crawlies, light from dark, life from death. It is when we stop and listen for Him, for grace, that we can remember the truth, that we can reframe what is happening. Though the facts remain the same, a simple reframing of the story can change the ultimate experience, and of course the ending. Then I can see the truth: I have not fallen into a deep dark pit that I cannot get out of. Rather, this darkness is forging my new being.

For there in the journey and stuck in the sting, the struggle . . . the struggle . . . is what gives you wings!
KAREN KINGSBURY

If I have learned anything, I know this to be true: there is no growth without pain.

The very things we struggle with actually give us the strength and character to become who we are. Think about the fact that the butterfly begins as such an ordinary bug. But then it becomes a stunning creature that can fly great distances. Did you know that monarch butterflies can fly up to three thousand miles during their migration? That they can fly at speeds up to twenty miles per hour? Some pilots have actually seen them at an altitude of eleven thousand feet. The beauty and strength of a simple butterfly remind me that with God all things are possible.

You can choose to stay a caterpillar, crawling on the ground your entire life. Or you can subject yourself to the transformation process, the pain of metamorphosis, and become someone who, with God's help, can fly to the highest heights, move at great speeds, and explore the world with wonder and gratitude.

I consider that the sufferings of this present time are not worth comparing with the glory about to be revealed to us.

ROMANS 8:18 (NRSV)

For Courage

When the light around you lessens
And your thoughts darken until
Your body feels fear turn
Cold as a stone inside,

When you find yourself bereft
Of any belief in yourself
And all you unknowingly
Leaned on has fallen,

When one voice commands
Your whole heart,
And it is raven dark,

Steady yourself and see
That it is your own thinking
That darkens your world,

Search and you will find
A diamond-thought of light,

Know that you are not alone
And that this darkness has purpose;

Gradually it will school your eyes
To find the one gift your life requires
Hidden within this night-corner.

Invoke the learning
Of every suffering
You have suffered.

Close your eyes.
Gather all the kindling
About your heart
To create one spark.
That is all you need
To nourish the flame
That will cleanse the dark
Of its weight of festered fear.

A new confidence will come alive
To urge you towards higher ground
Where your imagination
Will learn to engage difficulty
As its most rewarding threshold!

John O'Donohue

Japanese Bowl

I'm like one of those Japanese bowls
That were made long ago
I have some cracks in me
They have been filled with gold

That's what they used back then
When they had a bowl to mend
It did not hide the cracks

It made them shine instead
So now every old scar shows
From every time I broke
And anyone's eyes can see
I'm not what I used to be
But in a collector's mind
All of these jagged lines
Make me more beautiful
And worth a much higher price
I'm like one of those Japanese bowls
I was made long ago
I have some cracks you can see
See how they shine of gold

Peter Mayer

Thank you, God.
That though our hearts break
in this world,
You are always there.
Thank you, that during my
darkest moments,
You were carrying me.
Even as I felt so alone.
May I hold fast to the
hope that you provide,
that you can raise the dead,
that in the dark, light is coming,
that ultimately, all
brokenness will be healed,
relationship restored,
that wholeness and peace
is our birthright.

Like it or not, we either add to the darkness of
indifference and out-and-out evil which
surrounds us or we light a candle to see by.

MADELEINE L'ENGLE

It is better to light one candle
than to curse the darkness.

AUTHOR UNKNOWN

KINDNESS

two

KINDNESS

No one is born hating another person because
of the color of his skin, or his background, or his religion.
People must learn to hate, and if they can learn to hate,
they can be taught to love, for love comes more naturally
to the human heart than its opposite.

NELSON MANDELA

I WAS BORN in Derry City, Northern Ireland, a beautiful border town in the North West of Ireland. Yet throughout my childhood, my town was filled with tension and violence that began when I was about eight years old. I grew up in the midst of a war that became known in Ireland as "the Troubles."

Ours was a story of neighboring people wanting different things and being unable to find common ground. The Catholics desired independence from the United Kingdom, hoping to become part of the Republic of Ireland (Republicans); while the Protestants wanted to remain a part of the

United Kingdom (Loyalists). Both sides harbored animosity, distrust, and prejudice toward each other.

When the violence between the communities began to escalate, the British army arrived. But before long, it became clear that those sent in to establish peace became an army of occupation, and the conflict only increased with their presence.

As children, we would sometimes get detoured on our way home from school because of bomb scares or gun battles. We learned from an early age to hide behind cars and walls, quickly becoming little experts on telling how close the gunfire was. If it was a loud crack, you better take cover quickly; if it was more muted, you were probably safe for the moment and could continue on your way home.

We lived on the same street as John and Pat Hume. John was one of the great politicians of the day and was instrumental in bringing peace to Northern Ireland, and went on to win the Nobel Peace Prize. My mother and Pat became great friends, and their young daughter Mo was named after my mother.

Not long after my beloved mom passed away, I went to the cemetery to put flowers on her grave for Mother's Day. It was chilly and damp, and the wind blew sharply on the hillside where she was buried. I had bundled up in my favorite red woolen cape, with fake fur trim, to protect me from the sharp chill in the air. I was with my Auntie Ruby, my mother's only sister, and we brought with us some beautiful pansies, my mother's favorite flower.

The Town I Loved So Well

But when I returned how my eyes have burned

To see how a town could be brought to its knees

By the armoured cars and the bombed-out bars

And the gas that hangs on to every breeze.

Now the army's installed by the old gasyard wall

And the damned barbed wire gets higher and higher

With their tanks and their guns, oh my God,

what have they done

To the town I loved so well.

Phil Coulter

My eyes were filled with tears as I placed this small offering by her tombstone. Her absence in my life had broken my heart, and as we stood by her graveside, I missed her so desperately I could hardly breathe. I longed to hear her laughter and the sound of her voice calling my name. I ached to feel the warmth and safety of her arms around me. I didn't know if my mother could see me, if she could see the flowers I had so carefully selected for her. I longed to have her back.

My auntie's hand was on my shoulder when we heard the first loud gunshot. We both dropped to the ground instinctively, but this area of the cemetery offered no protection.

A wide, lonely hillside on a cold afternoon. And here I was, wearing a bright red cape.

My aunt pulled me to my feet and we began to run to see if we could find a large gravestone to duck behind. The shots rang out, and we saw a few others running for cover in the area around us.

"Get down, get down where you are!" a man yelled at us, seeing my bright red cape and realizing how much of a target it made me.

My aunt pulled me to the ground, just as we both smelled a scent like burned hair. She covered me with her body as we lay on the cold, wet earth, praying for protection and hoping that the battle would end.

Finally, the shooting stopped, and after we were certain it was over, we cautiously picked ourselves up off the ground and embraced in gratitude. Then, with my hand tight in hers, Auntie Ruby hurried me down the hill toward the safety of home.

As soon as we opened the front door, I ran to our kitchen, tears streaming down my face, to find my dad.

He held me close as my aunt told him what had happened.

He rubbed my back, calming me down. But then he grabbed the hood of my cape and said, "Ruby, come look at this."

And there, on the fake fur trim of my hooded red cape, was a large singed hole where a bullet had narrowly missed my head.

"Oh, thanks be to God," gasped my aunt as my father nodded. "Yes, thanks be to God indeed."

Years later, when Della heard that story, she said, "There were angels watching over you that day, baby." That is for sure.

Growing up in such troubled times planted in me the desire to work toward creating peace in the world.

The River Foyle divides Derry; and as the Troubles escalated, the communities on either side of the river became more and more segregated. It broke my heart to see our town split in two. So much anger and fear and sadness and loss on both sides. But my dad refused to give up hope. He always looked

You've Got to Be Carefully Taught

You've got to be taught to hate and fear,
You've got to be taught from year to year,
It's got to be drummed in your dear little ear
You've got to be carefully taught!
You've got to be taught to be afraid
Of people whose eyes are oddly made,
And people whose skin is a different shade
You've got to be carefully taught.
You've got to be taught before it's too late,
Before you are six or seven or eight,
To hate all the people your relatives hate
You've got to be carefully taught!

RICHARD RODGERS AND OSCAR HAMMERSTEIN II

for ways to build bridges. He always spoke of tolerance and love. He taught me that we should reach out to each other in neighborly love and support.

In those years, I listened to the music of Simon and Garfunkel and replayed their cassette over and over. They sang of a bridge over troubled water. Clearly we needed that in our community—and indeed we would rejoice to finally see a new Peace Bridge opened over the River Foyle in 2011. But back in the 1970s, my dad encouraged me to explore how we each could be that bridge in our own lives. How we could be angels of peace in the lives of others if only we were willing to let God use us. My dad reminded me that we just needed to have the eyes to see the opportunities and the openness of heart to see each calling to love. He taught me to pray and to ask God for His guidance in my life.

I always remember my father saying, "Love is a verb." Quiet by nature, he was more prone to performing small acts of kindness than peppering you with words of adoration. He was a thoughtful man, and I adored him. After my mother's death, I became more attached to him than ever. He was a schoolmaster, and later ran a mortgage-loan company; and in our predominantly working-class neighborhood, he was very well respected—not just because he had a college education and wore a shirt and tie every day but because he was never condescending to people. He was respectful and kind; and even though people in our community called each other by their first names, my dad remained Mr. Downey to many.

He volunteered to teach grown men in our community to read and write, yet did this discreetly to allow these men their pride and privacy. He was always seeking to help the world in little ways. And his acts of kindness spread far and wide.

His example has been an inspiration to me my entire life. It has caused me to commit to treating people with kindness and respect and to be on the lookout for ways to brighten someone's day. It's easy to get busy and forget to share simple kindnesses, but I know from experience that little acts of compassion add up to a life of great significance.

I've learned that people will forget what
you said, people will forget what
you did, but people will never forget
how you made them feel.

MAYA ANGELOU

Do all the good you can,

By all the means you can,

In all the ways you can,

In all the places you can,

At all the times you can,

To all the people you can,

As long as you ever can.

John Wesley

THE FLANNEL SHEETS

Actions speak louder than words . . .

MARK TWAIN

I was eighteen when I finally left Derry. As the Troubles continued with no sign of letting up, my dad knew an education would be my passport to a new and bigger life. So, with his blessing, when I graduated from high school I first went to Brighton College of Art, in the South of England, and then on to London and drama school. In London, I rented a room in one of those big Georgian houses that had been converted into flats. I missed my dad and went back to visit as often as I could.

It was late in the spring of my last semester in drama school, and I was planning a trip home to Ireland to stay with my father for the unexpected ordination of my eldest half brother, John. John was many years older than me, and had felt the calling to the priesthood late in his life, so it was a surprise for all of us. I knew how proud my father was that his oldest son was going to become a priest.

In the absence of cell phones, the lodgers in my flat shared a black pay phone in the chilly hallway by the front door. As I telephoned my father to confirm my travel arrangements the day before my flight, I pictured my small town and the grand celebration I knew was being planned. When I heard my father's voice on the other end of the line, a feeling of safety immediately washed over me. The sweet sound of his lilting voice was so comforting and familiar, even over the phone. We discussed my early flight the next morning from Heathrow Airport to Belfast, how I would be picked up at the airport and that I would be home in time for tea.

As we wrapped up our call, my father, a man of few words, said that he was so glad I was coming home and that, because of the ever-present dampness in our Derry air, he had hung my favorite yellow flannel sheets on the indoor line to air.

Our climate in the North of Ireland is damp at the best of times. To this day, when it rains in Malibu, I affectionately call it a "Derry Day." This was a time before dryers, and we just had a washtub and a wringer to do the laundry. In Ireland, we were rarely able to dry anything outside due to the rainy weather, so people in our town had indoor clotheslines, usually in the kitchen where there might be a stove to provide warmth and dryness.

I went to bed that night imagining the soft, cozy feel of those flannel sheets, prepared for me by my loving father. My little suitcase, packed for the trip and slightly frayed, was standing ready at the end of the bed.

In the middle of the night the guy from the front flat

began pounding on my door. "Wake up, Irish!" he yelled. "And tell your bloody family not to call in the middle of the night!" My heart skipped a beat as I rushed out of bed, fear flooding every step down the cold hallway in the dark. I lifted the heavy receiver, delaying a moment longer before I finally whispered hello.

My brother Lawrence was on the phone. My dad was dead. Lawrence told me it was sudden; apparently Dad's heart gave out.

I did not know what to do. I must have said something. I must have hung up the telephone. I know I slid down the wall and sat in the dark. I'm not sure for how long. I was in shock. I had just heard his voice. I had just spoken to him. How could he be gone? How had the very thing I feared most since my mother's death really happened?

I remembered how my dad had always said, "If you can bury your da, you can do anything." I knew I was no longer a little girl. I was making my way in the world, and I knew how proud my father was of my life in London, my dream of being an actress. But I still wanted him here. I didn't want to have to bury him.

I knew I could not sleep, so I went back to my room and waited until the sun came up. Then I took the flight I was scheduled to take, but now my journey home had a whole new, unwelcome purpose.

By the time I got to Derry, my father's body had already been returned to our brick row house for the wake, our front door displaying the black bow of mourning. In our loving Irish tradition, we still lay out our dead in our living rooms for the great parade of friends and family and neighbors, coming to pay their respects. The Irish wake is designed to provide the family with love and support as they send off their loved ones and say good-bye.

I walked into our dark little hallway and past the room where he lay. I was not ready yet to see him dead, needing first the courage that comes only from a cup of tea. Tea, the Irish solution to everything. So I slipped into our kitchen, so familiar to me in every way, and a vision took my breath away. For there, hanging on the indoor clothesline to air, were my favorite yellow flannel sheets, the last loving act of a most thoughtful man. I held them to my face, breathed in their kindness, and cried.

John walked into the room and saw me standing, holding the sheets. Not knowing of the last conversation I had with my father, he was focused on the practical, the fact that we would soon have countless friends and family streaming through the door to pay their respects. "Oh, we have to get these old sheets down before people come calling," he said as he went to put the teakettle on.

"Oh, not yet, not yet," I said quietly. I wanted those sheets there while I had my cup of tea, one final reminder of the kindness of my father, of how, during his last moments on earth, he was thinking of me, his youngest daughter, and how he could best welcome me home.

If I speak in the
tongues of men and
of angels but have not
love, I am a noisy gong or
a clanging cymbal. And if
I have prophetic powers and
understand all mysteries and all
knowledge, and if I have all faith, so as
to remove mountains, but have not love, I am
nothing. If I give away all I have, and if I deliver up
my body to be burned, but have not love, I gain nothing.

Love is patient and kind; love does not envy or boast;
it is not arrogant or rude. It does not insist on its own
way; it is not irritable or resentful; it does not rejoice at
wrongdoing, but rejoices with the truth. Love bears all
things, believes all things, hopes all things, endures all
things. Love never ends. As for prophecies, they will pass
away; as for tongues, they will cease; as for knowledge,
it will pass away. For we know in part and we prophesy
in part, but when the perfect comes, the partial will pass
away. When I was a child, I spoke like a child, I thought
like a child, I reasoned like a child. When I became a man,
I gave up childish ways. For now we see in a mirror dimly,
but then face-to-face. Now I know in part; then I shall
know fully, even as I have been fully known.

So now faith, hope, and love abide, these three; but the
greatest of these is love.

1 Corinthians 13 (ESV)

Lord,

make me an instrument
of Your peace.
Where there is hatred,
let me sow love;
where there is injury, pardon; where
there is doubt, faith;
where there is despair, hope;
where there is darkness, light; where
there is sadness, joy.
O, Divine Master,
grant that I may not so much seek
to be consoled as to console;
to be understood as to understand;
to be loved as to love;
for it is in giving that we receive;
it is in pardoning that we are
pardoned; it is in dying that we are
born again to eternal life.

PRAYER OF SAINT FRANCIS

Do not think that love, in order to be genuine,
has to be extraordinary. What we need is to love
without getting tired.

How does a lamp burn?
Through the continuous input of small drops of oil.
If the drops of oil run out, the light of the lamp will cease, and
the bridegroom will say, "I do not know you." (Matthew 25:12).

My daughters, what are these drops of oil in our lamps? They
are the small things of daily life: faithfulness, punctuality, small
words of kindness, a thought for others, our way of being silent,
of looking, of speaking, and of acting. These are the true drops
of love . . .

Be faithful in small things, because it is in them that your
strength lies.

Mother Teresa

WHAT IS A SMILE WORTH?

If you want to lift yourself up, lift up someone else.

BOOKER T. WASHINGTON

Many years ago, on the very first season of *Touched by an Angel*, we shot an episode that featured the organization Operation Smile. Operation Smile was founded to provide a safe, simple surgery to the countless impoverished children who are born with a craniofacial anomaly, usually a cleft palate or lip. This is a common issue, occurring in one out of every 500 to 750 births. Doctors can repair the lip or palate easily, and usually do so in the United States by the time the child is three months old for a cleft lip, or by the time the child is between twelve and eighteen months old for a cleft palate. Yet across the rest of the globe, many of these children do not have access to this straightforward, forty-five-minute surgery.

It was a powerful episode to film for both the cast and crew, and viewers across the world were touched deeply as well. I soon became actively involved in the organization as a spokesperson and began to travel around the globe, helping them on their mission to change the world one smile at a time.

Many of these children are born into cultures where stigmas are attached to such an anomaly, where it is viewed as a curse and a shame on the family, with no hope of a cure. Some children with cleft lips and palates cannot eat properly or smile or speak. The mothers of these children worry. They worry that their children will never have a normal life. The worry they will die. They pray for a cure, not realizing that one exists.

And then they hear rumors about this medical group coming, a group of doctors who supposedly have the ability to fix faces. And a seed of hope is planted. This seed of hope drives these women to walk miles or get on a bus to go to far-off places, all in hopes that their child might be chosen and given a chance at a normal life.

They arrive and see our faces and our smiles and our brochures with pictures that promise a fix, a solution to the problem that has plagued their beloved child since birth. And so they hand their babies over. They hand them over to strangers who don't even speak their language. Talk about a lesson in trust. They trust that with Operation Smile, there is a chance.

My favorite moment in every mission is when, forty-five minutes after a mother has handed over her baby to outsiders, she sees us emerge from surgery and give that baby back to her. It is like a rebirth. The child, whom that mother thought would never get to smile, smiles up at her for the first time. She is shrouded in joy and gratitude, tears stream down her face, and we all rejoice together in the power of healing, in the gift of second chances.

The first time I had the chance to give a healed child back to his mother, I was crying just as much as the mother. I looked at the child I held in my arms. His beautiful little face had been perfectly repaired, and I carefully carried him out to where his mother stood, alone and silent. She had been praying, fear and hope battling in her watchful gaze. Her face brightened

> *The only way you can serve God is by serving other people.*
>
> RICK WARREN

when she saw us walk toward her, and her eyes quickly found her child's face. There was her little son, perfectly restored. And she cried, this time tears of relief. Now her child would have a normal life.

It was one of the most amazing moments of my life, second only to the birth of my own little girl. To be the one to hand back a restored child to its mother, to see this mother's greatest prayer answered, felt like being one of God's angels.

And I've learned that the operation doesn't just change the life of that little boy or girl or mother. But when they travel back to their villages and the villagers see this little child restored, it creates a ripple of hope for the whole community. Because if that little baby's dreams can come true, maybe it can happen to them. Maybe taking a risk or taking a journey to see what might be out there could be the beginning of a new life.

I can't even begin to describe how powerful it is to see hope renewed in a person's life. When I go on these missions, of course I want to "help" people; but really, I do it selfishly, too. Because I, too, am transformed. To see the doctors and nurses who are volunteering their time to make these dreams come true fills me with a sense of hope and possibility. They are the angels. I watch as they train local doctors to perform these surgeries, so that after they are gone, hope will remain. Watching them reminds me of the gifts we all have to share with the world. As the old Chinese proverb says, "Give a man a fish, and he will eat for a day; teach a man to fish, and he will eat for a lifetime." When I witness the courage and trust that God instills in these mothers—the trust to bring their babies to these doctors—I am reminded of the goodness of God and how He truly performs miracles through His children every day if we are willing.

I love the founders of the Operation Smile organization, Dr. Bill Magee and his wife, Kathy. I am grateful to them for their example and their friendship. They possessed the empathic eyes to see the great need for this organization, the brave heart to see the possibilities, and the faith to try to help. "If we don't take care of that child, there's no guarantee that anyone else will," Kathy says.

What if they had just shrugged their shoulders and said "Oh, how sad" but did nothing? What if they had waited for others to step up?

But they didn't. They knew that God calls all of us to care for one another.

We sometimes think we have to do huge things to change the world. We don't. We just have to have the eyes to see the needs around us and to use the capabilities God has given us to help in small ways. God is waiting for us to be his hands in this world.

We should be shining lamps,
giving light to all around us.

CATHERINE McCAULEY

When I was a boy and I would see
scary things in the news,
my mother would say to me,
"Look for the helpers. You will always find
people who are helping."

FRED ROGERS

How wonderful it is that
nobody need wait a single moment
before starting to improve the world.

ANNE FRANK

AN UNEXPECTED ANGEL

You can preach a better sermon with your life
than with your lips.

OLIVER GOLDSMITH

For almost ten years, I was able to deliver a message of
faith, hope, and love on network television. More than
twenty million people tuned in each week to hear the message "God loves you." We would take them on a journey and
remind them that they are never truly alone. Because of that
message, when people ran into me on the street, they didn't
necessarily ask for an autograph. I wasn't just an actress they
admired. I was an angel. They wanted a hug.

When you play an angel on TV, people begin to think
you are an angel in real life. Sometimes when people met
me, they spoke quietly and reverently, as if they were in
the presence of someone holy! Now, I am the first person
to tell you that I am just as flawed as everyone else, that I
am far from perfect. But playing an angel for almost ten
years not only had a positive influence on the audience,

it had a huge impact on me as well. I began to realize that we all have the opportunity to be an angel if we are just willing to show kindness and grace and love to those around us.

For the almost ten years that I lived in Salt Lake City, I often went to Primary Children's Hospital to visit the children who were sick. The people of Salt Lake City treated us very well for the entire ten years that we filmed there. They took pride in what we were doing and embraced us like family wherever we went. I had gotten into the habit of stopping by the hospital when I could to provide a moment of joy for the many families who had sick children, and I would often visit the tiny babies in the NICU. If the parents weren't there, I would sometimes take a Polaroid of me visiting their baby and leave it on the incubator with a note saying that an angel had visited while they were gone. Over the years, I met many of these children in the neighborhoods where we filmed. A mom would show up with a now robust toddler to thank me and tell me that my visit had given them hope at a stressful time in their lives.

One day, around Christmas, I was at the hospital. I was wearing a Santa hat as a way to bring a festive spirit to the families who were sequestered in those halls. As I walked down the corridor, excited to see the next patient, I saw a family exiting one of the rooms. I quickly pulled off my hat and backed into a corner. There was no question what this family had just experienced. You could feel the grief gust like a wind out of this room. But the mother looked up, saw me, and gasped. She rushed over, saying, "Monica, here you are!" She grabbed my hands and said, "Oh, Monica, I prayed that an angel would come for my baby. And here you are! Here you are."

I stiffened, not knowing what to say. My heart ached for her.

Monica was the name of the angel I played on television, but *I* wasn't Monica, I was just Roma. I wasn't an angel; I was just a normal human being. I did not know what to say. This grieving woman had enveloped me in a hug, and she had just experienced the worst thing a parent can experience. So I just held her; I wrapped my arms around her and prayed quietly with her. I prayed with all my heart.

After a few moments, she pulled back and looked me in the eyes, tears still streaming down her cheeks. "Thank you," she said quietly, "that was just what I needed." And then she returned to her husband and family, still huddled just outside the room, and they all walked down the hospital corridor.

I stood there, my heart beating fast, overwhelmed with emotion, but also questioning whether I had been dishonest. That woman wanted and needed an angel, and all she got was me. But I also saw the comfort that my presence had provided. If I could make her smile through her tears, maybe I had done the right thing. If I had made her believe in God's faithfulness, perhaps everything was okay.

When I got home that evening, I sat down and called Della to tell her the story. "Oh, Della, I didn't know what to say. I was afraid to appear to be something I'm not. I should have said something, but I could not find the words."

Della laughed. "Baby, I don't understand what you're so upset about."

I tried to explain again. "But Della, she thought that God had sent an angel to her."

To which Della said, "And who said He didn't?" She paused. "That woman didn't need an actress, baby. She needed an angel. And if we are going to be used in this series for His highest good, then we need to learn to get out of the way."

As I hung up the phone that evening, I prayed, thanking God both for using me and for Della, who as always possessed the wisdom I desperately needed. Who was I to say God wasn't using me in that moment? How many other times had I limited Him and not been available to be a light to someone who needed it?

That moment has stuck with me through the years. And I've tried to be attuned to the ways that a simple act of kindness on my part might be the very thing a person needs, the very thing to remind them that they are not alone. The dictionary defines "angel" as "a spiritual being that serves especially as a messenger from God." We are all spiritual beings, and we all have the ability to be messengers of God. I know Della has been an angel for me, as has my own precious daughter, Reilly. My husband has been an angel for me more times that I can count, and for our boys. I pray that I will be an angel to others, every day. We are all here together—during the good times and the bad, the ups and downs—and sometimes we need a hand to pull us up, and at other times we have the strength to reach down and encourage someone else. That is what the family of God is here to do—keep walking forward, eyes heavenward, as we do the work of our maker.

In that moment, when that grieving woman probably felt so heartbroken and alone, God used me to remind her . . . *I'm here with you, I'm always here. Trust in me.*

Trust in me.

In my books, and sometimes even in real life, I have it in me at my best to be a saint to other people, and by saint I mean life-giver, someone who is able to bear to others something of the Holy Spirit, whom the creeds describe as the Lord and Giver of Life. Sometimes, by the grace of God, I have it in me to be Christ to other people. And so, of course, have we all—the life-giving, life-saving, and healing power to be saints, to be Christs, maybe at rare moments even to ourselves.

FREDERICK BUECHNER

Loaves and Fishes

This is not
the age of information.

This is *not*
the age of information.

Forget the news,
and the radio,
and the blurred screen.

This is the time
of loaves
and fishes.

People are hungry,
and one good word is bread
for a thousand.

David Whyte

Lord, may I be reminded
of your presence in my life,
may I have the eyes to see
the needs of your people,
may I have a heart to
feel them
and the willingness to see how
I might help.
May I see each of your children
as my own,
and seek only to be a
bringer of light.
May people see me and be inspired
by the goodness in the world.
May kindness be my mantle
and my sword.

I learned that courage was not the absence of fear, but the triumph over it. The brave man is not he who does not feel afraid, but he who conquers that fear.

NELSON MANDELA

---

*The Lord is my light and my salvation—
whom shall I fear?
The Lord is the stronghold of my life—
of whom shall I be afraid?*

PSALM 27:1 (NIV)

COURAGE

three

COURAGE

Promise me you'll always remember: You're braver than you believe, and stronger than you seem, and smarter than you think.

WINNIE THE POOH (A. A. MILNE)

THE WORD "en*courage*" means to embolden one with *courage*, and I'm so thankful for the many people in my life who have emboldened me, urging me to go after my dreams. It began with my mother and her loving enthusiasm, signing me up for dance and music classes, and her quiet, loving support from the back of the room at all those lessons. It continued with my father, who pushed me to pursue an education and who always told me I was strong, capable, and smart.

But they weren't the only ones who planted the seeds of courage and confidence in me.

By the time I graduated from art school in Brighton, I knew I wanted to be a professional actor. I had studied the work of the Dutch artist Vincent van Gogh, and he had said a curious thing in one of his many letters to his brother Theo. Growing dissatisfied with his work, he expressed that he no longer wanted to be the painter but rather he wanted to be the paint.

When I read this, I instantly understood it in some unspoken way. I wanted to become the "paint" in my work, too. To breathe life into a script, to become a character, to tell a story. I wanted to be an actor. I realized my dream was to be onstage. I decided the best way to achieve this was to further my studies at the Drama Studio in London. I interviewed twice and was finally offered a place at this prestigious school. I was thrilled and so excited about the quality of training I would receive, but my heart sank when I was turned down for a grant to cover the cost of the tuition. I knew I couldn't afford it on my own and was trying to process my disappointment when a miracle occurred.

Three extraordinary people who I had been working with on a summer theater project banded together and offered to put up the money for me to attend. They told me they believed in me and wanted to invest in my future. It wasn't a loan, they assured me, it was an investment in me. They didn't want me to have to turn down this wonderful opportunity. The only thing they asked was that I pay the kindness forward with my life. And I have tried to do that over the years to honor their generosity.

I had never experienced such unbelievable, unselfish kindness before. But before I could accept, I told them I had to talk it over with my father. My dad was stunned. Of course he wished he had enough money to pay the tuition himself, but it was more than our family could afford. Knowing this was an incredible opportunity for me, he said he couldn't let pride stand in the way, and he gave me permission to accept.

These three wonderful angels gave me so much more than just the tuition fees. They gave me encouragement and confidence. They stepped up and showed that they believed in me, a belief that made all the difference. It made me want to work as hard as I possibly could to show them their investment in me was worthwhile. I didn't want to let them down.

The agreement was that they would cover the tuition, but I needed to get a job to cover my rent and living expenses. I wasn't afraid of hard work, and I immediately got a job as a waitress so I could cover my costs.

I excelled in my studies in London, and even went on to win the highest award the school offered: "Most Promising Student of the Year." Then, just one month before graduation, my father died. I was devastated. Not having him with me at the pivotal moment of accepting my diploma broke my heart. I wanted to see his eyes shining with pride as I walked across the stage, his heart bursting with the knowledge that my whole life was still in front of me, beckoning.

So here I was, finally out of school, and my beloved parents had both passed on and my childhood home in Northern Ireland had been sold. I was trained and ready and eager to start my professional life. Some of my friends in the program were planning to move to New York after graduation. I began to wonder if I could take that leap of faith as well. I was a young woman with a big dream, and I knew that the journey of a thousand miles begins with the first step.

I was scared, of course. The unknown opened up before me. But when nothing is certain, everything is possible. I prayed I would know what direction to take, that I would be guided to each next step, and that I would have the courage to take it.

Looking back, I can see that if my father had still been alive, I might never have considered moving to America. But I was young and filled with a sense of adventure. So I packed my bags and joined the ranks of thousands of young actors and actresses who pour into New York City each year. I came looking for the American dream.

I remember those early years of walking all over the city in search of a job. I often didn't have the fare for a taxi, so it was walking or buses or the subway, uptown and downtown and crosstown, to readings and meetings, sometimes several a day. I came home each night hoping to see the light on the answering machine flashing with the offer of a job. But it rarely flashed, and I frequently felt tremendously insecure.

Even if you're on the right track, you'll get run over if you just sit there.

WILL ROGERS

To be an actor, you have to learn to live with fear.

Every actor, no matter how good, no matter how seasoned, must face the fear that inevitably arises when you walk onto a stage in front of hundreds of people. Rosalind Russell, the American actress from the 1940s and '50s, once said, "Acting is standing up naked and turning around very slowly." Of course, she was speaking about being emotionally naked, about appearing vulnerable in front of others.

Actors have to learn to live with the fear of being vulnerable, and to conquer it.

I knew that in order to survive pursuing acting as a

You never know how strong you are until being strong is your only choice.

BOB MARLEY

career, I had to develop a thick skin and the drive to keep going in the face of rejection. This was hard for me, as I am naturally tenderhearted and sensitive, but I knew that thick skin would provide an armor that would protect me. I had to learn not to take the setbacks to heart and not to take rejection personally.

There are often hundreds of actors pursuing just a few roles on each show. And the truth is that you could give the audition of your life, and they still might reject you just because of the color of your hair or because you are too short or too tall or too different from how directors envision the character.

Even though you know the rejection isn't personal, it often feels personal, and it hurts. That's when the thick skin is necessary.

But I had to learn to separate from the rejection. *It doesn't define who I am. The rejection isn't rejection of me. Acting is what I do, but it's not who I am.*

You can imagine that in those early days, before I had learned to disassociate, I struggled. I can see now that there was still within me a little child who felt the loss of her mother and a painful sense of abandonment. Rejections reopened old wounds that her death had created. And as these hurts reemerged, I no longer had my father there to offer his quiet words of encouragement and compassion.

Courage is resistance to fear, mastery of fear, not absence of fear.

MARK TWAIN

No matter what your profession, we all face those feelings sometimes. Feelings of unworthiness. Feelings of failure. Feelings of defeat.

But we don't have to stay in those places. I have found that the best remedy to negative self-talk is to try to move myself from a place of fear into a space of love. I start by simply thinking about the people I love. Remember Julie Andrews in *The Sound of Music* encouraging the von Trapp children to think of a few of their favorite things when they were afraid of the storm? Well, that's a version of what I do. I count my blessings, I pray, and I connect to God. Then I am reminded that God has a plan for my life, even when I do not always see it myself.

The time spent in that space of love restores me and gives me courage and joy, and my sense of purpose rises again. I

am filled back up to go out
into the world and chase my
dreams, energized, excited,
and full of faith.

*A journey of a thousand
miles must begin with a
single step.*

LAO TZU

I spent several years in
New York trying to make things happen. I booked some regional theater shows, which were good experiences but did
not pay much. In between shows, I went to acting classes and
voice classes and exercise classes, making sure that I was ready.
An acting teacher of mine always said that if opportunity
knocks, it needs to find you ready and prepared, not taking a
nap on the couch. You've got to stay well tuned in your craft.

During my years in Manhattan, I had the good fortune to
meet all sorts of wonderful people who respected the struggle
of the aspiring actors who populate the city and would do
their part to cheer them up. The first celebrity I ever met
came up to me one night when I was working as a coat-check
girl in a fancy Upper West Side restaurant. It was seasonal
work, but on a cold winter night I could pull in some decent
tips, making anywhere from twenty-five cents to a dollar per
coat. I would arrive at five o'clock to get set up for the night,
and most customers would arrive between seven and eight. I
would check people's coats, sit and read for a few hours while
they dined, and then retrieve their coats for them around
ten or eleven. One night, Regis Philbin walked up and asked
me what I was reading. I looked up and recognized his face
immediately. I told him the title of my book, and he looked

at me with that famous twinkle in his eye, and said, "Oh, do I detect a bit of an accent?"

I laughed and said, "Yes, I'm from Ireland."

We chatted for a bit, and then he went off to enjoy dinner with his lovely wife, Joy. He left me a twenty-dollar tip, and I will never forget his kindness.

Many years later, when I was doing publicity in New York City for *Touched by an Angel*, I went on his show with Kathie Lee Gifford, and I told him the story. Regis laughed at the end of it and pretended to wipe his brow. "Phew! I was worried for a bit that I had stiffed you!"

We soon became friends, and many years later Mark and I hosted a birthday luncheon for Regis and Joy at our Malibu home. Kathie Lee and I became very dear friends as well. She did a few guest appearances on *Touched by an Angel*, and I was honored to work with her as an actress. Kathie Lee is a talented, strong woman of faith and is just lovely to be around.

My coat checking soon gave way to some acting work, and I was finally cast Off Broadway, at New York's Public Theater and the Roundabout Theatre, doing Shaw and Ibsen and Shakespeare, wonderful roles in classical plays. I was thrilled to be finally doing what I was trained for and what I loved. It wasn't Broadway yet, but it was interesting, quality work, and it paid, supplementing my other part-time gigs. And then one evening at intermission, the stage manager popped into my room and said, "We have a special guest who wants to meet you."

Sir Rex Harrison had been in the audience, and he walked into my dressing room in his impeccably tailored suit. I practically fainted. It was such an honor to meet this movie star, most beloved for his role as Henry Higgins in *My Fair Lady*.

Sir Rex was mounting a production of W. Somerset Maugham's *The Circle* for Broadway, and he wanted me to come in the following Monday to audition for the role of the ingénue. My heart skipped a beat, and I of course said yes.

The following Monday I auditioned and landed the role. This was my first big break. The production also starred Glynis Johns and Stewart Granger, true old-time movie stars who, along with Sir Rex, were in the later stages of their careers. Between them they had so much experience and wisdom. We toured the country for three months and then ended up on Broadway for a six-month run.

I will never forget that first performance on the Broadway stage in New York. Taking my bow at curtain call, I was overcome with emotion. I was grateful to God for guiding me; to my mother, who instilled in me the love of theater; to my father, who gave me the belief that I had wings and could fly; and to the three angels who had helped put me through drama school.

Because of all of them and their love and support and belief in me, I saw my dreams come true that night.

And that was just the beginning. Appearing on Broadway in *The Circle* led to the title role in *A Woman Named Jackie*, which gave me the courage to move to Los Angeles. Which, of course, would eventually lead to me being cast on *Touched by an Angel.*

Nothing gets going from a stationary position. Energy begets energy; one thing leads to another. Each step of my journey opened the door for the next step, which led to Rex Harrison seeing me, which led me to my dream. Sometimes we say no to opportunities because they may not be exactly what we are looking for. But the truth is you never know where things might lead. You've got to stay open and have faith.

Life as an actor means living with a degree of uncertainty. It's

It's life, Sidda. You don't figure it out. You just climb up on the beast and ride.

REBECCA WELLS

a life that can create self-doubt and upset the natural urge we all have to feel safe. But we have to be bold and brave, because if we are not, we may miss the opportunity to do really great things.

I used to think I needed to have all my ducks lined up in a row before I could step out, that only when I felt certain of success should I move forward. But the truth is there is no certainty in this life. Pastor Rick Warren once said, "Living by faith isn't living with certainty. It's trusting God in spite of unanswered questions and unresolved doubts." If I had not put my trust in God, I never would have moved to New York or to Los Angeles.

Living a life of faith means learning to get our feet wet. When Jesus walked on water, only one disciple asked to join him: Peter. Peter slowly stepped out of the boat and began to do the impossible. When he looked down and began to doubt, Jesus stretched out his hand and encouraged him to trust, to look only at Him. And Peter walked on water.

I once heard someone say that the only difference between excitement and fear is your attitude.

Peter was afraid. But at least he got out of the boat.

Our God is not one who is content to keep us in our comfort zone. Jesus challenged his disciples to do more than they thought possible. The disciples weren't cut from theological cloth or raised on supernatural milk. But they were an ounce more devoted than they were afraid, and, as a result, did some extraordinary things.

MAX LUCADO

The Truelove

There is a faith in loving fiercely
the one who is rightfully yours,
especially if you have
waited years and especially
if part of you never believed
you could deserve this
loved and beckoning hand
held out to you this way.

I am thinking of faith now
and the testaments of loneliness
and what we feel we are
worthy of in this world.

Years ago in the Hebrides
I remember an old man
who walked every morning
on the grey stones
to the shore of baying seals,

who would press his hat
to his chest in the blustering
salt wind and say his prayer
to the turbulent Jesus
hidden in the water,

and I think of the story
of the storm and everyone
waking and seeing
the distant
yet familiar figure,
far across the water
calling to them,

and how we are all
waiting for that
abrupt waking, and that calling,
and that moment
when we have to say *yes*,
except it will
not come so grandly,
so Biblically,
but more subtly
and intimately, in the face
of the one you know
you have to love.

So that when
we finally step out of the boat
toward them, we find
everything holds
us, and everything confirms
our courage, and if you wanted
to drown you could,
but you don't,

because finally,
after all this struggle
and all these years,
you don't want to anymore,
you've simply had enough
of drowning,
and you want to live and you
want to love and you will
walk across any territory
and any darkness,
however fluid and however
dangerous, to take the
one hand you know
belongs in yours.

David Whyte

THE BIBLE PROJECT

Dream big and dare to fail.

NORMAN VAUGHAN

When *Touched by an Angel* wrapped after nine glorious seasons, my daughter, Reilly, who was six and a half at the time, and I moved back to Los Angeles. I wasn't sure what was to come next, but I was ready for a bit of downtime. I had worked consistently for almost a decade with hardly any time off, and I was tired. I needed some quiet space so I could gather myself, trusting that I would be guided to the next thing.

I enrolled Reilly in school; we found a lovely, welcoming church; and life began to find a new rhythm. Then, not long after returning to L.A., when I least expected it, I met Mark. We fell in love and knew we wanted to spend the rest of our lives together, so we married and merged our young families together. Mark and I hadn't worked together before, but of course we were in similar fields. He was producing television shows, and at that time had already achieved incredible success with the reality show *Survivor*. But we both longed for a chance to work on something together and hoped to incorporate our faith into that work. I had had the privilege of bringing my faith to my work for all those years on *Touched by an Angel,* and I wanted my work life and faith life to be aligned again.

As a family, we loved watching movies together. Given our professions, we watched a lot of new movies, but every now and then we would pull out an old classic. One year, around Easter, we put on *The Ten Commandments* and gathered as a family in front of the television set. But the film did not hold our young children's interest like we thought it would. Having been made over sixty years earlier, the film was just too old-fashioned for them; and while it is, of course, one of the classics, the truth is that our kids found it outdated and a bit slow.

One morning a few weeks after this, as we were sitting on our porch having a cup of tea, I mentioned to Mark: "You know, no one has ever done the Bible as a television show. We should do that."

Mark looked at me and laughed. "What, the whole thing?"

I laughed, too. "Well, there is certainly a beginning and an end. We'd just have to figure out what stories to include in the middle."

That conversation was the first step in one of the largest undertakings in our professional careers.

It was truly a Herculean task, to take a thousand-page document, beloved and revered by so many people, and bring it to the small screen in a way that honored our faith and glorified God. But what an exciting opportunity to bring these stories to life for a whole new generation. I felt ready to step outside my role as an actor and step into the role of producer.

Mark and I spent hours together, imagining what it could be. If we were going to pitch this idea, we had to know exactly what it was going to entail. The New Testament felt easier to figure out, as it has a clear narrative beginning with Jesus' birth and ending with his death and resurrection. But the Old Testament is more challenging. It spans so many years and has countless characters. There were obviously some stories we knew we had to incorporate, and then we had a wish list of others we thought might work well on the screen.

We soon reached out to a friend of ours, the president of Pepperdine University, and asked him to gather some of the theologians on his staff to be a sounding board about the project. We had an incredible meeting with these bright and faithful minds. They were encouraging but agreed it would be challenging. They promised to begin praying for us immediately.

You miss 100 percent of the shots you don't take.

WAYNE GRETZKY

When we would mention this project to other friends, we wouldn't always get such encouragement. In fact, many of our friends tried to dissuade us from pursuing it. They thought we were nuts. *It's too risky, too big, what if you get it wrong, it could be dangerous or you might look foolish. You*

can't win, you will fail. No one cares about the Bible anymore.
No one will buy it in Hollywood, and it could be a big, noisy,
humiliating flop!

We heard their concerns and didn't necessarily disagree
with them. We called in prayer, and we moved forward
in faith. We chose to listen
to the positive whisper of
encouragement in our hearts
rather than the loud negative
noises of the outside world.

> There is only one way to
> avoid criticism: do nothing,
> say nothing, and be
> nothing.
>
> ARISTOTLE

Eventually we found the
perfect partners at the His-
tory channel and Hearst. The team at History immediately
understood our hope for the scope and scale of the series,
and they stepped up and partnered with us. We compiled a
very large team of Bible consultants and theologians to make
sure we brought the story to life accurately. Our intention
was to bring the global audience closer to God through these
amazing stories.

As the writers were shaping the scripts, we began casting
in London and Los Angeles and scouting locations; and before we knew it, we were set to begin filming in Morocco.

Yet one cast member eluded us.

We were just weeks from beginning principal photogra-
phy, and we had not yet cast our most important role: Jesus.
To say this made us nervous would be an understatement. He
was, after all, our leading man.

Obviously it takes a special actor to portray Jesus, who is so much more than a character or historical figure. This person must have the special presence to portray someone both human and divine. In addition, he must be ready and willing to take on the role, which would be both daunting and difficult.

I was beginning to get worried, and I reached out to all my friends and church prayer circles with an email whose subject line made us all smile: "Looking for Jesus." I prayed fervently, asking God to send me the perfect actor to play the Lord, and then to let me know him when he showed up. Then, through a remarkable series of "coincidences," I was sent a videotape of an actor reading on camera. It got my attention right away, and the small voice within me told me to follow up. I found out the tape was of the Portuguese actor Diogo Morgado.

I called his agent and asked whether he could come in for a meeting. His agent thought I was calling from London and said, "I'm so sorry, but Diogo is out of the country right now."

"Where is he?" I asked.

"He's in L.A.," the agent replied.

I laughed out loud. "That's where I am," I said with glee. "Can he come by my home office tomorrow?" I asked.

"I'll find out," the agent said.

Sure enough, he was able to come.

I was waiting in the hallway with Mark when we received the call that Diogo had arrived. We have glass on our front door, so we were able to peek out as we watched Diogo open the garden gate and walk up the path to our house.

As he approached, a huge monarch butterfly the size of a small bird swooped down in front of his face, almost knocking him off his feet.

I was sure it was a sign.

I started to laugh and turned to Mark, who knew exactly what I was thinking. "There he is, Mark," I said with a smile. "There is our Jesus."

And Diogo walked through the door and into our lives.

If there had been any doubt in my mind before, it was all gone now—I believed that butterfly was a sign from God.

When *The Bible* finally began airing on the History channel in the spring of 2013, it exceeded everyone's expectations. The ratings were incredible, with over 100 million people eventually viewing it. Even more special was the personal feedback we began to receive from people around the country. They shared what it was like to watch these impactful stories together as a family and how it created an opportunity to discuss matters of faith with their kids. People were talking about Jesus around the water cooler. They were talking about *The Bible* on talk shows and morning shows; it was such a blessing to see how the series was being used to touch people's hearts and remind them of God's love.

Shortly thereafter, Mark and I were honored with the chance to speak at the National Prayer Breakfast in Washington, D.C., to an audience of leaders from all around the world, including the then president of the United States, Barack Obama. We talked about undertaking this project and the significance of bringing the Bible to national television, and shared about our own personal faith and what it felt like to be called "the noisiest Christians in Hollywood." We knew that with that title came great risk and great responsibility.

I think back to those many conversations with people who tried to convince us we would regret pursuing this project. They had only seen the reasons to be afraid.

I am sure that it helped that there were two of us. I'm so thankful I had Mark by my side. I know that pursuing this task together strengthened us in our resolve to move forward, and, I think, strengthened our marriage and friendship as well. I can't help but feel that God brought us together "for such a time as this."

Two was better than one, and together with God's help, we knew we could do it.

I hereby command you: Be strong and courageous; do not be frightened or dismayed, for the Lord your God is with you wherever you go.

JOSHUA 1:9 (NRSV)

That we are here is a huge affirmation; somehow life needed us and wanted us to be. To sense and trust this primeval acceptance can open a vast spring of trust within the heart. It can free us into a natural courage that casts out fear and opens up our lives to become voyages of discovery, creativity, and compassion. No threshold need be a threat, but rather an invitation and a promise. Whatever comes, the great sacrament of life will remain faithful to us, blessing us always with visible signs of invisible grace. We merely need to trust.

John O'Donohue

CARRIED IN HIS ARMS

God invites us to experience our not
being in control as an invitation to faith.

HENRI NOUWEN

I've always loved the poem "Footprints." My father first
shared it with me shortly after my mother's death. It reminded me of the song my mother used to sing to me as I was
falling asleep, "You'll Never Walk Alone." Ever since I was a
little girl, I've kept a copy of the "Footprints" poem in credit-
card size in my wallet, just in case I encounter someone who
needs encouragement. Then I share it with them.

As I prepared to go to Morocco for the filming of *The
Bible*, I knew I wasn't going to take my normal wallet. I was
going to take only the essentials into the desert with me, and
I certainly wouldn't need all my membership cards, credit
cards, and Starbucks cards! For some reason, I plucked the
"Footprints" card out of my wallet and stuffed it into the
little bag that would go with me on the film set. Perhaps
someone during the course of shooting might need it.

Morocco is beautiful, but the climate can be very challenging, with searing-hot sun during the day and sometimes freezing-cold temperatures in the evenings. Mark had been with me for the first couple of weeks, but he was in the middle of producing the NBC hit music show *The Voice* and needed to fly back to L.A. for the taping. We had a very skilled team in place, so while I would miss him, I knew I could handle things on the set while he was gone.

One day we were preparing to film the scene where Abraham walks up the mountain to sacrifice his son, Isaac. It is one of the most powerful and dramatic scenes in the Bible. Abraham is so faithful that he is willing to sacrifice his only son, the son that he and Sarah had prayed for, longed for, and that God had finally given to them in their old age. In the scene, we see Abraham trusting God; and even though his heart is breaking, he does not question God and is prepared to do as God asks. Mercifully, an angel of God intervenes and says, "Do not lay your hand on the boy or do anything to him; for now I know that you fear God, since you have not withheld your son, your only son, from me" (Genesis 22:12, NRSV). And before Abraham's eyes, there appears a lamb, the lamb he is now to sacrifice instead of his beloved son.

Obviously, we needed a lamb to film this scene, and in

What do you do when alone with God?
Many of us think, talk or ask.
But when alone with God it's also important to listen!
Solitude is the place where you can
hear the voice that calls you the beloved,
that leads you onto the next page of the adventure,
that says, as God said to Jesus early in the Gospels,
"This is my son, the Beloved,
with whom I am well pleased" (Matt. 3:17).
HENRI NOUWEN

the production meetings to prepare for this episode, I had requested two white lambs (I've learned through filming that you always need a backup animal in case the first one doesn't cooperate). We had reached out to some of the local people helping us with the shoot and requested that two white lambs be on the set first thing in the morning. It was all arranged.

When I arrived at our location that morning, I saw two lambs and a handler. And yet, these were not white lambs. One was a black lamb, and one was, let's just say, muddy-colored at best.

Through the translator, I did my best to communicate with their handler and asked him why he didn't bring a white lamb. But no matter how much I protested, it didn't change the fact that we did not have a white lamb; and because we were filming in such a remote location, it would likely take several hours for this mistake to be remedied.

We did not have several hours. We needed to start filming. *What difference does it make what color the lamb is?* I heard someone ask. But I knew that I wanted the lamb to signify Jesus, who came to be sacrificed for us. Jesus as the Lamb of God. Hans Zimmer had written a beautiful piece of music for the scene with Abraham. The music soared as Abraham and Isaac carried the wood up the hill for the sacrifice. We would play this same music in a later scene as Jesus carried the wood of the cross on which He would be sacrificed. The white lamb was significant and important.

I tried to hide it, but inside I was incredibly frustrated, thinking about how this would throw off our filming schedule for the entire day.

I walked off the set, feeling irritated and alone. I knew if I didn't take a moment to breathe and pray, I was going to cry.

I reached into my purse to grab a tissue, and the "Footprints" poem fell out.

I picked it up and began to read it for the thousandth time. When I got to the end, I smiled and thanked God for this reminder. I hadn't realized when I packed it that I was the one who would need it. That it was there for me. That in the middle of this arid desert, where we were trying to create this series to honor God and His story, I was the one who would need this reminder.

I'm here with you. I'm carrying you. You are never alone.

With my faith restored, I rejoined the team. We decided that we would film with the muddy-colored lamb and change his color in postproduction. It would require coming back to this very location with a white lamb so we could shoot a plate that we would drop into the scene with special effects at a later stage. But at least we had a plan for the day. God helped to keep me calm so that I could make a plan and move forward.

I believe that with faith, we can each do the impossible—that life is waiting for us to step up, believe, and do great things. There are always going to be times of anxiety and fear. But when we learn that even in those times, God is with us, it makes it all more tolerable. I've learned that God sometimes calms the storm, but at other times He lets the storm rage and calms the child. So when you feel like you are drowning in the sea of life, just remember that your lifeguard walks on water.

When I stand before God at the end of my life, I would hope that I would not have a single bit of talent left, and could say, "I used everything you gave me."

ERMA BOMBECK

May I dare to
dream big,
to see possibilities
instead of limits,
to believe that you, God,
can do impossible things
with your willing children.
Sometimes, God, I get afraid,
and I'd rather stay safe
than do what my
heart is calling me to do.
Please, Lord, help me
to reach out,
to get out of the boat,
and when I fear that
I'm sinking,
drowning,
look up, see you,
and keep walking in faith.

Spread love everywhere you go. Let no one ever come to you without leaving happier.

MOTHER TERESA

Dear friends, let us love one another, for love comes from God. Everyone who loves has been born of God and knows God.

1 JOHN 4:7 (NIV)

LOVE

four

LOVE

What we have once enjoyed, we can never lose.
All that we love deeply becomes part of us.

HELEN KELLER

I WAITED for a long time to have my daughter. I had always assumed I would have children one day but never felt the time was right. There was always one more mountain to climb, one more task to accomplish, and of course there was the question of finding the right mate.

A couple of years after I first moved to Los Angeles, I began dating a wonderful man. David was a film director, and we went on a blind date, set up by a friend of mine. We quickly fell in love. Within a few months, I booked the role of Monica and realized that I would be moving to Utah to film the show; so after we got married, he split his time between Utah and L.A. His work was in L.A., as well as his lovely seventeen-year-old daughter, Vanessa. I was already thirty-five by then, and so I knew that if we were to have children of our own, there was no time to delay.

When I found out that I was pregnant, we were both thrilled, and I couldn't wait to tell my other family, the cast and crew of *Touched by an Angel.*

The day came when I felt ready to share my news. We were filming in a jazz club, of all places, and the legendary musician B. B. King was on set. We had been filming onstage and had a lull in the action, so I told B. B. that I had some special news to share with the group. He said, "Can I play a little intro to get their attention?" and I smiled and said yes. He began to play his guitar, and everyone on set turned to see what was going on. When B. B. finished his musical introduction, I turned back to the cast and crew and said, "Well, thanks, B. B., for that lovely introduction to some wonderful news. I'm so thrilled to share with you all—you who have become my trusted friends and who are truly like family to me— that we are adding one more little angel to the family. I'm pregnant!"

Everyone cheered as B. B. began to play again. I turned around, and he came over and began to play to my tummy. My eyes filled with tears with the special introduction my precious baby was getting to the world.

We had quite an interesting time on the series keeping my pregnancy hidden from viewers. Given our filming schedule, we were expected to shoot until early May, and I was due in June. So there were countless scenes where I was carrying coats or large sun hats or shopping bags, or standing behind open car doors or a couch. With other kinds of shows, a pregnancy might have been written into the script, but that wasn't an option since I was playing an angel!

I chose not to find out whether we were having a boy or a girl, wanting that miraculous surprise at the moment my child was born. But the truth is, when I heard the words "It's a girl!" I realized just how much I had been hoping for a daughter. And here she was now, in my arms. My own precious, beautiful child.

I named her Reilly, to honor the memory of my mother, Maureen O'Reilly.

As I stared down at my sweet baby girl, I felt something happen within me. Tears streamed down my face, both for the miracle that I held in my arms and for the fact that something I so desperately missed was now restored. I cried in that moment for the mother I had lost and the mother I had now become. I had been filled with longing my whole life for this mother-daughter relationship. Now, with Reilly's birth, I was given a second chance at that relationship, a relationship I had been missing for more than half of my life. When my mother died, I missed her so much that there was truly a hole in me; the woman I became just grew up around that "hole." But it was as if Reilly's birth put a "W" in front of that word and made me "whole" again. As I held my beautiful baby girl in my arms, I cried tears of joy and healing. There is no question that love is a healer. It began in that hospital room;

and in the years since, the love has filled me and touched all the old hurts within me. The love Reilly brought to my life has ultimately healed me. She is my special angel. My sweet, beautiful girl. My gift from God.

Motherhood opened up a deep well of love in me, love I didn't know I had access to. Becoming a mother also helped my faith grow and deepen because it has given me insight into how much God loves us. His unconditional love, His perfect loving. I finally understood just how much God loves each and every one of us. We are, after all, His special children. The depth of my love for Reilly amazes me. And, of course, I then marvel at God's love for us.

Even though Reilly was born by caesarian section, I had to go back to work just a few short weeks after her birth. But I was blessed to have had the help and support of so many. I'm thankful for Debbie, our amazing nanny, and everyone on set who made me feel so loved. I could not have done it without Linda, my assistant, and the wonderful cast and crew who cared for us. And I was gifted with a schedule that offered some downtime, when I could rock and feed and love on my little baby girl in between my time filming.

Della was a doting grandmother, and our other regular cast member, John Dye, was the perfect, loving Uncle Johnnie. He always called Reilly his little lamb. In the embrace of this extended and loving family, Reilly grew and blossomed; but sadly, the same cannot be said for my marriage to her dad. My dreams of happily ever after were crushed around the time Reilly turned one. We decided to separate, and by the time she turned two, we had divorced.

So for many years, it was just the two of us. Reilly's dad came to visit her every few weeks, and he was always a good dad and a loving part of her life, but for the day-to-day of it, I was a single mom. Of course we always had Della by our side. I sometimes had family visits from Ireland, when my two half sisters, Ann and Jacinta, would come on their vacations. Reilly always loved the visits from her Irish aunties. But for the most part it was me, my girl, and our two doggies in our big house in Utah. We were best buddies

You don't know what unconditional love is. You may say you do, but if you don't have a child, you don't know what that is. But when you experience it, it is the most fulfilling experience ever.

REGINA KING

and so incredibly close. We spent all our time together. Once while shopping in a local mall, someone asked me for an autograph. Reilly, who was only four at the time, tugged at my hand and said, "This is *my* mommy, not TV mommy."

Reilly and I had such fun together. We had tea parties for her dolls and stuffed animals, we painted pictures, we played hopscotch, and we pretended to be characters in the movies we watched together while curled up on the couch. We swam in the summer, and we built snowmen in the winter. I adored her and passed all my loving and nurturing into my sweet little girl. I knew Reilly was sometimes confused about the fact

My Little angel

Oh, my little angel,
you are the flesh and blood
of my flesh and my blood.
It was God who breathed life into you,
and, for me, that was His greatest gift of all.

And now as I watch you sleeping,
I'm still lost in wonder
at the miracle of your birth,
and lost for words to describe
the blessings you have brought me.

Where once my life seemed sometimes empty and futile,
now you fill me up and give me reason to live.

In a world full of suspicion, dishonesty, and distrust,
you, my little angel, are an open book.

When I am weak, you give me strength;
when I am drifting, you are my anchor.

Yesterday I found you weeping over a broken doll,
and I wanted to cry as I held you in my arms.

And when the day comes that I find you
weeping over a broken heart,
I know I'll want to die,
but I'll still be here to comfort you.

Oh, my little angel,
whate'er befalls you in the years ahead,
may the Lord above, who gave you to me,
hold you in the hollow of His hand.

Phil Coulter

that our family didn't look like a traditional family. I knew she longed to have a mom and dad and siblings who all lived together as other children do. Her dad and sister, Vanessa, lived in another state, and though she saw them regularly, it wasn't the same. One day a little girl at school said that we weren't a real family because it was just the two of us. That upset Reilly, and she came home to me in tears.

I tried to explain that no matter what, it's *love* that defines a family. I tried to share how much I felt like Della Reese was my mama, no matter that we came from two different places. I went on to tell Reilly about the fact that my family didn't look "normal" growing up, as I lost my mother when I was ten; so I was a little girl without a mother, and with just my dad to raise us. Other family members helped out when they could, but my father really was a single parent again. He learned to braid my long hair and took me shopping for dresses, and he never wanted me to feel the void that was obviously there from missing Mom. Bless him, he strove so hard to make things okay.

This story seemed to comfort Reilly. She held me tight and said, "It's you and me, Mama. We are a family." I kissed her little head and reassured her, "Yes, baby, I will love you forever, and I will always be your mommy."

I tried to show Reilly that she was part of a big family, too, by taking her to Ireland once a year so we could see my siblings and she could play with her many Irish cousins. I wanted her to know what it means to be Irish, to know the richness of our culture and beauty of our country, since it is such an integral part of who I consider myself to be.

It was a few more years before Reilly and I found the family we'd always dreamed of. And when we did, it was so fun and joyful to be welcomed into the family of Burnetts and feel like we all belonged together. We blended two families into one, often joking that we were like the Brady Bunch; we all felt so fortunate to have found one another. We weren't a traditional family, so we felt that much more special. We had created something of our own, had taken what could have been just wounds and made something beautiful from them. Love is a healer, a mender. Love has the power to make things whole.

The Beatles were right. All you need is love. Love makes a family, not DNA or background. Love. Just love. Simply love.

All those years ago, as I was in the midst of my divorce, heartbroken and hurting, I didn't know what was to come. I didn't know then that many years later, I would sit at my Thanksgiving table, under the tree in my garden, with my family, my husband and my daughter and my two fine stepsons. And that one year we would also include my ex-husband and his nephew, and my husband's ex-wife and her father, and we would all break bread together, and hold hands and pray, and be thankful to God together for the blessings we have, and for the gift of family, no matter what it looks like.

We must let go of the life we have planned,
so as to accept the one that is waiting for us.

JOSEPH CAMPBELL

For a Mother-to-Be

Nothing could have prepared
Your heart to open like this.

From beyond the skies and the stars
This echo arrived inside you
And started to pulse with life,
Each beat a tiny act of growth,
Traversing all our ancient shapes
On its way home to itself.

Once it began, you were no longer your own.
A new, more courageous you, offering itself
In a new way to a presence you can sense
But you have not seen or known.

It has made you feel alone
In a way you never knew before;
Everyone else sees only from the outside
What you feel and feed
With every fiber of your being.

Never have you traveled farther inward
Where words and thoughts become half-light
Unable to reach the fund of brightness
Strengthening inside the night of your womb.

Like some primeval moon,
Your soul brightens
The tides of essence
That flow to your child.

You know your life has changed forever,
For in all the days and years to come,
Distance will never be able to cut you off
From the one you now carry
For nine months under your heart.

May you be blessed with quiet confidence
That destiny will guide you and mind you.

May the emerging spirit of your child
Imbibe encouragement and joy
From the continuous music of your heart,
So that it can grow with ease,
Expectant of wonder and welcome
When its form is fully filled

And it makes its journey out
To see you and settle at last
Relieved, and glad in your arms.

John O'Donohue

LOVE STORY

I love you without knowing how, or when, or from where.
I love you simply, without problems or pride:
I love you in this way because I do not know
any other way of loving but this, in which there is no I or you,
so intimate that your hand upon my chest is my hand,
so intimate that when I fall asleep your eyes close.

PABLO NERUDA

The most magical things can have the humblest of beginnings.

The magic of my love story with Mark began with my feet in a bucket of water. Not the most glamorous of images, I know, but a girl needs a pedicure every now and then!

I had recently moved back to Los Angeles after wrapping nine seasons of *Touched by an Angel*. I was being very prayerful and thoughtful about the next steps in my career. I didn't want to plunge ahead without God's gentle guidance. It was a time of great soul-searching and of discovering a deeper sense of self, now free of the attention that had rained down on me during the success of *Touched by an Angel*. For nine years, I had been in the limelight, on countless magazine covers, doing daytime and nighttime talk shows, walking the red carpet, and receiving accolades and awards. I had tried very hard to stay grounded and in gratitude during that time; but the truth is, when it all goes away, it can feel very quiet. The silence can be deafening. In my industry, you can be recognized as one of *People* magazine's "Most Beautiful People in the World" one year, and the next year get no public attention at all. If you don't have a strong sense of self or a spiritual life, you can feel adrift and lost. If you don't have a sense of humor, the lack of attention can be painful. And let's face it, if you allow yourself to be defined by what you do, then it raises the question, Who are you when you aren't doing that?

Most of us know in our heads that our sense of self should not be dependent on what we do or how we look. But in real life, that's hard to pull off. I look at my daughter and her friends, and it pains me to see the pressure these girls feel to be thin or beautiful. Our culture puts such an unhealthy emphasis on looking a certain way in order to be loved or valued.

I know firsthand how illusory beauty is. Over the years I appeared on magazine covers, but it wasn't me just showing up with that kind of beauty. There was always a hair and makeup team and a stylist selecting beautiful clothes.

But young women don't realize how fake this beauty is. They see it and think they should look that way.

I wanted to instill in Reilly an appreciation for real beauty.

Real beauty is of the heart; it's the glow that lights your face when you are doing something kind, it's the tears you cry in appreciation of someone else's pain. Real beauty is kindness, gratitude, love.

If you get too attached to being beautiful on the outside, what happens when that "beauty" starts to fade? As we naturally age, fear can start to emerge. It can be a painful struggle, and I am not immune to this fear. Fear of letting go of that illusion of beauty. Fear of no longer being valued and accepted.

But the real freedom is to be found in letting go of fear. Letting go of the need to look a certain way, to be accepted by the masses. Who you are is perfect. God made you that way. He loves who you are becoming on the inside. This body will fade away. That's what it was made to do.

Your heart and spirit will be with you forever.

If we can remember this, fear dissolves.

Consider Mother Teresa, a woman who aged gracefully and didn't let it slow her down. Her beauty was apparent until the day she died. It glowed in the warmth of her smile as she helped God's people. She was radiant. She emitted a light that you cannot buy in a bottle.

She displayed the true beauty of grace, compassion, and love.

I knew that this time in Malibu—in between my role as Monica and whatever God had planned for me next— was an important season of growth . . . a time of letting go of the experience of *Touched by an Angel* and the deep connection I had to playing and being Monica, and a time of expanding and deepening my understanding of self and trusting in God for whatever was next. In fact, I discovered a beautiful sense of freedom after we moved back to Malibu and I enrolled Reilly in the local grade school. I loved being Mom at the park and queen of the carpool and living a normal life. I didn't know what was next, but I knew God would guide me.

One afternoon, Della came over for lunch. And in her sweet, direct way, she said, "Are you lonely, baby? Isn't it time you trusted your heart to love again?"

Well, I felt very happy with my life the way it was. "Oh, I don't know about that. It's hard to meet quality guys," I said, shaking my head.

"Well, honey, it's simple. You've got to hand it over. You have to ask God to choose a partner for you."

I laughed. It was simple, but I hadn't ever thought of that. I'd never really thought to ask God to choose for me.

Della said, "Well, think about what you want, and you bring that to God. Don't pray it over and over. Pray it once, and then just trust."

As usual, Della, the great loving and wise woman, was guiding me in a way that I am so thankful for.

And so I took some time to think about what I truly wanted in a man. I would be mindful of those qualities and pay attention. I wanted a man who would be strong and caring, a man to love me and my daughter, and a man who loved God. I wanted a man who was kind and loving and funny. I wanted a good man, an honest man, a man with integrity. I wanted him to be smart and to have his own success so there wouldn't be anything competitive between us. I wanted a man who would make me feel safe. I wanted him to love kids, and I wanted him to share my love of the ocean, of Ireland . . . to be honest, it was a long list!

And then I took a moment and picked up my list and handed it over to God. "God, this is what I think I need, but I didn't choose well in the past, so all I ask is that you let me know when he gets here."

So on an ordinary afternoon, a few months later, I was getting a pedicure in a salon. And as I sat there with my feet in a bucket of water, wearing a tracksuit with an elastic waistband, for goodness' sake, I noticed a man getting his hair cut across the room from me. His back was to me, but I noticed him because he was laughing a lot and generally being pretty noisy. My eyes caught his in the mirror, and my heart started to race. I mean, it was racing. I couldn't ignore it. And I thought, *Really? Is this happening?*

I quickly looked away, embarrassed that he had caught me watching. But I looked up again, and our eyes met again. I felt my cheeks heat. He was so handsome and joyful. Again I thought, *Really, is that him?* and I stared back down at my book. I had never reacted this way to seeing someone before. It was a physical reaction, like my body was trying to let me know . . . *something is happening here. Pay attention.*

I couldn't help myself. My eyes were drawn back to the mirror one more time. And yet again, he was looking at me!

I vowed not to make that mistake again.

A few minutes later, his haircut was finished, he spent a few moments checking out with the receptionist, and he was gone.

When my nails were dry, I carefully put on my flip-flops and walked up to the same checkout desk.

My curiosity got the best of me.

"Excuse me," I said to the receptionist, casually. "But do you happen to know the name of the man who just walked out of here?"

She looked at me with a smile. "Oh, isn't that funny," she said, "he just asked me who *you* were."

We laughed together, and she told me his name was Mark Burnett. He was local, but originally from the UK; he was divorced with two little kids and was a producer of reality TV.

I thanked her for letting me know and wondered when he might show back up in my life. He certainly had piqued my interest.

A few days later, I got a call from that receptionist. Mark had called the salon and asked if they might give him my number. She, of course, wanted to check with me first, before giving out personal information.

I said, "Yes, please give him my number!"

Shortly after that, she called back again.

"Yes?" I said, confused.

"I'm sorry to bother you again, but he wanted me to ask whether you would say yes if he called and asked you out?" the receptionist said with a laugh, probably feeling a bit like a schoolyard go-between, stuck back in the seventh grade.

I had to admit, I found it kind of adorable that he had her call and ask me that. I told her she could give him my number; of course I was going to say yes!

Well, a few moments later, he called, we went out, and I soon realized that this was it. My love had arrived.

Our first date was a Stevie Wonder concert at the House of Blues. Mark and I hit it off immediately. We both came from the same corner of the world, were born the same year, were both divorced with young children of a similar age (he had two boys, I had my little girl). We were both self-made, working in the same field. We lived on the same beach, drove the same car, laughed at the same jokes. It was better than anything I had ever experienced. It was the kind of love I knew could last my entire life.

We were married in a small ceremony presided over by Della, with just our new little family in attendance, and Mark's dad, Archie, and stepmom, Jean. Our oldest boy, James, served as best man; our little boy, Cameron, as ring bearer; and my beautiful Reilly was my bridesmaid. It was not just the marriage of two people but the coming together of a family of five. It felt like it was meant to be. Each child got to keep his or her position in the family. James was still the oldest, Cameron still the youngest, Reilly still the only girl.

We said our vows under a beautiful arbor in our backyard, where I had entwined three silk butterflies to represent my parents and Mark's mom, our angels in attendance. But they also made their presence known in other ways. That morning, as Mark and I gazed out at the ocean, saying prayers of gratitude for the special day that was under way, three butterflies fluttered right in front of us, a sign of God's presence and our loved ones' spirits. When Della arrived, she carried with her an ornate purse with butterflies embroidered on it. And finally, later in the day, despite the fact that we hadn't shared the news of our wedding with any of our friends, planning instead to send a marriage announcement after the fact, a gift arrived via FedEx, and within was a picture frame with three butterflies in the corner.

God made it clear that He was with us and blessing us with this day.

We had such a lovely time creating a new family from our five disparate parts. I love kids and had always wanted more children, and here I had these two beautiful young boys in my life! James and Cameron are a blessing to me. We certainly had to make some adjustments—Reilly had to learn to play with the boys and be a part of a larger family, since it had been just the two of us for so long. And the boys had to learn what it was like to have a sister in their lives. I'll never forget one morning, a few months after we were married, when everyone was rushing around, getting ready for school. Reilly and I were walking down the stairs as Mark was trying to get James and Cameron to find their backpacks, and in Mark's noisy fashion, he used a louder tone than Reilly was accustomed to with me. She looked at me and said, "Mom, I can't believe you fell in love with a military man!"

Oh, how I laughed. Mark had served time in the British military, which I know impacted the man he is today and how he handles himself, but to hear my little girl put it that way just cracked me up. We still laugh about it today.

Now, of course, all three of our lovely children are grown, and Mark and I are practically empty nesters. They are each following their own dreams. Reilly is back east at college studying theater, James recently graduated and is pursuing his love of the music business, and Cameron is in film school. It is so special to see them all making their way in the world, pursuing their dreams; but we're so happy when they take the time to come back home so we can be together as a family— as we know not to take family for granted.

As I look back, I know I got the family I'd always dreamed of; but I also got so much more. For Mark and I became not just husband and wife together, not just parents together, not just best friends, although all of those have made me happier than I could ever have dreamed. Mark and I also be- came business partners. We had the privilege of making *The Bible* together—it was a large, challenging undertaking but also a project that came to affect so many people. We went on to create our production company, LightWorkers Media, and produced many TV series and films together. We truly believe God brought us together to create such projects and bring them into the world, to shine a light for such a time as this. God's plans are so much bigger than we could have imagined. Isn't that always the case? Our vision can be small, while He is working things together for a greater good, the ultimate good. Our partnership has

> Love does not consist in gazing at each other, but in looking outward together in the same direction.
> ANTOINE DE SAINT-EXUPÉRY

helped to deepen our marriage and our friendship. We are so grateful that, with God's help, we found each other.

The love I share with Mark is the love I've always dreamed of receiving. He loves me the way I always wanted to be loved. One story provides a great example of this. About ten years ago, all five of us were in Australia together as a family. The boys were thirteen and nine, and Reilly was about ten. And as we wandered the streets of Sydney, we saw a little painting in the window of an art gallery. I don't remember who saw it first, but we were all soon gathered around this window, marveling at this particular piece of art. It was a small painting of a dog that looked just like our great big Irish wolfhound, Finn. And surrounding the dog were three butterflies.

Of course my entire family knows how much I love but-terflies and how symbolic they have been in my life. We all marveled at the dog's resemblance to Finn, and how there were three butterflies, one for each of the children.

After a bit of conversation and much laughter, we kept walking, exploring the town.

That afternoon, as we went back to the hotel for a rest, I sneaked back to the little gallery. It was June, and Mark's birthday was in July. I wanted to get the painting for him as a birthday surprise.

> *If God only used perfect people, nothing would get done. God will use anybody if you're available.*
>
> RICK WARREN

When I got back to the hotel with the painting, the kids were lying around a tad jet-lagged, reading and re-laxing, and Mark was in the other room on the phone. So I quietly showed the kids my surprise, and then quickly buried it in the bottom of my suit-case.

The next month, as I handed Mark his present, he opened it with care and then looked up at me with delight when he saw what was inside.

"I can't believe it!" he said, with a laugh.

"I know, I just had to get it for you," I said, remembering our trip and our family's joy in the discovery.

"No, no, you don't understand," Mark said, shaking his head with a smile. "I went back the next day to buy the painting for *you* because you had loved it so much. But it was already gone."

My mouth dropped open in shock. Cameron piped in at this point.

"He took me with him, and I had to pretend I didn't know you had already bought it!" he said.

Mark's eyes met mine. We smiled and laughed, that we had each had this same instinct to do something loving for the other one. It reminded me of that lovely O. Henry story "The Gift of the Magi." She sells her hair to buy him a chain for his watch, but he has sold his watch to buy beautiful combs for her hair. I know without a doubt that love is a verb. Anyone can say the words "I love you," but love is an action. Mark and I had the same loving instinct for each other.

This is how good love can be.

I sometimes marvel at the blessings in my life, but none more than my partnership with Mark. It was always my greatest dream to find someone who loved me the same way I loved him. I have that in Mark.

Thank you, God.

The minute I heard my first love story
I started looking for you, not knowing
how blind that was.
Lovers don't finally meet somewhere.
They're in each other all along.

RUMI

My children, our love should not be only
words and talk. Our love must be true love.
And we should show that love
by what we do.

1 JOHN 3:18 (ICB)

THE MOTHER OF GOD

Love anything and your heart will be wrung
and possibly broken. If you want to make sure
of keeping it intact you must give it to no one.
To love is to be vulnerable.

C. S. LEWIS

As I shared earlier, it was quite a journey to find our Jesus for the *Bible* series. Once Diogo walked up our drive and into our lives, it felt as if it was meant to be. Both Mark and I felt a deep connection to him and trusted him inherently to take on this important role.

This role required a lot from the actor. Once filming had started, I began the practice of praying before each scene. Diogo would often join me in prayer. Sometimes we would read the scene as it appeared in the Bible first, and then he would walk onto the set; and I knew the Holy Spirit was with him.

As the weeks passed, we were still looking for someone to play Mary, Jesus' mother. We had already cast a beautiful young actress to play Mary for the nativity scene. We now needed someone older, who looked like that actress might look in thirty years and who could play Mary as she walks beside her grown child as He fulfills the mission God has given Him.

I sat in our production office, looking online at links of actresses to be considered. And I just couldn't seem to find the right one. Mark walked in and saw what I was doing. And he looked at me with a twinkle in his eye. "I don't know why you are missing the obvious. You need to take on this role yourself. You've been like a mother to Diogo anyway."

I stared at Mark in shock. I had never even considered it. I was a producer for this series, not an actress.

And yet, as his words sank in, I began to realize he was right. I was believable as an older version of our young Mary. And I, of course, felt very connected to Diogo. I had promised him that if he took the role of Jesus, I would walk with him every step of the way.

I prayed about it that night and felt a knowing and peace. Yes, this was the answer. I was so thankful to Mark for opening my eyes to the solution that had been in front of us all along.

Taking on the role of Mary touched my heart profoundly. It also made me consider her experience in a way I never had before. I had grown up in a household of faith, and since I was a child, I had reflected on Jesus' sacrifice on the cross and was always filled with gratitude to Him. But as I stepped into the role of His Blessed Mother Mary, I suddenly had to watch this scene through the eyes of a mother and feel this scene with a mother's heart. It must have been unbearable for Mary to see her own son being crucified. Yet she showed such faith and courage. I tried to imagine the faith she must have possessed to not completely fall apart at the foot of the cross. There, up there, is her baby boy! There was the son she had raised and nurtured and loved so much.

While Jesus paid the ultimate sacrifice, sweet, tender Mary also made a sacrifice. Oh, how my heart broke while filming that scene. When she runs up to Him as He carries the cross, He falls to the ground, no longer able to carry the heavy wood. And the guards continue to whip Him. Mary reaches out her hand and can only say, "My son!"

In our film, Jesus looks into His mother's eyes and says, "Don't be afraid. Everything is possible with God."

In the darkest of times, Jesus could still see the light. In His most difficult moment, He was still a man of encouragement and faith.

When we see the cross, we are reminded that to be human is to experience pain. But this, too, shall pass.

I will always carry the memory of that moment and the faith Jesus had as He sought to encourage and strengthen His mother, whom He knew was close to despair. We know, too, that the Lord said only seven things from the cross, yet one of those was to the disciple John, telling him to take care of His mother. Even as He was dying, Jesus was loving His mother.

During filming, in the heat of the desert sun, I kept hearing a tune in my head. I started humming it repeatedly and soon realized that this song had been placed on my heart for a reason. The song was the beautiful Mark Lowry and Buddy Greene song "Mary, Did You Know?" I heard it over and over in my mind. And then I paid attention.

I found the song online and began to play it as I watched the scenes between Jesus and His mother in the editing bay. As I worked with Tessa, one of our talented young editors, I felt inspired. The combination of the song and the imagery was powerful. Maybe God could reach people through it.

And Mary said, Behold the handmaid of the Lord; be it unto me according to thy word. And the angel departed from her.

LUKE 1:38 (KJV)

Mark was back in L.A. filming *The Voice* at the time, and one of our favorite singers was a coach on the show. So I sent Mark the edited material, and he shared it with CeeLo Green. CeeLo grew up going to church, and loved the song "Mary, Did You Know?" He decided to record the song for his new Christmas album, and using the edited footage from the *Bible* series, we pulled together a beautiful music video using CeeLo's extraordinary version of this song. It was released on TV and immediately went viral. It gave people the chance to consider the life of Mary in a new way.

Mary said yes to the angel Gabriel, and her "Yes" changed the course of history.

Mary, Did You Know?

Mary, did you know that your Baby Boy would one day walk
on water?
Mary, did you know that your Baby Boy would save our
sons and daughters?
Did you know that your Baby Boy has come to make you
new?
This Child that you delivered will soon deliver you.

Mary, did you know that your Baby Boy will give sight to a
blind man?
Mary, did you know that your Baby Boy will calm the storm
with His hand?
Did you know that your Baby Boy has walked where angels
trod?
When you kiss your little Baby you kiss the face of God?

Oh Mary, did you know?

The blind will see, the deaf will hear, the dead will live
  again.
The lame will leap, the dumb will speak the praises of
  The Lamb.

Mary, did you know that your Baby Boy is Lord of all
  creation?
Mary, did you know that your Baby Boy would one day
  rule the nations?
Did you know that your Baby Boy is heaven's perfect
  Lamb?
This sleeping Child you're holding is the Great I Am.

Mark Lowry and Buddy Greene

Mary is a living example of deep, loving surrender, and of the power of sacrifice.

The Blessed Mother inspires all of us to recognize what it means to love God and let go and trust that God always knows best. I know this can be hard sometimes. We strive to control and manage our lives, and it can be a challenge to let go and surrender, to hand it all over to God. But Mary teaches us it is possible. Mary teaches us what love is. Love wants to protect and save, but love also knows that sometimes sacrifice and surrender are what is called for.

When we let go and empty our hands, God is there to fill our open hands.

Think about Mary's darkest days. She didn't know what would happen in three days. That her son would rise from the dead. That His mission was far from over and had, in truth, just begun. Mary trusted God.

This is how we know what love is:
Jesus Christ laid down his life for us.
And we ought to lay down our lives
for our brothers and sisters.

JOHN 3:16 (NIV)

AN ANGEL AMONG US

*We do not draw people to Christ by loudly
discrediting what they believe, by telling them how wrong
they are and how right we are, but by showing them
a light that is so lovely that they want with all their
hearts to know the source of it.*

MADELEINE L'ENGLE

I first met Maya Angelou when she appeared in an episode of
Touched by an Angel that also featured the lovely and talented
Natalie Cole. Della and Maya had been friends for years,
and the entire crew was so honored that she agreed to be a
part of our show. I had long been an admirer of her and her
voice, literally and artistically. She and Della often referred to
each other as sisters, and Della had introduced me to her as
her "daughter." Maya laughed when she met me. "Well," she
said, "since Della and I are sisters, and you are her daughter,
I guess that makes me your aunt!"

Meeting her in person did not disappoint. She is one of
those people who you just know has much to say. When she
spoke, you listened. Even so, she had the gift of giving peo-

ple her full attention. When she turned her gaze on you, you felt truly seen and heard and recognized. She had an extraordinary gift for raising everyone up and making every single person feel very special. There was a presence about her—of greatness, of humility, of spirit. She embodied her own words: "I have learned that people will forget what you said, people will forget what you did, but people will never forget how you made them feel."

I took Reilly to meet her once, years later when Maya was on tour for her book *Letter to My Daughter*. Maya considered the world her family and each person her child. That is how she looked at you, with eyes full of love and with a heart full of faith and promise. When Reilly met her after her reading, Maya turned her attention to Reilly fully, just as she had to me those many years before back in Utah. It is a moment Reilly has never forgotten.

I also had the chance to visit her a number of times at her home. One time, she was filming a cooking show, and she asked Della and me to appear on it. I flew in the night before and was able to stay at her beautiful home in North Carolina. We sat at her kitchen table, just the two of us, talking and laughing, and then she asked, "Would you care to have me read anything?"

I said, "Oh, yes, anything."

She read "Still I Rise," and then, as a special treat, she read the poem she had written for *Touched by an Angel*. As she began to read, in the quiet half-light of her kitchen, time stood still. It was one of those moments that will forever be imprinted on my heart. Having this amazing woman breathe life into those beautiful words. Just the two of us at her kitchen table drinking tea.

There are people in the world who really get it. Who embody the great possibility that dwells within each one of us. The potential we all have to love, to speak truth, to connect no matter our differences. To understand that we are all one, that we all belong to each other, that we are one big, beautiful family of God.

Maya was one of those people. Maya always said: Be a rainbow in someone else's cloud. Truly, she was an angel.

"Touched by an Angel"
aka
"Love's Exquisite Freedom"

We, unaccustomed to courage
exiles from delight
live coiled in shells of loneliness
until love leaves its high holy temple
and comes into our sight
to liberate us into life.

Love arrives
and in its train come ecstasies
old memories of pleasure
ancient histories of pain.
Yet if we are bold,
love strikes away the chains of fear
from our souls.

We are weaned from our timidity
In the flush of love's light
we dare be brave
And suddenly we see
that love costs all we are
and will ever be.
Yet it is only love
which sets us free.

Maya Angelou

You, God, are love.

We know that love is your essence.

and that you call us

to spread that love.

Help us, Lord.

Help us to become vessels

of your love,

Your peace,

Your kindness,

Your spirit.

Not just to those who

are easy to love,

not just those we

think belong to us,

but all of your children.

May we be part of

a love revolution,

in Your name,

and smile by smile,

hug by hug,

change the world.

When you can't put your prayers into words,
God hears your heart.

UNKNOWN

The Lord is the everlasting God, the Creator of the ends of the
earth. He does not faint or grow weary;
his understanding is unsearchable. He gives power
to the faint, and strengthens the powerless.
Even youths will faint and be weary,
and the young will fall exhausted;
but those who wait for the Lord
shall renew their strength,
they shall mount up with wings like eagles,
they shall run and not be weary,
they shall walk and not faint.

ISAIAH 40:28–31 (NRSV)

STILLNESS

five

STILLNESS

During my days of deepest grief, in all of my shock,
sorrow and struggle, I sat at the feet of God.
I literally spent hours each day reading God's word,
meditating on scripture and praying.
I intentionally spent a significant amount of time
being still before God.

RICK WARREN

AFTER THE SUCCESS of The Bible series on the History channel, Mark and I had the chance to do a follow-up series for NBC called *A.D.: The Bible Continues.* By this time, we had only one child left at home, Cameron, who was in his last year of high school. James and Reilly were both off at college in Boston. This kind of series can require a lot of travel and the need to be gone for long periods of time. Cameron, who had dreams of going to film school when he graduated, decided to take a semester off to come with us to Morocco and work on the crew. Mark and I were thrilled. We loved that we would be able to provide this incredible learning opportunity for Cameron, and we loved that we'd have him with us during the long months on location.

But just a few weeks into filming, Cameron got incredibly sick. At first we thought it was food poisoning, which can happen in foreign countries where the food and water are quite different from that in the States. Simultaneously, we were also filming a series in Malta called *The Dovekeepers* for CBS, so we took him with us to Malta, hoping that the change in diet might help. At first, much to our relief, he seemed to improve, but after a few days, it became clear that it was a much more serious issue than food poisoning, and he was admitted to the hospital.

Mark and I waited anxiously, holding each other close and praying, as the doctor examined him. We just wanted him to be okay. Cameron was very brave, and though we tried to appear strong in front of him, we were incredibly worried. After scans and tests and hushed conversations, the doctor finally pulled us aside to share his diagnosis.

Cameron had a brain tumor. Our hearts sank. But the doctor returned with what he promised was good news. The tu-

---

Do not worry about anything, but in everything by prayer and supplication with thanksgiving let your requests be made known to God. And the peace of God, which surpasses all understanding, will guard your hearts and your minds in Christ Jesus.

PHILIPPIANS 4:6–7 (NRSV)

mor was operable. He advised we get Cameron back to the States and have surgery performed as soon as possible.

Mark immediately arranged a plane for a medical evacuation from the location, and an ambulance was waiting in Los Angeles to take Cameron straight to the hospital.

And thus began a time that truly felt like the darkest of days, where all that we had taken for granted was now held in the hands of God. Of course, it had all been in His hands before, but now we acutely felt the reality that we had no power over the situation.

It was a frightening time for all of us, and we found ourselves clinging to hope but ultimately having to surrender to God.

Here we were at the peak of our careers. The Bible series had been a huge success; our company, LightWorkers Media, had just merged with MGM; and we were filming two network shows at the same time. But this incident with our son brought us to our knees, literally. None of that success mattered; we would have traded it all just to have Cameron completely well again.

We were so grateful to have access to the very best care and a fantastic team of doctors at UCLA Medical Center. But Cameron's issues were complicated, and we immediately called in prayers. We reached out to friends and family and our church community all across the country, knowing that we needed a miracle. We needed Cameron to be covered in prayer. We didn't know what would happen, but we knew we needed God. Both for his healing and for strength for our family to withstand these days.

Mark and I are both producers. In our day-to-day lives, members of the cast or crew come to us with situations that need fixing, and we help to figure things out. We help solve problems. But the situation with Cameron was filled with unknowing and uncertainty. We felt powerless to solve this "problem." There was nothing to be done except to call on God.

Mark was an absolute pillar of strength in this crisis. He is a natural leader, and he moved to make the smartest medical choices on behalf of Cameron. I can honestly say that if you were hanging off a cliff on the end of a rope, you would want Mark Burnett on the other end. He never gives up and he never lets go. He is completely loving and reliable and dependable. He stepped into this situation, taking whatever actions were needed, holding tightly to his boy, and he never let go. With no quick fix in sight, it became a waiting game, and we soon knew we would be at the hospital for some time. At the nurse's suggestion, we decided to take shifts to give each other a break to get home to have a quick shower or grab a change of clothes. The hospital told us we were in this for the long haul, and we had to be smart or we would not endure.

There is no pit so deep that God's love is not deeper still.

CORRIE TEN BOOM

Before we left for Morocco, we had started some renovations at our home, thinking it was the perfect time, as we

The Lord will fight for you, you need only to be still.

EXODUS 14:14 (NIV)

would be gone and out of the country for several months. Now we were unexpectedly back, and our house was in chaos. It was a shock to walk in and discover walls removed, plastic sheeting all over the place, and a coating of dust everywhere.

We have always called our home "the Sanctuary," and if ever we needed a space of peace and calm, it was now. We needed a sanctuary, but with builders in the house, we certainly weren't going to find it at home. We thought about checking into a hotel, but ultimately decided we still wanted the comfort and security that comes from being in your own home and being able to crawl into your own bed. We would deal with the chaos. The physical mess in our home was an outer reflection of what was going on in our emotional and spiritual lives.

Looking back, I see this time of our lives as a blur. We were all barely coping, in survival mode, and acting on pure instinct. Friends and family flew in from the UK to be of support. Of course Cameron's mother and her family were there, and James and Reilly flew home from college on the East Coast as often as they could to be at the hospital as well. James was such a great big brother, sitting for hours at his brother's bedside, holding his hand and refusing to leave even for a moment. It was a time of great worry for our little family, but looking back, I can see that it brought us all closer together, as we leaned on one another for support and strength.

I remember driving back and forth from the hospital, and those times alone in the car provided my most intimate moments with God. There were times I had to pull over on the side of the road and sit in the quiet of my car, weeping and listening for His still, small voice. There was no real peace at the hospital, where I tried to remain strong and be a good partner for Mark, and there was no stillness in our home with all the construction going on. Only in the privacy of my car could my soul allow itself to feel. *God, please heal him. Please, Lord, please, please heal him.* It was here, alone, where I could finally cry out to God and try to find the stillness within myself.

Prayer is a lifeline to God.
REV. BILLY GRAHAM

Days became weeks, and the worry was taking its toll. Mark, who stood watch over his son like a warrior angel morning, noon, and night, was just about worn out. Indeed, we all were exhausted. We were practically living at the hospital, and the uncertainty was frightening. When our dear friends Pastor Rick and Kay Warren came by and prayed with us and prayed over Cameron, it was not only a blessing to Cameron but it lifted our spirits as well.

Indeed, we were so grateful to all the friends who rallied around us—those who visited and those who reached out to us on email or on the phone, and we were particularly grateful to all those who reached out to us in prayer. We could feel the love that

Worry does not empty tomorrow of its sorrow, it empties today of its strength.

CORRIE TEN BOOM

surrounded us, and we were uplifted and strengthened by it. The whole experience had brought us to our knees. For in the fear and uncertainty, there was nowhere else to go but to God.

We cried out in our darkness and despair, and, mercifully, the Lord heard us. Cameron began to slowly recover.

Once we knew he was out of the woods and we had all breathed a sigh of relief together and cried tears of gratitude, I went out to my car and was finally alone, about to drive home to the Sanctuary. I fell to my knees in the parking lot. *Thank you, God. Thank you, God. Thank you, God.*

I'm not sure if I said the words, but I know God felt my prayer of gratitude through the tears that were streaming down my face.

In the midst of the crisis, there was a moment when we did not know if Cameron would ever walk or talk again, and yet when he was released from the hospital in time for an incredible Thanksgiving feast, he practically ran through our front door with a giant smile on his face. Healed and re-stored, talking a mile a minute. There was no doubt what we were all thankful for that year. We held hands tightly around our table and prayed together, thanking God for healing

Cameron, for giving him back his health, and for returning him to his loving family.

In many ways, the experience brought our little family closer together, which is an additional blessing. We no longer take each other or anything in our lives for granted. Our three wonderful children are all now young adults, making their way in the world, reaching for their dreams. We love them so much and are proud of each one of them. We are very close, and we try to gather as often as we can as a family, sharing laughter and love and food and conversation around the dining table. We always take time to give thanks and pray together before every meal, a practice we began with our children when they were very young. Our hearts are full of gratitude for all our blessings and each other.

You don't choose your family. They are God's gift to you, as you are to them.

DESMOND TUTU

Prayer can mean so many things. It is most definitely the crying out to God for help. In those dark days of uncertainty, all I could do was simply call out, *Help him, God, heal him, God.* I feel certain God welcomed those prayers. I believe He welcomes us anytime we come to him, even if we have no words.

But prayer is more than asking. It is a conversation with our Beloved. It is a quieting of the soul, so we can hear. It is a stilling of the chaos, so we can see how God is all around us, if we only take the time to notice.

The bond that links your true family is not one of blood, but of respect and joy in each other's life.

RICHARD BACH

We are a nation of doers. Rather than human beings, we are human do-ings. We work and strive and talk and move and go, go, go.

But if we want to be at peace, we must stop.

Stop our working. Stop our talking. Stop even our praying.

Breathe in, breathe out.

Make space. Listen to the whispers of our hearts.

It is only in the quietness, in the stillness, that we can hear the voice of God.

Prayer is as natural an expression of faith as breathing is of life.

JONATHAN EDWARDS

Therefore I tell you, do not worry about your life, what you will eat or drink; or about your body, what you will wear. Is not life more than food, and the body more than clothes? Look at the birds of the air; they do not sow or reap or store away in barns, and yet your heavenly Father feeds them. Are you not much more valuable than they? Can any one of you by worrying add a single hour to your life?

And why do you worry about clothes? See how the flowers of the field grow. They do not labor or spin. Yet I tell you that not even Solomon in all his splendor was dressed like one of these. If that is how God clothes the grass of the field, which is here today and tomorrow is thrown into the fire, will he not much more clothe you—you of little faith? So do not worry, saying, 'What shall we eat?' or 'What shall we drink?' or 'What shall we wear?' For the pagans run after all these things, and your heavenly Father knows that you need them. But seek first his kingdom and his righteousness, and all these things will be given to you as well. Therefore do not worry about tomorrow, for tomorrow will worry about itself. Each day has enough trouble of its own.

Matthew 6:25-34 (NIV)

Praying

It doesn't have to be

the blue iris, it could be

weeds in a vacant lot, or a few

small stones; just

pay attention, then patch

a few words together and don't try

to make them elaborate, this isn't

a contest but the doorway

into thanks, and a silence in which

another voice may speak.

Mary Oliver

A SPACE FOR GRACE

You cannot in one glance survey this most vast and beautiful system of the universe, in its wide expanse, without being completely overwhelmed by the boundless force of its brightness.

JOHN CALVIN

When life begins to get messy and chaotic and loud, I have to take time away. I have to find a moment of stillness. And I find that stillness through prayer and in nature.

When I was growing up, we of course learned the Our Father, and I remember getting on my knees with my father and praying that prayer. And how important that prayer is. It is how Jesus Himself taught us to pray. But prayer can be much more than words that we say to God. T. S. Eliot says, "If we really want to pray, we must first learn to listen, for in the silence of our hearts God speaks."

We are sometimes too busy to notice that God is trying to speak to us.

*May we all grow in grace and peace,
and not neglect the silence that is printed in the centre of our being.
It will not fail us.*

THOMAS MERTON

Our culture is bombarded on all sides by demands. We live in a noisy world, with texting and emailing and music and TV and on and on. We used to be able to get away and have space . . . on the weekend, on a plane, at dinner. But now we are expected to be available at all times. To respond immediately.

It is only when we slow down that we are able to breathe. To connect with the spirit of God. To *hear* God. It is only in that peace that we can see the butterfly and notice the miracles unfolding all around. When we are still, we can get out of the way.

Stillness brings you into the present moment. We are often so fixated on something that happened in the past or worried about what might happen in the future that we completely miss the now.

Prayer can involve a time that you set aside to commune with God, but I like to try to bring prayer into every moment.

To call Him in, to invite Him into each moment. I feel this the strongest when I'm in nature. When we are surrounded by nature, we can finally commune with God and His creation. Walking out into a field or looking up at the sky allows us to breathe and recharge and reminds us how big our God is.

God is also in the small things. The song of a bird, the feel of the sun on

Yesterday is history. Tomorrow is a mystery. Today is a gift. That's why it's called the present.

ALICE MORSE EARLE

our skin, the buzz of the bumblebee, the flight of the butterfly. In every blade of grass we can see the beauty of creation.

In every walk with Nature one receives far more than he seeks.

JOHN MUIR

And there, in that space, we will find God.

I try to get out in nature each morning, either with a brisk hike along the mountain trails near our home or a quiet stroll on the beach. For you, it might mean walking your dog in your neighborhood or stepping out onto your porch and looking up at the sky. Spending time outside allows us to make space in our hearts for God. It gives us a chance to fill up, to nurture our souls so we can go into our day feeling in tune with what truly matters. No matter what you think about meditation, there is something to be said for developing the skill to quiet your mind. Whether you say the Rosary, simply count your breaths, or call out to God, meditation frees your mind of the noise and chatter; it gets you into a space of openness and availability.

This is one of the reasons I love living by the ocean. The constant sound of the waves becomes a meditation, washing in and out, as steady and consistent as my heartbeat, like a massage for my mind and my spirit.

I've also created rituals for myself throughout the day that allow me to stop and find stillness. Of course, since I am an Irishwoman, a cup of tea is the solution to everything! For in the process of making tea, there is space, there is waiting, there is quiet. There is ritual. First, you put water in the kettle, and then you wait for it to boil. Then you warm the pot, then put the tea in, pour in the boiling water, and wait for the tea to brew. By the time you sit down to your steaming cup of tea, all is well in the world. You have created what I like to call a "space for grace." Every moment in my past, big or small in memory, involved a cup of tea.

I See His Blood upon the Rose

I see his blood upon the rose
And in the stars the glory of his eyes,
His body gleams amid eternal snows,
His tears fall from the skies.

I see his face in every flower;
The thunder and the singing of the birds
Are but his voice—and carven by his power
Rocks are his written words.

All pathways by his feet are worn,
His strong heart stirs the ever-beating sea,
His crown of thorns is twined with every thorn,
His cross is every tree.

Joseph Mary Plunkett

You can find this space for grace anywhere, in any moment. When you go outside and look at the sky, when you read a book of poetry, or when you turn on a piece of music that you know stirs your soul. These are tools that can create in you a feeling of well-being and connect you with the spiritual and with God. And, of course, reading the Bible and spending time in the Word of God is the ultimate way to invite Him into your heart and into each moment.

When anxious, uneasy and bad thoughts come, I go to the sea, and the sea drowns them out with its great wide sounds, cleanses me with its noise, and imposes a rhythm upon everything in me that is bewildered and confused.

RAINER MARIA RILKE

We have to remember to take care of ourselves, to slow down, and to nurture our relationship with God. Building a relationship with God is like building any other relationship. While God never stops loving us, we can feel disconnected from Him if we don't make space for Him, if we don't take the time to be quiet, to still the chatter and make room for His thoughts and His grace.

There are so many rituals from across different cultures that share the same intention, and those rituals can help us stop and remember and bring Him in. Whether they are performing the sign of the cross, splashing holy water, or lighting a candle as you make your prayer. These are all designed as gentle reminders. I have candles scattered throughout my house, and I light them wherever I go. For me, there is something about the scratch of the match against the carbon and the *whish* that comes when the flame bursts to light that ushers in the holy.

I have heard it said that we either live our lives as if nothing is a miracle or as if everything is a miracle. I, of course, believe that everything is a miracle, from the healing power of God to the stunning beauty of creation to the magical emotion that comes from a particular piece of music.

I strive to live each day making room to recognize these miracles and thank God for them. When you do that, you realize how close He is. That He is always right there, waiting for you, in your heart and mind. In times when you feel close to Him, and even times when you feel desperately far away, He is always there, waiting for you to call on Him.

Look within.

Look without.

He is there.

*Faith is the bird that feels the light
when the dawn is still dark.*

RABINDRANATH TAGORE

In the middle of sentences loaded with action—healing suffering people, casting out devils, responding to impatient
disciples, traveling from town to town and preaching from
synagogue to synagogue—we find these quiet words: "In the
morning, long before dawn, he got up and left the house, and
went off to a lonely place and prayed there." In the center of
breathless activities, we hear a restful breathing. Surrounded
by hours of moving, we find a moment of quiet stillness. In the
heart of much involvement, there are words of withdrawal. In
the midst of action, there is contemplation. And after much
togetherness, there is solitude. The more I read this nearly
silent sentence locked in between the loud words of action,
the more I have the sense that the secret of Jesus' ministry is
hidden in that lonely place where he went to pray, early in the
morning, long before dawn.

Henri Nouwen

In our lives in the world, the temptation is always to go where the world takes us, to drift with whatever current happens to be running strongest. When good things happen, we rise to heaven; when bad things happen, we descend to hell. When the world strikes out at us, we strike back, and when one way or another the world blesses us, our spirits soar. I know this to be true of no one as well as I know it to be true of myself. I know how just the weather can affect my whole state of mind for good or ill, how just getting stuck in a traffic jam can ruin an afternoon that in every other way is so beautiful that it dazzles the heart. We are in constant danger of being not actors in the drama of our own lives but reactors. The fragmentary nature of our experience shatters us into fragments. Instead of being whole, most of the time we are in pieces, and we see the world in pieces, full of darkness at one moment and full of light the next.

It is in Jesus, of course, and in the people whose lives have been deeply touched by Jesus, and in ourselves at those moments when we also are deeply touched by him, that we see another way of being human in this world, which is the way of wholeness. When we glimpse that wholeness in others, we recognize it immediately for what it is, and the reason we recognize it, I believe, is that no matter how much the world shatters us to pieces, we carry inside us a *vision* of wholeness that we sense is our true home and that beckons to us. It is part of what the book of Genesis means by saying that we are made in the image of God.

Frederick Buechner

Today

Today I'm flying low and I'm
not saying a word.
I'm letting all the voodoos of ambition sleep.

The world goes on as it must,
the bees in the garden rumbling a little,
the fish leaping, the gnats getting eaten.
And so forth.

But I'm taking the day off.
Quiet as a feather.
I hardly move though really I'm traveling
a terrific distance.

Stillness. One of the doors
into the temple.

Mary Oliver

The Lake Isle of Innisfree

I will arise and go now, and go to Innisfree,
And a small cabin build there, of clay and wattles made:
Nine bean-rows will I have there, a hive for the honey-bee,
And live alone in the bee-loud glade.

And I shall have some peace there, for peace comes dropping
    slow,
Dropping from the veils of the morning to where the cricket
    sings;
There midnight's all a glimmer, and noon a purple glow,
And evening full of the linnet's wings.

I will arise and go now, for always night and day
I hear lake water lapping with low sounds by the shore;
While I stand on the roadway, or on the pavements grey,
I hear it in the deep heart's core.

William Butler Yeats

THE FIELD

O Beauty, you are the light of the world!

DEREK WALCOTT

My father had a quiet stillness about him. When we would go to Moville in the summers, my father loved to walk along the shore at Greencastle. We would walk along that rocky seashore, me beside him, in complete easy silence, sometimes for hours.

Many years later, I finally had a bit of money saved after the success of *A Woman Named Jackie.* I still didn't own a car or a home in the U.S., yet I had this idea that maybe I would buy a wee cottage in Ireland, a little corner for myself in the world. I looked around at some different towns but didn't find anything I liked. I soon found myself back in Greencastle, and there, along the very shore that I used to walk with Dad, was a small field for sale. Now, there was no cottage on it. Just a field. I had no idea or real plan for what I was going to do with a field. But I wanted that field. I wanted that field for my dad.

In a matter of days, I was signing the contract with the

village solicitor. And then
I took my rented car and
drove out to what was now
my field. It had been raining
earlier, and so I had my Wel-

*Out beyond ideas
of wrongdoing and
rightdoing, there is a field.
I will meet you there.*

RUMI

lington boots on, and the ground was still damp and muddy.
I climbed the fence and went and sat in the middle of the
field, staring out at the waters of Lough Foyle. And I laughed
and cried, thinking, *Fine lot of good this old field is going to
do me!*

But then the breeze blew, and I'm sure I felt my dad's hand
on my shoulder. And I imagined him saying, "Aren't you a
great girl, now. Good on ya."

And I smiled. I had bought this field for my dad. And I
knew wherever he was, he was pleased. He would have just
loved it, of that I am certain.

I kept that field for many years.

And yes, I can see that it was a very impractical purchase.
I still laugh to think that the very first thing I bought with
the money I earned was a field for my dead father. But we all
so want our parents to be proud of us. He wasn't around to
see what I had done, to see the life I was creating for myself. I
bought that field as if to say, *See, Dad, look what I did!*

And I know I felt his pride in that field that day.

To me, a field can be just as holy as the largest cathedral.
It can usher in a moment just as profound as the greatest
sermon.

You see, the holy is everywhere. It is in the sun and the moon and the stars. It is in you and me. We often go looking for it. We think we will be able to find space on vacation or when we go to church. We are always waiting. When we get there, then we will be happy or whole or complete. But it is here. Already here. In you and in me.

We just have to stop, and breathe, and listen. And see that it has been in us all along.

What wings are to a bird, and sails to a ship,
so is prayer to the soul.

CORRIE TEN BOOM

Lord, you have been our dwelling place
throughout all generations.
Before the mountains were born
or you brought forth the whole world,
from everlasting to everlasting
you are God.

Psalm 90: 1-2 (NIV)

I know, God, that you are only
as far away as my next breath.
That you are always there, waiting, in
the stillness inside,
if only I would stop and find you.
Thank you for the reminders you put
in our lives.
To slow down.
To breathe. To wonder.
Thank you for the ocean,
that magnificent display
of your glory
and your power.
Thank you for the sun
that warms our skin,
for the breeze that
makes our hair dance,
for the flowers that
not only delight our eyes
but tickle our noses
with their delicious scent.
You have made our world
a wonder of beauty.
Thank you.
Thank you for reminders,
for stillness,
for grace.

If there is light in the soul, there will be beauty in the person. If there is beauty in the person, there will be harmony in the house. If there is harmony in the house, there will be order in the nation. If there is order in the nation, there will be peace in the world.

CHINESE PROVERB

Everything is possible for one who believes.

MARK 9:23 (NIV)

GRATITUDE

six

GRATITUDE

I wouldn't have dared ask God for all He has given me.
I couldn't have done it on my own.
I thank God every day for what I have.

LORETTA LYNN

IT ALL COMES down to one thing: gratitude.

Every morning when I get out of bed and my first foot hits the floor, I say, "Thank." Then the other foot hits the floor, and I say, "You." And all the way into the bathroom, I am whispering, "Thank you. Thank you. Thank you." A pitter-patter of gratitude as I begin my day.

I began this practice when I was filming *Touched by an Angel* in Utah. I don't remember where I read or heard about it, but as soon as I discovered this practice, I knew it was something I wanted to integrate into my daily routine. And I've done it every day ever since.

I've now added another routine to remind me to give thanks

throughout the day. Each time I wash my hands and feel the water run over my skin, I say it again. "Thank you. Thank you, God." It helps me take a step back from whatever is happening in my day to remember my blessings. It's a reminder for me to acknowledge God; and from that space, I am brought into a place of strength and wholeness and fullness. I find when I attach an attitude to an action—something I am bound to do throughout the day—it helps me remember the attitude more. And so every time I wash my hands, my perception of whatever is going on around me instantly changes.

I think that practice spoke to me while I was in Utah because I was so grateful during that season of my life. So grateful to be cast in a starring role on a TV show, so thankful that the series had been picked up and that it had finally found its audience. While *Touched by an Angel* eventually went on to become the number one show on the network, the first year or two it really struggled to find its audience. We shot the pilot not knowing if it would be picked up, and CBS initially ordered only six episodes, then increased it to thirteen. They kept moving our time slot, and we were even placed on an early hiatus for a while—which often signals that the end is in sight and that the show will be canceled. But then, finally, they put us in a Saturday-night time slot, and we began to pick up some ratings. We realized, as a cast and crew, that if we didn't do something to spread the word, this show would be over before it even had a chance to begin, which often happens. So we reached out to youth groups and churches all across the country and let them know that there was a TV show on the air that celebrated God and was hoping to spread the message of God's love. And slowly the faith community began to mobilize, word of

One more day to serve.
One more hour to love.
One more minute to praise.
For this day I am grateful.
If I awaken to the morning sun,
I am grateful.

MARY LOU KOWNACKI,
ORDER OF SAINT BENEDICT

mouth began to spread, the churches began to pray, and we became the little engine that could. *I think I can, I think I can, I think I can.*

Finally, the network moved us to Sunday night. That was the sweet spot. Families could gather at the end of the weekend to watch this show together. Parents and grandparents could snuggle on the couch with their kids and know they didn't have to keep their finger on the remote control. They trusted the show and enjoyed the message of hope. Soon millions of people were watching each week.

Talk about gratitude. It was more than any of us could have hoped for.

And we soon realized that it was more than entertainment; we came to believe that God was truly using our show to reach His children.

I was so moved by letters I received from people who shared how a particular episode impacted them and deeply touched their lives. Because I was the face of the show, many of these letters were addressed to me, but I would bring them to set to share with my cast and crew. We would laugh and cry and hug, hearing the messages from these viewers, so grateful for the opportunity to be part of something that was clearly bigger than all of us. As Della would say, "It's a God thing, baby."

One time I was at a bookstore in Los Angeles doing a signing for a children's book I had written, and a young woman came up to me, tears in her eyes and fresh scars on her wrists. And she told me the most remarkable story.

She hadn't had an easy life, and one night she found herself full of despair and ready to take her own life. She slit her wrists and slid down the bathroom wall, filled with anger at her family because she felt abandoned and alone, feelings that had plagued her throughout her life. And now here she was, feeling abandoned and alone again. She cried out to God, "Even now, there's no one here! There's no one here." And she let her head sink to her knees, waiting for death to take her.

But then she heard something from the living room. It was the television. She didn't even remember turning it on. *Touched by an Angel* was on, and it was the angel revelation scene. And this woman heard the words of Monica the angel come wafting through the bathroom door: "You are not alone. You are never alone. Don't you know that God loves you?"

I am the light of the world. Whoever follows me will not walk in darkness, but will have the light of life.
JOHN 8:12 (ESV)

When she heard those words, she lifted her head. She felt those words were just for her. And she picked up a towel and wrapped up her wrists and called an ambulance.

I stared at her in shock and gave her a hug, tears flooding my eyes, and all I could say was, "Thank you, God."

Thank you, God.

Over and over. I was so humbled by what God was able to accomplish with that little show of ours.

God is willing and able to use any of us to do His work. We just have to be ready. How do you prepare yourself to be God's angel? We've touched on it throughout this book. You slow down so you can hear His whisper. Find the stillness. You look for ways to perform small acts of kindness. You dare to do something courageous and step out onto that water. You look for ways to love. For that's who and what God is. Love. You want to be His angel? Spread love.

Love.

Love.

After the show wrapped, I went through a time of mourning. I missed my cast and crew family, but I also missed Monica. I missed playing her and inhabiting her spirit. Playing Monica for many hours a day, over many years, taught me so much. She made me a better friend, a better listener, a more faithful servant. I enjoyed living in her skin, and I think she brought out the best of me. She was able to truly, fully show up for someone. She listened, not just with her ears but also with her heart. When people come to you with a heart-load of hurt, they aren't always looking for solutions or answers. It's often enough just to listen and love. When people feel they are truly heard, healing can happen.

I also missed the important work we were doing, the purpose that I felt in my life. Reilly and I had come back to Malibu, and I wasn't sure what I was going to do next; but I knew I didn't want to just jump into another role.

One of the first things I filmed after the show wrapped was an infomercial for Operation Smile, a short film to increase awareness of the good work that they do. I had been meaning to do it ever since I had gotten involved with this wonderful organization after the first season of the show, but I hadn't had enough time to go on location to shoot it. So I packed my bags and headed off to Vietnam. I spent a week at the mission hospital, working to tell the story of children whose lives had been forever changed with this restorative surgery. I was grateful to be able to help bring attention to the cause and to help raise millions of dollars for this organization that brings so much hope and light into the world.

After that, I just waited. I waited, knowing that God would bring forth the right next step for me. I poured myself into being a mom. I loved being there for Reilly in a way I hadn't been able to do when I was putting in twelve-hour days on set. A number of job opportunities presented themselves, but I kept waiting. I didn't want to say yes to something out of fear of becoming irrelevant. If a job wasn't going to bring light and hope, I wasn't that interested.

But I had been chasing work for my entire life. It was scary to not work. I had to trust that space, even when waves of panic came crashing in.

The Bible says there is a time for everything. A time for sowing and reaping. Even Jesus took time to be alone and away from the crowds, time to pray, to gather Himself, before he went back out to do the good work.

I had no idea at the time that the next big thing for me would be the *Bible* project, but of course Mark had to come into my life before that could come to fruition.

I'm so thankful that God gave me the courage to wait. For Mark. For the Bible series. For Him.

Many people are surprised that my husband and I are able to work together. I have girlfriends who joke that they can hardly wash dishes with their husbands without getting into a disagreement! But I know God brought Mark and me together for a greater purpose. I often tell people that he and I have different skill sets and that we are quite a team when put together. Sometimes, to get a project made, you need to kick down a door; and there is no better man to kick a door down than my husband! But sometimes the door requires a gentle knock, and that's what I am able to do. Either way, the doors opened for us together. Our production company is named LightWorkers Media, and we believe it's better to light one candle than to curse the darkness.

Thank you, God. For my beautiful family. Thank you for my husband, Mark. For the important work you are guiding us to do together. Thank you for helping us find a way to bring your light into the world in an industry that isn't always interested in the light.

Sometimes it feels as if there is so much darkness in the world. I want to be a helper to bring people to the light. To spread the light. To shine the light. God is the Light, and He is always there.

Oh, there were many times when I was not as patient as I sound now. There were times when I would call out to Monica and say, somewhat jokingly, "Where are you when I need you? I miss you!"

> I don't think of all the misery, but of the beauty that still remains.
>
> ANNE FRANK

But of course, she *was* there, wasn't she? The angel is just the conduit of spirit. And in those moments, those moments when I was laughing as I called on Monica, I was calling out to God. And I would feel Him come alongside me, just as He came alongside those footprints in the sand, and say, *I'm right here, it's okay. Just sit. You don't have to be doing all the time. Just trust. You are doing enough.*

You are not alone. I'm right here with you.

Thank you, God.

There are two ways of spreading light: to be the candle or the mirror that reflects it.

EDITH WHARTON

If the only prayer you said
in your whole life was "thank you,"
that would suffice.

MEISTER ECKHART

STOP LOOKING
FOR LACK

Acceptance doesn't mean resignation; it means
understanding that something is what it is
and that there's got to be a way through it.

MICHAEL J. FOX

I've learned one thing from being in this industry for almost thirty years now. Theodore Roosevelt probably said it best: "Comparison is the thief of joy." No matter what you have accomplished, there will always be someone with "more." More awards, more work, longer legs, bigger house. Trust me, the list can go on and on. I have more than I could have ever imagined in my wildest dreams, and yet there are still people with way more than me, if I choose to live my life in comparison.

That's why gratitude is so essential. There is no room for comparison within the words "Thank you." Thank you is fullness. Thank you is overflowing. Thank you is blessed beyond measure. There is no lack; there is only abundance. That's why we must learn to say thank you all the time. For every gift, big or small. For a home to live in, a job that pays the bills, a person to love, a child to raise. Saying thank you not only acknowledges all we've been given but also makes room for more to arrive.

To lift up the hands in prayer gives God glory, but a man with a dungfork in his hand, a woman with a slop pail, give Him glory, too. God is so great that all things give Him glory if you mean that they should.

GERARD MANLEY HOPKINS

I find that when I live with an "attitude of gratitude," I am attuned to the blessings of God. I am always looking for the next gift He might bestow, the next butterfly that will encourage me, the next quiet whisper of His voice.

When I am focused on what I don't have, I miss the blessings all around.

Perhaps you've heard the story of God's lifeboat. I'm not sure who wrote it, but it's become a kind of epistle of the many ways we can miss God.

As the story goes, there was a huge storm, and the emergency personnel sent a warning to the community that a flood was likely. They encouraged people to evacuate to keep themselves safe.

And a man said to himself: *I trust God and know that He will send a miracle to save me.*

His neighbors came by and said, "We are leaving, and there is room for you in our car. Please, come with us!"

But the man said, "No, I know that God will save me."

A few hours later, as the waters continued to rise, now licking at his front porch, a man in a canoe paddled over to his porch. "The waters are rising quickly. Come into my canoe, and I will get you to safety!"

But the man said, "No, thank you, God will save me."

A few hours later, the water had entered the house, and the man had to go up to his second story. A police boat arrived. The police saw him through his window, and said, "Come on, get in before it's too late!"

But again the man refused, saying, "No, thank you, God will save me."

By this time, the waters had reached the second floor, and the man had to climb onto his roof.

A helicopter was searching the area and found this lone man sitting on top of his roof as the sunset glimmered and darkness threatened.

"Sir, here is a rope, take hold, and we will pull you up and take you to safety!"

And sure enough, the man refused. "No, God will save me."

The waters continued to rise, and the man was washed away and drowned.

When he reached heaven, he walked up to God and said, accusingly, "God, I put my faith in you! Why didn't you save me?"

And God looked at him and said, "I sent you a warning,

a car, a canoe, a boat, and a helicopter. What more were you looking for?"

It's a silly story, but I think one that can show the power of thank you. What if, instead of saying "No, thanks" to every miracle God provided, the man instead had said, "Thank you"? He would have been safe at the very beginning. He would have been filled with wonder at the way God provides. He would have been a part of the chorus singing God's praise.

"Thank you" changes everything.

There have been times in my life when I have been disappointed, when I didn't book a job I thought should have been mine, or when God didn't answer my prayer the way I expected.

It's not always easy. That's why simply saying thank you throughout the day attunes you to what is right—not what is wrong—and reminds you where God has shown up, rather than where He is missing.

You don't want to miss the boat, do you?

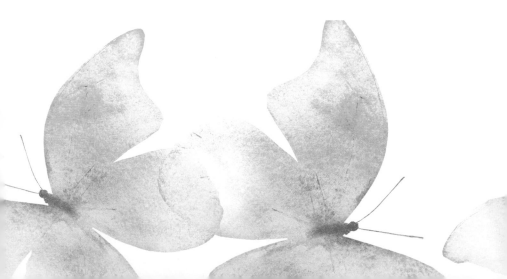

Christ with me, Christ before me, Christ behind me,
Christ in me, Christ beneath me, Christ above me,
Christ on my right, Christ on my left,
Christ where I lie, Christ where I sit, Christ where I arise,
Christ in the heart of every one who thinks of me,
Christ in the mouth of every one who speaks to me,
Christ in every eye that sees me,
Christ in every ear that hears me.
Salvation is of the Lord.
Salvation is of the Christ.
May your salvation, Lord, be ever with us.

Saint Patrick

A CAUSE FOR CELEBRATION

Find a place inside where there's joy, and the joy will burn out the pain.

JOSEPH CAMPBELL

When I experienced great loss very early in my life, I could have let that loss define me. I might have felt justified to walk around with a chip on my shoulder, feeling as if life had dealt me a bad hand. Those losses could have shaken me to the core of who I am. But my father helped me to see the butterfly, remember? So early in my life, his example taught me to . . . look for the miracle.

Gratitude helps us see the light in the darkness, the potential of healing among the sick, the hope among the hopeless. In spite of what I've lost, I haven't lost everything. I know gratitude is the key. The key to everything.

When I'm out in nature . . . thank you.

When I see a butterfly . . . thank you.

When I see good people doing their best to make this world a better place . . . thank you.

Viktor Frankl, who experienced the horrors of the concentration camp, famously said, "Between stimulus and response, there is a space. In that space is our power to choose our response. In our response lies our growth and our freedom."

That someone who experienced one of the darkest moments of our human history can see hope still, gives me hope. He would not be defined by what happened to him. Instead he said: "Everything can be taken from man but one thing: the last of the human freedoms—to choose one's attitude in any given set of circumstances, to choose one's own way."

We can choose darkness and lack. Or we can choose light, hope, and gratitude.

May we all choose light.

My life has been geared toward a search for light, a desire to see the helpers, not just the helpless. Perhaps that has been why I've been so drawn to the work of Operation Smile. The people in this organization are bringers of light. They see the children in need of surgery; they see the hole that no one is filling. And

> *Life is 10% what happens to you and 90% how you react to it.*
>
> CHARLES SWINDOLL

they take time out of their busy lives to go and fill that hole. To heal that child. What they do truly changes lives. Those healed children go forth into their lives with a new call, a renewed hope, and a beam of light that shines brightly wherever they go. Those children know the call of gratitude. It is in their eyes, in their now-bright smiles, in their hugs and kisses.

Thank you. To the doctor who healed me. The person who donated. And God, who is the ultimate healer.

There is a parable that tells the story of a man walking on a beach covered with thousands of starfish. They literally litter the beach, making it hard to walk. And as the man gazes along the shore, he notices a little boy walking carefully through the starfish and every now and then stopping, gingerly picking up a starfish, and throwing it into the sea. The man walks up to the boy to ask him what he is doing. And the boy explains that when the tide goes out, all these starfish will die, no longer close to the sea, and unable to reach their home. The man knows this is true and says, "But there are too many out here for you to save. You won't really be able to make a difference."

The boy stops, picks up another starfish, and throws it into the water.

"It made a difference to that one," he says triumphantly.

No, we cannot save the entire world, but, one child at a time, we can make a difference. Let's not be paralyzed by the huge need in our world or overwhelmed by all the pain—and end up doing nothing. We must do *something*, and if we each do something, give something, help someone, then together we *can* make a difference.

In that way, we can live our lives as a chorus of gratitude. There is no time to waste.

When I was growing up, we had a room that we called "the good room." It was the room where we would entertain guests, and in it lived a little china cabinet with glass doors, and within this was my mother's greatest treasure: a set of fine china that had been given to her as a wedding gift. Oh, how she loved that china. It was her most expensive and luxurious possession. As children, we were not often allowed in the good room, because she didn't want us playing in there and perhaps jostling the cabinet and breaking one of her precious dishes. The cabinet was locked with a little key, and my mother would only open it to wash the china, carefully dry it, and then arrange it back nicely inside.

One afternoon during the height of the Troubles, after the British army had arrived, we were all gathered in the kitchen. The army had brought these humongous armored Saracens that would rumble through our narrow streets. And when this happened, the entire house would shake.

This particular afternoon, we heard the telltale growl of a Saracen turning down our street, and then we began to feel the tremors as its large mass made its way up the hill. And as the house began to shake, we heard a loud crash come from the good room. My mother's hand flew to her face and she ran down the hallway, grabbing the key to the china cabinet as she went. But there was no need to open it. It was clear what had happened as soon as we walked into the room. The top shelf had collapsed onto the bottom shelf, and every single piece of her china was shattered.

My mother fell to her knees, opened the cabinet door, and cried, touching her precious china that was now destroyed for good.

You can cut all the flowers but you cannot keep Spring from coming.

PABLO NERUDA

That image has stayed with me for my entire life.

We all have things we want to save, that we want to preserve. But my mother was keeping that china for what? A special day sometime in the future? Sadly, she never got to enjoy it.

And I've learned from that to enjoy each moment for the blessing it is, because none of us is guaranteed anything more than right now.

I'm someone who wants to jump in and seize the moment. I'm not locking up any rooms. Let's thank God for every gift and use it to its fullest.

An attitude of gratitude means every day is the best. Every day is a cause for celebration. From the beauty of the sunrise to the splendor of the sunset, may we all bask in the glory that God has given.

Thank you, God.

Thank you, God.

Thank you, God.

There is treasure buried in the field of every one of our days, even the bleakest or dullest, and it is our business, as we journey, to keep our eyes peeled for it.

FREDERICK BUECHNER

The belief that *happiness has to be deserved* has led to centuries of pain, guilt, and deception. So firmly have we clung to this single, illusory belief that we've almost forgotten the real truth about happiness. So busy are we trying to *deserve* happiness that we no longer have much time for ideas such as: *Happiness is natural, happiness is a birthright, happiness is free, happiness is a choice, happiness is within,* and *happiness is being.* The moment you believe that happiness has to be deserved, you must toil for evermore.

Robert Holden

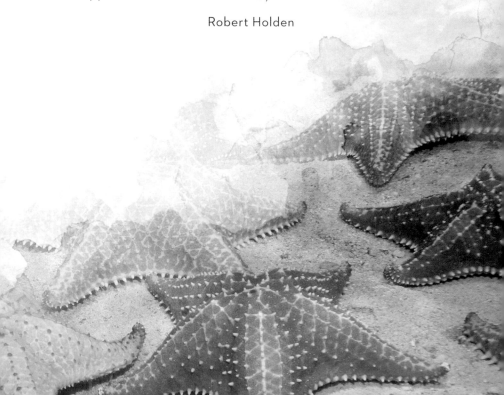

Thank
You,
God.

There's no place like home.

Praise be to the God and Father of our Lord Jesus Christ, who has blessed us in the heavenly realms with every spiritual blessing in Christ. For he chose us in him before the creation of the world to be holy and blameless in his sight. In love he predestined us for adoption to sonship through Jesus Christ, in accordance with his pleasure and will—to the praise of his glorious grace, which he has freely given us in the One he loves.

EPHESIANS 1:3–6 (NIV)

HOME

seven

HOME

My soul is from elsewhere, I'm sure of that,
and I intend to end up there.

Rumi

I KNOW THAT the reason I was able to keep going after the loss of my mother was that my faith had taught me I would see her again. My faith told me, *Yes, this hurts. Yes, life is hard. But take heart. This is not the end. Jesus rose after three days, and our spirits, too, are immortal. There is a place waiting for you. It is filled with God and your loved ones. All tears will be dried. All hurts will be healed. It is paradise, and it is forever.*

I'm not sure where I would be if I didn't have that hope as a guiding force in my life.

I found a Welsh word the other day that I had never come across before: *hiraeth*. It is defined as a homesickness for a home to which you cannot return, a home that maybe never was; the nostalgia, the yearning, the grief for the lost places of your past.

Of course I responded to that word as a girl whose childhood essentially ended at age ten when her mother's bright light was taken from this world. I do feel as if I've carried a longing for that home ever since . . . the home that was filled with laughter and joy and a mother's love.

But I also respond to the part of the definition that speaks of a home that maybe never was. Because this world is filled with longing. None of us have perfect lives. I can attest that all the money and success in the world doesn't fill our hearts. There is a void in each of us that I believe can only be filled by God and will only be fully healed when we reach heaven.

For all the gifts I've been given, I still long. I long for my mom and dad. I long for Reilly to meet her grandparents. I long to share stories with my parents of where life has taken me.

I long to feel that completeness of being with all of my loved ones together.

And I know I will have that in heaven. That not only will I be able to walk with my mom and dad again but one day, I hope many years after I've arrived, I will see my own baby girl walk through those gates. And I will embrace her. And then I will pull her over to my mother

Death is no more than passing from one room into another. But there's a difference for me, you know. Because in that other room I shall be able to see.

HELEN KELLER

and my father. And they will see their beautiful granddaughter. And we will hug and laugh and cry at the good and the bad and the love and the joy. And the grace that allowed us to finally be together, forever.

Billy Graham famously said, "My home is in heaven. I'm just passing through this world." Sometimes we search so hard to find home. We think we will find it in the perfect job or perfect relationship, or maybe if we build just the right house or move to the right neighborhood, everything will fall into place. But true home is within us. True home is in God. We're like Dorothy in *The Wizard of Oz*: she thinks she needs certain things to make her whole and get her back home. She thinks she needs courage and heart and a brain. She thinks that if she could just pull back the curtain and find Oz, all would be well. But when she gets back home, she realizes that what she truly needs has been with her all along.

> We shall not cease from exploration
> And the end of all our exploring
> Will be to arrive where we started
> And know the place for the first time.
>
> T. S. ELIOT

I hope that in this book you have begun to see the beauty in your journey. How it may have twisted and turned, and had ups and downs, but ultimately that you were never alone on the Yellow Brick Road. That even in the dark forest, God was preparing you. That even as you danced in Munchkinland, it was time to say *thank you*. That even though when you arrive back home and nothing has changed on the outside, you'll see that you've been changed on the inside. And that is all that matters. When we awaken fully to God, it's as if we finally remember that we are not merely caterpillars but that we are, in fact, beautiful butterflies with wings to fly.

*Human spiritual longing is, finally,
the humility of realizing that we have forgotten
who we are. . . . There can be times in the process
of seeking that we are reassured that however
much we are searching, we are at some level
even more devoutly being searched for. There may even
be times when we are reassured that the
frenzy of searching is not really needed, that in
fact we have already been found. But the longing
will persist, and so will the seeking, and unless we
are unusually fortunate we shall search
in a multitude of blind alleys.*

GERALD MAY

When We All Get to Heaven

Sing the wondrous love of Jesus,
Sing His mercy and His grace.
In the mansions bright and blessed
He'll prepare for us a place.

(Refrain)
When we all get to Heaven,
What a day of rejoicing that will be!
When we all see Jesus,
We'll sing and shout the victory!

While we walk the pilgrim pathway,
Clouds will overspread the sky;
But when trav'ling days are over,
Not a shadow, not a sigh.

Let us then be true and faithful,
Trusting, serving every day;
Just one glimpse of Him in glory
Will the toils of life repay.

Onward to the prize before us!
Soon His beauty we'll behold;
Soon the pearly gates will open;
We shall tread the streets of gold.

Eliza E. Hewitt

The Journey

Above the mountains
the geese turn into
the light again

painting their
black silhouettes
on an open sky.

Sometimes everything
has to be
inscribed across
the heavens

so you can find
the one line
already written
inside you.

Sometimes it takes
a great sky
to find that

first, bright
    and indescribable
       wedge of freedom
          in your own heart.

Sometimes with
    the bones of the black
       sticks left when the fire
          has gone out

someone has written
    something new
    in the ashes
       of your life.

You are not leaving,
    even as the light
       fades quickly now,
          you are arriving.

David Whyte

GOD'S CALLING CARD

See, I am sending an angel ahead of you to guard you along the way and to bring you to the place I have prepared.

EXODUS 23:20 (NIV)

I love the saying that some attribute to Albert Einstein: "Coincidence is God's way of remaining anonymous." I love to look for how beautiful things come together in a way that shows there was a plan, that there were greater forces at work. Either there is no God or there is only God. I, of course, strive to live my life believing that it is all God at work.

Sometimes you have to look for those "coincidences," and other times they are so obvious you can only laugh and thank God. These gifts, these simple moments that show that He is here and that your loved ones are still surrounding you, are the ones that lift my heart and give me strength. They show me that the veil between this world and the next is just that, a thin veil. We are closer than we think, though we may feel so far. Separation is just an illusion.

Several years ago, Mark and I hosted a table at an Operation Smile gala. I have been an ambassador for this wonderful organization for many years, and on this particular night we joined a group of friends all there to support this worthy cause. We were sitting down to dinner when a young girl came around the tables trying to sell raffle tickets. We had already donated, so my first impulse was to politely decline. But this girl was hovering around the table, and she reminded me a bit of Reilly, so I dug into my purse to see what cash I had. I had forty dollars, and the tickets were twenty dollars each, so I bought two tickets and wrote my name on them, and the girl moved on to the next table.

One of my dear friends, Brooke Burke-Charvet, was the MC for the night, and as dinner was wrapping up, she went up on-stage with a very large hat filled with raffle tickets. And as she put her hand deep into that hat, she pulled out a ticket and said, "Well, it's my friend Roma Downey!"

I jumped up like I'd just won an Oscar. I'd never really won anything like this before and was so excited. Mark pulled me back to my chair, laughing, as there was nothing to go up and receive; you would find out later what the prize was.

It turned out that the prize was choosing a piece of jewelry from the designer Thanh Hoang. They gave Thanh my contact information, and a few weeks later I invited her out to my house to look at her beautiful jewelry collection and share some tea.

After Thanh arrived and we'd settled in for our tea, she reached into her bag and pulled out a few pieces of jewelry for me to choose from her collection, Le Dragon d'Or.

She sat there with her hand in her bag, and she looked me in the eye.

"Roma, I have one piece of jewelry I made about fifteen years ago. No one has ever bought it, so I have stopped showing it. It is an unusual piece. But as I was leaving this morning, I had a strong feeling I should bring it. You may not like it, which is fine—I have a few other pieces as well—but I wanted to show you this one first."

And she pulled out a beautiful butterfly ring.

Tears sprang to my eyes. Immediately, I knew it was from my mom. That it was a message from her. *I'm still here, Roma. All these years later, I'm still right here.*

Of course I chose that piece of jewelry. Nothing else would do. That ring was a gift from my dear mother. It was meant for me.

I later learned that when Brooke picked the second raffle ticket out of the hat, as there were two prizes to be won that night, my name was on the ticket again! But she, of course, put it aside. She couldn't have me winning both prizes; it might have looked rigged. What are the chances my name was pulled out twice?

But to me, that shows how much my mother wanted me to get her message. What are the odds? That I would end up

Sometimes the heart sees what is invisible to the eye.
H. JACKSON BROWN JR.

buying a raffle ticket despite my initial resistance. That my name would be the one to be called, out of the hundreds in that hat. Twice! And that unbeknownst to me, the prize would be a butterfly ring.

Those moments were so validating to me. I then understood that my mother is still reaching out to me. That I will see her again. That I will be reunited with the loving energy of my mom and dad, even though I don't know exactly what heaven may look like.

Now, some may say that it was just a coincidence that my name was called and that that designer felt called to bring a butterfly ring.

But I like to see those coincidences as signs of God's love, as reminders of his constant presence, and that I am truly a beloved child of God. And He is taking care of me in moments big and small.

For all who are led by the Spirit of God are sons of God.
For you did not receive the spirit of slavery to fall back
into fear, but you have received the Spirit of adoption as
sons, by whom we cry, "Abba! Father!" The Spirit himself
bears witness with our spirit that we are children of God,
and if children, then heirs—heirs of God and fellow heirs
with Christ, provided we suffer with him in order that we
may also be glorified with him.

ROMANS 8:14–17 (ESV)

Late have I loved Thee, O Lord; and behold,
Thou wast within and I without, and there I sought Thee.
Thou was with me when I was not with Thee.
Thou didst call, and cry, and burst my deafness.
Thou didst gleam, and glow, and dispel my blindness.
Thou didst touch me, and I burned for Thy peace.
For Thyself Thou hast made us,
and restless our hearts until in Thee they find their ease.
Late have I loved Thee,
Thou Beauty ever old and ever new.
Thou hast burst my bonds asunder;
unto Thee will I offer up an offering of praise.

Saint Augustine

Danny Boy

Oh, Danny Boy, the pipes, the pipes are calling
From glen to glen, and down the mountainside;
The summer's gone, and all the roses falling
It's you, it's you must go and I must bide.

But come ye back when summer's in the meadow,
Or when the valley's hush'd and white with snow;
It's I'll be there in sunshine or in shadow,
Oh, Danny Boy, oh, Danny Boy, I love you so!

But when ye come, and all the flow'rs are dying
If I am dead, as dead I well may be,
Ye'll come and find the place where I am lying,
And kneel and say an Ave there for me.

And I shall hear, though soft you tread above me,
And all my grave will warmer, sweeter be,
For you will bend and tell me that you love me,
And I shall sleep in peace until you come to me!

Frederic Weatherly

THE REMEMBERING

Define yourself radically as one beloved by God.
This is the true self. Every other identity is illusion.

JOHN EAGAN

I hope that throughout this book you've come to remember:
We are all beloved children of God.

No matter what you've done, no matter what mistakes
you've made or pain you've caused, that truth doesn't change.
We are His children. We are His beloved. There is nothing
God won't do to bring us back to Him.

God shows us this in the Bible.

The Prodigal Son is not just a story to tell. It is our story.

Then Jesus said, "There was a man who had two sons.
The younger of them said to his father, 'Father, give
me the share of the property that will belong to me.'
So he divided his property between them. A few days
later the younger son gathered all he had and trav-
eled to a distant country, and there he squandered
his property in dissolute living. When he had spent
everything, a severe famine took place throughout that coun-

try, and he began to be in need. So he went and hired himself out to one of the citizens of that country, who sent him to his fields to feed the pigs. He would gladly have filled himself with the pods that the pigs were eating; and no one gave him anything. But when he came to himself he said, 'How many of my father's hired hands have bread enough and to spare, but here I am dying of hunger! I will get up and go to my father, and I will say to him, "Father, I have sinned against heaven and before you; I am no longer worthy to be called your son; treat me like one of your hired hands."' So he set off and went to his father. But while he was still far off, his father saw him and was filled with compassion; he ran and put his arms around him and kissed him."

LUKE 15:11-20 (NRSV)

I am that son, and God is that Father. The Father who doesn't sit there shaking his head, wanting me to know the depth of my sin, but He is the Father who rejoices that I have come back and cannot wait for me to reach His door, and He comes running to envelop me in His arms. This is the kind of love God has for us. He doesn't reluctantly allow us back in; rather, He celebrates us and gives us robes and feasts and more than we could ever deserve.

We are His beloved.

My good friend and childhood parish priest Father Paddy O'Kane told me the following story: A young boy had been warned by his parents not to play with matches, and yet he was a curious boy and sneaked out to the barn with a box of matches to see how they worked. He loved the sound of the match striking, the smell of the sulfur as the match burst into flame, and, most of all, seeing the small flame glow. After a few minutes of this thrill, he accidently dropped one of the flaming matches, and the straw underfoot caught fire. He tried to stamp it out, but it caught too quickly, and before he knew it the floor was covered in flames. The boy ran out and looked on in horror as the entire barn was soon engulfed. Knowing that he was responsible, the boy ran out into the tall grass and hid, watching in shame as the entire barn burned to the ground.

When he saw his parents emerge from the house, he stayed hidden. He knew he had let them down and they would be angry. He watched as the fire engines arrived along with friends and neighbors. He saw his parents crying, and he knew they were so upset. And it was his fault.

The boy stayed hidden, even as night fell, afraid to confront his parents. *They must be so mad at me*, he thought.

But soon the night began to get very cold, and he was so hungry. He quietly walked up to the house and sneaked in the back door, hanging his head in shame.

*But when the set time had fully come, God sent his Son, born of a woman, born under the law, to redeem those under the law, that we might receive adoption to sonship. Because you are his sons, God sent the Spirit of his Son into our hearts, the Spirit who calls out, "**Abba**, Father." So you are no longer a slave, but God's child; and since you are his child, God has made you also an heir.*

GALATIANS 4:4–7 (NIV)

When his father saw him, he gasped.

"I'm so sorry, Daddy," the wee boy said.

And his father ran over to him and swept him up in a hug, kissing him, calling out to his wife, tears streaming down his face.

"Oh, my boy, my boy, we thought you were dead," the father whispered into his ear. "Thank you, God, thank you, God!"

It did not matter in that moment that the boy had done something he shouldn't have. They were just so relieved to have him home. They were overjoyed to have their little boy back.

That is how God loves us. His love for us is unconditional. No matter how much we may have messed up, He always welcomes us back.

I know I forget this often, and that is why I always come back to stillness. In stillness and quiet, I can remember who I truly am. I am not my fear or insecurities. I am not Monica, the angel. I am not Roma, the celebrity. I am Roma, God's beloved. No matter how far I have strayed or how much I may have forgotten, that identity never changes. Sometimes I feel far from God. Sometimes I feel close to God. But God is not the variable in that equation. I am. The illusion of separation is just that, an illusion. God is always there. I've just turned away and cannot see Him.

If we are all God's children, it means that we are all one family. If you have lived your life wondering where you belong, searching for home, it is here. We are all the family of God. We forget. We get caught up in separation. But we are all one family. We all belong to each other, like Mother Teresa taught. Like Maya Angelou showed us.

Remembering this will change everything.

So while we go out in the world, searching and searching and searching for home, it is within that we will find it. Our home is knowing that we are God's beloved children; and no matter how dark life can feel, He is always there to guide us, comfort us, and shelter us.

He is our home.

Thank you, God.

Ultimately the only way that I can be myself is to become identified with Him in Whom is hidden the reason and fulfillment of my existence.

THOMAS MERTON

It has always seemed to me, ever since early childhood, that, amid all the commonplaces of life, I was very near to a kingdom of ideal beauty. Between it and me hung only a thin veil. I could never draw it quite aside, but sometimes a wind fluttered it and I caught a glimpse of the enchanting realm beyond— only a glimpse—but those glimpses have always made life worthwhile.

Lucy Maud Montgomery

We are above all things loved—that is the good news of the gospel—and loved not just the way we turn up on Sundays in our best clothes and on our best behavior and with our best feet forward, but loved as we alone know ourselves to be, the weakest and shabbiest of what we are along with the strongest and gladdest. To come together as people who believe that just maybe this gospel is actually true should be to come together like people who have just won the Irish Sweepstakes. It should have us throwing our arms around each other like people who have just discovered that every single man and woman in those pews is not just another familiar or unfamiliar face but is our long-lost brother and our long-lost sister, because despite the fact that we have all walked in different gardens and knelt at different graves, we have all, humanly speaking, come from the same place and are heading out into the same blessed mystery that awaits us all.

Frederick Buechner

I'm sorry, God, for
forgetting the truth.
That you are my Father,
and I am your child.
That we all belong
to one family.
And that is where
we will find home.
Help us remember,
daily,
moment by moment,
our true identity
as yours.
Always yours.
Forever yours.
That you are preparing
a place for us.
A place where all that
we've lost is now found.
A place where all is fulfilled,
nothing is lacking.
And we have you.
You.
Always,
You.

Everything Is Waiting for You

Your great mistake is to act the drama
as if you were alone. As if life
were a progressive and cunning crime
with no witness to the tiny hidden
transgressions. To feel abandoned is to deny
the intimacy of your surroundings. Surely,
even you, at times, have felt the grand array;
the swelling presence, and the chorus, crowding
out your solo voice. You must note
the way the soap dish enables you,
or the window latch grants you freedom.
Alertness is the hidden discipline of familiarity.
The stairs are your mentor of things

to come, the doors have always been there
to frighten you and invite you,
and the tiny speaker in the phone
is your dream-ladder to divinity.

Put down the weight of your aloneness and ease into
the conversation. The kettle is singing
even as it pours you a drink, the cooking pots
have left their arrogant aloofness and
seen the good in you at last. All the birds
and creatures of the world are unutterably
themselves. Everything is waiting for you.

David Whyte

YOU NEVER WALK ALONE

At the beginning of every episode of *Touched by an Angel*, they played our theme song. The lovely Della Reese sang it, and the themes it touched on were those that appeared on every show. It was called "Walk with You," and it told the story that no matter what, there was someone by your side. You were never alone. It could be an angel or God. But no matter what, there was someone there.

At the time, I don't think I even recognized how similar the themes in this song were to those in the song my mother sang to me, "You'll Never Walk Alone," and how similar they were to the theme of the poem "Footprints," which my father shared with me shortly after my mother's death. Over and over, the theme of my life story has been that we are never alone. Though I was an orphan in my early twenties, an age when most still want the guidance of their parents, I was never alone.

Here I am, so many years later, and that is still what I want to share.

Look for the butterflies. Look for the helpers. Look for the angels.

They are everywhere.

Our lives probably look very different—yours and mine. None of us traverses the same path. But I know that we all share one thing in common, and that is that our Father in heaven loves each of us equally and fiercely. He is forging a beautiful butterfly out of whatever cocoon you may be enduring.

Take heart. Have faith. And when the light comes, as it always does, enjoy the flight to the rest of your life.

I know that, one day, we will meet. It may be on this earth, but probably not. But I know we will meet in heaven.

I'll see you there.

Death is not extinguishing
the light; it is only
putting out the lamp
because the dawn has come.

RABINDRANATH TAGORE

So do not fear, for I am with you;
do not be dismayed, for I am your God.
I will strengthen you and help you;
I will uphold you with my righteous right hand.

ISAIAH 41:10 (NIV)

Walk with You

When you walk down the road
Heavy burden, heavy load

I will rise and I will walk with you
When you walk through the night
And you feel like you wanna just give up,
give up, give up on the fight
I will come and I will walk with you
Walk with you
Until the sun don't even shine
Walk with you
I'll be there all the time

I tell you I'll walk with you
See you through
When you walk from this place
And you gotta go to meet Him face to face
Take my hand and I will walk with you

Oh, oh walk with you
Till the clouds fade away
I tell you I'll walk with you
Each and every day

Oh yes I'll walk with you

Lyrics by Marc Lichtman,
additional lyrics by Martha Williamson
Theme song from *Touched by an Angel*

May

the road rise to meet you,
May the wind be always
at your back,
May the sun shine warm
upon your face,
The rains fall soft upon
your fields and,
Until we meet again,
May God hold you
in the palm of His hand.

IRISH BLESSING

Acknowledgments

My Angels along the Way

There have been countless people who have come into my life at times when I greatly needed them. I know these were angels sent by God to encourage and strengthen me. I am so fortunate to have been blessed by incredible friends, family, colleagues, and partners in my life, and this book wouldn't exist without them.

Gone but not forgotten, of course, are my precious mom and dad and my beloved Auntie Ruby.

Across the ocean in Derry, I thank my family for their constant love and support over the years: my brother Lawrence and his wife, Fiona; my half sisters Ann and Jacinta, and their husbands, John and Michael; my half brother Pat and his wife, Ann; my half brother Fr. John; our dear family friend Fr. Paddy O'Kane; and all my many nieces and nephews.

A thank-you to my lovely mother-in-law, Jean; I'm so grateful that she and her late husband, Archie, came into my life when I married Mark.

I thank friends and mentors and wise hearts along the way for enriching my life and helping me discover my gifts and giving me the courage to dream: my sincere thanks to Roy Grant, Sandra Freeman, and Faith O'Reilly for believing in me. To directors Jack Going, who gave me my first big theater break, and Larry Peerce, who gave me my first big television break. Who knows where I'd be without you!

Thank you to my beloved *Touched by an Angel* family. I am so grateful for the love we shared after so many wonderful years spent together: to

Martha Williamson and the cast and crew, in particular the late John Dye and my own beloved momma, Della Reese.

Thank you to all my *Bible* and *A.D.* family, the entire cast and crew who brought so much light to my life, and in particular Richard Bedser.

Thank you to Gary Barber and my MGM family and all of my Light-Workers family, who stay as committed as I am to telling positive and encouraging stories and trying to change the world through kindness, and especially to John Kilcullen and Katherine Warnock for their input on this book.

Thank you to all the folks at Operation Smile who volunteer to give of their time and talent, changing the world one smile at a time.

Thank you to everyone who helped with *Box of Butterflies*, breathing life into its pages with love and support and creativity. To Jan Miller and Shannon Marven for helping me find the right publisher for this project and your unwavering support throughout. To Pam Reynolds, Brian Edwards, and Christina Tajalli, for their legal expertise. To Judith Curr, Carolyn Reidy, Philis Boultinghouse, Stephen Fallert, Jonathan Merkh, and the entire team at Simon & Schuster and Howard Books. To Torrey Sharp and Min Choi for their beautiful design; Jetty Stutzman, Linda Medvene, and Austin Hargraves for their incredible work on the cover; and Lina Plath and Clareanne Darragh from Frank PR, my tireless PR team. To Cindy DiTiberio, who came alongside at just the right time to help me envision what this book could be, who helped me get the stories out of my heart and onto the page, and whose tireless dedication to the process has helped this book emerge into the beautiful treasure it is.

A special thanks to all the writers and contributors who granted me rights to use their material, which so greatly enhanced this book. They have been butterflies for me along the way, and I'm so grateful that I can share them with you. A special thanks to Mary Oliver, Martha Williamson and Marc Lichtman, Anne Neilson, Karen Kingsbury, Phil Coulter, David Whyte, and the dear Dr. Maya Angelou.

A thank-you to Ashley Chase, my invaluable assistant, who handles so many details and keeps me focused, on time, and on schedule.

I'm so grateful for the special friends who have graced my path. There are way too many to mention here, but in particular, I thank my girlfriends close to home and overseas, friends whom I can count on no matter what, my true angels along the way, including Joanna, Moira, Cynthia, Elizabeth, Carol and Kay, Irena, Brooke, Lisa, Marilyn, and Valerie.

I've been humbled and overwhelmed by the generosity of so many people and their kind words on behalf of *Box of Butterflies*. There has been so much support from friends, colleagues—people I so deeply admire and respect—and I am incredibly grateful. Given the immense response, I regret we were not able to print all of the gracious words offered. I thank each and every person listed below from the bottom of my heart and have created a special place where you can read everything that people have been saying about *Box of Butterflies* at www.boxofbutterflies.com.

My deepest thanks go to:

Megan Alexander, Moll Anderson, Raymond Arroyo, Pastors Caroline and Matthew Barnett, Pastor Luke Barnett, Bishop Robert Barron, Pastor Mark Batterson, Bob Beltz, Lisa Bevere, Rev. Msgr. J. Brian Bransfield, Bishop Dale C. Bronner, Brooke Burke-Charvet, Rev. William Byrne, Phil Cooke, LL COOL J, Jeremy and Jessica Courtney, Pastors David and Nicole Crank, Cindy Crawford, Laurie Crouch, Jim Daly, Juan Pablo Di Pace, Shannen Doherty, Fran Drescher, Joshua DuBois, Rev. Jonathan Falwell, Dr. Ronnie Floyd, Pastor Ken Foreman, Bob Goff, Kathie Lee Gifford, Archbishop José H. Gomez, Jon Gordon, Pastors Craig and Amy Groeschel, Pastor Bobby Gruenewald, Pastor John C. Hagee, Billy Hallowell, Michelle McKinney Hammond, Patricia Heaton, Pastors Bobbie and Brian Houston, Arianna Huffington, Dr. Joel C. Hunter, Jackelyn and Donald Iloff, Jerry Johnson, Jason Kennedy, Lauren Scruggs- Kennedy, Karen Kingsbury, Ali Landry, Pastor Max Lucado, Gabe and Rebekah Lyons, Dr. Bill and Kathy Magee, Pastor Erwin Raphael McManus, Santiago "Jimmy" Mellado, Dr. Carl A. Moeller, Johnnie Moore, Pastor Phil Munsey, Anne Neilson, Nancy O'Dell, Cardinal Seán O'Malley, Pastor Victoria Osteen, Dr. Mehmet Oz, Sister Rose Pacatte, Kevin Palau, Tony Robbins, Willie and Korie Robertson, Rev. Samuel Rodriguez, SQuire Rushnell, Rodrigo Santoro, Joel and Luke Smallbone, Pastor Judah Smith, Michael W. Smith, Pastors Andy and Sandra Stanley, Pastor Dave Stone, Cal Thomas, Pastor Brian Tome, Nick Vujicic, Pastor Holly Wagner, Pastor Rick and Kay Warren, and Cardinal Donald Wuerl.

Last but not least, I must thank my closest family. My own little Brady Bunch! I am so grateful to my beloved husband, Mark, my best friend, partner, soul mate, and the absolute love of my life. He is the true leading man in my life. Loving him and being loved by him is more than I could have ever dreamed of. I am grateful for the two amazing sons he brought into my life. I have cherished helping to raise James and Cameron, and I love them dearly and am so proud of the young men they have become.

And to Reilly, my beloved daughter: your birth blessed me more than you could ever know. You are a part of my heart, and loving you brings me so much joy. Thanks for being the best daughter a mother could have.

Credits

ed by permission of The Random House Group Limited. © John O'Donohue 2007. Audio Rights: excerpted from *To Bless the Space Between Us.* Copyright © 2008 with permission of Sounds True Inc.

Page 110: Photo: Kevin Lynch, art direction by 30sixty Advertising, History®.

Pages 118–19: "My Little Angel."
Words and Music by Phil Coulter.
Copyright © 1999 Spirit Catalog Holdings, S.a.r.l.
All rights controlled and administered by Spirit Two Music, Inc.
International Copyright Secured. All Rights Reserved.
Reprinted by Permission of Hal Leonard LLC.

Pages 124–25: "Blessing: For a Mother-to-Be," from *To Bless the Space between Us: A Book of Blessings,* by John O'Donohue. Copyright © 2008 by John O'Donohue. Used by permission of Doubleday, an imprint of the Knopf Doubleday Publishing Group, a division of Penguin Random House LLC. All rights reserved. Any third-party use of this material, outside of this publication, is prohibited. Interested parties must apply directly to Penguin Random House LLC for permission. For the United Kingdom: Excerpts from *Benedictus* by John O'Donohue. Published by Bantam Press. Reprinted by permission of The Random House Group Limited. © John O'Donohue 2007. Audio Rights: excerpted from *To Bless the Space Between Us.* Copyright © 2008 with permission of Sounds True Inc.

Page 139: "Angels," original artwork by Anne Neilson, used by permission.

Pages 144–45: "Mary, Did You Know?" Mark Lowry/Buddy Greene. © 1991 Word Music (ASCAP), LLC, Rufus Music (ASCAP) (adm. at CapitolCMGPublishing.com). All Rights on behalf of Word Music, LLC, administered by WB Music Corp. International Copyright Secured. All Rights Reserved. Used by Permission.

Pages 150: "Touched by an Angel" aka "Love's Exquisite Freedom" by Maya Angelou. Copyright © 1975 by Maya Angelou. Reprinted by permission of Caged Bird Legacy, LLC.

Pages 164: "Praying," from the volume *Thirst,* by Mary Oliver, published by Beacon Press, Boston. Copyright © 2006 by Mary

Praise for *Box of Butterflies*

"Regardless of the season of life you are in, Roma Downey's hope-filled book powerfully reveals the love, grace, and kindness waiting for you in Christ. Roma warmly guides you through a reading experience that will build your faith, renew your mind, and encourage your heart. Open this book and prepare to be blessed as you experience God's grace in a new, fresh, and intimate way."

—Craig and Amy Groeschel, pastors, Life.Church, and authors, *From This Day Forward*

"We all need inspiration in our everyday lives to give us strength as we face obstacles, challenges, and setbacks. I am grateful that Roma offers such a beautiful compilation of so many wonderfully wise and thoughtful sentiments. Thank you, Roma. I am proud to call you a friend."

—Fran Drescher, author, actress, health advocate

"Equal parts deeply personal and profoundly inspirational, as you turn these pages you won't just find a story about Roma; this is a book about how God paints on the canvas of our lives with many beautiful colors. We have all experienced pain and loss, joy and celebration. You'll find words in this book that will lift you up."

—Bob Goff, author, *New York Times* bestseller *Love Does*

"In the time that we have known Roma, we have found her to be like a breath of sweet air from above. We are confident this book will enlarge your perception and revelation of a God who fails not. The imprint of His kindness and goodness is all around us, and Roma is certainly one capable and gifted in helping others to see it. *Box of Butterflies* is a testament of gratitude, offering comfort and assurance for the hungry soul."

—Bobbie and Brian Houston, global senior pastors, Hillsong Church

"Roma's beautiful soul shines through in *Box of Butterflies*, reminding us that despite the struggles and difficulties of life, God is always with us. Her personal stories, quotes, and words of encouragement will be the inspiration you need to remember God's presence and rediscover the beauty found in the life around you."

—Lisa Bevere, *New York Times* bestselling author and cofounder, Messenger International